Millennials in
Architecture

Millennials in Architecture

Generations, Disruption, and the Legacy of a Profession

Darius Sollohub

UNIVERSITY OF TEXAS PRESS   AUSTIN

Requests for permission to reproduce material from this work
should be sent to:
    Permissions
    University of Texas Press
    P.O. Box 7819
    Austin, TX 78713-7819
    utpress.utexas.edu/rp-form

⊚ The paper used in this book meets the minimum requirements
of ANSI/NISO Z39.48-1992 (R1997) (Permanence of Paper).

Library of Congress Cataloging-in-Publication Data

Names: Sollohub, Darius, author.
Title: Millennials in architecture : generations, disruption, and
    the legacy of a profession / Darius Sollohub.
Description: First edition. | Austin : University of Texas Press,
    2019. | Includes bibliographical references and index.
Identifiers: - $ $/ 2018052869
    ISBN 978-1-4773-1855-3 (cloth : alk. paper)
    ISBN 978-1-4773-1894-2 (pbk. : alk. paper)
    ISBN 978-1-4773-1856-0 (library e-book)
    ISBN 978-1-4773-1857-7 (nonlibrary e-book)
Subjects: LCSH: Architecture and society. | Architecture,
    Modern—21st century. | Generation Y—Attitudes. |
    Generation Y—Psychology.
Classification: LCC NA2543.S6 S6375 2019 | DDC 720.1/03—dc23
LC record available at https://lccn.loc.gov/2018052869

doi:10.7560/318553

For Richard Sweeney,
who taught us all about Millennials,
and about ourselves.
1946–2016

Contents

Preface

> No matter how contrasts between generations have been created, one fundamental fact of life remains true in the United States: Generations matter. To understand other people, and even to fully understand ourselves, we must consider generational identity at least as carefully as we consider any other social characteristic.
>
> **ELWOOD CARLSON**

In the fall semester of 2009, I taught a studio class in collaboration with the local chapter of Habitat for Humanity. Habitat's architect joined me one day a week in class and Habitat staff periodically reviewed progress. Families already living in Habitat homes also offered their input. Students used building information modelling (BIM) software to ensure that their houses met Habitat's budget and to empirically prove the cost-effectiveness of each home's featured sustainability. At the semester's final review, a jury selected one student's design to advance toward construction, with Habitat's architect offering the winning designer and the first runner-up paid internships to finish the construction documents over winter break. The students' solidarity was so high that they continued working together, submitting the semester's work to a National Council of Architectural Registration Boards (NCARB) competition, and the project won the coveted $25,000 grand prize. That accomplishment was pivotal in my being appointed director of the New Jersey School of Architecture in 2010.

Great story, right? The part I have withheld thus far is how much I absolutely *dreaded* teaching that studio. My dread centered on the belief that no student would want to design an affordable house in what was known as the

"Options" year, when our curriculum typically offered a choice of formally exotic or theory-driven studios. Our faculty expected students would crave the artistic freedom of Options after three years of an extremely rigid core curriculum. Things had been this way since I began teaching, and along with my faculty colleagues, I saw no reason for change. Habitat's property committee chair, who is a neighbor and friend, had been pestering me for years to take on the task of the collaborative class. Each year I found an excuse, knowing Options presented the only slot in our curriculum to fit a studio like Habitat's. But when a research studio's funding fell through weeks before the semester began and I needed a design assignment, I finally gave in; "Let's get this out of the way," I thought. Setting expectations exceedingly low, I forecast to Habitat that we would be the last choice in the studio lottery, as few students would voluntarily choose a project assignment with the profound constraints of a small affordable house amidst such a rich array of other choices. And given the role GPA played in prioritizing choices, I surmised that this would also mean that the lowest-performing students would be "stuck" with the studio and it would feel remedial. They would toil away while others forayed into the esoteric. I braced for the worst.

To my shock and surprise, demand for the studio was exceptionally high; many students listed it as their first choice. The studio filled mostly with honors students, so many that the associate dean respectfully asked if I could share some with the other studios. When I later queried students about what attracted them, their responses were largely consistent: they spoke of wanting to do something real that would matter to them. I learned, to my surprise, that many considered the typical Options studios to be faculty indulgences that offered students few practical lessons in preparation for their careers. One student even referred to them as "fantasy studios." And in the economic recession in which we then found ourselves, many students considered formal exploration for its own sake to be irresponsible. Students also jumped at the opportunity to use BIM and its range of functionality, expecting that proficiency would give them a leg up when vying for jobs after graduation. They knew those faculty members interested in formal exploration typically frowned upon BIM, preferring more formally generative software. The most prominent attraction students cited was the civic purpose of the studio, which would allow students to play an active role in providing for those in need. To a local newspaper, the winning student described the studio's mission as "noble." "You're not trying to give people a shelter, but a home," he said.[1]

I recognized only later that this was my personal introduction to the Millennial generation. The overarching practicality and civic focus of those students were characteristics I later learned to be significant to their generation. That the studio functioned successfully in a highly collaborative manner, not only among students but also within the larger Habitat community, revealed another Millennial tendency: team-centeredness. While this kind of studio was not entirely novel—community-focused studios had been around since the sixties—its use of digital strategies was a key to its success. Differing from the traditional design-build studio, it achieved a high level of virtual resolution, both aesthetic and practical, in a relatively short period of time, with designers obtaining community buy-in through both highly realistic renderings and data-supported rationales. The studio also exhibited other, more quirky Millennial characteristics; students quickly taught themselves how to use the cost-estimating functions of BIM and developed work-arounds for the finicky relationship between BIM and the environmental modelling software, which at that time was poorly integrated. To my amazement, they did so by largely ignoring the computer industry reps brought in to lecture them, instead opting to scan the web for online tutorials and chat rooms to teach themselves. To make his project the most environmentally sustainable, the winning designer not only found a newly developed heat exchanger but also convinced the company to discount it for Habitat and found a state program to fund it. He pursued this winning strategy entirely online and on his own initiative.

The following year, as one of my first acts as director, I convened a faculty colloquium to discuss our current pedagogy. It was in that undertaking that I first became aware of Millennials. The experience of the prior year snapped into focus after our university librarian, who had been assiduously studying Millennials for many years, spoke to our group. I was surprised (and somewhat embarrassed) to find that the generation had then been in higher education for about a decade. How did I miss this, especially with a leading scholar on the subject on campus? I discovered that many different kinds of writers had been studying this generation, some from the time Millennials were small children; somehow, they not only knew they were coming, but forecast their features. Collectively, these writers had identified distinct Millennial characteristics, and their scholarship had reached a point that healthy disagreement and discussion had emerged between different camps. I also learned that Millennials are digital natives, and as a pure function of when I was born, I will always remain a digital immigrant. To my distress,

I found that their digital inheritance was instrumental in Millennials' ability to profoundly change industries, social structures, politics, you name it. I nervously came to realize that any organizational structure was vulnerable to this large wave of youth empowered with digital know-how and that this reorganizational phenomenon had a name: a disruption.

Why was I not aware of these disruptors in our midst? I asked others about Millennials near and far and got raised eyebrows; "You mean Gen Y or those Nexters?" some responded. Few knew anything about them. Among my faculty colleagues, most shared the misconception that students' aspirations had not changed significantly in the years since we were in school—the same fallacy that caused me to dread the Habitat studio. I soon began to realize that changes occurring around me, those that I simply chalked up in the vague category of technological progress, were driven by Millennials' active and total embrace of technology as digital natives. This also made me worry. After all, the recording industry had lost half its value in less than a decade, newspapers were closing all around us, and MIT, Harvard, and Stanford had begun offering their courses online, and for free. Closer to home, enrollment in architecture schools, including my own, progressively began to slip. While most attributed this to the recession, I wondered if other factors were at work and if my complacent academic community was next to be disrupted. When in early 2013 the American Institute of Architecture's journal *Architect* put a Millennial on the cover and called for "drastic changes to pedagogy, licensure and firm management,"[2] I realized that my community had stirred and something needed to be done. That awakening drives this book.

Millennials in Architecture: Generations, Disruption, and the Legacy of a Profession calls for architectural practice and education to embrace and take seriously this catalytic generation. Doing so will utilize the Millennial generation to its greatest advantage as we move forward through a turbulent period, one in which the architectural community will be asked to play a disproportionately large role in shaping our physical world. In the coming decades the earth's population will increase by over a third, with two-thirds of its people moving to cities. This reconfiguration will be largely driven by demographic change, with Millennials playing the lead role, and the success of this transformation will depend increasingly on Millennial leadership. The degree to which climate change and political unrest will further induce migration may dramatically increase urbanization and its associated issues. Rising to the challenge of solving them will test the organizational abilities of the practices doing the work and the ability of academia to teach those who will undertake it. Acknowledging Millennials in architecture as disruptors, grooming them for leadership, and accepting the standards of education they expect will have great bearing on the future quality of life of the whole population.

Focusing directly on these coming challenges, this book emerges at a critical moment as Millennial architects near becoming a majority in the workforce and are and will for some time remain a majority in schools. This vantage allows for the evaluation of early writing on Millennials and the comparison of those findings and predictions with contemporary data and personal testimony specific to architecture. To use a meteorological metaphor, architecture also finds itself at a kind of midpoint, in the eye of a slow-moving storm of Millennial disruption. In the calm of its eye, architectural practices enjoy renewal after the deepest economic recession in recent memory caused severe layoffs. As the economy revives and Millennials fill vacant seats, taking advantage of this pause to understand and accommodate the generation will best prepare architecture practices for the trials ahead when the tempest resumes. This will involve mobilizing the many Millennial assets, but also reckoning with the challenges some have identified in dealing with the generation. The second half of the storm, I believe, will bring a dramatic disruption that will not leave architectural schools unscathed. And how the architectural academy weathers this disruption will in turn have direct bearing on the success of the architectural profession.

The stakes are indeed high. For years architects have been complaining about erosion to their agency. But if the needs of architecture's Millennials go unanswered, the changes to come may be marshaled forward by sectors other than architecture, leaving the profession yet further marginalized and perhaps permanently damaged after this disruptive storm passes. Examples of Millennial-driven disruptions now abound. Who could have predicted that a search engine company, Google, would usurp the lead from the once all-powerful automobile industry in the development of autonomous vehicles?[3] And the fact that BIM software is creeping toward automation should make every architect shudder. The coming years will decide which side of the algorithm architects will be on: writing the software or being dominated by those who do.

The organizational structure of this book places the reader at the eye of the storm, in the present. This allows the reader to pivot three times: looking first to the past, then analyzing the present critically through a generational understanding, and, finally, speculating about the future. Part One begins with a critical assessment of Millennials' relationship to architecture in the beginning of the twenty-first century and continues with a close examination of the generation and its relationship to previous ones going back to the early twentieth century. I apply the methodology of different generational writers to this examination, including that of the historians William Strauss and Neil Howe, two of the most prolific and controversial contemporary writers on generations. Part One concludes by applying a generational overlay to the history of American architecture going back to modernism. Part Two pivots to reconsider the present, beginning with a review of recent texts that reveals generational layers in architecture's profession and academy. Recognizing these layers is essential in moving forward, allowing the highest possible mobilization of Millennial assets by turning perceived challenges into opportunities for change. This examination looks closely at Millennial behaviors and characteristics and how they positively or negatively affect architectural practice and education, including each attribute's digital underpinnings. *Millennials in Architecture* concludes in Part Three by scouting the profound disruption that digital technology will bring, a reconnaissance that informs on how to embark on the drastic changes to pedagogy, licensure, and firm management that the American Institute of Architects expects.

This book targets multiple and overlapping audiences. While its primary focus is on the community of architects in practice—designers, managers, and employees—and those in the academy—administrators, teachers, and students—it should also resonate among the broader design community, the boundaries of which seem to be fluid. While an important purpose of this book is to make all aware of the disruption ahead, its larger intent is to position architecture to take advantage of generational characteristics to effectively prepare for what will be a major building age. In its lowest form, this work begrudgingly accepts its role as a self-help book that explains to managers and employees in the profession why each group seems befuddled by the other's expectations, to the academy why students question whether a career in architecture is worth the effort, and to professors whether Millennials' efforts can withstand architecture's historically difficult demands. Yet the explanation of each of these conflicts underscores the loftier aspiration of this book: to show how an awareness of the special relationship between Millennials and the practice of architecture can reorganize and expand its domain in both pedagogy and practical methodology. The general characteristics that we ascribe to Millennials, such as civic-mindedness and a team focus, have always been central to the architect's identity. That architecture embraced digital practices in both the profession and the academy well before other disciplines suggests another alliance. If understood as proto-Millennial in its makeup, the architecture community can take advantage of its unique gifts to empower the rising generation for future leadership positions in architecture and beyond. For those that share this argument—whatever generation they identify with; whether they are part of the architectural community or outside it—this book serves as a manifesto.

My most coveted audience is also this book's primary subject. I truly hope that you, the disruptors, whether employed, still in school, or somewhere on a margin—and whether you identify as Millennial or not—read this book. While some of you may agree with the generalized findings, surely as many will respond to some characteristic with skepticism, saying, "That's not me." To those skeptics, I ask you to first consider the arguments in their entirety and not to invalidate the whole undertaking because of individual or local points of disagreement. This book is meant to inspire precisely this consideration, as it is my sincerest goal that you bring the debate it incites to your studios, offices, agencies, social media, blogs, and beyond. Any study that describes and contrasts the generalized characteristics of an entire generation must spark contention not only from the generation described but also from its elders and its juniors. I have faith that your generation of disruptors will use this book as a call to action.

In igniting this discussion, I see tremendous profit in positing the characterizations I have isolated and in describing the rich interplay between generations past, current, and anticipated for an audience to consider and debate. My own Habitat epiphany regarding Millennials came after a combined thirty years of practice and teaching, and I bring to this new understanding the zeal of a convert. I have spent the time since immersed in generational scholarship while at the same time carefully observing the many students I serve and how my faculty colleagues interact with them. Parallel to this, I have also taken the time to query architects, both Millennial and older, through online polling and in focus groups. Serving as a form of architectural correspondent from the eye of this storm, I render here as accurate an assessment as possible, using my professional awareness tempered by an academic's skepticism to prompt a long overdue discussion, one that I hope can lead to lasting change. In its most fundamental ambition, this book calls those in architecture to see themselves in a manner that some of us have seldom, if ever, done: as an active participant in a generation. This simple step will cause us to give renewed attention to the remarkable time we live in, to who we are, to the students we teach, the individuals we employ, and the people we learn from and work for, and most importantly to the constituents we all serve, as together we contemplate our place in time and history.

Millennials in
Architecture

PART ONE

A Twenty-First-Century Generation

CHAPTER 1

Introduction
Millennials, Architecture, Disruption

**The fateful act of living in and with one's generation
completes the drama of human existence.**

MARTIN HEIDEGGER

Millennials. So named as the first generation to rise to adulthood in the third millennium of the Western calendar. Yet the coincidence of when they matured distinguishes them in name only; their significance stems from the epochal technological and social changes that form who they are. These factors make them worthy of close attention. Millennials have a recognizable personality with a unique blend of behaviors and traits that studies and data reveal. They regard themselves as distinct, and based on the ever-increasing scrutiny society is giving them, older generations seem to agree. Some have great hopes for them; others are wary. While every generation is distinct in some way, who the Millennials are, the era they find themselves living in, and how they act will profoundly influence us all. Millennials constitute a demographic army who will disrupt all that lies before them. And a combination of factors renders Millennial architects to be prime disruptors among these legions.

Millennial behaviors and traits, both positive and negative, can be traced to three historical factors. First, Millennials are the debut generation of the global and systemic digital revolution. Second, growing up, they received an unprecedented level of care and attention from their parents. Third, their whole lives have been subject to exhaustive examination, with extensive comparison to previous generations. This last factor is largely a consequence of the previous two; their digital aptitude attracts our collective curiosity (and awe), and their doting parents take every opportunity to track and explain how special they are.

Understanding Millennials' attributes enables the architectural community to best take advantage of the generation's mindset and to position the architects among them to one day lead the profession, a demographic reality that will come sooner than many expect. Preparing this generation—whose priorities are significantly different from their predecessors'—is an imperative not to be ignored. Architecture is reinventing itself after enduring the Great Recession, an economic shock that typically comes once in a century. The effect of this shock on higher education may be even greater. As some forecast, the disruptions rolling through every industry and institution, led by Millennials and their digital mantle, will fundamentally change the way knowledge is passed from one generation to the next. Architectural education will be no exception. Given that current universities are essentially still medieval in nature, this may be a shock that comes once in a millennium.

Architecture is a cyclic industry that often painfully anticipates each economic downturn. As recovery does come, the discipline finds itself privileged to imagine a new and different world. The challenges presented in the most recent downturn's aftermath are historically severe. In the coming decades, the earth's population will increase by more than a third, with two-thirds of its people moving to cities.[1] Globally, Millennials are the disruptors prompting this migration, and whether it brings turmoil or success will depend increasingly on their leadership. Understanding Millennials as the cause of the disruption is also, ironically, the key to advancing after it passes. The looming dread that climate change and political unrest will only further induce migration raises the stakes even higher. The discipline of architecture is the one best poised to take on the vast physical transformation before us, but only if it mobilizes Millennials among its ranks to lead. If architecture does not bear this responsibility, it will release Millennials to other modes of thinking, and its agency will be further eroded and perhaps permanently damaged. Given this outlook, understanding Millennials today as emerging practitioners and students—their digital aptitudes, how they were raised, and what researchers have revealed about them—provides the essential self-reflexivity to fully rally them to action. Following their lead through the disruption ahead will earn the discipline of architecture the privilege to build a new and better world in its aftermath.

Digital Natives

Millennials came of age with the computer. Considered to be those born from the early 1980s up until the mid-2000s, Millennials knew the computer's potential by the time the first Millennial reached high school. And for the youngest, many parents placed digital devices in their cribs. While these changes may seem monumental to those who knew of the world before, Millennials take the digital world for granted. They have grown symbiotically with digital devices that have become smaller, cheaper, more mobile, and ever more powerful. Millennials have come to expect and even demand the opportunities that a digital world offers. As the first Millennials graduated high school in 2001, Marc Prensky described them as "digital natives," meaning that Millennials were born to this new world. As "digital immigrants," the rest of us came to it from another.[2] Undoubtedly, this epochal birthright has affected the Millennials' cognition. How could it not?[3]

For Millennials, the internet is instantaneous and ubiquitous. Accelerated by the widespread deployment of broadband infrastructure in the mid-1990s, the web became the primary tool for information gathering by the time Millennials entered college. Wireless zones and later wireless cellular networks untethered the internet from the desktop computer and made it available just about anywhere. This transformation radically compressed the time required for almost all tasks. Millennials complete in seconds research that once took hours if not days. The operative task in the twenty-first century is not to gather what information one can find, but to select which is most relevant (and most accurate). Most Millennials never had to pursue these tasks in a predigital age, so their response to instantaneous information is less one of incredulity than one of pondering what to do next. This information revolution has reorganized libraries, closed newspapers, influenced elections, and created an informal, decentralized information-sharing system in the blogosphere that is as ubiquitous as it is difficult to verify.

Entertainment—in some form or another—seems to fill every moment of free time the digital revolution liberated for Millennials. Most played digital games before venturing onto the web. Once online, they responded en masse to digital music downloads that disaggregated the traditional record album. Their preferences brought on taste-defining artificial intelligences that now influence what music to enjoy. After the immersive fantasy films Millennials grew up watching, animation engines became so real they spawned fully engrossing games now played in vast networks on the web. It seems to follow logically (and with little remaining irony) that the US military adopted the same interactive platforms used for entertainment to fight proxy wars using drones.[4] For Millennials, the streaming of video has become an unlimited visual resource. Videos now assist with the most prosaic tasks, such as learning how to tie a bowtie or cook an omelet. They also circulate humor and promote dramatic talent, elevating unknowns to celebrity stardom. For many, online connectivity has changed lives by finding them life partners. Those using online digital media affirm their success or popularity using an apt yet unnerving biological metaphor: going viral.

Most profound, the ubiquity of the internet has created clusters of entirely new kinds of communities whose sheer connectivity itself is unprecedented. According to a 2018 survey by the Pew Research Center, more than nine in ten Millennials (92 percent) own smartphones, compared with 67 percent of Boomers. A remarkable 28 percent of Millennials are smartphone-only internet users, meaning they access the internet anytime, anywhere, without relying on traditional broadband service at home.[5] By 2010, three years after the release of the smartphone, 83 percent of Millennials slept with digital devices on their bedside table,[6] and by 2015, 92 percent of teens reported going online daily, with 24 percent saying they were online "almost constantly."[7] Eighty-five percent of Millennials have a social media profile, compared to 57 percent of Boomers. (I will discuss Baby Boomers, Generation X, and their predecessors in subsequent chapters.) And significantly large shares of Millennials have adopted relatively new platforms such as Instagram (52 percent) and Snapchat (47 percent).[8] Millennial connectivity is constant, leading some to refer to them as the "always on" generation. To the exasperation of older generations, Millennials text those sitting next to them and often text while doing multiple tasks, including driving (64 percent admit to having sent or received a text while at the wheel, according to Pew).[9] This hivelike connectivity has spawned new genres of self-expression and created instantaneous swarms for both celebrations and the toppling of dictators.

One simply cannot overemphasize the profound changes brought by all things digital in which Millennials have participated. Chroniclers have and will continue to write extensively about this revolution. Thus it is surprising that, until a cover story broke in the January 2013 issue of *Architect* magazine, little had been written about Millennial-driven change in the context of architectural practice and education. This is especially surprising given how critical this revolution has been to design thinking. Many of the digital devices used by Millennials, most notably Apple products, are paradigms of design, part of a larger Gesamtkunstwerk that integrates everything from software to the iconic Apple store. The kind of beta-tested, iterative processes that rest at the core of architectural practice also formed the 3-D digital entertainment of the games Millennials play and the films they watch. And the free flow of information through software such as building information modeling (BIM) allows for integrated data and global collaboration. The last events of comparable magnitude in architecture may have been the Renaissance or the machine age, but I would say that each pales in comparison.

Scheduled

Millennials are the product of a rigorously scheduled upbringing. The reasons for this include who raised them, the social change they grew up amidst, and the highly specialized care given them. This hyperscheduling affects many of their character traits, with both significant positive and negative implications.

One begins understanding this scheduling protocol by recognizing that the first Millennials were the children of Baby Boomers. Baby Boomers, or Boomers for short, set a new standard for child rearing, largely rejecting the laissez-faire parenting style of their 1950s parents and opting instead to take a highly active role in raising their own children. Then the most highly educated generation in US history, Boomers wanted the same if not better for their offspring. Understanding the value of well-regarded universities and their selectivity, many Boomers set a high bar: their children would receive whatever preparation necessary to gain admission. Noted for their own transgressive behaviors with alcohol, sex, and drugs—and the toll they took—many Boomers strategized that keeping their children busy would help prevent similar circumstances.[10]

Societal changes also contributed to a more structured upbringing for Millennials. The sexual revolution of the 1960s propelled twice as many Boomer women to complete a four-year college program (26 percent) than in the previous generation (13 percent).[11] As a result, more women entered the workforce to increase household income and the subsequent quality of life. The same sexual revolution also led to higher divorce rates, resulting in more single-parent households: only 79 percent of Millennials under age ten grew up in a household with both parents present, compared to 86 percent of Boomers of the same age.[12] In a newly mobile and increasingly suburban nation, parents could no longer rely on a grandparent nearby to watch the kids. For all of these reasons, many Millennials grew up in households without a parent at home during the day. As a result, Boomer parents opted for preschool and after-school care, which increasingly became highly programmed and goal-oriented. In summer, camps changed from aimless canoeing to "career discovery" mini-semesters often on university campuses. Because families were having fewer children—the average household size was 22 percent smaller in 1990 than 1950—two working parents could afford this option.[13]

From a combination of Boomer high standards and external societal pressures, the typical Millennial received structured and sometimes highly focused care, often with other children, outside the home and under another's supervision. A parent carefully managed these activities from afar, and when required, often intervened directly. Abuse of this watchfulness eventually earned them the nickname "helicopter parents."[14] In primary and secondary schools, seasonal clubs and sports expanded to become year-round activities to meet two needs: doubling as extracurricular activities for future college applications and as an extended form of day care.

This structured upbringing made Millennials inclined to respect authority and work and fare well with others. They also get along with their parents, something few Boomers can claim (at least as young adults).[15] Most research recognizes an increase in civic-mindedness among Millennials that may be a corollary to their respect for authority.[16] They are generally practical and goal-oriented; they scored higher than previous generations on standardized SAT and NAEP tests when scores were adjusted for other factors.[17] Later findings in 2015, however, suggest a decline, especially when gauged internationally.[18] These attributes give many Millennials high expectations of themselves that can test their confidence once they leave the range of a hovering parent. Negative attributes include overthinking and choosing preconceived life paths without truly testing their own affinities.[19] Many Millennials are prone to impatience if someone fails to provide service equal to standards set by their parents or caregivers.[20] Observers debate whether their tendency to move home after college as "boomerang kids" is a result of their inability to spread their wings, a consequence of the stalled economy, a pragmatic choice not to waste money, an expression of abiding affection for their parents, or a combination of all the above.[21] Perhaps the most scathing negative attribute, leveled at Millennials in a controversial 2013 *Time* magazine cover story, is that their overarching confidence has resulted in three times the cases of narcissistic personality disorder compared to those 65 or older.[22]

As Paul Taylor from the Pew Research Center summarizes in his book, *The Next America*, Millennials are distinguished by two seemingly incompatible characteristics. First, compared to other generations, many Millennials seem to be ambling along on an excruciatingly "slow walk to adulthood." In 2012, 40 percent of Millennial men and 32 percent of women over eighteen were living in their parents' homes, only 20 percent were married by their mid-twenties when over half their parents were at the same age, and when polled in 2007, only 18 percent considered the main purpose of forming a lifetime union in marriage to bear and raise children, compared to 33 percent of those 65 and older.[23] By 2018, a position taken in *The Lancet Child & Adolescent Health* journal recommended expanding the period of adolescence, commonly accepted since the mid-1950s as between ten and nineteen, to twenty-four years of age.[24]

The second characteristic seems to counter the first's hesitancy with an almost unshakable optimism in the future, even in the face of extraordinary challenges that have, nonetheless, taken their toll. In a 2015 American Psychological Association survey, adult Millennials reported a stress level of 5.5 out of 10, where researchers consider 3.6 to be healthy.[25] Yet after studying Millennials for more than a decade, Taylor still writes that they seem undeterred:

> Despite inheriting the worst economy since the Great Depression, despite rates of youth un- and underemployment that are the highest since the government began keeping such records, despite the growing albatross of student loan debt, and despite not being able to think about starting a family of their own, Millennials are America's most stubborn optimists. They have a self-confidence born of coddling parents and everyone-gets-a-trophy coaches. They have the look-at-me elan that comes from being humankind's first generation of digital natives. . . . And they have the invincibility of youth.[26]

If one accepts viral circulation on the internet as anecdotal evidence, Norman Foster's statement that "if you weren't an optimist, it would be impossible to be an architect" would suggest an alignment between architecture and the Millennials' unshakable optimism. And this may bode well for the architectural profession. In contrast, the Millennials' slow path to adulthood may impede a commitment to architectural education's intense training period, which for the undergraduate professional degree starts while still a teenager. Awareness of this demand may be a contributing factor to current declining enrollment and retention.

As I discuss later in this book, architecture may be able to draw as many benefits from Millennials' characteristics and behaviors as it needs to reckon with what research reveals as their negative traits. From a positive standpoint, when the Millennials' self-confidence eventually hitches itself to the architectural profession's traditional work ethic, early results show new modes of leadership outside the discipline (I discuss these in Chapter 2). In the academy, the Millennials' predisposition to collaborative and goal-oriented learning environments makes them favor studio-based education. This trend compels some design schools to migrate studio learning to other disciplines in order to meet new demand. How the architectural academy responds to the Millennials' penchant for social networks and video games remains an open question. For some educators, they are a distraction; others—following the lead outside the discipline of architecture—see an opportunity. Perhaps the greatest challenge to the profession and academy will be to reconcile an age-old design process, one committed to a slow, patient, and iterative search, with the Millennial generation's collective demand for immediate results. And their overriding quest for a balanced quality of life only complicates this reconciliation further.

Studied

Writers began profiling Millennials even before they became adults or acquired a name. In addition to their digital birthright and proud Boomer parents, scrutiny comes from the growing ranks of researchers whose forebearers first began studying generations in prewar Germany. This research community now has at its disposal enough data on both Millennials and their predecessor generations to make comparisons using social science data, market research, neurological experiments, and ever increasingly, the data-mining logs of web activity: big data. In most, but not all cases, these empirically support an earlier historiography that was largely based on cultural understanding.

The dramatic economic changes wrought by their digital upbringing has driven the desire to study Millennials. Now commonly referred to as "disruptions," these began to appear when the first Millennials reached young adulthood around 2000. Their coming-of-age helped upend the music industry through internet file sharing, with US sales of recorded music falling from $14.6 billion in 1999 to just $6.3 billion ten years later.[27] In another sector, print newspaper ad revenues declined by 50 percent between 2005 and 2015 as advertisers flee print media to the internet sites that Millennials prefer, especially social media.[28] Anyone in the business community has strong reason to believe that a disruption to their industry might be next. For them, understanding Millennials is a matter of survival.

The magnitude of the Millennials' disruptions has spawned an entire intellectual community focusing on the generation. Activities range from blogs to articles in academic journals, from op-eds to significant polling exercises, from popular press pieces to books and even series of books. Writers include self-declared gurus trying to create a generalized Millennial profile, soothsayers trying to tell the future, and data analysts, including scholars, trying to validate or deny both. While I will use many of these to form a profile for this book, let me introduce three often-referenced examples of the different forms this examination takes.

First, the work of the Pew Research Center stands out for its focus on Millennials, an endeavor the *New York Times* described in 2014 as "the most illuminating literary project of our era."[29] Led by Paul Taylor, executive vice president for special projects, Pew leverages its examination of Millennials with the center's extensive experience with public opinion polling, demographic research, media content analysis, and empirical social science. In 2010, it debuted its Millennial research in an optimistically titled report, "Millennials: Confident. Connected. Open to Change." The report profiles Millennials then between the ages of eighteen and twenty-nine, examining "their demographics; their political and social values; their lifestyles and life priorities; their digital technology and social media habits; and their economic and educational aspirations."[30] A later 2014 report, entitled "Millennials in Adulthood: Detached from Institutions, Networked with Friends," offers a less rosy forecast. Profiling those eighteen to thirty-three, the study confirms the generation's persistent optimism, but also reveals an ominous and growing detachment from organized politics and religion, as well as an increasing distrust of others. Pew also finds that Millennials, burdened by debt, are in no rush to marry. On a less somber note, the report confirms that social media increasingly binds the generation in positive ways.[31] In 2018, based on its own reasoning, Pew declared the Millennial birthing period closed, deciding that the last had been born in 1996[32] (others project the bracket into the mid 2000s, which I will continue to cite in this book). Writing on his own but with data support from Pew, Taylor published *The Next America* in 2014, its book jacket describing an America headed "toward a future marked by the most striking social, racial, and economic shifts the country has seen in a century."

Second, an academic study published in *Academic Medicine* in 2006 by Nicole Borges and her colleagues stands out as one of a few longitudinal (meaning long-term) studies relevant to professional education. "Comparing Millennial and Generation X Medical Students at One Medical School" finds that Millennial students at the Northeastern Ohio Medical University College of Medicine had significant personality differences from their predecessors, Generation X. Borges's team tested two groups: the first matriculated between the years 1989–1994 and the second from 2001–2004. Separating more than eight hundred medical students from both periods into three groups by age—Millennials, Generation X, and a third overlapping group they refer to as Cuspars—their analysis shows significant differences between Generation X and Millennial students in ten of sixteen personality factors. And by including the Cuspars, whose scores ranged between Generation X's and Millennials' in several categories, the study strongly suggests the personalities of the generations were gradually shifting over time.[33]

Finally, any comprehensive examination of Millennials must reckon with over two decades of writing by William Strauss and Neil Howe and the controversy surrounding it. Strauss and Howe were the first to use the term "Millennial" to describe the generation, beginning with the book *Generations: The History of America's Future, 1584 to 2069* (1991). With *The Fourth Turning* (1997), the duo mapped out what has come to be called Strauss-Howe generational theory, a proposition that considers Millennials to be the latest in a line of Anglo-Saxon generations cycling back five hundred years. With the publication of *Millennials Rising* (2000), they announced the generation's debut in the first year they turned eighteen as per their generational theory timeline. As Millennials came of age Strauss and Howe produced two editions of *Millennials Go to College* (2003, 2007), and Neil Howe completed *Millennials in the Workplace* (2010) with Reena Nadler after William Strauss passed away in 2007. This body of work became the foundation of a consultant enterprise that advised industries and included its own publishing and polling apparatus. Most notably, Strauss and Howe first set forth the generational profile that Pew has advanced and others continue to question: that Millennials are confident, dynamic, and optimistic. When compared to their predecessor generation, Strauss and Howe stress that Millennials are "good kids," and framed by their generational theory, they consider Millennials as archetypal members of a "hero" generation.[34]

Given Strauss and Howe's early prominence, their deep connections to industry, the fact that both authors rose from the ranks of Washington's congressional and agency support infrastructure, and their lightly footnoted writing outside of peer-reviewed academic journals, Strauss and Howe receive much criticism, and it began early. Reviewing *The Fourth Turning* for the *New York Times*, Michael Lind described their theories as elastic, unfalsifiable, and "as vague as those of fortune cookies."[35] Some indict Strauss and Howe for their "failure to deal adequately with the demographics and social reality of race, ethnicity, and class in American society."[36] Others seem most skeptical of the "good kid" tag, seeing narcissism and arrogance instead of self-confidence and questioning the altruistic motives associated with their respectfulness.[37]

Controversy over Strauss and Howe's writing extends to politics, where it initially had an impact across a broad spectrum. The book jacket of *Generations* describes how Al Gore and Newt Gingrich, two leaders from opposing political camps who squared off in the "culture wars" of the 1990s, both hailed the work. Decades later, Strauss and Howe's work gained new attention and notoriety in 2017 when *Time* and *Politico* revealed *The Fourth Turning* to be a critically influential book to Donald Trump's political strategist and adviser, Stephen Bannon.[38] Given the political controversy, one might consider setting aside Strauss and Howe's work, yet doing so leaves a difficult-to-bridge void in understanding the Millennial generation. The authors first identify Millennials as a distinct generation from childhood and frame the twenty-first-century broad discourse for when they became adults. Their characterizations have largely stood the test of time, and most writers on generations, whether scholarly or not, make reference to their work. I use their timelines and categorizations to frame a discussion of architectural generations and also to understand the dynamics between contemporary age groups. To prepare the reader to join in this analysis, I both summarize and critically evaluate Strauss and Howe's schema. Doing so helps to contextualize their findings with those of Pew, Borges, and others, including their critics, to form a more comprehensive understanding of Millennials in architecture.

To validate these many findings as they pertain to Millennial architects,

I conducted an online poll in early 2016 in cooperation with the American Institute of Architecture Students, the New York chapter of the American Institute of Architects, and the American Architectural Foundation. The poll drew responses from over 350 self-described Millennial participants and over one hundred from older generations. The poll had two goals. The first was to discern if any deviation exists between Millennial architects and the general characteristics ascribed to the entire generation by Pew Research and others. The survey found concordance with broader research with some significant deviation in certain areas. In focus groups I conducted both before and after the poll, I probed these deviations, and use the responses culled to formulate reasons why they might exist. The second goal was to test findings that emerged in my attempt to form a general profile of the Millennial architect, and these slant toward education in questions about pedagogy and career choices. I presented my findings at the Center for Architecture in New York in January of 2016 and at the AIAS FORUM in Boston in December of that year. The results are discussed throughout Part Two, and the entire poll is included as an appendix.

Disruptors

The proliferation of research—offering both conjecture and rebuttal—indicates that something is indeed going on here with Millennials. Yet while their being the digitally savviest, best-parented, and most scrutinized generation may be sufficient cause alone to study them, Millennials may be remembered less for who they are than for their role as the disruptors of economies, politics, and academia in a turbulent era.

Twenty-first-century business media first began using the term "disruption" to define these upheavals. Like a fierce prairie thunderstorm moving through time, these events describe a technology and its associated values overtaking an existing market, typically employing digital hardware and software as the primary agents of disruption. Since 2015, disruptions have become ubiquitous and are sometimes the subject of stand-up comedy. Awareness of them has spawned conferences such as TechCrunch Disrupt,[39] which jumps from city to city, and have compelled the University of Southern California to launch a new program branded as a "degree to disrupt."[40] In his 2014 book *The Road to Reinvention*, venture capitalist Josh Linkner uses survival-of-the-fittest rhetoric in challenging his readers to "disrupt or be disrupted."[41]

While disruptions might appear as simply another sign of laissez-faire capitalism in the digital age, one must not underestimate the Millennials' critical role as disruptors in these market transformations, as their large numbers and social media–linked mindset provide the crucial swing block necessary to change a market. Until sufficient numbers massed around 2000, innovation alone did not bring on disruption. Compare, for example, Apple's 1993 introduction of its Newton device with the 2007 iPhone debut: both have the same basic function and both encountered early technological glitches and poor marketing, yet the Newton proved to be a colossal business embarrassment while the iPhone propelled Apple to become the world's most profitable corporation within three years.[42] Whatever latent disruptive capacity the pioneering Newton held, it emerged too soon to take advantage of the adult Millennial demographic. Another example is Fathom, a 2000 online learning project in which Columbia University and many well-regarded partners invested $25 million. The venture failed after three years, with a Columbia administrator admitting, "It's unclear what the market is."[43] Within a decade, other prestigious universities along with numerous startups would offer online courses in a growing market of Millennials who grew up comfortable with the concept of learning online. These universities now hold a decisive advantage, as academia stands poised to be disrupted.

While the word "disruption" conjures an image of millennial hordes coordinated through social media storming every industry's fortress, another essential word often accompanies it in the twenty-first century: innovation. Appropriated by the Millennial digital native mindset, technological innovation makes this battle so lopsided, the same way cannons suddenly made medieval fortifications obsolete. In a 2014 essay, Jill Lepore traces the history of both words and how they apply in a contemporary business lexicon. Lepore writes that after 9/11, "innovation" as a term gained ubiquity (again, coincident with the arrival of adult Millennials) among major news venues, with *Time* magazine, the *New York Times*, and *Forbes* all publishing special innovation issues. Surprisingly, the word once held negative connotations, signifying excessive novelty without purpose or end. Edmund Burke referred to the French Revolution as a "revolt of innovation" and American Federalists declared themselves to be "enemies to innovation." The word only took on a positive meaning in the mid-twentieth century with economist Joseph Schumpeter using it in the context of bringing new products to market. In his writing, Schumpeter also introduces the concept of "creative destruction."[44]

In his 1997 book, *The Innovator's Dilemma*, Clayton Christensen elaborates upon creative destruction as a form of innovation and as a means of survival in contemporary business. A professor at Harvard Business School, Christensen studies why companies fail. The word "dilemma" in the book's title alludes to the critical instance when a business leader must choose between two kinds of innovation: sustaining or disruptive. Sustaining innovation refers to the progressive improvement of production to maintain competitive status. Disruptive innovation creates a new market by applying a different set of values that ultimately eclipses the prevailing one. Christensen writes that all too often, business leaders choose sustaining innovations because the disruptive option offers little initial profit and takes away investment necessary to maintain an existing product's competitiveness.[45] Twenty-first-century startups, financed as privateers by venture capital, hold no responsibility for sustaining any existing production. For these entities, disruptive innovation has become the battle cry; they either disrupt an existing market or, failing to do so, reconstitute themselves for an entirely different onslaught. Drawn to new markets created by Millennials, and increasingly driven by Millennial know-how, these disruptors, for better or worse, have become the leadership icons of the Millennial business age.

Architecture has always practiced a form of disruptive innovation; it is how the profession continually grows to stay competitive. And of all the forms of professional education, design pedagogy, as it has evolved through many generations in architecture schools, is arguably best equipped to teach future innovators how to disrupt. One need only look at the business programs that have appropriated this pedagogy as evidence. A contemporary doctrine of innovation also argues that failure is an essential component of disruption; only through continual trial and error can a disruptor discover the right combination of technological prowess and market vulnerability. The iterative process developed in architecture schools and practiced by successful professionals closely parallels that of contemporary Millennial disruptors. Well-trained architects have been tempered by a constant interrogation in reviews while at school, and this compels them to continually innovate as professionals. As described throughout this book, other affinities bind architects and Millennials, each following a common creed of disruption.

After initially upsetting business practices, by 2010 unexpected Millennial disruptions erupted in sectors of society not directly connected to the economy, each suggesting an era of increased turbulence. The faster-than-anticipated passage of marriage equality laws reveals the growing and steady pressure of Millennial social values. Pew's Paul Taylor predicts a potential generational disruption to the social welfare safety net, as the entitlement needs of retiring Boomers must someday be reconciled with the slowly rising incomes of Millennials.⁴⁶ The global disruption to cities that the UN predicts is already beginning in North America. Vehicle miles traveled (VMT) decreased 25 percent among sixteen-to-thirty-year-olds between 2001 and 2009, while public transit ridership has increased 36 percent since 1996, indicating the generation's preference for the mobility patterns of urban living.⁴⁷ Globally, Millennials sparked the political sea change in the Middle East that began with a whiff of optimism as the Arab Spring, but has in most cases devolved into chaos. The disconcerting at-traction of global Millennials (including a sizable number of Americans) to the barbaric campaign of the Islamic State—made notorious by the horrific content of its social media—is a chilling reminder of how easily the Millen-nials' "good kid" tag can flip to its polar opposite.

Disruption crescendoed in the US with the 2016 upset election of Donald Trump, the culmination of a period of worldwide political upheaval the *Christian Science Monitor* end-of-year issue painted as a "Year of Disruption."⁴⁸ Millennials had earlier played a disruptive role when they emerged from political passivity and, mobilized by social media, swept Barack Obama into office in 2008 and reelected him in 2012 (albeit in diminished numbers). But in 2016 they disrupted the election in favor of the opposite party through inaction by returning to their pre-Obama political abstention, or for oth-ers, by registering a protest vote for a third-party candidate. According to a *Bloomberg News* analysis of exit polls, had Millennials voted for Hillary Clinton in the same numbers as they did for Obama in 2008, Clinton would have won in a landslide by over two hundred electoral votes.⁴⁹ The switch represented less a party realignment and more a consolidation of disillu-sionment in traditional political parties, leaving Millennials waiting in dor-mancy for leadership to realign disruption with innovation, whether through another Obama or someone like Senator Bernie Sanders, who captured their imaginations during the 2016 primaries. Given that Millennials' affiliation with the Republican Party has stubbornly remained around 30 percent, it seems unlikely that they will rally behind President Trump, although that, too, remains uncertain.⁵⁰ It is equally uncertain whether they will subscribe to *New York Times* opinion columnist Charles Blow's exhortation to use their "power of disruption" to mobilize through grassroots activism.⁵¹ There is some indication, however, that this is occurring. A heightened Millennial sense of propriety seems to be fueling the Me Too movement that felled the Hollywood mogul Harvey Weinstein and the starchitect Richard Meier.

The cohort also leads the country in a revitalized stand on gun control. Despite these trends, the only given seems that the Millennial generation will remain a potent, disruptive force well into the twenty-first century, bringing change both through action and inaction. Knowing who or what mobilizes them will be a powerful strategic asset.

It is against this backdrop of economic, social, and political disruption that it seems imperative to better understand Millennials as architectural practice and pedagogy contend with their own respective disruptions, ones that will be increasingly associated with a large generational cohort whose influence is as great as it is unpredictable.

Millennials in Architecture: Practice

If one brackets the years when the Millennial generation turns eighteen—approximately 2000 to 2022—the Great Recession forms a deep economic and psychological indent in the middle third of this time span. In architecture, the impact's magnitude echoes that of the recording and publishing industries' declines earlier in the decade. The AIA's Architecture Billings Index lost almost half its value, from a high of 60.5 in 2005 to a low of 34.4 in 2009.[52] The severity of the downturn forced architecture firms to cut almost a third of their staff.[53] Many of those laid off, including the older generations, have not returned to architecture, especially those without computer skills who did not retool themselves. Of the younger generation, 30 percent of Millennial interns laid off who were surveyed in 2012 expressed their unlikelihood to return to architecture.[54] And as also reported in a 2012 Georgetown study, many of the one in six Millennials who could not find work upon graduating architecture school opted never to join the profession.[55] The economic upheaval dramatically reorganized the practice, causing firms to shrink, forcing many to merge, and cleansing the market of all but the smallest nondigital firms. By mid-2014, the recovery seemed to have begun, with the Billings Index rising to 55.8 by July.[56] And as the rebound continues, firms hire mostly Millennials with strong digital skills, but at lower salaries than older workers. Due to the absence of older generations who did not return to architecture, postrecession firms employ disproportionately more Millennials than if the recession had not occurred. And as Boomers retire at an increasing rate in the coming decades, the ratio of Millennials in architectural practices will dramatically increase. This comes with benefits and challenges as we enter a period of global transformation.

It is a stretch to argue that Millennials caused the disruption to the architecture profession in the same way their consumer practices affected other industries. Architecture is a highly reactive and cyclic industry that is often the harbinger of market vicissitudes, but seldom the cause. It is safe to say, however, that Millennials will and already have begun to play a critical role in reshaping architectural practice in the disruption's wake in a pattern that will last for some time. In an article in the January 2014 issue of *Architect* magazine, Thomas Fisher lays out an emergent future consistent with many Millennial attributes. He forecasts that postrecession practices will be digitally nimble, small-scaled, smart city–focused, public interest–driven, and "polyculturally" collaborative.

Fisher frames much of the article from an understanding of Jeremy Rifkin's book, *The Third Industrial Revolution*.[57] According to Rifkin, industrial revolutions occur when innovations in communication technology join with new energy sources to change the form of production. If the first industrial revolution resulted in the steam engine and the assembly line came from the second, then according to Rifkin, 3-D printing will mark the third. He argues that spiking fuel costs jump-started the Great Recession to begin a new industrial era in which renewable energy will render fossil fuels uneconomic and archaic. As a result, both energy production and manufacturing—using 3-D printing—will decentralize in an entirely new social formation.

According to Fisher, architects may be aligned well to contribute extensively in this new critical epoch. In addition to having helped pioneer 3-D printing, architecture can combine Millennial connectivity and team-based skills to participate in the emergence of "deep play." In the previous revolutions, as Rifkin explains, "we lived to work"; in the third, "we will live to play." As he describes it, deep play is not frivolous, but "the way we experience the other, transcend ourselves and connect to broader, ever more inclusive communities of life in our common search for universality."[58] Deep play resonates with the creative, patient, and iterative search that design has traditionally embraced, and may position architecture well in the third industrial revolution and the new world built around it. While it will be the Millennials' great privilege to bring about change aligned with their values if this revolution happens, it will also be an enormous challenge to lead the currently fragmented society in doing so.

Millennials in Architecture: Academia

Economic uncertainty has largely clouded the experience of Millennials in architecture schools. When they first entered, the country had just experienced the burst of the dot-com bubble, followed shortly by the economic fallout of the 9/11 attacks. And then the Great Recession greeted the first graduating classes. The impact of these events shrank professional program first-time enrollments by 22 percent between 2009 and 2014.[59] And while enrollment began to creep up after the recession's low, by 2017, total enrollment was still 17 percent below its 2008 high.[60] Many schools were also making up for the deficit by enrolling more foreign students,[60] whose presence in American architectural schools increased from 12 percent in 2009 to 24 percent by 2016.[61] This strategy may ultimately prove no panacea for schools if more restrictive federal immigration policies deter international students from applying. An 18 percent drop nationwide after the 9/11 attacks serves as a reminder of just how volatile foreign enrollments can be.[62]

Picked up by national media in 2012, a Georgetown study reported unemployment among architecture graduates as twice that of those with engineering or business degrees.[63] A follow-up 2015 report found unemployment among architecture graduates still high, even though the general economy had begun to improve. Most alarming, architects had the highest unemployment levels of the professional groups surveyed, even exceeding those of experienced workers with only a high school diploma.[64] Through most of the recession, architects were buoyed by the US Bureau of Labor Statistics projecting a 17 percent increase in demand for architects by 2022.[65] But by 2016, it had scaled back its projection to no growth, suggesting that the decrease in architecture's labor force caused by the Great Recession could be more permanent than many had thought.

While gloomy job prospects undoubtedly hinder enrollment in architecture schools, other factors might also contribute. These could include recent memories of relatives or family friends who suffered in the recession, lower pay compared to other professions, the lure of other creative fields related to the internet, and architecture's reputation for long hours. Millennials' practical tendencies—especially when enforced by parental oversight—might make any of these reason enough to choose a different career path. Yet while today's poor architecture school enrollment may seem significant, it pales when compared to the Millennial-driven disruption to academia that many see ahead.

In 2012, the Stanford University president, John Hennessy, used the phrase "there's a tsunami coming" to describe the magnitude of what looms over academia. Hennessy's tsunami refers to the great changes that he believes digital media and online learning will have on higher education, changes in which Millennials have and will continue to play a significant role.[66] In a subsequent editorial that uses Hennessy's metaphor in its title, *New York Times* columnist David Brooks places these changes in the context of the Great Recession. Brooks describes how the recession caused students and their parents to balk at the high cost of tuition and fees, which have outpaced inflation in the United States for decades. With recent graduates unable to find jobs and overwhelmed by debt, younger Millennials are carefully considering which educational models will get them the employment and compensation they expect for the right price.[67] This relatively recent shock occurs against the backdrop of a long-term transition in which higher education is increasingly regarded less as a public good than a private one. In this sense, many Millennials consider a college degree to be a commodity, one that ultimately leads to career development and personal advancement, rather than an accepted societal ritual.[68]

Online education—once considered an inferior mode—is an option Millennials increasingly are using. Undergraduate students taking online courses rose from 15 percent in 2008 to 47 percent in 2014, although many report doing so more as a matter of convenience or necessity and not necessarily preference.[69] The sudden proliferation of massive open online courses (MOOCs) in 2008, and their early adoption by elite universities such as Stanford, MIT, and Harvard, caught the education community by surprise, with many confused as to why a highly selective university such as MIT would offer the exact same course through digital media to everyone, and for *free*. Although reviews remain mixed, and few students complete these courses, the numbers signing up for them are staggering. For now, it seems that these top-tier universities sense the changes ahead and are responding in advance. They have the resources to experiment and absorb the high initial costs as a loss leader to establish early brand dominance.[70] In 2012, a dozen top-tier international universities committed to working with Coursera, a for-profit company formed by two former Stanford faculty, to integrate MOOCs into their curricula.[71] Universities not able to join this and other consortia, or to invest in producing their own online curricula of comparable quality, may suffer. These include public universities hampered by decreases in state support, private universities without strong endowments, and for-profit universities operating on thin financial margins.

The Millennial disruption to academia is occurring swiftly, and success may not be as simple as offering online courses. Even Sebastian Thrun, the Stanford professor who hosted the first MOOC, is nervous about the pace of change.[72] Yet the academic leaders looking ahead recognize that one need go no further than sectors of the entertainment and journalism industries to know that there will be winners and losers in this shake-up. Those that do not understand the Millennial wave and begin some form of transition soon may find themselves suddenly outpaced and engulfed by the coming tsunami. Echoing Hennessy's concerns, Kevin Carey, in his book *The End of College*, predicts that perhaps only fifty American colleges and universities will survive the disruptions of the twenty-first century.[73] Digital technology driven by the preferences Millennials set forth will either cause schools to be absorbed or cease to exist.

Course correction—a major theme throughout this book—can help architecture schools survive and even profit from higher education's re-organization. Without it, the tsunami may indeed drown many schools. As an advantage, the architectural academy crossed the digital divide in the previous generation, entering the twenty-first century technologically pre-pared for the new cohort. In almost all schools, studios maintain broadband access—either wired, wireless, or both. That Millennials prefer the experi-ential learning aspect of a studio environment, especially one meeting their digital expectations, is another distinct advantage. By exporting the proven experience of this teaching method and its digital infrastructure to other disciplines, architecture schools can maintain and diversify their enrollment. And schools that link this to AIA's prescribed degree and licensure reforms will be better positioned to do so.

A sobering reality is that architecture schools will need to catch up. When the first wave of Millennials entered graduate programs in 2005, Stanford's mechanical engineering department, in conjunction with its business school, adopted a studio-based, experiential learning model as the showcase of their Institute of Design (a.k.a. the d.school). Stanford guessed right in anticipating Millennial educational preferences in disciplines without a previous tradition of studio learning. If architecture schools fail to seize upon this opportunity, other pedagogies will. To be cost-effective, schools will have to balance the studio's relatively high student-to-faculty ratio with other forms of less expensive course delivery. Blending its popular studio model with some form of online learning, even applying the instant feedback loop of digital games, will make architecture schools more competitive and also exporters of pedagogy, potentially emerging as winners in the coming shake-up.

These opportunities and vulnerabilities in the face of future dramatic disruptions should compel American architectural practices and schools to remain relevant and competitive with other disciplines, other continents, and, increasingly, one another. As *Architect* magazine urges, this will require a complete reappraisal of pedagogy, licensure, and firm management to take full advantage of what Millennials have to offer.[74] Given that Millennials are prompting change systemically, a close examination of the generation currently in architecture offices, classrooms, and studios is in order if not grossly overdue. There are many questions to ask: Who are they? How have technology and upbringing given them distinct characteristics and what are those? How and why are they different from other generations of architects? How do we take advantage of their optimism and help them overcome any hesitancy? Overshadowing each of these questions is the looming threat of disruption, perhaps massive, in our future. How we simultaneously both anticipate and groom these Millennial disruptors for leadership in architecture will be fateful. The survival of the discipline as we know it may hang in the balance.

CHAPTER 2

Who Are the Millennials?

> Dating back to their first births in the early 1980s,
> you could see this millennial generation coming.
> Everywhere they've been, from bulging nurseries
> to the new "Baby on Board" minivans, from day-care
> to kindergarten to high school, they have changed
> the face of youth—and transformed every institution
> they've touched.
>
> **WILLIAM STRAUSS AND NEIL HOWE**

Millennials are the junior architects in firms and the students currently in architecture schools. The first entered college in 2000, and the last will graduate in the late 2020s. Millennials are populous in number and know that they are distinct from their forebearers. From various studies, one can generate a broad profile that finds them to be self-confident, team-oriented, and outwardly focused, with a pervasive digital acumen affecting each aspect of this characterization. Skeptics contest the Millennials' altruism, intellect, distinctiveness, and digital aptitude. Comparing their general characteristics with the contemporary practice and teaching of architecture reveals significant correspondence. How architecture as a mindset relates to the Millennial profile refined by critics lays the groundwork for how the profession and academy can adapt to the generation.

Millennials form one of the largest and most distinct demographic groups in US history. Pew Research places them at about the same number as their Baby Boomer parents, 77 million, while Eric Greenberg and Karl Weber, using an earlier birth year to begin the cohort, count them at 95 million, a US majority.[1] More than half have attended or will attend some form of college, a larger number than any previous generation,[2] and standardized tests measure them as the most intelligent generation, when controlled for other factors.[3] Sixty-one percent of Millennials say their age group is unique and distinct, a response twelve percentage points higher than that of their predecessors, Generation X.[4] With the ever-growing abundance of data, many studies and surveys find Millennials to be statistically different from previous generations at the same age in several ways, with every indication that these characteristics will remain part of their lifelong culture.[5]

Millennial Characteristics and Their Critics

The three overarching positive Millennial categories—self-confidence, team orientation, and outward focus—are consistent among most profiles of Millennials. Confidence appears first in the title of the 2010 Pew report and has remained among Strauss and Howe's seven core Millennial characteristics since they began listing them in 2000. Through the 2010s, Millennial confidence is so solid that even diminished prospects in the labor force after the Great Recession fail to deter their optimism.[6] Most writers concur that their faith in themselves comes from an upbringing of encouragement and support, and it is without surprise that "special" and "sheltered" are first and second among Strauss and Howe's core characteristics.

The nurturing of the Millennials' self-confidence began at birth when Millennial babies suddenly dominated the national agenda in the United States in the early 1980s. Their Boomer parents (recast as yuppies) lobbied for school reform and legislation that lessened their children's exposure to negative influences, especially alcohol and drugs. Boomers had firsthand experiences with those excesses and wanted none of them for their children. A culture of "do as I say, not as I do (or did)" became common.[7] Protectiveness prevailed; the drinking age changed, drug laws were strengthened, driver's licenses became more restrictive, and bicycle helmets suddenly became ubiquitous on children and adults alike.[8]

By certain measures, sheltering and nurturing have led to a Millennial sense of well-being. For the 2000–2010 decade, Millennials maintained consistently lower suicide rates than middle-aged and older adults;[9] 67 percent considered themselves happy or very happy most of the time,[10] and 88 percent believed that they would earn enough in their future.[11] A dissenting voice on this topic is Texas A&M's Fred Bonner, who questions the universality of Millennials' sense of "specialness," complaining that this has little bearing on Millennials of color. When Professor Bonner asks minority students if they are special, he typically receives blank stares.[12]

With regard to personality, Nicole Borges's 2006 *Academic Medicine* study finds them to be socially bold and adventuresome, open to change and experimental, and organized and self-disciplined.[13] Strauss and Howe's additional core characteristics find them to be "achieving" but also characterize them as feeling "pressured." Indeed, society has placed tremendous pressure on Millennials to live up to their reputation as what Ron Alsop describes as "trophy kids."[14] Pressure seems to be increasing for Millennials; a 2013 American Psychological Association report cites that 39 percent of Millennials say their stress has increased in the previous year, compared to 36 percent of Generation X and 33 percent of Boomers.[15] Despite the evident strain, Strauss and Howe—who often use cultural avatars as representatives of generations—believe Millennials will remain upbeat, saying, "Like their cartoon hero SpongeBob SquarePants, Millennials believe that the irrepressible optimism can overcome all obstacles."[16]

Their confidence also stems from their prowess with digital technology and the opportunity it affords. Nearly one in four Millennials believe that technology makes them different, twice the number of the next closest polled category (musical taste).[17] Millennials learn by doing and typically learn technology from one another or online rather than from printed instructions or lectures. Among Millennials, 73 percent believe that the internet has been mostly a good thing for society. The internet is used by 97 percent of Millennials, while 82 percent of adult Millennials say they use Facebook.[18] Marc Prensky, who coined the term "digital native," writes that for this generation, "the locus of 'knowledge' has, in the twenty-first century, moved to a great extent from the teacher to the Internet."[19] Millennials effortlessly navigate the internet's new and continually transforming realm, giving them a seemingly decisive advantage over other generations and the corresponding self-assurance that comes with it. Businesses, institutions, and academia increasingly use the terms "reverse-" or "up-" as a prefix to mentoring, referring to the phenomenon of younger individuals teaching older ones about all things related to the digital revolution.[20] Emory University Professor Mark Bauerlein takes an opposing view of their digital aptitude. His provocatively titled book, *The Dumbest Generation: How the Digital Age Stupefies Young Americans and Jeopardizes Our Future*, argues that the Millennials' overreliance on all things digital infantilizes them.[21]

A second common characteristic of Millennials is their team orientation. Strauss and Howe again list this as a core characteristic, attributable to a youth spent continuously clustered with their peers. Millennials became "who they are" by watching Barney on PBS, playing organized sports where no one loses, and collaborating in Montessori-style learning with a focus on community service. As a result, Millennials both work and play well with others. In 2007, only three teens in ten reported that they usually socialize with only one or two friends, as Millennial teens more often associate in packs held loosely together by social media.[22] Peer pressure to a Millennial is a means of promoting good behavior that binds a group, rather than the slippery slope toward transgression that it meant for earlier generations. The Millennial team spirit uses technology to create an unprecedented degree of connectivity. Through social networks, starting with Myspace, Friendster, and Facebook and later branching off into a maze of others, Millennials maintain digital linkages that have spawned an entirely new subeconomy.

Outward focus is the third aspect of a Millennial's generalized profile. Millennials are largely respectful, generous, and convivial toward others, including those in authority, and are significantly less critical of government than other generations.[23] More than 57 percent say they volunteered in the past twelve months.[24] This overarching respect also leads to tolerance; in a 2010 study, 55 percent of Millennials say their generation is more tolerant of races and groups different from their own compared to 37 percent of people fifty and older.[25] Ninety-three percent of Millennials agree that it is OK for blacks and whites to date when less than 60 percent of Boomers agreed at the same age.[26] Nearly 58 percent of Millennials say that immigrants strengthen the country, compared to 43 percent of older generations.[27]

Not since the 1950s has a generation been more respectful toward parents and authority. Unlike with Boomers—who famously announced "don't trust anyone over thirty"—almost no "generation gap" exists between Millennials and their parents. According to Pew, only 26 percent of all polled say that there are strong conflicts today between young people and older people, and 68 percent say that conflicts are either not very strong or are nonexistent.[28] The percentage of teens who say that their values are "very or mostly similar" to their parents was 76 percent in 2007.[29] Beyond respect, Millennials consider parents their friends, even sharing tastes in clothing, music, and other entertainment. Musical preference, in the past an aural weapon used by the young against older generations, Millennials instead regard as a bonding opportunity. Part of the success of shows like *American Idol* rests in their ability to attract old and young media markets to the same genre.[30] When prompted for a preference, by two-to-one margins, Millennials report listening more to rap and hip-hop than alternative rock.[31] That a white majority overwhelmingly favors music associated with black culture is a further reflection of Millennial interracial acceptance. Their preference for hip-hop has, however, caused the genre to shed its earlier associations with brutality and cynicism, replacing them with a "new style more open to humor, to manners, to commitment, to religion, and to success."[32] If a generation gap does exist, it centers on technology. A 2009 Pew survey found that nearly three-quarters of all adults said young and older people are very different in the way they use computers and technologies.[33]

With outward focus comes a sense of responsibility and adherence to rules. As early as 1998, Millennials were tending to "embrace traditional values of home, family life, community, and education."[34] Their most significant but disputed characteristic seems to be their aura of being "good kids." Strauss and Howe cite this as a conscious attempt by Millennials to counter their Boomer parents' inner focus and their assault on norms and rules that disrupted the Millennials' early childhood. A majority of Millennials identified the "major causes" of America's problems to be "people who don't respect law and authority."[35]

A 2012 rebuttal to the Millennial "good kid" claim, published in the *Journal of Personality and Social Psychology*, casts much doubt on this positive image. Using data from the annual freshman survey by the University of Michigan's Cooperative Institutional Research Program, San Diego State University professor Jean Twenge found the Millennials' aspirations related to money, image, and fame more important than those related to self-acceptance, affiliation, and community.[36] The data also found that fewer Millennials considered empathy for others, charity, and the importance of having a job worthwhile to society when compared to Generation X. While the Millennials' community service involvement was higher, Twenge contended that this is because it became a high school graduation requirement. She found similar declines in the Millennial generation's much-touted interest in social problems, political participation, and trust in government when compared to Generation X. Some of the largest declines related to interest in the environment, directly countering the assertion of Greenberg and Weber.[37] This recent body of Twenge's research builds on her 2006 book, *Generation Me: Why Today's Young Americans Are More Confident, Assertive, Entitled—and More Miserable Than Ever Before*, in which she disparagingly characterizes Millennials as a generation of narcissists.[38] The 2013 *Time* magazine cover story citing increased narcissistic personality disorder among Millennials is rooted in Twenge's challenge.[39]

To sort out whose data is correct is one of the problems social scientists face in studying generations, and I focus on these in Chapter 3. In some respects, the pro and con views are subjective: what Pew and Strauss/Howe describe as confidence for Twenge has crossed a line into overconfident narcissism. The lively debate does however indicate that the Millennial generation is significant enough to attract attention from multiple viewpoints. While the danger of stereotyping is large, clear patterns have emerged to make Millennials as different from their predecessors as Generation X is from the Boomers. A combination of empirical study with a historical comparison of generations leaves much information that can be useful in repositioning architecture at a critical time. And if the remaining findings are controversial, it is better to digest them than to ignore them entirely.

Architecture and Millennial Characteristics

While discussion of Millennials by Strauss and Howe and others developed enough to attract strong antithetical positions by Twenge, Bauerlein, and Bonner, the community of architects has largely ignored this area of inquiry. A wide literature search in architectural practice and education prior to the 2013 *Architect* article yields only a limited awareness of Millennials coming from the practice and from interior design educators.[40] While one can speculate on the reasons for this indifference, the fact remains that by the time the article appeared, Millennials had been in architectural practice for a decade, with the oldest elevated to associate-level in many large firms.[41] And by 2013, the academy had felt their presence even longer, with the oldest going up for tenure. Despite the complete lack until recently of references to Millennials by name or by cohort in the architectural academy and the profession, the community has written self-reflexively enough about practice and pedagogy in the twenty-first century to correlate a relationship with the Millennial characteristics and behaviors that have emerged. While on the surface one might believe this shift to be practitioner- or faculty-initiated, it is also the result of external forces, such as computing, which have both transformed architecture and formed the Millennial generation. Another correlation is architecture expanding into landscape urbanism, exhibiting confidence and a trend toward an interdisciplinary approach, which are both Millennial characteristics. A gradual shift within architectural discourse from the critical to the practical, combined with an increased sense of social responsibility and involvement in civic work, often voluntary and uncompensated, shows a heightened outward focus. Whether or not these trends were initiated from the bottom up by Millennials or from the top down by older generations may be moot; these are distinct attributes that twenty-first century architectural practice and pedagogy share with Millennials.

Digital Architects

By the time the first Millennials arrived in architecture schools as undergraduates around 2000, the computer was increasingly moving out of windowless rooms and onto drafting tables in many studios in North American schools. Stan Allen writes of the 2000s as a decade when the computer "ceased to be a technology to be either celebrated or resisted; it is simply a fact of life. Its logic has been fully absorbed into work routines and habits of thought."[42] This development had been many years in the making. The advent of CAD software in the 1970s, followed by the affordability of desktop computers in the mid-1980s, allowed architects to transition from manual methods of calculation and representation to digital ones. The crossing of this so-called "digital divide" soon allowed architecture schools to introduce the use of computers at the earliest stages of a student's development. In this sense, digital practice became "native" to the community of architects early, well before it was adopted by other professions and well before the widespread use of email and the emergence of the internet in the mid-1990s.

The computer rapidly allowed architects to use a formal vocabulary that was unimaginable when they first crossed the divide. The innovation of building information modeling (BIM) in the 1990s, which combines 3-D formal exploration with all manners of measurability, gave the arriving Millennial architecture student a stout toolbox to access. Finith Jernigan's expansive definition of what he calls "Big BIM" seems to predict the networked sensibilities of Millennials, describing the software platform as "the management of information and the complex relationships between the social and technical resources that represent the complexity, collaboration, and interrelationships of today's organizations and environment."[43] For those entering the profession in the early twenty-first century, a robust array of matured and tested technology gave the young architect a strong sense of confidence. Seemingly acknowledging the Millennial characteristics outlined in this chapter, Allen writes that this technological confidence allowed an architect to explore "beyond the architect's traditional relationship with clients and builders, making possible newly pragmatic, inventive, and hands-on approaches."[44]

Areas Beyond a Traditional Purview

The Millennials' capacity to both work and play well with others correlates to a renewed interest in cross-disciplinarity found in an expanded design practice emerging in the new century. One example of cross-disciplinary expansion is landscape urbanism, which reinvigorated the often-sidelined practice of landscape architecture, synthesizing it with the disciplines of architecture, planning, infrastructure, urban design, ecology, hydrology, horticulture, civil and environmental engineering, among others. Spearheaded by the practitioner-academic James Corner, landscape urbanists rallied these varied disciplines around a new focus on the environment and ecology, made imperative by sustainability concerns. This interest engages the postindustrial city with large parcels of land open for potential development.[45] That both concerns, the environment and moving back to cities, are high on the Millennials' agenda (at least for architects, as we shall see later) has added their support to the landscape urbanism movement.[46] Corner's signature work, Manhattan's High Line, designed collaboratively with architects Diller Scofidio + Renfro and horticulturalist Piet Odoulf, exemplifies landscape urbanism's potential. Within five years of its opening in 2009, the High Line had become, per acre, the most visited park in the United States,[47] and cities around the world are taking a second look at abandoned infrastructure that may offer the same reward. The High Line has catalyzed changes in zoning, attracted adjacent projects by prominent architects, and become a go-to site for design studios in many schools.

Team Orientation by Design

Awareness of the Apple brand exposed Millennials to the concept of high design as the result of extensive team coordination. After the restoration of Steve Jobs to the helm, the rise of Apple's market share in the 2000s coincided with the rise of Millennials as a distinct adult cohort. Whether Millennials use Apple devices or some of the many copycats, Jobs became a legendary design disruptor. Apple uses integrated collaborative teams of computer programmers, hardware engineers, industrial designers, interior designers, architects, logisticians, packaging experts, fashion designers, and marketers to design its products. Until his death, Jobs led his team and carefully watched over every detail from inception to the spectacle of each product's launch. He was like a proxy "helicopter parent," obsessing over every aspect of products that were like his children. Whether Millennials knew of Jobs and his tyrannical nature (which may not have meshed with their high standards for respectfulness) is immaterial; the objects transmit a sense of paternal control that seems awfully familiar. Like Boomer parents, Jobs and his team seemed to have anticipated every Millennial need. In each new product release, Jobs foresaw what they wanted and made it for them. First came desktops and laptops that were "not their parents'" computers, neither boxy nor beige, but pulsating like lanterns and emulating robotic toys. Apple's portable MacBooks were cool: silver, sleek, and impossibly thin.

When Millennials stumbled upon how to pillage the internet for pirated music, Jobs gave them the iPod, a minimalist device to play their haul, one they could slip in the pockets of their T-shirts or jeans. But like a moral parent, with iTunes he also created the revenue model that restored their methods of music consumption to lawfulness. Jobs satisfied their need for connectedness with the iPhone, which could take calls and texts, surf the Web, and stay logged into social media. The iPhone's artificial intelligence, Siri, became the Millennials' proxy caretaker. Jobs's swan song was the iPad, which merged all his creations into one portable and omnipotent device for digital natives. Whether they use the proprietary products or the many knockoffs that have brought patent infringement suits, Millennials have evolved symbiotically with devices pioneered by Apple. Jobs formed a Gesamtkunstwerk made for Millennials. And that these products are the

Figure 2.1. Apple iPod Silhouettes. The Pop History Dig. From http://www.pophistorydig.com/topics/ipod-silhouettes-2000-2011, accessed October 9, 2016.

result of Jobs—who grew up in a fifties modern Eichler home, who respected the typography of Herbert Bayer, who mimicked the purely geometric minimalist product design of Dieter Rams, and who commissioned the architect Peter Bohlin[48] to design a fleet of stores of Miesian transparency and rich materials where gods lurk in every detail—means that an appreciation of quality modern design deeply intertwines with the Millennial neural network. Nothing describes this symbiosis better than the iPod advertising campaign using female and male silhouettes of dancing Millennials, with synaptic white lines connecting the devices on their hips to their brains.[49]

From Criticality to Projectivism

The Millennial embrace of the practical and a penchant for civic-mindedness parallels the swing in architecture from an emphasis on theory and discursive practice to a renewed engagement with the real and the public, all seen anew through the lens of technology. In 2004, Allen described a "new model of practice," one "committed to public legibility, to the active engagement of new technologies, and to creative means of implementation," one that "takes as its object not self-referential theories but real problems—the difficult moments when architecture takes its place in the world."[50] Through fabrication, design-build, and community design, by the first decade of the twenty-first century—whether aware or not—architectural practice and its academies would increasingly ally with Millennial values.

Digital technology accelerated the transition from criticality to the "projective," fostering an ability to circumvent traditional production protocols. Beginning in the mid-1990s, SHoP Architects helped pioneer confident strategies of mass customization, bringing design from the virtual to the real using computer-controlled manufacturing technology. Using BIM software, SHoP quickly expanded into a full-grown design-build practice with extensive forays into production and prefabrication. This expansion was formalized with the establishment of SHoP Construction in 2007. The firm later built on this momentum to form SHoP Real Estate in 2012. Like the field of landscape urbanism, SHoP expanded its range beyond the traditional architect's purview. Robert Somol and Sarah Whiting describe the objectivity of enterprises such as SHoP as "new practice strategies that were less invested in critique and resistance, and instead worked with the speed and intensity of contemporary urban life."[51] This technological confidence to produce had parallels in the academy, as experiments with stereolithography matured into 3-D printing by the 2000s. Different forms of digital manufacturing became so ubiquitous in schools that by 2010 they had expanded beyond architecture to spawn the "maker movement."

Renewed Outward Focus

A spirit of confidence and an expansive scope also fueled renewed interest in the academic variant of design-build, a hands-on pedagogy pioneered in the late 1960s. Academic coursework focused on designing and then building real projects found new leadership in Samuel Mockbee, whose Auburn University Rural Studio program brought quality design to poor communities that seldom know its benefits. After Mockbee's death in 2002, design-build studios spread throughout North America, with students appreciating the combination of hands-on experience and results-oriented work that touched a sense of civic awareness, all of which appeal to Millennial tendencies.[52] In another reprise of the sixties, the growing interest in civic work propelled an increase in community design. By 2000, forty-six North American schools already maintained community design programs, which blossomed into service-learning opportunities for Millennial students to affect change in many areas, often working at the grassroots level.[53] During the same period, professional firms also leaned toward civic work. Leading among these efforts, the nonprofit organization Public Architecture began asking firms to commit a minimum of 1 percent of their time to pro bono service in 2002. By 2011, more than 900 firms, including prominent ones such as SHoP, had engaged, representing $28 million in in-kind support. Participating firms acknowledged that such efforts boosted firm morale.[54] As the Great Recession began to subside, firms correlated these efforts with Millennial characteristics and actively positioned their civic activity as a means of attracting and retaining new talent.

With almost unanimous affirmation by climate scientists that global warming was causing an increased frequency of environmental catastrophes, the architectural discipline expanded its engagement with communities at every scale. In 2005, Hurricane Katrina was the first disaster to stimulate a "call to conscience, prompting people in all fields to reevaluate their priorities in the face of human suffering."[55] Architects (including masses of Millennial students) responded by helping to survey damage, clear homes, and hold charrettes. For Millennials, these environmentally induced crises provided the opportunity to become "innovative change makers" trying to "design their way to a more beautiful, just world."[56] In 2013, efforts expanded after Superstorm Sandy in the Northeast; the catastrophic event instantly formed an entirely new subdiscipline: resiliency. On the day in 2014 when resiliency proposals were due for the Rebuild by Design competition, a US government–funded initiative, program director Henk Ovink was hopeful that fifty entries, perhaps seventy-five (if they were lucky) would arrive. To his surprise, design teams submitted 148 entries.[57] These included one from OMA, Rem Koolhaas's high concept design concern. Koolhaas is a protégé of the highly conceptual Peter Eisenman; his involvement indicates that by 2014 even the highest levels of practice had transitioned to the objective with an outward civic focus.

Millennials in architectural practices and schools clearly share the characteristics of self-confidence, team orientation, and a sense of outward and socially responsible focus with their larger cohort. Arguably, their early and strident efforts even qualify them as hyper-Millennials. They have expanded their digital skills beyond those of their non-architect peers to deploy them to physically make things. They fully understand the new design Gesamtkunstwerk that governs digital devices as a strategy and can apply it to their own work. And they have answered the call to take their actions to the community and respond to crises. Some suggest that Millennials fail to take initiative; the evidence of Millennials in architecture suggest otherwise, perhaps to a fault. Instructors applying leadership tests to Millennial students in the Yale Building Project found Millennial architects to be far more autocratic than their peers.[58] In better understanding the characteristics of Millennial architects, all challenges help foster a dialectical relationship, leading to a more realistic profile of the generation. Why, until recently, architectural self-examination neglected to identify Millennials remains unclear, although this may become better understood in an examination of Millennials in the twentieth century. Further applying a generational schema to a century of US architectural practice and education reveals synchronicity, often identifying architecture in the generational vanguard of prevailing movements and their epochal shifts. This historical context provides the provisional framework for both empowering and adapting to the Millennial generation.

CHAPTER 3

Generations in Historical Context
Generation X, Boomers, Silents, GIs

> **Submerged in the great anonymous multitude, and save for the final individual nucleus of our life, to ask ourselves to which generation we belong is, in large measure, to ask who we are.**
>
> **JULIÁN MARÍAS**

The concept of generations has always been part of history, with roots in folk and religious traditions dating back to antiquity. A contemporary focus on generations begins with the work of the German sociologist Karl Mannheim, who examines generations as a historical phenomenon, laying out the basic parameters for what constitutes a generation and how it relates to others. Since Mannheim, empiricists from the social sciences have attempted to isolate various generational characteristics, yet are challenged by multiple variables that defy categorization, as the precise duration, attributes, and even generational names vary considerably among researchers. Virtually all studying them place generations in a chronological context, a longitudinal comparison to those that came before. This juxtaposition sharpens a generation's profile. When a new generation emerges, sometimes subtle, sometimes abrupt changes tell us this occurred. The predecessors to the Millennials—Generation X, Boomers, Silents, and the GIs—are known to us by their culture, experiences, and accomplishments. The parents and grandparents who raised Millennials came from these historical groupings. It is the rippling of our antecedents' personae through time that, as Marías writes above, contributes to who we are.

The Problem of Generations

All comprehensive studies of generations pay homage to Karl Mannheim's "The Problem of Generations," first published in German in 1927 and translated into English in 1952.[1] In his seminal work, Mannheim postulates that "the social phenomenon of 'generations' represents nothing more than a particular kind of identity of location, embracing 'age groups' embedded in a historical-social process."[2] Mannheim uses the term "location" (*generationslagerung*) to refer to a period of time shared by a well-defined age group in a generational setting. As a "community of date and space," a generation encounters "the same concrete historical problems" that bind it together culturally. When used in reference to culture, the term "generation" differs from a kinship or familial one, which alludes to a given family's offspring. While kinship generations are defined biologically, the duration of a cultural generation falls somewhere between 15 and 25 years. For William Strauss and Neil Howe, generations must pass a three-part test to achieve a "peer personality" to be recognized as distinct. Also known as a "generational persona," this grouping organizes according to: (1) a common age location; (2) common beliefs and behavior; and (3) perceived membership in a common generation.[3] The German art historian Wilhelm Pinder uses the term "generational entelechy" to describe the "social and emotional center of gravity pulling at a larger group of slightly older or younger peers."[4] In Pinder's view, society begins to understand a generation's boundary when the pull of one entelechy supplants that of another. In many cases, this boundary is only recognized years later.

While generations are often discussed in generalities, the characteristics of each are never uniform. In fact, a given generation typically consists of different and opposing personality types that find themselves grouped together. Mannheim writes, "Within any generation, there can exist a number of differentiated antagonistic generation-units. Together they constitute an 'actual' generation precisely because they are oriented toward each other, even though only in the sense of fighting one another."[5] José Ortega y Gasset's writing on the generational experience comes to a similar conclusion, arguing that each generation is a "dynamic compromise between the mass and individual." He continues that despite a generation's "most violent opposition of 'pros' and 'antis,' it is easy to perceive a real union of interests. Both parties consist of men of their own time; and great as their differences may be their mutual resemblances are still greater."[6] The German sociologist Julius Peterson goes further, subdividing members of a generation into three types of individuals: directive, directed, and suppressed. The directive personality sets a generation's tone, the directed follows and legitimizes it, and the suppressed either withdraws or spends a lifetime in opposition. Whether active, passive, or opposed, each personality type realizes its part in a single generational unit. The suppressed of one generation often inspire the directives of the next.[7] Mannheim refers to these as "forerunners."[8] This idea of a vanguard group is central to Strauss and Howe's concept of preseasonality, further elaborated in the next chapter.

As a form of research, Mannheim, Ortega y Gasset, Pinder, and Peterson all follow a largely historical approach in their analysis of cultural generations. At the other end of the spectrum, and more recently, academic empiricists from the disciplines of sociology and psychology have sought data to fortify these cultural conjectures. The results remain largely mixed as many studies have been dogged by multiple variables, including effects and biases, which can dull or skew the imprint of a generation. In their 2010 study "Generational Differences in Work Values," Emma Parry and Peter Urwin cite several of these effects, including age, period, cohort, and sex. Each makes categorizing Millennials difficult.[9] Age effects are those that most individuals experience at a given period of maturation regardless of their generational affiliation. For example, critics of Jean Twenge claim such an age effect when they assert that all young adults, not just the Millennials whom Twenge singles out, are prone to narcissism.[10] Period effects are those caused by events, location, or social status. Millennials' generalized confidence—which intensive parenting and affluence may have brought some of them—can be less pronounced for those who did not share the same experiences growing up because of family structure, race, or class. "Little Emperor" syndrome, an extreme example of a period effect, describes the highly entitled tendencies of the disproportionate number of male children born during China's one-child policy.[11] "Cohort" is a term often used in the social sciences for a generation as a whole. A cohort effect describes variations common to groups or subgroups who share similar life experiences, such as those who go to college or serve in the military. My own American Institute of Architecture Students polling reveals a cohort effect among Millennial architects. Sex effects refer to variations according to gender, such as the much greater propensity of male Millennials to remain at home after college compared to females.[12]

Another difficulty of generational studies that Parry and Urwin cite is disagreement on the exact beginning and ending dates of a generation, or in other words, when Pinder's entelechy transitions to the pull of a new group. While most agree that the first Millennials were born in the 1980s, some like Eric Greenberg and Karl Weber, go back as far as 1978, seemingly for little reason except to perhaps enlarge their total number to add emphasis to their argument.[13] Pew Research's decision to unilaterally declare the last Millennial birth year may be an attempt to project their authority on the subject matter. Nicole Borges identifies a distinct transitional group she calls "Cuspars," whose generational characteristics blend two generations at their point of transition. This introduces a buffering period instead of a single transitional year.[14] Jean Twenge argues that the beginning and end dates are pointless, as generational changes are nonlinear and happen incrementally.[15] Chroniclers of generations typically only recognize the common attributes of a generation many years into their adulthood. The contemporary focus on Millennials, which Strauss and Howe began when its members were small children, may represent a significant historical shift in generational awareness. If the events their theory projects come to pass, future generations may be identified as they are being born or even anticipated years in advance.

Of all writers on generations, Strauss and Howe are most strident about the precise year when generations shift. They base this on their own monitoring of cultural change, and thus their bracketing is typically a few years divergent from more accepted timelines. For example, while demographers such as Pew Research bookend the Baby Boomer generation as many do, beginning with the 1946 spike in births after World War II and ending with a corresponding drop in 1964, which coincided with the availability of birth control pills, Strauss and Howe instead use 1943 and 1960, respectively. Citing shifts in cultural production such as films, literature, and music, Strauss and Howe also relay the accounts of many born from 1943 to 1945 who identify as Boomers and others born after 1960 who state how they stand apart from them.[16] Notable among these is Barack Obama (born 1961), who when describing the generation he feels precedes his, writes, "I sometimes felt as if I were watching the psychodrama of the baby boom generation—a tale rooted in old grudges and revenge plots hatched on a handful of college campuses long ago—played out on the national stage."[17]

The pursuit of empirical evidence to define Millennial characteristics has led to healthy debate. A 2012 study by Kali Trzesniewski and Brent Donnellan seeking to replicate Twenge's research using the same raw data found little to correlate her characterization of Millennials as egotistical,

Table 3.1. Generational Age Brackets

	Millennial	Generation X	Baby Boomer	Silent
Alsop (2008)	1980–2001	1965–1979	1946–1964	1925–1945 (Traditionalists)
Appelbaum et al. (2005)*		1961–1981	1943–1960	
Borges et al.	1981–1999	1965–1980 cuspar: 1975–1980		
Broadbridge et al. (2007)	1977–1994			
Cennamo and Gardner (2008)*	1980–	1962–1979	1946–1961	
Chen and Choi (2008)*	1978–	1965–1977	1946–1964	
Greenberg and Weber (2008)	1978–2000 (Generation We)	1965–1977	1946–1964	
Gursoy et al. (2008)*	1981–2000	1961–1980	1946–1960	
Jurkiewicz and Brown (1998)*	-	1961–1981	1943–1960	1925–1942 (Matures)
Lamm and Meeks (2009)*	1981–2000 (Generation Y)	1961–1981	1943–1960	
Lyons et al. (2007)*	1980–	1965–1979	1945–1964	–1944 (Matures)
Parker and Chusmir (1990)*			1946–1964	–1945 (Matures)
Parry and Urwin (2010)	1982–	1961–1981	1943–1960	1925–1942
Pew (2018)	1981–1996	1965–1980	1945–1964	1928–1945
Sessa et al. (2007)*	1983– (Generation Y)	early: 1964–1976 late: 1977–1982	early: 1946–1954 late: 1955–1963	1925–1945
Smola and Sutton (2002)*		1977	1946–1964	
Strauss and Howe (2007)	1982–2005	1961–1981	1943–1960	1925–1942

Table 3.1. Generational Age Brackets (continued)

	Millennial	Generation X	Baby Boomer	Silent
Twenge and Campbell (2012)	1980–1999 (Generation Me)	1965–1979	1946–1964	1925–1945
Wong et al. (2008)*	1982–2000	1965–1981	1945–1964	

*After Parry and Urwin. See Emma Parry and Peter Urwin, "Generational Differences in Work Values: A Review of Theory and Evidence," *International Journal of Management Reviews* 13 (2011): 89.

entitled, and narcissistic. The null findings may support the conclusion of other Twenge skeptics that late adolescence may be too early to discern generational characteristics that will only emerge later. The authors also explain other bias factors that help to explain the inconsistency in findings when studying generations.[18]

The naming of a generation as it is forming often reveals one such bias. For example, Strauss and Howe may have favored 1982 as the first birth year of a generation it would call Millennials, knowing that its first high school graduates would debut in the pivotal year of 2000 to better fit their narrative. Chroniclers of generations typically start out using a variety of names for the same cohort, finally settling on one or two that stay the course of time. A generation's provisional name also often borrows from previous ones, revealing a bias toward a more linear view of history; writers still refer to Millennials as Generation Y, Generation Next, and Echo Boomers. The name Generation Y uses the next letter in the alphabet after Generation X, the Millennials' predecessors; Generation Next or the Nexters refers to a similar serial placement; and the term Echo Boomers references the Boomer parents of the first Millennials to reach adulthood. Echo Boomer also alludes to the demographic reality that the Millennials' numbers are large (depending of course on how you count them), almost as large as Boomers'. Generational names often focus on a single event or series of related events or to drastic social or demographic change.[19] Given the poor employment prognosis in 2012, *Newsweek* magazine showed an explicit bias in referring to Millennials as the "screwed" generation. Generational names often reveal the partialities of those who study them, whether they sing Millennials' praises for being civic-minded (Greenberg and Weber: "Generation We") or chastise them for their narcissism (Twenge: "Generation Me").

While still not as universal as Boomer, the name Millennial, first introduced by Strauss and Howe in 1992, is increasingly becoming widely accepted. As they contend, it is the name the generation overwhelmingly prefers.[20]

The contemporary interest in Millennials thus represents a blend of cultural assertions and empirical analysis with mixed conclusions. Part of the difficulty may be because, as Mannheim and his followers set forth, generations are less a homogenous group and more a collection of distinct cohorts of the same age bound together in a conflict over issues. And while the positions of one group might be pronounced, the underlying issues that separate them from other groups might be harder to pin down using social science metrics. As in the chronicling of any conflict, the many variables at play become evident only after the proverbial smoke clears. To isolate these variables, comprehensive studies of a generation often compare it to previous ones, sometimes extending the comparison to all the adult generations alive at the time of writing. For the remainder of this chapter I follow this approach, contextualizing Millennials by describing their predecessors back to the GI generation. In Chapter 5 I reverse this chronology to examine five distinct American architectural generations beginning with the GIs, a cohort that also includes architecture's modernists. With architecture primarily recognized as a form of cultural production, I will follow in the tradition of Mannheim, using the cultural markers of generations to identify differences, and where available, using empirical evidence to support my assertions. In this chronology, I will also test Strauss-Howe generational theory, which I summarize in Chapter 4, and its relevance to the recent architectural past. While I understand that my approach may carry its own bias, it nonetheless begins an examination of architecture as a serial progression of generations, an examination proceeding in search of empirical validation to correct for biases and effects that may take years—or, to use the timelines of this book—many generations to assemble.

Generation X

At first glance, the characteristics of Generation X (often shortened to Gen X) are almost exactly opposite those of Millennials, summarized in the previous chapter. Whereas Millennials tend to be self-confident, team-oriented, and outwardly focused, Gen Xers tend to be wary, independent, and skeptical, if not outright cynical, as the lyrics of their grunge and hip-hop music memorialize. Generation X experienced a childhood where divorce and single-parent households were increasingly common. Many were latchkey kids, glued to the television and forbidden to leave the house. While Millennials may have grown up sheltered, Generation X sheltered themselves, alone. Theirs was an era when youth crime increased and test scores fell. In 1984, the US government identified them in their adolescence as so wild and uneducated that the Nation at Risk task force was initiated to rein them in. When Generation X ventured out, it was into a world beset by AIDS, where one in six high school students knew a victim of a shooting. Their disaffection characterized a cohort of largely unaligned political pragmatists.[21] Generation X's employment profile has trended toward free agency over corporate loyalty, all overshadowed by a cloud of decreased expectations. Pew Research and others found that, adjusted for inflation, Generation X males in 2004 made 12 percent less than their fathers did in 1974, becoming the first American generation to experience an income decline.[22] The hip-hop that appealed to Generation X in the 1990s differed markedly from what Millennials would later appreciate. Taking on pseudonyms like their graffiti-writing contemporaries, performers like Dr. Dre, Ice Cube, LL Cool J, and Mike D projected a pragmatic, cynical, and "all-business" attitude that embraced realism, exalting urban hedonism and violence, to increasingly multiracial audiences.[23] Nirvana's Kurt Cobain expressed a different manifestation of Generation X's angst in the refrain of the 1991 grunge anthem "Smells Like Teen Spirit," singing "with the lights out, it's less dangerous, . . . I feel stupid and contagious, here we are now, entertain us." Cynically fitting, the name of the album is *Nevermind*.

Cultural writers generally attribute the name Generation X to the Canadian Douglas Coupland, author of the 1991 book *Generation X: Tales for an Accelerated Culture*.[24] Coupland intends the letter *X* to stand for the random, ambiguous, and contradictory ways of the generation. The letter *X* also connotes a variable or blank, in mathematical terms, as in the song "Blank Generation" by the 1970s punk band Richard Hell and the Voidoids. Pew Research refers to Generation X also as the Baby "Bust" generation because of their relatively small numbers compared to those of the Baby "Boom." Strauss and Howe remark that their low numbers were because many were unwanted, either prevented by birth control or terminated through abortion, going so far as to write that Generation X suffers a form of survivor guilt, "resenting the lasting damage done by an era in which they now realize *they* were the babies adults were trying so much not to have."[25] Strauss and Howe first called them "Thirteeners" in their 1993 anthology *13th Gen: Abort, Retry, Ignore, Fail?* The name refers not to the unlucky number but to the authors' contention that they are America's thirteenth generation since the Founding Fathers. Although they used the word Thirteener in subsequent writings, by 2007 Strauss and Howe refer to them, as most others do, as Generation X.

Generation X finds itself bookended and outshone by both Millennials and Boomers (as described in the next chapter, Strauss and Howe classify Generation X as a "recessive" generation). Generational writers seldom define the years of Generation X by core values that bind. Instead they identify persons born in the early 1960s who no longer align themselves with Boomers, and continue the group through the early 1980s, when a critical mass of Boomers started having Millennial children. This suggests, rather cynically, that Generation X has no values. Strauss and Howe described them in 1998 as "a generation less knowable by its core than by its bits and pieces." A 1982 *Newsweek* article heralding the arrival of Boomer-born, Millennial toddlers with the cuddly Cabbage Patch Kids dolls serving as their avatars also announced, by default, that the generation Allan Bloom later derided in *The Closing of the American Mind* had stopped being born. Strauss and Howe also mark the end of Generation X's birth years with the emergence of certain films featuring Millennials as "angelic" children—*Raising Arizona*, *Three Men and a Baby*, and *Baby Boom*—replacing those depicting the "demonic" children of Generation X—*The Exorcist*, *It's Alive*, *The Omen*, and *Halloween*.[26] Strauss and Howe contend that the Boomer birth years ended in 1961, not 1964 as popular chroniclers accept. Strauss and Howe mark Kennedy's 1963 assassination as a milestone of awareness between generations, suggesting perhaps that anyone without some memory of his murder lacks the cathartic imprint to be a true Boomer.[27]

The fragmentation of values, randomness, and ambiguity associated with Generation X showed themselves in built form as the generation began entering architectural practice. The architectural style referred to by many as deconstructivism highlighted jagged and arbitrary forms, which like their hip-hop and grunge musical counterparts, seemed confrontational. Cobain's howling and searing guitar riffs, along with hip-hop's valorization of street violence, found allegiance with discordant form-making and the clashing use of materials sampled from an urban industrial vernacular. Announcing the design style's arrival in a debut show at the Museum of Modern Art, Philip Johnson introduced the catalog using words akin to Strauss and Howe, describing what this new architecture was *not* more than what it stood for: "Deconstructivist architecture is not a new style. We arrogate to its development none of the messianic fervor of the modern movement, none of the exclusivity of that catholic and Calvinist cause. Deconstructivist architecture represents no movement; it is not a creed. It has no 'three rules' of compliance."[28]

Deconstructivism may not have been a long-lasting movement, but it did ultimately supplant the style associated with the previous generation. That it was the 85-year-old Johnson who heralded its arrival in 1988 underscores a major theme of this book: that while society might focus on one generation, as it is now on Millennials, it is how all the generations alive interact over time that changes culture. Throughout his long career, Johnson, who received the first Pritzker prize in 1979, possessed an uncanny ability (many consider it shrewdness) to sense shifts in sensibility coincident with generational swings. Although the outcomes were almost always derivative, he successfully, and at times dramatically, reshaped his practice to fall into alignment with the newest trends. As we move back through generations in this chapter, I will check in at each transition to see how Johnson repositioned, setting up a further discussion of his mercurial behavior in the timelines I reconstruct later in the book.

Younger generations often attract the kind of scorn doled out on Generation X as older adults seem shocked by the Sturm und Drang of adolescence.[29] In a 1998 study, in the midst of the condemnation of Generation X, only 16 percent of adult Americans agree that people under the age of thirty shared their moral and ethical values.[30] It is not surprising that contempt for Generation X comes largely from Boomers of Strauss and Howe's age. This tendency to denounce the generation immediately junior may also account for the stridency of Jean Twenge's claim that Millennials are narcissists and Mark Bauerlein's that they are dumb; both are Generation X academics. Certain Generation X writers have responded to these characterizations with a mixture of emotions. Douglas Rushkoff, author of the 1993 *GenX Reader*, writes, seemingly with envy, "Instead of getting free love, we got AIDS."[31] With the cheeky title *X Saves the World: How Generation X Got the Shaft but Can Still Keep Everything from Sucking*, Jeff Gordinier fumes at being unappreciated, ranting against Boomer self-righteousness that culminates in incessant talk and no action, sneering, "Great, you had a party in Haight-Ashbury in 1967, I'm thrilled for you." In defense of his cohort, Gordinier boasts that Generation X instead busied itself with revolutionary changes in media such as Jon Stewart's *The Daily Show* and business's colossi, Google and Amazon.[32] *Time* magazine, in its review of Gordinier's book, describes best the umbrage of this much smaller cohort sandwiched between Boomers and Millennials: "It's something like a national case of sibling rivalry, with millennials playing the part of the spoiled, naive baby and boomers acting as the self-righteous firstborn. Gordinier's book, then, is like the earnest ranting of a forgotten middle child."[33]

Boomers

Baby Boomers are Generation X's immediate predecessors and the parents of the first wave of Millennials. Millennial characteristics and behaviors are as much a result of following Boomers' direction as they are of rejecting their values. Boomers came of age enjoying a childhood of privilege during the sustained American economic expansion after World War II. Their parents, who had endured both the depravations of a childhood in the Depression followed by the trials of wars, wanted to bestow on their children the best they could give. Most Boomers grew up indulged in spacious suburbia, with unprecedented mobility and brand-new schools. It may be nostalgia for this upbringing that Boomers wanted to bequeath to their Millennial children. Boomers' numbers alone make them significant if not special; they are almost twice the size of their predecessor generation, and their size made them a "superclass" with an economic power bigger than some GNPs.[34] As the first Millennials were being born in the early 1980s, Boomers numbered more than 70 million Americans, one third of the country's population.[35] Boomers created a specific rhetoric and a strong sense of identity about themselves that Millennials inherited. While 61 percent of Millennials described themselves as unique and distinct in 2012, nearly as many Boomers (58 percent) still thought the same.[36]

Television connected Boomers, giving them a shared sense of popular culture that they would pass to their children. Shows like *Leave It to Beaver*, *Father Knows Best*, and *Dennis the Menace* provided Boomers universal, if stereotypical, TV characters. Advertising laced these shows with indelible jingles that many Boomers grew up humming. Boomer-targeted media affected all Western countries, with a significant impact in Asia and Africa and even the Soviet bloc. The Boomers' cultural philosopher, Marshall McLuhan, places the focus on media itself, arguing in *Understanding Media: The Extensions of Man* that the content is secondary; media itself binds people together. A lightbulb proffers no content, McLuhan argues; it is a "medium that shapes and controls the scale and form of human association and action."[37] Beginning with radio, this media knit together McLuhan's "global village." Most prescient, McLuhan imagines the world of the internet that Millennials so fluidly began to occupy as they grew up. The next media, he accurately predicted in 1962, "would obsolesce mass library organization, retrieve the individual's encyclopedic function, and flip into a private line to speedily tailored data of a saleable kind."[38] McLuhan's distinction between "hot" and "cool" media, where hot media demand attention while multiple cool media could operate simultaneously in a kind of background, antici- pates Millennials' propensity toward multitasking: the juggling of many cool media to be heated up on demand. McLuhan first popularized the term "surf- ing," as in web-surfing, with the statement "Heidegger surf-boards along on the electronic wave as triumphantly as Descartes rode the mechanical wave."[39] As densely argued as they were, McLuhan's books were popular throughout the 1960s and 1970s, forecasting a future that arrived just in time for Boomers to buy their Millennial children expensive computers to connect globally and surf the "World-Wide-Web," later shortened to WWW.

Locally, Boomers marshaled an inclusion of the marginalized—blacks, Latinos, women, gays, and the disabled—into mainstream society. Through loud protest, they injected tolerance into every realm from entertainment to sports to politics. Millennials have inherited this cause and are today the most tolerant generation in American history.[40] Boomers' tolerance and acceptance did not extend to older generations and especially those in authority. Their level of recrimination defined them as they endorsed the lyr- ics of The Who's anthem, "My Generation," singing: "Why don't you all fade away, . . . Hope I die before I get old." This ethos defined the Boomers' cult of impetuous youth, whose coming of age ushered in a period of unrest and rupture that shook the Western world. Yet the generation that began with a mission to challenge the status quo never fully agreed upon its replacement.

It is the Boomer sense of rebellion that the Millennials have not inherited. Except for Twenge and other minority reporters, most observers see Millen- nials getting along well with their parents; a majority say they "hardly ever" or "never" disagree with them.[41] Millennials respect their elders, including those in authority and government. Many leave for college expecting to come back home.[42] Projecting a positive image may be the Millennials' own form of rebellion, an inverse kind of Sturm und Drang.

And while the Boomers may be distinct, they are far from consistent and constantly changing. That many socialist-leaning hippies discovered materialism and reinvented themselves as yuppies in their thirties shows a distinct protean tendency of Boomers. The name "Boomer" only became commonplace in 1980 with Landon Jones's bestseller about them.[43] Before that the cohort cycled through many names associated with the period, including war babies, Spock babies, Sputnik generation, Pepsi generation, Now generation, and, as Twenge refers to their children, the Me generation. Those who mistake the more outspoken hippies as defining the generation need only remember the "silent majority" of Boomers who gave the conservative Richard Nixon a landslide presidential victory in 1972. Despite an early display of tolerance, deep divisions later developed among Boomers as the silent majority found a voice to counter the outspoken and liberal hippies. As Mannheim predicted, Boomers remained oriented toward each other, if only to save the biggest fight until after the older generation eventually faded away.[44] In the mid-1990s, two self-avowed Boomers—Bill Clinton and Newt Gingrich—led opposing camps in the culture wars, a conflict that still flares, the same conflict Obama wants no part of. In politics, that conflict rages at the core of the partisan gridlock that plagues the 2010s; in religion, the conflict is among factions polarized around issues of abortion and homosexuality. The term "culture wars" refers to early Boomer sparring over the US government's role in funding museum content and to proponents of rock and roll shouting down emergent genres with chants of "rock lives" and "disco sucks."

In a separate front of the culture wars, a renewed appreciation for historical forms challenged a modernist architectural language its critics associated with the broader establishment. In one camp stood the "Whites," architects who clung to the modernist architectural language first laid down in the 1920s. Challenging them were the "Grays," who indulged in a new appreciation for vernacular, populist, and historicist forms previously considered off-limits for serious architecture. Given that the discord began in a recession with little building being done, combatants often sortied through many unbuilt, theoretical projects. These came to be known derisively as "paper architecture," often accompanied by a quarrelsome "talkitecture" of the same ilk that Jeff Gordinier ridicules as incessant Boomer prattle. Philip Johnson, who played a pivotal role in establishing the modernist canon as a young man in the 1930s, famously abandoned his compatriots to join with the Grays. By first using historical forms to complement the neo-Renaissance Boston Public Library with his addition in 1972 and later fashioning buildings to look like glass castles or granite Chippendale furniture, Johnson sought to appeal to Boomer design values while forsaking the earlier values for which he stridently advocated in his youth.

While Millennials accepted much of what their Boomer parents directed them to do, quietly embracing their parents' early tolerance and showing an eclectic acceptance toward most cultural forms, they show little signs of a Boomer rancor or divisiveness. Millennials identify "the excess of adult individualism" as one of the "major causes" of America's problems today, clearly pointing a finger at their parents' generation.[45] Millennials remain largely united, with majorities supporting abortion rights and gay marriage.[46] And in contrast to the Boomers' disquiet, their children seem more content; in 2009 some 41 percent of Millennials said they were satisfied with the way things are going in the country, compared with just 26 percent of those aged thirty and older.[47] In 2013, 85 percent of Millennials (both employed and unemployed) said that they either have enough earnings or income now to lead the kind of life they want or they believe they will in the future, while only 68 percent of Generation X and 60 percent of Boomers said the same.[48] Compared to their elders, Millennials' contentment and optimism remain high, as Pew Research maintains: "Whatever toll a recession, a housing crisis, a financial meltdown, and a pair of wars may have taken on the national psyche in the past few years, it appears to have hit the old harder than the young."[49] As to the fuming of their aging parents' political leaders, Millennials seem to be patiently waiting for them to just fade away.

Silents

The Boomers' predecessor generation was as quiet as its successors were outspoken. The first of the Silent generation were born in the mid-1920s and the last around the end of WWII. This was the cohort of "Depression kids" and "war babies" whose generational name refers to their tendency to not complain, to follow direction, and to conform.[50] Silents were the first generation in US history with fewer people than the preceding one. With a government-induced period of productivity meant to house and educate returning GIs, unemployment stayed low and household incomes grew at the fastest pace ever measured in the United States. Many Silents skipped blue-collar work entirely and immediately embarked on white-collar careers. Because of the ratio of low population to high productivity, the demographer Elwood Carlson calls their generation the "Lucky Few."[51]

The Silent generation remained at once contented and complacent, with the soothing lyrics of Frank Sinatra and other crooners serenading them as they came of age. They prospered in a state of ease at a time when the country seemed to breathe a decades-long sigh of relief after the Depression and war. Adhering closely to the directives of those who had fought in it, a group best exemplified by President Eisenhower, the Silent generation presided over one of the most sustained periods of technological expansion in American history, which culminated in members of their generation being the first to set foot on the moon.

The work produced at Bell Labs represents one of the most prolific examples of this expansion. This government-subsidized monopoly developed a cozy relationship with the military, taking advantage of the momentum it had achieved during the war in advancing telecommunications and developing radar. Bell Labs nurtured an environment where profit was seldom a motive, allowing for the slow cultivation of a remarkable string of inventions. These would one day underpin the twenty-first-century digital world and included the transistor, binary code, cellular telephony, videophones, telecommunications satellites, photovoltaics, lasers, and fiber optics. All were produced in the sylvan New Jersey suburbs of "grassy campuses where deer would graze at twilight," in facilities that Arthur C. Clarke described as a "factory of ideas," where "production lines are invisible."[52] The last of these, designed for Bell Labs by Eero Saarinen, staff fondly referred to both literally and figuratively as "the black box." Within these idea factories, theoretical physicists worked with skilled technicians of all kinds in environments with disciplinary boundaries left porous by intent. Following a strictly enforced open-door policy, every employee, even the Nobel Prize winners (who were many) had to engage in discussion when prompted, even with the most junior employee. The ethos of Bell Labs created inventions so advanced they warranted the description commonly used by twenty-first-century disruptors: "solutions looking for problems."

In the prime of his career and recently graduated from Harvard with a degree in architecture, Philip Johnson influenced the built landscape of the Silent generation in different ways at a variety of scales. Johnson was instrumental in steering the commission for the Seagram Building to Ludwig Mies van der Rohe, whose cool minimalism became the prevalent corporate style for the postwar period. Johnson also assisted Mies with the design of Seagram and maintained a leadership role in crafting its interiors. The Seagram tower inspired office buildings like it to sprout in cities. Emerging suburban office campuses like Bell Labs were often laid out as long, horizontal buildings, as if they were towers on their sides. Johnson later shrewdly followed Mies's lead in pioneering a new domestic architecture, building his iconic Glass House in rural Connecticut as an homage to Mies's earlier

Farnsworth House. Both set an example, albeit an unattainable one for the rising middle class, of an ideal house in the newly accessible outskirts of the city. Johnson would later populate his rural compound with structures that reflected the styles associated with each generation he astutely recognized.

The pervasive WWII regimentation of both civilian and military populations carried over into the postwar period, albeit in subtler ways. Women doubled down at home and men wore a different kind of uniform, the "gray flannel suit," in the new corporate environment that Johnson and his contemporaries popularized. The relentlessly regular gridded surfaces of the new glass architecture telegraphed a similar gridding of equal-sized cubicles that could cover vast acreages of interior space, all illuminated by newly developed cheap fluorescent lighting. Yet while the surface of the Silents' society appeared ordered and quiet, exuding an image of peace, prosperity, and progress, it masked an inward anxiety that only further abetted conformity. W. H. Auden's 1947 book-length poem, *The Age of Anxiety*, echoes the inner mood of the postwar Silents, each with vivid childhood memories of newsreels reporting Hitler's horrors. As adults, Silents now imagined Stalin as the new threat, a despot who at any second could launch nuclear weapons to bring on the apocalypse. The great constructions of the time—interstate highways and suburbia—were built by the government in the name of defensibility. All told, the mix of worry and productivity created the "cultural underpinnings for thrift and teamwork, with everybody pitching in like good neighbors sharing lawn mowers"[53] to stay happy and keep together in case the worst should happen.

While Boomer children played in brand-new suburbs, largely oblivious to these perceived threats, some of their elders began to complain about the superficiality and sameness in which Silents found themselves living. Malvina Reynolds's song mocked the "little boxes made of ticky-tacky," the domestic counterparts to office cubicles.[54] Lewis Mumford railed against their homogeneity, describing a "multitude of uniform, unidentifiable houses, lined-up inflexibly, at uniform distances on uniform roads, in a treeless command waste, inhabited by people of the same class, the same incomes, the same age group, witnessing the same television performances, eating the same tasteless prefabricated foods, from the same freezers."[55] Prosperous as it was, homogeneity brought racial segregation; any comingling of races during the war had since returned to prewar norms, with whites decamping for the suburbs, leaving the older inner cities to minorities and the poor. That Silents include the smallest share of immigrants of any generation in the twentieth century only furthered the trend toward sameness.[56]

Thus, when the time came, there was much in the stultifying uniformity of Silent postwar culture for Boomers to rebel against. Yet they rebelled as much against the Silents who implemented this comfortable world as they did against the GIs who fought for and envisioned it. In many regards, Silents carried on the characteristics of the GIs who preceded them, perhaps to a fault. But without wartime necessity, the virtue of GI unity eventually became the Silent vices of homogeneity and complacency.

The GI Generation

While they would only acquire the name after World War II began, the GI generation is known as the American generation that patiently endured the Depression and later enlisted in droves to defeat foreign enemies. Tom Brokaw in his eponymous 1998 book dubbed them the "Greatest Generation." Born between the turn of the last century and the mid-1920s, young GIs benefitted from reform-era ideals; they played in new parks, enjoyed outings through scouting, and self-organized as clubs. A focus on public health brought them vitamins and better hygiene. Child labor laws protected their innocence, and they were to become the best-educated American generation to date. The Depression renewed their sense of civic discipline, and scouting and clubs prepared them for the uniformed recovery work of the Civilian Conservation Corps (CCC) and the Works Progress Administration (WPA). The GI generation grew up with a belief in a beneficent government. Their sense of order and commitment differed markedly from the previous generation's dissipation, as the so-called "flappers" partied through the Roaring Twenties with a recklessness many in the rising generation associated with causing the Depression.

Once the United States entered WWII, CCC and WPA uniforms changed to combat fatigues as peer pressure incented most young people to enlist. The sense of outward focus the Depression instilled allowed older World War I officers to rapidly organize them into fighting divisions. It also silenced the dissenting voices of the isolationist and older veterans who remained fixated on the horrors of the previous war. The GIs' sacrifices overseas encouraged those at home, both young and old, to ration and recycle. The war reorganized the world, and upon their return, GIs set out to continue the transformation of the United States they began before they left. The continuation of FDR's strong central government during the Depression and war years rewarded the returning GIs with subsidized education and housing. City dwellers spilled out into newly developed suburbs and urban leaders razed and rebuilt, often clumsily, what they left behind. In the stability of this newly formed landscape, the GIs prospered and propagated, giving birth to scores of Boomer children. Strauss and Howe describe this period as "an era when large institutions were regarded as effective, government as powerful, science as benign, schools as good, careers as reliable, families as strong, and crime as under control."[57] Through their unity, GIs led Silents in transforming America with remarkable speed and efficiency, building highways to alter cities and airports to better connect them. Within twenty years of the war's end, GIs largely built out the futuristic template that Norman Bel Geddes had laid out in the General Motors pavilion at the 1939 World's Fair. Assisted by the younger Silents, GIs achieved major civil rights legislation and mobilized technologically to put a man on the moon. The GI generation's prominence rippled through time as they maintained an unprecedented thirty-two-year hold on the American presidency, beginning with John Kennedy in 1960.

While the GI generation may have shared a sense of civic responsibility with their younger Silent siblings, GIs were strident while Silents evolved a culture of complacency. Still in his twenties, Philip Johnson expressed this GI stridency when he joined the architecture department of the newly opened Museum of Modern Art in New York. There he helped organize the first exhibition on modern architecture in 1932, which along with its accompanying catalog confidently declared how the rising generation would build according to newly imported European precedents. To this mission he brought the "messianic fervor," exclusivity of its "catholic and Calvinist cause," and defining principles that he would later declare conspicuously absent from deconstructivist architecture (although this diagnosis of deconstructivism's vacuity did not prevent him from later mimicking its forms). Johnson would later apply his generational stridency to his domestic tastes, which we will further examine in Chapter 8. It must be noted that before he emerged as Harvard-trained corporate architect in the 1950s, Johnson entertained a fascination with Nazism, traveling to Germany before the war. Only after significant vetting would the army allow him to join the ranks of other GIs. After his early influence as a young member of the GI generation, he seldom again led generational change, although throughout his long career until his death in 2005 his notorious opportunism would signal that the mantle of design leadership had recently changed.

Eventually, the GIs' stridency turned to hubris, and it was their own Boomer children who rejected their utopian goal of creating what B. F. Skinner called a "technology of behavior." Ever complacent, Silents seemed caught in the crossfire, forced to choose a cohort with whom to side. The clash of values that became the generation gap between the GIs and their children extended to hygiene, apparel, sexual mores, and even tone of voice. At every opportunity, Boomers opposed and undermined GI ideals, with their dissent ultimately achieving enough momentum to force a withdrawal from Vietnam, expose Watergate, and topple a president. By the time the GIs retired, their youthful optimism and obedience had come fully into question and their vaunted projects attacked. Cities declared their urban renewal efforts unlivable and imploded them; San Francisco and Boston removed GI-built highways. And for as long as they continue to hold office, right-leaning Boomer politicians relentlessly seek to undermine the GIs' social programs. Despite these setbacks, society remembers the Greatest Generation not for the failure of their ambitions, but rather for the optimism, teamwork, and outward focus of their youth.

That both the GI and Millennial generations share common characteristics, such as optimism, teamwork, and outward focus, rests at the root of Strauss-Howe generational theory, which the next chapter outlines. Contrasting Millennials with the personae, cultural expressions, and achievements of Generation X, Boomers, Silents, and GIs sharpens the profile of the Millennial generation by placing them in historical context. While social science empiricists remain in disagreement in their attempts to isolate various generational characteristics, the historical-social viewpoint, first brought into focus by Mannheim, remains relevant if one can see through the fog of its ambiguity. Mannheim alludes to these difficulties in the conclusion to his seminal work when he remarks that when understanding generations biologically, one can benefit from the uniformity of natural law, but when reckoning with them at the cultural and social level, "its effects can be ascertained only with great difficulty and by indirect methods."[58] In the current age of disruption, Strauss-Howe generational theory presents itself as one of these indirect methods, perhaps the most prominent. It also happens to be the most controversial.

CHAPTER 4

Working with Generational Theory

Demographic transformations are dramas in slow
motion. They unfold incrementally, almost imper-
ceptibly, tick by tock, without trumpets or press
conferences. But every so often, as the weight of
change builds, a society takes a hard look at itself
and notices that things are different. These "aha"
moments are rare and revealing.

PAUL TAYLOR

In their many books, William Strauss and Neil Howe attempt to organize
Paul Taylor's rare and revealing events into an overarching framework that
has come to be known as Strauss-Howe generational theory. Fundamental
to their writing are two essential propositions: first, generations follow re-
peating archetypes, and second, each generation as young adults sets the
tone for an era, a tone that also repeats in type. The Millennial generation's
similarity to GIs, along with linkages between the transformations of World
War II and the social upheaval of the 1960s, are aspects of how Strauss-Howe
theory explains history. Going back hundreds of years, their historiography
includes much detail with many layers of organization, and although highly
formulaic, it attempts to maintain variability. Strauss and Howe's prescient
forecast of current disruptions has brought renewed popular interest; it
has also stirred anew the controversy that has surrounded their work since
first posited. Biases brought out by their theory and fueled by controversy
cloud an understanding of generations, while at the same time focusing
great attention on Millennials. If generational transformation indeed plays
a role in current disruptions, then an awareness of Strauss and Howe may
be a necessary guide, although one to be used with caution.

The reverse chronology of the last chapter ends with the identification of the GI and Millennial generations as sharing in common the characteristics of optimism, teamwork, and outward focus. This is an assertion at the root of Strauss-Howe generational theory. Their embrace of a cyclical theory of history fundamentally challenges the views of those who believe history to be linear. These linear beliefs include an Augustine-influenced Christianity marching inexorably toward the return of the Messiah, a Marxist class struggle continuing from feudalism to capitalism to communism, and an Enlightenment view of a constant forward march toward reason. Instead, Strauss and Howe align with a mythopoetic tradition that draws from the Old Testament and ancient Rome and extends through the German Romantic philosophies of Hegel and Heidegger, drawing from these a belief in major themes cycling through time on a periodic basis, including acknowledgment that the pace of events speeds toward a crisis, to then slow again.

Archetypes

Strauss and Howe's theory has two interrelated and primary components. First, they argue that archetypal generations repeat in cycles of four in the same order, with each generation following its prescribed archetype. Second, they claim that there is a distinct and recurring time period associated with each of the four generations' coming of age. When added together, these four time periods sum up to a cycle of approximately ninety years, the same as that of a long natural life. Strauss and Howe's four generational archetypes (see Table 4.1) as described in their 1997 book *The Fourth Turning* are, in order: *artist, prophet, nomad,* and *hero*. These names update those provided in their 1992 book *Generations*, which, in the same order, are: *adaptive, idealist, reactive,* and *civic*. The greatest impact on the atmosphere of a given era occurs when each archetype reaches young adulthood (young twenties to mid-forties). A crisis ends one cycle of archetypes to begin another. This makes the GIs and the Millennials hero-types who each end a cycle.

A new cycle begins with artist-types implementing the external changes to society that hero-types had set forth while resolving the predicament of the previous era. Most recently, Silents played the artist-type role. Like the orderly technicians at Bell Labs after the war, they built out the world the GI hero-types had envisioned and fought for. Following the GI lead, Silents reorganized the physical landscape through urban renewal, suburbia, and highways and the social realm with civil rights and expanded education. The prophet-type then follows the artists to change society's internal order.

Table 4.1. Strauss-Howe Generational Archetypes

Artist generations (adaptive) grow up as the overprotected children during a Crisis, come of age as the sensitive young adults of a post-Crisis world, break free as indecisive midlife leaders during an Awakening, and age into empathetic post-Awakening elders.

Prophet generations (idealist) grow up as increasingly indulged post-Crisis children, come of age as the narcissistic young crusaders of an Awakening, cultivate principles as moralistic midlifers, and emerge as wise elders guiding the next Crisis.

Nomad generations (reactive) grow up as the underprotected children during an Awakening, come of age as the alienated young adults of a post-Awakening world, mellow into pragmatic midlife leaders during a Crisis, and age into tough post-Crisis elders.

Hero generations (civic) grow up as the increasingly protected post-Awakening children, come of age as the heroic young teamworkers of a Crisis, demonstrate hubris as energetic midlifers, and emerge as powerful elders attacked in an Awakening.

William Strauss and Neil Howe, *The Fourth Turning: An American Prophecy* (New York: Broadway, 1997), 84.

By questioning the spiritual and moral values of the GIs, prophet-type Boomers undermined the status quo and set out to establish a new value system based on equality and social justice. Boomer dissent led to a stalemate in Vietnam and brought down the government. Next, Generation X filled the nomad-type role. Reverting to free agency after the societal disquiet incited by previous prophet-type discord, their vagrancy presided over the era, giving them a "bad kid" reputation of hyperindividualism. In the climax of Strauss-Howe generational theory, it falls upon the hero-type as a young adult to influence the resolution to a perpetual discord that has descended into crisis. Strauss and Howe's formulation designates Millennials as the hero-types who will close this cycle.

Strauss and Howe's archetypes must pass a three-part test to qualify for this sequence: (1) they must have been born within a certain range of years, (2) they must have common beliefs and behavior; and (3) they must perceive of themselves as members in a common generation.[1] Building upon the observations of their generational studies forebearers, Strauss and Howe absorb the findings of Karl Mannheim and his contemporaries, asserting that while archetypal generations might share a great deal, they are far from monolithic; each generation includes "differentiated antagonistic generation-units"[2] who nonetheless "perceive a real union of interests."[3] These antagonists further subdivide each generation into three types: the *directive* personality, who set a generation's tone, the *directed*, who follow and legitimize it, and the *suppressed*, who either withdraw or spend a lifetime in opposition. The suppressed group in opposition often inspires the directives of the next.[4]

This variegation makes generations seemingly difficult to categorize, yet Strauss and Howe work much of these differences into the details of their theory. For example, they build on Peterson's assertion that the suppressed of one generation become the cultural change agents of the one that follows. This occurs when a critical mass is suddenly achieved, an event that typically comes as a surprise. They refer to this preview tendency as *preseasonality*, which is similar to Mannheim's identification of an advance guard as "forerunners." Preseasonality explains culturally how the Silent Beat movement's obscure writing suddenly influenced many Boomers, or when Boomer punk musicians, playing largely unnoticed in urban ghettoes, laid the groundwork for Generation X's grunge to later go mainstream. Strauss and Howe use the culture of professional baseball to describe how certain types of players repeatedly show preseasonality generation upon generation. They cite Cal Ripken Jr.'s diligence and team focus as predicting the Millennial persona, Curt Flood previewed Generation X's free agency, Jackie Robinson lived as a vanguard of the Boomer social conscience, and the stoic Lou Gehrig forecast the taciturn Silents.[5] When later validated, preseasonality, or being "ahead of one's time," confers a heroic nobility on those who bravely stood up to the status quo. Strauss and Howe also describe how events can be *postseasonal*, meaning that they are out of sync with the spirit of a time, or to use the common pejorative, "on the wrong side of history." Postseasonal actors miss the turnoff toward a cyclical timeline and proceed unwittingly on the straight path to obscurity. Strauss and Howe developed these patterns by categorizing American generations going back centuries (see Table 4.2).

Strauss and Howe note that distinctions between a generation's first and second half often prompt these inflections. The first group, referred to

Table 4.2. Strauss-Howe Generations

Reformation Generation	1483–1511	*Prophet*
Reprisal Generation	1512–1540	*Nomad*
Elizabethan Generation	1541–1565	*Hero*
Parliamentary Generation	1566–1587	*Artist*
Puritan Generation	1588–1617	*Prophet*
Cavalier Generation	1618–1647	*Nomad*
Glorious Generation	1648–1673	*Hero*
Enlightenment Generation	1674–1700	*Artist*
Awakening Generation	1701–1723	*Prophet*
Liberty Generation	1724–1741	*Nomad*
Republican Generation	1742–1766	*Hero*
Compromise Generation	1767–1791	*Artist*
Transcendental Generation	1792–1821	*Prophet*
Gilded Generation	1822–1842	*Nomad*
Progressive Generation	1843–1859	*Artist*
Missionary Generation	1860–1882	*Prophet*
Lost Generation	1883–1900	*Nomad*
GI Generation	1901–1924	*Hero*
Silent Generation	1925–1942	*Artist*
Baby Boom Generation	1943–1960	*Prophet*
Generation X	1961–1981	*Nomad*
Millennial Generation	1982–2004	*Hero*
Homeland Generation	2005–?	*Artist*

William Strauss and Neil Howe, *The Fourth Turning: An American Prophecy* (New York: Broadway, 1997), 123–138.

as "early" or "lead-edge," establish a generation's character by selectively accepting or rejecting characteristics of both their parents and the generation immediately prior according to their archetypal script. A second "late" group carry most of these characteristics but shift subtly in key areas that hint at the primary character of the generation to follow. This change occurs when the generation immediately preceding their children rises to become the new majority parent of their children's generation.[6] Despite these shifts, it is important to remember that a generation's archetypal character is forged by the leading edge of a generation. The latecomers only hint at the characteristics of the generation to follow through a distinct but highly visible minority, like the Beats or punks.

Tracing archetypal characteristics across several recent generations reveals this gradual transition. For example, Boomers rejected the GI generation's uniformity and their Millennial children rejected Boomers' outspoken politics, but when the majority of Millennials began to have Generation X parents, Millennials reversed their political silence and suddenly voted in much larger numbers in the 2008 elections. They also began vocalizing through outlets such as the "Occupy" movements, a pattern that differed noticeably from lead-edge Millennials with Boomer parents.[7] By rejecting the political skepticism of their Generation X parents, some late Millennials opted instead to idealize one Boomer aspect—political outspokenness—while otherwise remaining consistent with most characteristics of their generation. The Black Lives Matter and Me Too movements offer additional examples of this late emergence. One might consider whether the emergence of today's "hipsters" qualifies as another vanguard outlier. Like "Beat" and "punk," the "hipster" brand is rife with stereotypes and used pejoratively (especially by Millennials). The Urban Dictionary, a crowdsourced online dictionary, describes hipsters as pretentious, hypocritical, and self-absorbed, but also creative, intelligent, and independent-minded.[8] While their name concedes some allegiance to their predecessor "hippies," they remain distinctly Millennial in most respects. To support their relationship across archetypes that are two phases of life distant, Strauss and Howe often revert to anecdotal testimony from history; Igor Stravinsky once observed that "it is one of nature's ways, that we feel closer to distant generations than to the generation immediately preceding us."[9]

Strauss and Howe use preseasonality and the midgenerational shift to rationalize a high degree of differentiation within a generation, perhaps as a device to tidy up the loose ends of their theory that do not fit neatly into categories. Their theory contains several explanations for related anomalies, and these are largely to be expected, since Mannheim and his followers find that generations are less a homogenous group and more a collection of difficult-to-categorize cohorts of the same age, bound together in conflict over issues. In the chapters that follow, preseasonality describes an advantage held by architecture, one that has been largely unrecognized. This advantage, however, may also bring drawbacks that are only now making their appearance.

Turnings

The imprint of each of these four generations on a corresponding cycle of periods is what Strauss and Howe refer to as *turnings*, when the young adults of each era give it a distinct social mood. They name the roughly 90-year cycle of four turnings a *saeculum*, using the Latin word for a human lifetime.[10] Strauss and Howe historiography, when applied to 500 years of Anglo-Saxon history, counts six saecula. The four turnings of Strauss and Howe's saeculum, in order, are: a *high*, an *awakening*, an *unraveling*, and a *crisis* (see Table 4.3). The high is an "upbeat era of strengthening institutions and weakening individualism." In our time, the high era occurred in the prosperous postwar years. In the previous saeculum it happened during the Gilded Age, a period of comparable economic growth and expansion of higher education and infrastructure. The awakening is a "passionate era of spiritual upheaval." This occurred as prophet-type Boomers brought about the morals and consciousness-raising of the late 1960s. The previous awakening era occurred when reformers at the turn of the last century raised awareness to rein in monopolies and secure rights for labor. The unraveling is a "downcast era of strengthening individualism and weakening institutions." Dominated by Generation X, this recent unraveling period recalls the previous unraveling of the 1920s, characterized by bad-kid molls and racketeers who Gertrude Stein dubbed "une génération perdue," the Lost Generation. This period ended with renegade banks causing cascading economic collapse. Closing out a saeculum, heroes contend with a crisis as young adults in a "decisive era of secular upheaval, when the values regime propels the replacement of the old civic order with a new one." According to a Strauss-Howe timeline, Millennials will leave their mark on the current period just as the GIs did before them.[11] (For a list of saecula in American history, see Table 4.4.)

As they often do, Strauss and Howe rely heavily on metaphor to add texture to their argument, with seasons of the year playing a prominent role (their use of the word "turning" derives from this reliance). Using this poetic analogy, they write: "In a springlike High, a society fortifies and builds and converges in an era of promise. In a summerlike Awakening, it dreams

Table 4.3. Strauss-Howe Turnings (Generational Eras)

High: an upbeat era of institutions and weakening individualism. Nomads replace prophets in elderhood, slowing the pace of social change and shunning old crusades in favor of simplicity and survivalism. Powerful heroes replace nomads in midlife, establishing an upbeat, constructive ethic of social discipline. Artists replace heroes in young adulthood to become sensitive helpmates, lending their expertise in cooperation to an era of growing social calm. Prophets replace artists in childhood and are nurtured with increasing indulgence by optimistic adults in a secure environment.

Awakening: a passionate era of spiritual upheaval. Heroes replaced nomads in elderhood, orchestrating ever-grander secular constructions, setting the stage for the spiritual goals of the young. Artists replace heroes in midlife, applying expertise and process to improve society while calming the passions of the young. Prophets replace artists in young adulthood challenging the moral failure of elder-built institutions, sparking a society-wide spiritual awakening. Nomads replace prophets in childhood and are left unprotected at a time of social convulsion and adult self-discovery.

Unraveling: a downcast era of strengthening individualism and weakening institutions. Artists replace heroes in elderhood, quickening the pace of social change in shunning the old order in favor of complexity and sensitivity. Prophets replace artists in midlife, preaching a downbeat, values-fixated epic of moral conviction. Nomads replace prophets in young adulthood, becoming brazen free agents and lending their pragmatism and independence to an era of growing social turmoil. Heroes replaced nomads in childhood and are nurtured with an increasing protection by pessimistic adults in an unsecured environment.

Crisis: a decisive era of secular upheaval, when the values regime propels the replacement of the old civic order with a new one. Prophets replace artists in elderhood, pushing to resolve ever-deepening moral choices and setting the stage for the secular goals of the young. Nomads replace prophets in midlife, applying toughness and resolution to defend society while safeguarding the interests of the young. Heroes working in teams replace nomads in young adulthood, challenging the political failure of elder-led crusades and fueling a society-wide secular crisis. Artists replace heroes in childhood and are overprotected at a time of political convulsion and adult self-sacrifice.

William Strauss and Neil Howe, *The Fourth Turning: An American Prophecy* (New York: Broadway, 1997), 145–271.

Table 4.4. Strauss-Howe Turnings in the Anglo-American Saeculum

REFORMATION SAECULUM

Tudor Renaissance	1487-1517	High
Protestant Reformation	1517-1542	Awakening
French and Indian War	1542–1569	Unravelling
American Revolution	1569–1594	Crisis

REFORMATION SAECULUM

Merrie England	1594-1621	High
Puritan Awakening	1621-1649	Awakening
Reaction and Restoration	1649–1675	Unravelling
Glorious Revolution	1675–1704	Crisis

REVOLUTIONARY SAECULUM

Augustan Age of Empire	1704-1727	High
Great Awakening	1727–1746	Awakening
French and Indian War	1746–1773	Unravelling
American Revolution	1773–1794	Crisis

CIVIL WAR SAECULUM

Era of Good Feelings	1794–1822	High
Transcendental Awakening	1822–1844	Awakening
Mexican War and Sectionalism	1844–1860	Unravelling
Civil War	1860–1865	Crisis

GREAT POWER SAECULUM

Reconstruction and Gilded Age	1865–1886	High
Third Great Awakening (Reform Era)	1886–1908	Awakening
World War I and Prohibition	1908–1929	Unravelling
Great Depression and World War II	1929–1946	Crisis

MILLENNIAL SAECULUM

American High	1946–1964	High
Consciousness Revolution	1964–1984	Awakening
Culture Wars	1984–2005?	Unravelling
Millennial Crisis (Great Recession)	2005?–	Crisis

William Strauss and Neil Howe, *The Fourth Turning: An American Prophecy* (New York: Broadway, 1997), 138.

and plays and exults in an era of euphoria. In an autumnal Unraveling, it harvests and consumes and diverges in an era of anxiety. In a hibernal Crisis, it focuses and struggles and sacrifices in an era of survival."[12]

Two pivotal events dramatically highlight the Strauss-Howe saeculum. Called *social moments,* these occur at the metaphorical solstices "when everyone senses—at the time and afterward—that history is moving swiftly, that the familiar world is disappearing and a new world is emerging."[13] Social moments come in two types and only occur during crisis and awakening eras: *secular* during a crisis era, when society focuses on reordering the outer world of institutions and public behavior, and *spiritual* in an awakening era, when society shifts attention to changing the inner world of values and private behavior. Crisis-era social moments are triggered by exogenous, outside events, which congeal generational forces when they occur. Awakening-era social moments begin when the young adults of a prophet generation "burst forth spiritually upon coming of age."[14] These can be either spontaneous or sparked by an outside event. Social moments always alternate in type and last about ten years, normally arriving in time intervals separated by two phases of life, approximately forty to forty-five years apart.[15]

Strauss and Howe provide additional descriptors for their archetypes to define the role they play during social moments. Hero- and prophet-types are "dominant" generations who are either the young adults or elders during a social moment, depending on whether it is secular or spiritual. When young, these dominants recast society's "active agenda"; later, as elders, they react to it. As their theory evolved, Strauss and Howe modified the terms they used for archetypes. Below I combine them using the previous word from *Generations* as an adjective in italics. Therefore, during a secular crisis-era event, *civic* heroes set the agenda as young adults, led by *idealist* prophets as elders. Later, the relationship flips, as inner-focused *idealist* prophets challenge the values set forth by their *civic* hero parents, now elders, during the upheaval of a spiritual awakening era. Strauss and Howe describe how dominant generation hero- and prophet-types give a saeculum a kind of two-stroke pulse during social moments. Going backwards chronologically, the downstroke of the secular crisis of World War II and the Depression came after the previous crisis occurring in the spiritual awakening of the reform era; before that, the Civil War crisis followed transcendentalism, before that, the American Revolution came after the Great Awakening, and so on.

A "recessive" generation experiences social moments as children and later in middle age. By presiding over the upstrokes of these pulses as young adults in either a high or unraveling era, they give pause between the driving events of social moments. In a corresponding arrangement as before, *reactive* nomad-types continue the internal questioning begun in a spiritual crisis, while *adaptive* artist-types maintain the momentum of external transformation begun in a secular crisis. Because of their supporting role, Strauss and Howe refer to members of these recessive generations as "helpmates" who continue many of the characteristics of their predecessor generations. Although less outspoken than their dominant counterparts, helpmates eventually develop their own voice in distinct contrast to their precursors', generally occurring after the midgeneration inflection described earlier. The features then expressed often predict characteristics their successor generation will adopt. For this reason, other writers also refer to recessives as a "hinge" generation.[16] For example, the artist-type Silent generation eventually found a voice to bring forth diversity and social equality, which were less on the minds of their GI forebearers but were issues that Boomers later championed. The nomad-type Generation X continued the Boomer inward-focused speculation to its nadir, but ultimately chose free-agency pragmatism over process, a trait that now is a hallmark of Millennials.

Strauss and Howe rely on multiple forms of cultural expression, such as literature, film, music, and clothing, to argue their theory. In their one significant mention of architecture's archetypal activity in each phase, they curiously pair it with fashion:

> Consider architecture and fashion. A High produces styles that are expansive yet functional, and features romantic revivals that combine confident masculinity (and large constructions) with yielding femininity (and standardization). An Awakening returns to natural, spiritual, folk, rural and primitive motifs, always starting with a thaw in conventional social discipline and the emergence of conscience-driven lifestyle fetishes (regarding food, dress, language, sex, and leisure). An Unraveling is the most eclectic era, with a deliberate mixing and crossing of styles, periods, and genders. A Fourth Turning (Crisis) brings new interest in the rational and classical, in simplicity, restraint, and decorum—while gender-related fashions begin to reformalize and return to elegance.[17]

As with much of Strauss and Howe's theory, ambiguity accompanies an attempt to correlate. If one considers the period of American modernism to be a crisis-era turning, the characteristics of rationality, simplicity, restraint, and even decorum certainly apply, but Strauss and Howe's use of the term "classical" remains vague. Are they referring to a Greco-Roman-derived architecture, or simply a return to a "classic" convention (in a fashion sense) after a period of eclectic free agency? Or does "classic" apply to the lingering pre–WWII governmental style in the United States best exemplified by the Roosevelt era's build-out of Washington, DC? But if so, this work is seldom associated with the rationality, simplicity, and restraint tradition-ally linked with modernism. Similarly vague, the attributes of a Strauss and Howe awakening era—a return to natural, spiritual, folk, rural, and primi-tive motifs—can apply to the postmodern architecture associated with the awakening era and also to modernism, as each mined the vernacular to unencumber architecture from bourgeois taste. Suffice it to say, one can read Strauss and Howe's description of architecture in various ways to cover many possible interpretations.

Generational Constellations

In any given era, young adults set a generational mood, with every liv-ing generation playing its role within a grouping Strauss and Howe call a "generational constellation." In addition to its tone-setting young adults, each constellation has its elder stewards, midlife managers, and upstarts watching as children (see Figure 4.1). As a society enters a new season, each archetype simultaneously enters its next phase of life to play one of these roles. It is important to note that these seasonal cycles are slightly out of phase with generational shifts, occurring two to five years after a new gen-eration of children starts being born. Strauss and Howe describe this pause as necessary for each archetype to sense the mood of the old era turning stale and ripe for replacement with something new.[18]

The dynamic between these cohorts—different for each age because of archetypal characteristics—sets the ethos for every Strauss-Howe turn-ing. Another way Strauss and Howe describe their constellation is as a "generational diagonal," based on a graphic depiction of generations mov-ing through time diagonally. A verbal description of this close chronology is as follows: The last Strauss-Howe high era begins when the GIs return from WWII in 1946 to manage Silents and raise Boomer children. This ends in 1964 with the first societal rumblings of the awakening era. During this next period, the Lost generation, who managed GIs during the war, recedes from the scene. Boomers now dominate the awakening era, clashing with their GI parents as Silents in midlife choose sides and their Generation X

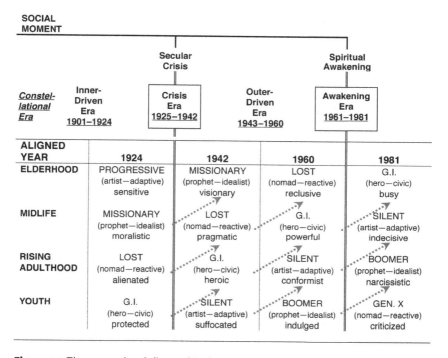

Figure 4.1. The generational diagonal in the twentieth century. After Strauss and Howe, 1991, 79.

children observe. This clash lasts until 1984, in the middle of the Reagan administration, when the unraveling era begins. An era of disquiet imprinted with Generation X values, this interval features still outspoken Boomers, who are now also raising and sheltering their Millennial children. The Silents begin slipping away as the unraveling era ends with the economic crash of 2008. The crash signals the beginning of a crisis era; as Boomers' culture wars reach a climax, Generation X must manage the discord, and everyone waits for Millennial values to present themselves. The crash is preceded in 2005 by the arrival of the successors to Millennials, who Strauss and Howe provisionally name the "Homeland" generation (less descriptive, linear-minded writers refer to them as Generation Z; Pew simply refers to them with the placeholder "Post-Millennial"). Mirroring how Silents performed in the last crisis, Generation X will guide Millennials in bringing the crisis to some resolution by the early 2030s, according to Strauss and Howe's script. Afterward, Millennials will lead the adaptive, artist-type Homelands in refining a new civic order as their Boomer parents fade away. Strauss and Howe's concept of preseasonality would assert that hipsters are a preview of the cultural characteristics of the coming artist-type Homeland generation.

A summary of Strauss and Howe's archetypal roles includes one final character type they call a *gray champion*, a role occurring once per saeculum and only in a secular crisis. To describe this elder, Strauss and Howe derive characteristics from an archetypal figure in Nathaniel Hawthorne's *Twice-Told Tales*. This quote, taken from *Generations*, uses the earlier terminology for the Strauss-Howe archetypes to describe this figure:

> In each of America's decisive moments of secular crisis—the Glorious Revolution of 1689, the American Revolution, the Civil War, and the twin emergencies of the Great Depression and World War II—this society has witnessed the cyclical return of a special breed of elder. . . . At each of these four history-turning moments, America turned for guidance to aging Idealists, spiritual warriors possessed of strong inner vision, patriarchs commanding the respect and obedience of their juniors. All four of these generations of patriarchs had previously been young adults during an era of spiritual Awakening; none of them had come of age facing a secular crisis even remotely similar to the one they faced as grandparents.[19]

The protagonists in Hawthorne's story are anonymous and mythic although Strauss and Howe identify them as being akin to Samuel Adams, Ben Franklin, Abraham Lincoln, and Franklin Roosevelt, all public figures who motivated every generation of a secular crisis era constellation to the full potential of their peer personalities. Strauss and Howe assert that it is the gray champion's sudden rise to prominence that heralds the arrival of a crisis.

In Strauss and Howe's closely timed six saecula going back to North American colonization, they cite the American Civil War as the one anomalous event when the regular transition of generational constellations did not follow an orderly transition and a generation failed to fulfill its archetypal destiny. In this secular crisis era, a dominant hero-type never emerged, and the generation that should have risen to dominance went on to follow the recessive (and less prominent) artist-type role. Strauss and Howe offer several reasons for this. First, the war erupted early according to their timeline, almost a half phase of life sooner than other crises. Second, the three adult generations involved in the war formed a "dangerous constel-

WORKING WITH GENERATIONAL THEORY

lation," allowing each of their worst peer instincts to prevail. And third, the war came to an exhausting and "untriumphant" end, lacking in the lasting civic reconstitutions that followed other crises.[20] Strauss and Howe largely stress the second reason, a "calamitous miscommunication between young and old,"[21] as precipitating the first and third reasons. Through the Civil War anomaly, Strauss and Howe remind their audience that despite the high causality otherwise present in much of their theory, variability still prevails. And while the generational constellation provides each cohort with a "location in history, a peer personality, and a set of possible scripts to follow ... it leaves each generation free to express either its better or its worse instincts, to choose a script that posterity may later read with gratitude or sorrow."[22]

Crisis

Strauss and Howe's depiction of a crisis is the most controversial aspect of their theory and for some its most seductive. According to their timeline, as written in 1997, by the 2010s the world should be in the throes of a secular crisis. Adherents to Strauss-Howe theory can find much evidence to support this, arguing that the crisis likely began with the economic collapse of 2008 and continues with the unexpected election of Donald Trump and other worldwide destabilizations. Ten years prior to the market slump, Strauss and Howe forecast a "Great Devaluation," writing that it would begin a few years before or after the year 2005, basing its likely trigger less on theory than on the demographic reality of a critical mass of Boomers retiring.[23] They also predicted with uncanny accuracy aspects of the mortgage crisis, which they wrote would leave "the world arbitraged and tentacled: Debtors won't know who holds their notes, homeowners who owns their mortgages."[24] The 2008 crash came as foretold and, within the elastic Strauss and Howe timeline, close to being on saecular schedule. In global politics, direct parallels to the 1930s seem to abound, including showcase Olympic Games hosted by controlling regimes in Beijing and Sochi (Berlin), revanchism in Crimea and the Ukraine (Sudetenland), a proxy war in Syria (Spanish Civil War), and the rise of democratically elected, populist, and authoritarian regimes across the globe as a much expanded twenty-first-century version of the Axis powers. These regimes rule in Russia, India, Pakistan, Saudi Arabia, the Philippines, Myanmar, Venezuela, Egypt, Turkey, Hungary, and Poland. Trump's campaign reprises the language of Charles Lindbergh's America First movement of the 1930s, as does the nativism of Britain's surprise Brexit vote to leave the European Union.

As enthralling as Strauss and Howe's predictions might be, and drawing comparisons to the 1930s can indeed become intoxicating, the question remains: how can reasonable people, and especially academic scholars, act on this knowledge? Before one begins to answer the question, it is important to again take note of the high degree of variability surrounding the study of generations. One must also account for the biases of those interacting with the work, those of the researchers themselves, and the effect that close scrutiny has had on Millennials, the object of generational theory in the current context of crisis.

For example, to search for proof for Strauss-Howe theory by creating a list, as I do above, one must apply a bias toward linear history, which Strauss and Howe so bemoan. All of the six secular crises from which their theory derives are as different as they might be archetypal. Overlaying past events on the current crisis exposes a bias toward assembling superficial symptoms, causing one to potentially overlook the underlying causes. In his 2017 book, *On Tyranny: Twenty Lessons from the Twentieth Century*, Timothy Snyder remarks how crises require society to call upon "deep anchoring" to successfully negotiate between the biases of naiveté and cynicism. Yet Snyder begins his book by writing how "history does not repeat itself, but it does instruct" and continues with how it can familiarize and also warn. In his last chapter, Snyder recommends a historical focus rooted in culture to comprehend the circumstances following Trump's election. He parallels Strauss and Howe's use of literature as a resource by invoking a line from the end of Shakespeare's *Hamlet*: "The time is out of joint. O cursèd spite, that ever I was born to set it right! Nay, come, let's go together."[25] In explaining his appreciation for the passage in a 2017 interview, Snyder perhaps unknowingly again echoes Strauss and Howe: "I was trying to describe to the students their situation, which is that they have to feel the time is out of joint, but also I was trying to get across to them that they were born to set it right. It is really up to them—not that people of other generations don't have to participate—but I have this very strong intuition that it's going be people in their 20s who end up being the decisive voices of change for our country."[26]

Strauss and Howe's comprehensive writings recommend how to contend with a secular crisis, and this may have attracted those with a bias toward survivalism. Again referring to seasons, Strauss and Howe use the metaphor of preparing for a winter storm, but one that lasts many years. They list an abstract string of action verbs as headings for preparative recommendations: rectify, converge, bond, gather, root, brace, and hedge. Perhaps it is their survivalist pitch that has attracted Stephen Bannon and other denizens of extreme politics who seem to revel in conspiracies and end-of-days predictions. From the archconservative website *Breitbart News*, Bannon joined the Trump campaign and later served a seven-month stint as White House chief strategist before moving on. His ascendance brought renewed attention to his 2010 documentary *Generation Zero*, which situates the 2008 financial crisis squarely within Strauss-Howe generational theory and includes speaking parts by Neil Howe, among other pundits. The film aligns Bannon's stated goal, to dismantle what he terms the "deep state" of American government, with Strauss and Howe's forecast of a coming "decisive era of secular upheaval, when the values regime propels the replacement of the old civic order with a new one."[27]

A barely disguised contempt for Strauss and Howe among some of the media due to the Bannon association reflects a corresponding bias on the left. An April 2017 *New York Times* article, whose title includes "Winter Is Coming," derides their implied survivalism along with the Bannon connection, and dismissively refers to Neil Howe as an "amateur" historian, although in fact he holds a PhD in history from Yale. Nowhere does the article mention Howe's lifelong writing on Millennials or the impact of their theory; it instead gropes snidely for personal details, such as where Howe is currently employed (a financial research firm—he also studied economics at Yale).[28] Strauss-Howe theory is so intricately woven into generational studies that to purge it because of the *Times*' and other media's derision would constitute a form of intellectual censorship. After all, a 2013 *Architecture* magazine article that recommends "drastic changes to pedagogy, licensure, and firm management" begins with a lengthy quote from Strauss and Howe; in their survey of academic Millennial research, Emma Parry and Peter Urwin cite their generational diagonal as an "explanation of the complex way in which historical events and moods shape a generation's members' lives"; and Paul Taylor in his book *The Next America*, written with Pew Research, describes a "looming generational showdown" and after discussing Strauss and Howe, states, "I see some value in generalizations about generations." Biases from both right and left, who seem to consistently select from Strauss and Howe only what is most useful, can create a cloud of controversy that obscures that which remains.

An examination of Strauss and Howe would not be complete without a discussion of the authors' own biases, which become apparent on close examination of their work over several decades. That both are Boomers with Millennial children reveals a too-close-to-the-subject bias: both the parents' and children's generations are dominant cohorts who figure prominently as protagonists in their writing, while other cohort groups are less distinguished. One can discern this in how Strauss and Howe's timelines have changed as their theory has evolved. In an earlier version outlined in 1991 in *Generations*, they have not yet named the saeculum but have established the four archetypal eras as a poetic parallel to the seasons. They privilege their Boomer generation as beginning this cycle with their archetypally signature awakening, although the cycle perplexingly begins in summer and not winter. By *The Fourth Turning* in 1997 they have brought this cycle into alignment with a more typical calendar, with the newly named saeculum ending with a dramatic crisis now associated with their Millennial children. Between the two texts, Strauss and Howe went from privileging their own position in the first timeline to later upgrading their children's position, following a pattern of Boomer parents bestowing a specialness on their children that they once reserved for themselves. A similar bias is evident in their renaming of their 1991 generational archetypes, adaptive, idealist, reactive, and civic, in 1997 as artist, prophet, nomad, and hero, respectively. While this is arguably a dramatic character promotion for all, it is especially so for the Boomers' children, now elevated from civic to heroic.

And what if Millennials cannot rise to the occasion? Well, a cynic might argue that Strauss and Howe—being the stereotypical helicopter parents that Boomers are born to be—have identified an historical precedent to get Millennials off the hook. Their Civil War anomaly provides ready-made excuses one can apply to contemporary conditions: the 2008 financial crisis coming early and a "dangerous constellation" of partisan bickerers staying relevant well beyond their years. Together, in the wake of a future "untriumphant" conflict (whatever that may mean), these conditions might all align to excuse the Millennial generation from performing in their debut. Thus, whether Millennials step up to meet the crisis's challenge or retire from the field early, it seems that Strauss and Howe may have built in alternative futures for them. It also conveniently keeps the integrity of the Strauss-Howe historiography intact.

I write this last description for effect, to show how easily skepticism of Strauss-Howe theory can degenerate into sarcasm. The study of generations is still relatively young and largely unverified, so applying their theory to understanding the present—let alone foreseeing the future—can indeed seem as dubious as relying on a horoscope or almanac. On the other hand, enough circumstantial evidence exists to cause one to look at history, as Snyder suggests, less for repetition and more for instruction when trying to comprehend current disruptions. When dealing with change and generational dynamics in the architectural academy and profession, a reasonable strategy for applying Strauss and Howe would be to utilize one of their action verbs: to hedge. To do so asks the reader to straddle between cautious usage and vigilant skepticism. While their generational chronology may be compelling, whether their theory has any validity will be demonstrated by how Strauss and Howe's social moment, currently underway, will play out over the next decade and how its events and characteristics are measured. The voluminous data the digital age produces, if organized with longitudinal forethought, may either prove or disprove whether the current challenges play out as predicted and if the hero-type profile will hold up for Millennials. Whether Strauss and Howe's theory stands the test of time, the fact that the digital age has no borders will likely extend their American focus into a global one, an expansion that will bring yet even more bias.

Millennials are the first generation in history to come of age under such scrutiny, with Strauss and Howe leading the effort by prophesying their futures when the youngest were barely ten years old. Given the gravity of these predictions, some may question whether Millennials have the pluck to take on this burden—notably the Millennial skeptic Jean Twenge, who considers them spoiled narcissists, or Mark Bauerlein, who concludes they are dumb. The weight on the cohort of what Strauss and Howe call an "American prophecy" is only compounded as many rising adult Millennials find themselves struggling as they emerge into a sour economy with fraught politics.[29] The unprecedented scrutiny may have also created a sociological effect analogous to Heisenberg's uncertainty principle in physics, which posits that the closer one gets to a subatomic particle, the more any attempt to measure it precisely will disturb it. In an age of hyperconnectivity, one must consider whether the intense focus on Millennials has had a similar effect on them.

If there is a single literary body of work that conveys the anxiety that Millennials might feel under this scrutiny, it is J. K. Rowling's *Harry Potter* saga. Beginning with the first of seven volumes in 1997, this escapist, young adult story synchronizes with the puberty of lead-edge Millennials. That a significant majority of Millennials report some exposure to the books and more to the films suggests alignment with not only the tone but also the

values that define the narrative.[30] Moreover, it identifies many of the stories' conflicts as generational following a Strauss-Howe script: set amidst
a parallel universe of witches and wizards largely invisible to a nonmagical
world, the epic begins as Harry reaches puberty and suddenly discovers that
he is destined to resolve the crisis of his squabbling elders, a quarrel that
by the end of the narrative devolves into an epic battle between good and
evil. Millennial profiles and Strauss-Howe archetypes figure prominently:
Harry's friends are a diverse group from different races and strata of society,
including those discriminated against because of their nonmagical parents.
Of mixed ancestry himself (his mother was murdered because of it), Harry is
counseled by various nomad-type advisers, while a gray champion presides
over it all until he dies (Roosevelt-like) just as Harry and his companions
must go on to fulfill their destiny. Rowling is British, and through eight
movies, audiobooks, and translations into seventy-two languages, the
worldwide Harry Potter phenomenon makes apparent how the Millennial
anxiety underlying this epic saga may now be global.

For those attempting to understand generations, hurdles of bias and
controversy remain to be surmounted. Strauss and Howe's classification of
the current period as one of crisis only heightens the level of ambiguity. Their
theory applies great specificity to the cyclical eras of the past, populated
by archetypes that acted out each drama. Using this knowledge twenty
years ago, Strauss and Howe attempted to predict a future that is now our
present, but despite their many accommodations, the unruliness of history
may be too chaotic to fully project by formula. Nonetheless, Strauss and
Howe's legacy is a set of observations ranging from the self-evident to those
potentially manipulated by bias. For those seeking to better understand
generations in order to navigate the destabilizations of the early twenty-first
century—and emerge better off for it—appraising Strauss-Howe theory with
a cautious hedge remains an advisable strategy.

CHAPTER 5
Architectural History by Generation

> The influence of the third generation of modern archi-
> tects is making itself felt. The contribution of this new
> generation (and I use this term in reference to philo-
> sophical stance and not to age) must be seen in rela-
> tion to the two which preceded it: the heroic generation
> of *form givers*, Le Corbusier, Mies van der Rohe, Frank
> Lloyd Wright, and the second generation of *formalists*,
> refiners and redefiners, Phillip Johnson, Eero Saarinen,
> Paul Rudolph et al. among the Americans who, com-
> ing to maturity in the postwar years, sought stability
> through strong personal statement often removed from
> considerations of program and context.
>
> **ROBERT A. M. STERN**

The generation Robert Stern introduces in his 1969 book, *New Directions in American Architecture*, would later be associated with the postmodern movement, a style in architecture that arose during the societal tumult instigated by Boomers. Similar to the way social scientists use longitudinal comparisons to validate their positions, Stern traces momentum back several generations. Reversing the longitudinally directed chronology of Chapter 3 and organizing a generationally aligned history of four successive eras in American architecture since modernism propels us into the present.[1] As each era of this chronology opens, the profession and academy shift to adopt themes, with a canonical text debuting the period and new firms that put the emerging generational values of that era into practice. Prior vanguards in previous eras anticipate the action of the next period, with later mainstream acceptance validating their foresight. Overlaying a Strauss-Howe timeline on Stern's chronology shows significant synchronization and common appellations. An abundance of twentieth-century architectural movements never fully correlate with Strauss-Howe theory, although their exceptions reconcile some of the ambiguities and inconsistencies. This leaves a provisional framework laden with as much risk as opportunity. Whether or not one accepts Strauss and Howe's formula, entertaining an alternative view of the architecture since modernism based on the interplay of generations may help architecture benefit from current and future disruptions. And accepting any associated epistemological risks may help the profession and academy fully assimilate a cohort that generational theory suggests may become, to reapply Stern's term, a new generation of "form givers."

Modernism

The stock market crash of 1929 announced the emergence of American modernism, marking a decisive rupture in architectural chronology with a past rooted in eclecticism. After the crash, US building construction dropped by 75 percent, causing a sustained pause that lasted until the end of World War II.[2] After his election in 1932, Franklin Delano Roosevelt's government intervened to maintain the construction economy thorough the Civilian Conservation Corps and Works Progress Administration. These programs benefitted from a large generation of relatively well-educated and self-organizing young adults who responded with can-do practicality, team spirit, and outward focus, qualities that history now associates with the GI generation, or as Brokaw calls them, the Greatest Generation. Their values would pervade building throughout the rise of American modernism. While neoclassicism and other historical styles lingered in the civic architecture of Washington and other government centers, economic hardship and later wartime necessity helped a practical new architectural language eventually displace historicism throughout the rest of the country. Leading the way were the vast infrastructure works of the Tennessee Valley Authority and others around the country.[3] Even Rockefeller Center, a rare private sector project of the Depression era and an icon of the new emerging language, was noteworthy for being broadly collaborative.[4] Rem Koolhaas would later refer to it as a "masterpiece without a genius."[5] By the end of the war, modernism had become the accepted national form of the architectural profession. Firms that established themselves during this period to become stalwarts of American modernism include Skidmore, Owings & Merrill (1936), Edward Durell Stone (1933), and Perkins+Will (1935).

In American architectural schools, a parallel shift away from Beaux-Arts curricula was occurring at the same time. In 1932, William Hudnut shocked the architectural community by announcing that studio projects should focus more on the practical than the exotic, his pronouncement seeking to change the long-accepted practice of having all academic work produced in the United States judged according to Beaux-Arts standards.[6] Hudnut would reform the academic program at Columbia and later Harvard, where he would lay the groundwork for the arrival of Walter Gropius. Hudnut and Gropius together formed a pedagogy that would drive modernism into the postwar era (although Hudnut would later famously break with Gropius).[7] While Hudnut's transformation of elite design programs may have had broader long-term ramifications, the movement away from the Beaux-Arts had quietly begun more than a decade earlier in regional schools far from the East Coast, at Oregon and Cincinnati. Most notable about these vanguard pedagogies was their return to basics, focusing on practical technical issues, interdisciplinarity, and an increasing spirit of civic-mindedness.[8]

The publication of *The International Style: Modern Architecture Since 1922* represents the first significant appearance of Philip Johnson in a generational reconstruction of American modernism. Johnson wrote the book along with Henry-Russell Hitchcock to accompany an exhibition with a similar name at the Museum of Modern Art (MoMA), an epochal institution that opened a week after the 1929 crash. Although the exhibition was initiated by Alfred Barr, MoMA's first director, he left the curating of the show and writing to two young curators, both then in their twenties. The book and exhibition focused on international modern architecture's leaders (including Le Corbusier and Ludwig Mies van der Rohe), housing, and modernism's global impact. Noticeably absent from the publication (but not the exhibition) was Frank Lloyd Wright, the third of Stern's heroic trio. By proselytizing the publication's canonical and largely practical principles—an emphasis of volume over mass, the standardization of elements, and the avoidance of ornament—it became an architectural pattern book of functional pragmatism for American architects through the coming decades. The show traveled throughout the United States, and its wide exposure helped convince American schools to later invite Gropius and Mies to administer their programs.[9]

Though the *International Style* catalog and exhibition may have been influential in the United States, it drew its content from nearly ten-year-old examples and influences from a continent away. Indeed, significant shifts toward modernism in both the European profession and the academy had begun well before 1929, with some historians tracing those origins as far back as the nineteenth if not the eighteenth century.[10] And while the MoMA exhibition included the work of emerging American modernists, many of those practicing in the United States—Rudolph Schindler, Richard Neutra, and William Lescaze—were European émigrés. In the European design professions, modernism under many names—purism, de Stijl, functionalism, objectivity (*sachlichkeit*), and constructivism—had begun almost a full generation before their American counterpart picked it up. In a parallel concurrence in architectural education, Gropius founded the Bauhaus in 1919, and Vkhutemas, the Russian state art and technical school, opened the following year. While each shared a similar modernist pedagogy, the Bauhaus would go on to heavily influence design education in the United States well into the twentieth century, perhaps because it was less associated with Communism in an increasingly sensitive ideological climate. The influence of both Frank Lloyd Wright and American industrial vernacular on emergent European modernism suggests reciprocity rather than a one-way flow of ideas across the Atlantic.[11]

Postwar Modernism

Government-driven consolidation and the empowerment of public and private US institutions characterized the postwar modernist era. Following a pattern set before the war, federal leadership now delegated a new generation of technocrats to both expand and create a new civic environment, except this time on a massive scale. This new generation of what Stern calls "formalists, refiners, and redefiners" carried through with "strong personal statements" cleansed of historical association but somehow less in touch with the considerations of program and context that drove their predecessors. A rapidly expanding economy also allowed aging heroic modernists like Mies to fulfill schematic proposals developed during or before the wartime crisis. Mies now benefitted more directly from the boosterism of those of the prewar generation, like Philip Johnson, now entering midcareer. With Johnson's design support, Mies finally realized the Seagram Building, the glass skyscraper he first began imagining in 1922. In parallel, Le Corbusier completed the high-rise Unité d'habitation in Marseille, a form derived from ideas first proposed for La Ville Radieuse in 1924. A new generation of American architects soon began replicating towers inspired by both designers across the US. Mies's Seagram Building served as the prototype for the modern corporation to house the Silent generation's "man in the gray flannel suit," and Le Corbusier's apartment block became the preferred form to remedy the problems of American urban poverty. Occupants later referred to buildings like it generically, often sarcastically, as the "projects." Beyond the city, various modernist prototypes for dispersed housing gave creative license to sprawling suburban expansion by oftentimes lesser talents. These concepts ranged from those inspired by Frank Lloyd Wright's Broadacre City, which he first proposed in *The Disappearing City* in 1932, to the more practical homestead developments of the New Deal, and to Clarence Stein and Henry Wright's garden cities.[12]

In many ways, Johnson's change of character represents both the continuity and dissimilarity between the generation of prewar young adults and those after it. While still maintaining his prewar modernist progressive ideology, after his earlier misadventures with fascism Johnson traded in his vanguardist persona for a newly minted professional image as he trawled for corporate clients. Firms that established themselves after World War II included Johnson's (1949) and the other two Stern formalists': Eero Saarinen (1950) and Paul Rudolph (1951). Another practice also became emblematic of the period, the cooperative grouping of The Architects Collaborative (1946). Founded by Benjamin Thompson and others in a spirit of intergenerational conviviality, the firm included Gropius as their "idealistic, tolerant, worldly mentor."[13]

Empowered with a mission to train for expansion, architecture schools absorbed the shockwave of spiking enrollments caused by returning GIs who joined the younger Silents entering higher education. Between 1945 and 1950, thirteen new schools of architecture opened in the United States and Canada, and Georgia Tech's enrollment grew from twenty-two during the war to 450 students after it.[14] By the war's end, most schools had fully embraced modern design pedagogy in what would coalesce to become a progressive national style representing the country's imperative to reshape itself and also to project its global ambitions. As if to make up for lost time, most schools fully incorporated curricula to inculcate students with those heroic qualities that won the war: pragmatic, technical focus, interdisciplinary teamwork, and progressive civic-mindedness. A renewed emphasis on finding practical solutions to technical problems educated a corps of experts, often focused on housing or industrialized building techniques.

A corollary to this specialization was the identified need to collaborate with colleagues in related fields. To achieve this, many schools followed Hudnut's lead at Harvard to interweave architecture, landscape architecture, and planning into one institution. These included the University of Pennsylvania under G. Holmes Perkins and UC Berkeley under William Wurster. By naming the new entity UC Berkeley's College of Environmental Design, Wurster even dropped the word "architecture" from the masthead entirely, emphasizing the new interdisciplinarity that positioned architecture less as a stand-alone discipline than as part of a larger system whose scale had yet to be defined.[15] While some European cities were replacing (often with exactitude) what extensive bombing had destroyed, America took on an abstract technocratic focus that attempted to simultaneously solve overlapping urban difficulties. This multidisciplinary effort spawned an entire new discipline: urban design, a postwar invention meant to guide urban renewal and respond to suburbanization, which ironically was the very pattern that federal subsidies and policies were perpetuating.[16] This national focus on the civic realm—in which the architectural academies actively participated—was as much an attempt to correct problems as to project an image of a government in control, all to bulwark against the seemingly ever-present threat of Communism that loomed prominently during the era.

As occurred with prewar modernism, those who would guide the postwar period in both the American profession and the academies came from across the Atlantic, most notably the pedagogue-practitioners Gropius and Mies, followed by Ludwig Hilberseimer and László Moholy-Nagy. One academy that in the 1930s quietly made an early and lasting impact on the succeeding generation in espousing a radical interdisciplinarity was Black Mountain College in North Carolina, a place where European modernists and their values were welcome. Bauhaus faculty Anni and Josef Albers and Xanti Schawinsky found refuge there, while the college commissioned Gropius and Marcel Breuer to design its campus. The Dutch painter Willem de Kooning later influenced the American engineer and inventor Buckminster Fuller. And while teaching there in 1943, A. Lawrence Kocher and Howard Dearstyne (Dearstyne had studied at the Bauhaus) together conceptualized an "architectural center" that stressed organizational management, applied research, and connections to industry—all values that would later dominate the postwar era.[17]

Sigfried Giedion's *Space, Time and Architecture: The Growth of a New Tradition*, first published in 1941, legitimized a broad mandate of values for several decades of the postwar era by laying deep thematic and historic foundations for both modern architecture and urban planning. Rather than freeze his observations in time, Giedion regularly inserted new material into what became a kind of living document (and also to maintain the ongoing renewal of his status as a professional kingmaker) in 1949, 1954, 1962, and finally, 1967, just as Stern's reactionary postmodernism was beginning to emerge. Giedion argues for a deep generational awareness, writing that

"Only when he (the historian) is permeated by the spirit of his own time is he prepared to detect those tracts of the past which previous generations have overlooked."[18] Giedion's scope and progressive outlook spoke directly to the postwar practitioner and student in the United States, where he predicted with a conviction what succeeding generations would condemn: that design would attain a perpetuating autonomy "apart from questions of economics, class interests, race, or other issues."[19] In his "Nine Points on Monumentality," joined by the architect José Luis Sert and the painter Fernand Léger, Giedion laid out a specific prescription in the postwar era for "human landmarks which men have created as symbols for their ideals, for their aims, and for their actions." These would be urban-focused, the products of close collaboration aimed at aiding in the "organization of community life in the city which has been practically neglected up to date."[20]

As the postwar era progressed, each copy of the modernist prototype lost fidelity to the refined clarity of the original. By the period's end, many had become completely debased and targets of attack. Outside the cities, much of the complex richness of the prewar efforts fell away as a technocratic, almost martial, imperative took hold to mass-produce homes that carried a vague whiff of the hominess of housing built before the Depression. At the regional scale, politicians both federal and local authorized the building of Norman Bel Geddes's 1939 vision of a nation of highways and airports. With the original little more than a comprehensive advertising initiative to sell fuel and automobiles, designers gave little consideration to any unintended consequences.[21] The sudden, massive, and unprecedented impact on the American landscape shocked many. Cities lost residents and businesses to greener (and cheaper) pastures, often abetted by the clearing of whole neighborhoods, whether because of so-called renewal, the fatal piercing of highways, or a coordinated combination of both. By the end of the era, the massive change caused cities to stagnate and regions to expand chaotically. The time progressively became riper for a new generation to reject the values that two succeeding generations had accrued.

Postmodernism

Unlike during the previous changeover before the war, the academies, not the government or the architecture profession, led the next significant shift in generational values, with students literally on the front lines. Beginning in 1965, inner-city rioting, political assassinations, and growing protests toward the Vietnam War created an unease across the United States that caused bloodshed. By 1968, architecture students led by those at Columbia and UC Berkeley joined the unrest by vociferously rejecting the technically driven and practical values then taught. They demanded the old values be replaced with ideas of social relevance, especially those emerging from grassroots participation, finding suspect any civic work initiated by the government or institutions. And while many community-oriented projects ushered in a new form of collaboration, the rejection of systems-based design rooted in pure technology or pragmatism led to a more personal exploration of design as "a return to the notion of architecture as an art."[22] Thus, the hallmarks of their forebearers' generations, held dear from the onset of the Depression—practicality, interdisciplinarity, and civic-mindedness—many in the rising generation of architects found as corrupting as youth in the general population found them.[23]

The questioning of its formulaic methods by the rising generation stunned the architecture profession. In retreat, the government retracted sponsorship of urban renewal projects, and a series of economic crises through the 1970s furthered a cessation of commissions. As a result, architecture's focus moved from built work to the speculative investigations of the academy, where a polarized debate emerged between a core group of young teacher-practitioners. This face-off between "Whites" and "Grays," which Phillip Johnson observed carefully and later joined, paralleled the broader rancor of the culture wars crisscrossing the nation. Colin Rowe and Kenneth Frampton anthologized the architects who held fast to modernism's orthodoxy in their book *Five Architects*. (Taking after the period's larger-than-life Chicago Seven, these "Whites" also became the New York Five.) In the opposing camp, Robert Stern led the "Grays," a faction adopting inclusivist and overt references to vernacular, populist, and historicist forms, which up to then the modernist canon had devalued. Both sides made their arguments through unbuilt projects, conceptual work, or domestically scaled buildings.[24] The Grays quickly seized the initiative, and when the economy revived, postmodernism (a.k.a. POMO) thrived as the prevalent style into the 1980s. Noteworthy firms founded during this period and known for their early postmodernism included Stern's own Robert A. M. Stern Architects (1977), Kohn Pedersen Fox (1976), and Michael Graves, who achieved notoriety in 1974 when he publicly switched sides. Effectively defecting from the New York Five to join the postmodernist Grays, he perhaps inspired Johnson to definitively do so several years later when he began building skyscrapers inspired by Chippendale furniture, castles, and cathedrals.[25]

In 1966, Robert Venturi's theoretical treatise *Complexity and Contradiction in Architecture* launched postmodernism and precipitated the challenge to modernism's status quo, which would later rage rampant. His self-described "gentle manifesto" of polemics encouraged active rebellion that echoed the rhetoric of people in the streets, asserting that architects could "no longer afford to be intimidated by the puritanically moral language of orthodox Modern architecture."[26] Venturi's manifesto decisively broke with modernist conventions in its liberal reference to historical forms, a resource that modernists largely avoided. Asking rhetorically if it is "almost all right," his text relegitimized the heterogeneity of America's iconic Main Street, the vulgar urban space that the previous era's newly formed urban design tried to sanitize. Venturi's text would become the guidebook for a new generation practicing Stern's inclusive approach, who believed that this path would achieve a greater alignment with society's values.

Many foreshadowings predicted the sea change in architecture well before it began. Hudnut himself is said to have first used the term "postmodernism" in a 1946 article in which he repudiated the direction of Gropius, turning on the very visionary modernist he brought to America years before. Hudnut instead called for a return to the lessons of history and a renewed civic engagement in urban culture twenty years before the uproar of the 1960s began.[27] As occurred before the rise of modernism, significant previews of postmodernism came from across the Atlantic. The Team 10 consortium's rebuke of the orthodoxy of the Congrès Internationaux d'Architecture Moderne (CIAM) led several US schools to invite its members, namely Aldo van Eyck and Herman Hertzberger, to teach a more value-based, humanist pedagogy. And beginning in 1961 via a series of cartoon-inspired pamphlets, the British group Archigram disseminated a formal language inspired by pop art and psychedelia, "targeting youth as potential agents for change, portraying architecture as being in the throes of a generational struggle."[28] Once again, an American brand of anticipatory action emerged not from eastern cities but from the heartland, with a rediscovery of the rural vernacular led by the writing of J. B. Jackson, whose work Venturi and his wife and partner Denise Scott Brown both later championed.

Deconstruction

A noticeable shift in style and tone occurred in the late 1980s as the primary thrust of postmodernism began to splinter and Generation X raised its voice over the din of the Boomers. An economic downturn followed the financial crash of 1987; triggered by abuses in real estate development, it deeply impacted architecture. The end of easy commissions brought on an era of wariness, skepticism, and self-motivation many in architecture refer to as "deconstruction." The era also coincided with widespread adoption of the computer in the production and teaching of architecture, a technological advancement that only furthered the ever-increasing variety of modes of expression. By the early 1990s, premodern historical references in architecture had lost their primacy, challenged by the rediscovery of other earlier practices of modernism, especially those excluded from the International Style canon, such as constructivism and expressionism. An initial preoccupation with jagged forms that recalled constructivist art (and helped coin the era's name) gave way to a computer-driven emphasis on fluidity and smoothness that recalled the expressionist work of Erich Mendelsohn and Frederick Kiesler, a style that drew the name "blob architecture." In stark contrast, at the urban scale the embracement of the premodern prevailed and even strengthened with the formation of the Congress for the New Urbanism in 1993. This group sought to force into law policy frameworks of premodern town-planning principles that heroic modernists categorically rejected. The declining standards of this era led the US General Services Administration to launch the Design Excellence Program in 1994 to remedy the mediocrity that a broad, undisciplined architectural eclecticism had brought to public building. Critics mocked the large projects of the era, such as Boston's "Big Dig" and the early rebuilding at the World Trade Center site, for their banality, inefficiencies, and inability to control costs.

In response, a growing pragmatism about building at a manageable scale hearkened back to both constructivist architecture and the grittier methods of the vanishing industrial city. Using unfinished materials such as plywood, metal mesh, and exposed—even purposely messy—detailing, architects built an analog to the gritty and raw grunge and hip-hop music of the era. This pragmatic drive, combined with an abiding sense of hyperindividualism, free agency, and digital practice, took aim at the dependent relationship with the construction industry and the legal forces that architecture had fallen prey to, while also looking beyond the all-consuming theoretical argumentation of the academies. Firms that emerged in this era and that shared these characteristics include SHoP Architects (1996), Office dA (1991), and Foreign Office Architects (1993).

In architectural schools, stylistic pluralism became the norm, with a strengthening belief in individual expression and a growing disengagement from the social issues that drove teaching in the previous era. Individual architects associated with singular positions traveled to different schools as visiting studio critics or to give lectures in ever-expanding nomadic circuits. As in the profession's quest for noncanonical stylistic references, academicians sought architectural relevance in the ever-more-obscure humanities, especially literary criticism, to be "reconceived as a kind of discursive, text-based practice."[29] Academies fostered a new kind of pedagogue: the professional architectural theorist. Holding forth at different schools, often in direct competition with one another, these critics accelerated the tendentiousness of the previous postmodern era, drawing lines of opposition on many fronts in architecture's form of the culture wars. Some attacked postmodernism's tendency toward nostalgia, associating it with the right-leaning Reagan administration's attempt to restore traditional cultural values. In opposition, others promoted an open-ended pluralism, promoting formal experimentation as an arm of ever-evolving liberalism. All seemed to grapple with what postmodernism was or should now be: "Was it humanist, marked by a desire to recover tradition and cultural expression; or was it posthumanist, a radical break with both modernism and its premodern past, celebrating heterogeneity and the new?"[30] The greatest conflict was between theory that sought to "destabilize the certainties of received architectural knowledge"[31] and reemergent pragmatism focusing "around the idea of practice and engagement in the real world, usually through fabrication, construction performance, or program."[32] It was the rise of computers in architectural schools beginning in the late 1980s that empowered a new generation with a sense of free agency focused on building that began to suppress the squabble.

At the height of postmodernism, the emergence of an "LA school" of architecture in the 1970s anticipated the values of the deconstructivist period. Consistent with other geographical precursors, this formal experimentation came not from the established firms and academies of the Northeast, which at the time skirmished over the validity of historicism, theory, or practice, but from the West Coast, with Frank Gehry's pioneering practice and the opening of the Southern California Institute of Architecture (SCI-Arc). Gehry's iconoclastic use of materials such as chain-link fencing and corrugated metal siding, first employed to formally reshape his own home in Santa Monica in 1978, prefigures both the free agency and the penchant for industrial or deliberately unfinished materials that later characterize the deconstructivist period. Despite a slight nod to historical forms at his

Loyola Law School campus, Gehry's formal explorations liberated a whole generation of younger architects from both historical interpretation and orthogonal building. Perhaps most important, his adaptation of the aviation-based 3-D software CATIA for the Lewis Residence (1989) pioneered both the digitally mediated form-making *and* the information-based modeling that would underpin architecture practices of the following generation.

Concurrently, the founding of SCI-Arc by Ray Kappe as a nonhierarchical school committed to both regional modernism and a broad-based understanding of environmental concerns resonated with Gehry's pioneering effort. It became a fertile laboratory for its faculty-practitioners, Thom Mayne, Michael Rotondi, and Eric Owen Moss, who took inspiration from Gehry's architecture to emphasize their own "perceptual qualities, formal experimentation, and, most of all, as Rotondi put it, a practicality grounded in 'how to make stuff.'"[33] Los Angeles's detachment from the cultural churnings back east made it seem the perfect place to evolve an individualistic and nomadic persona for future deconstructivists, a place Gehry described where "historicism and contextualism are empty words in a city that has no history, no tradition, and no context."[34]

As with the heroic modernist generation before it, a MoMA exhibition and seminal catalog announced the new destructivist era and helped disseminate its name. *Deconstructivist Architecture* furthered the link with the previous epochal publication and exhibition some fifty years earlier, asking Phillip Johnson to co-curate the show and write the introduction. Yet rather than express continuity with the previous event, Johnson instead seemed intent on erasing any relationship, writing emphatically how deconstructivism is *not* a style or movement, with *no* messianic fervor or exclusivity associated with modernism and *no* rules.[35] Johnson seemed to be at once maintaining the prominence of his generation's earlier contribution while also describing the lawless free agency of the new cohort. Johnson's embrace of this style in his own work, continuing his regular reinvention upon a generational changing-of-the-guard, would be his last.

Despite Johnson's disavowal, the stylistic debut bore significant similarities to the previous *International Style* premier show and book. Like its predecessor, the show's curatorial position, and especially its name, seemed superficial. As if searching for purpose, the exhibition connected Jacques Derrida's theories on deconstruction to the previous Russian constructivist movement, revealing vague curatorial notions, "the bits and pieces," to use Strauss and Howe's term, of what bound the era together. While the show recognized Americans Frank Gehry and Peter Eisenman, the former for his groundbreaking West Coast explorations and the latter for continuing an East Coast postmodern foment (Eisenman was a member of the New York Five), it introduced mostly European-trained architects—Zaha Hadid, Coop Himmelb(l)au, Rem Koolhaas, Daniel Libeskind, and Bernard Tschumi—to a broad American audience (although all had already spent considerable time in the United States). Each European would go on to establish robust practices (two would win Pritzker prizes), although at the time of the show they had even fewer built projects than their modernist forerunners had in 1932. As an exhibition and document, *Deconstructivist Architecture* helped to evangelize a design movement distinctly different than the one it suc-ceeded. Like its predecessor two generations prior, it marked the beginning of an era, set its tone, and introduced its protagonists.

Strauss and Howe Overlaid

Before bringing this timeline to the present, it is worth pausing to consider the overt generational rhythms evident in the previous four periods as described. The common use of the term "heroic" and the synonymity of "deconstruction" and "unraveling" suggest at least a superficial similarity to Strauss-Howe generational theory worth further discussion. The four distinct eras from modernism to deconstruction show consistency with Strauss and Howe's archetypal eras: the first is an era of epochal change; the second shows a spirit of refinement; the third is a period of reform; and the fourth diverges momentum. Each seminal text I have selected marks the beginning of a new period and espouses its standards, while the actions of Phillip Johnson's serial opportunism also signal the changes in mood.

There are two critical milestones in this four-part trajectory. Modernism arises in the first, a period of secular transformation when, as Strauss and Howe project, society reorders the "outer world of institutions and public behavior." This transition occurs during a period of global economic hard-ship and war, when all "perceive that historic events are radically altering their social environment."[36] The second, an inward-focused reappraisal, corresponds to the postmodern rebuke that followed the first rupture. This era challenges the results of the prior reordering and refocuses attention to the "inner world of values and private behavior."[37] Consider for comparison Stern's call for a renewal of values, written at the time of this milestone and several decades before Strauss and Howe. Stern advocates for an inclusive approach that "rejects the heroic stance which orthodox modern architecture assumed to itself as the source of cultural values in favor of a more modest and flexible position in which architecture embodies the values which society, not just other architects, values and supports."[38] His use of the word "values" (if grammatically one time too many) correlates with Strauss and Howe's proposition that in an awakening era, values emanate from an inner world to reject external orthodoxy.

Young adult protagonists drive these course corrections. A practical, team-driven, and outwardly focused cohort finds direction in a global modernist movement whose functionalist and communitarian values appeal to their own. Their appellation as heroes only further binds them to a period known for heroic architecture. By rejecting their forebearers' technocratic and unfeeling orthodoxy, young postmodernists later find their own mission. Each of these dominants leads the next recessive generation. Those who follow the modernists, in Stern's wording, "the second generation of formalists, refiners and redefiners," advance the mission of consolidation set forth by their predecessors. The later deconstructivists follow a reverse trajectory in extending postmodern disagreements toward fragmentation.

A vanguardist tendency is evident in each period. Prior to the modernist upheaval in America, ripples of change came both from Europe and the American heartland. The instigators of Stern's second generation also came from Europe but incubated first in American schools. The influencers of postmodernism continue the pattern of previous generations, drawing ideas from both Europe and an American vernacular. And while many of the protagonists of deconstruction were European, they all benefitted from Gehry's pioneering formal experimentation enhanced by digital technology, which he cultivated in Los Angeles, far from Europe and the East Coast.

While Stern and Giedion allude to generations of architects, the wide variety of architectural expression that expanded in the twentieth century overwhelms a historiography as comprehensive as anyone might construct following Strauss and Howe. One attempt is Charles Jencks' famous "Evolutionary Tree" (see Figure 5.1), first drawn in 1973 and later supplemented in 2000.[39] He organizes this index of global architectural trends, movements, and practitioners throughout the twentieth century into six traditions: logical, idealist, self-conscious, intuitive, activist, and unselfconscious. The last—unselfconscious—Jencks claims accounts for 80 percent of gross activity. He depicts graphically the century's ebbs and flows, and these correspond to Strauss and Howe's basic rhythm. Blobs of activity in black correspond to course-corrective periods when action frenzies. A distinguishing

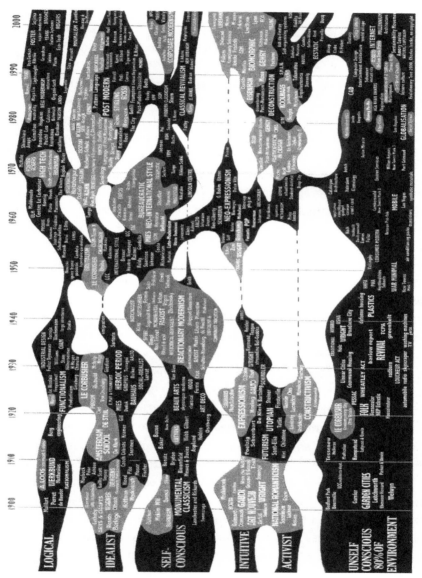

Figure 5.1. Jencks' theory of evolution. From Charles Jencks, "2000 July: Jencks' Theory of Evolution, an Overview of 20th Century Architecture," *Architectural Review*, December 7, 2011.

difference occurs during the rise of modernism, when activities increase and the bulges swell but remain distinct. During postmodernism's ascent, the black zones merge briefly, only to have white areas fragment their unity. As deconstruction commences, these white zones increase in numbers greater than at the timeline's beginning as the black clouds balkanize. In contrast, when pragmatism prevailed and dissent laid dormant at midcentury, white areas, most notably among the idealist, intuitive, and activist traditions, are completely free of action. Jencks' "Evolutionary Tree" anticipates later "Wordles," or word clouds, graphic models commonly used on the internet to represent web activity or other inputs. Many architectural bloggers have since formed their own trees of Wordles inspired by Jencks, continually evolving them as history moves forward.

Delving further beyond the superficial and graphic, one encounters significant ambiguities when applying a Strauss-Howe chronology to architectural history. The first is Strauss and Howe's overwhelming bias toward an American instead of a European timeline. For example, while Strauss and Howe and architectural writers such as Stern all use the term *heroic* to describe individuals bringing about radical change in the twentieth century, they seem to be following different calendars. Straus and Howe's young adult heroes (born 1900–1925) follow their archetypal script in a crisis era beginning in 1929, but the architects Alison and Peter Smithson write with definitiveness that "the [heroic] period *ended* when absolute conviction in the movement died, around 1929" (italics mine). The period ended, according to the Smithsons, largely because European economic and political upheavals forced many to leave the chaos of Europe for the United States.[40] Clearly, the two periods influenced one another, but it remains unclear when Strauss and Howe's critical rupture, prompting society's rejection of "the ossifying and dysfunctional roles" of an earlier order, actually transpired. Did it first happen in Europe, ending in 1929, and then migrate across the Atlantic, thus placing American and European cycles out of phase with each other? Strauss and Howe offer little to sufficiently explain the interface between generations of different continents, although they reference such geographically, ethnically, and historically diverse writers as Arnold J. Toynbee, José Ortega y Gasset, and Ibn Khaldun. They do, however, concede that "generations in America have often shared a similar mind-set, a sort of sympathetic vibration, with their transatlantic peers."[41] They also anticipate the rest of the globe one day fully synchronizing; as cultures "grow more open and mobile, this distinction between America and other societies may be disappearing."[42]

A related ambiguity is who qualifies as a hero in a Strauss-Howe description of a hero generation. Stern's heroic modernists are all much older than Strauss and Howe's young adult hero-types, born 1900–1925, and Wright, the only American in Stern's trio, is significantly older. Even if one assumes a separate European cycle one decade ahead of an American one, when Mies (b. 1886) and Corbusier (b. 1887) produced their early seminal work as young-adult heroes, it still fails to explain Stern's inclusion of Wright (b. 1867), who was approaching retirement when the other modernists were acting heroically. Stern's parenthetical qualification, that he uses this term "in reference to philosophical stance and not to age," suggests he considers the grouping less demographically and more as a device to unify the trio around a common belief.

Rather than demanding consistency within the formula, applying Strauss and Howe's more general construct of generational constellations may help to explain this confusion and ultimately prove more useful in navigating present turbulent changes. According to the generational constellations construct, the four generations active during a secular crisis interact with one another fluidly to move history forward. While rising adult hero-types create a receptive mood, nomad-types lead them and prophet-types guide the larger operation. If one applies this understanding, both Mies and Corbusier led during the heroic period of modernism *not* as members of a classic Strauss-Howe hero-type generation, but instead as nomadic, with their independence and sense of free agency better fitting that character profile.[43] In this scenario, Wright parallels Roosevelt's unflinching leadership of iconoclastic nomad-type generals Dwight Eisenhower, Douglas MacArthur, and George Patton as they led the well-educated and self-confident GIs in the war.

In this four-part construct of the generational constellation, Frank Lloyd Wright more than any other figure fits the role of the Strauss-Howe gray champion, a title he might have even found worthy of applying to himself.[44] Wright first influenced and later simultaneously both challenged and absorbed the impact of MoMA's European-focused International Style in a way that would revive his career, filling the role of the wise if irritable elder who would help consolidate American modernism beginning in the mid-1930s until his death in 1959. Like Roosevelt, Wright was born into the prophet-type generation (1860–1882) that rose to adulthood during the awakening of the reform period. After apprenticing to Louis Sullivan and adopting his strong directives, Wright radically changed American architecture with his practice, and to anticipate the widespread emergence of modernism that he presided over late in his career constitutes an entirely separate front of preseasonality. Beginning with the Wasmuth Portfolio of 1910, Wright's work profoundly impacted a younger European generation, and despite the later chilly relations between him and its heroic leaders—Corbusier and Mies—his age and greater experience left them less his peers (as Stern's grouping might suggest) and more his protégés. As their elder, Wright always stayed ahead of them, masterfully absorbing the International Style's signature white horizontality at Fallingwater. There he juxtaposed bright horizontal bands in cantilevered extensions against rough-stone verticals, all set in a sublimely picturesque landscape that captured the imagination of a despondent country. Wright decisively led American modernism as it emerged from the Depression, and despite his protean nature, many insults, and general cantankerousness, he exerted a powerful hold on generations of architecture students.[45] Beginning in 1932, many came as fellows to learn directly from the master at Taliesin East and later West, where he sat literally on a dais, and figuratively as patriarch, fully in the Strauss-Howe mold. Whether one accepts Wright's elevation to patriarch status, Strauss and Howe's mythopoeic standards may be of use in defining leadership in the disruptive periods of this century.

The Twenty-First Century
Like the crash of 1929, the financial crisis of 2008 had a significant global impact, and history will remember Trump's upset election as unprecedented, if not disruptive. And if the dramatic economic and political upheavals are not significant enough, scientists' nearly unanimous environmental warnings about climate change should be crisis enough to focus future generations.[46] If a financial crash archetypally links Millennials and the GI generation, a looming environmental catastrophe may be the exogenous crisis that differentiates them. Notwithstanding political upheavals and conflicts, climate change may be the signal crisis of a Millennial architect's lifetime. Whether or not one needs Strauss and Howe's generational theory to take action, a crisis of significant proportions is or will soon beset society, and it is architecture's choice as to whether it will lead in contending with it or follow others.

If it opts to lead, the discipline will need to rely on the shared Millennial traits of confidence, team-spiritedness, and outward focus in addressing the future technological and interdisciplinary issues related to solving environmental problems, if not the economic and political issues associated with them. Future leaders, whether they come from within the Millennial cohort or from older generations, will depend on a well-articulated message delivered with confidence. Within the realm of architecture, the neo-Millennial trends already established can serve as proven methodology. The expansion of scope pioneered by landscape urbanists, with its renewed focus on environmental sustainability in a postindustrial world, can guide architects to accomplish this in other realms. Practical, actionable initiatives at the civic scale—which must take priority over theoretical, procedural, and conceptual undertakings not directly leading to a sustainable future—can set a standard for tangible results. Rather than striving for beauty as an end in itself, architects must use aesthetics to play a role in maintaining a consistent message, binding together myriad disciplines under the umbrella of design and sustainability as a singular Gesamtkunstwerk. Unlike modernism, which championed the master builder, the coming era can build upon the learned experiences of architects working hands-on with communities to empower master organizers to serve as the binding agents who will lead disruption through innovation.

If the environmental crisis is the external burden thrust upon Millennials, their digital birthright is the single most important endogenous characteristic that distinguishes them from the GI generation. This culturally inborn digital acumen gives them confidence, enhances their social connectivity, and enables a sense of self-awareness even deeper than that which bound together their Boomer parents. The digital revolution in all its manifestations has allowed us to understand our world in wholly new ways. The 2013 *Architect* magazine article about Millennials sums up well how the digital has pervaded a triad of Millennial attributes: "What is distinct about this generation's pursuit of [a] broader vision is its access to information and to one another. Fueled by technological connectivity and the belief that what they do matters, Millennials tend to trust in the agency of the individual in work as a service to the greater good."[47]

The digital underpinnings of Millennial characteristics began to show themselves in design schools about the time that most embraced the computer, an example of architecture's preseasonality that I often mention in this book. This timing may explain why the architectural community paid less attention to the arrival of the new generation. While other professions were collectively waking up to the economic and cultural shock that Millennial-driven technology began to cause in the 2000s, the architectural profession and academies had absorbed the transition with little fanfare a decade prior. For architects around the turn of the millennium, the economy was expanding, and as Stan Allen writes, the computer had become "simply a fact of life. Its logic fully absorbed into work routines and habits of thought."[48] Preseasonality—being "ahead of one's time"—can be a powerful credential, but only if recognized and acted upon accordingly. Otherwise one falls prey to being "postseasonal," or on the wrong side of history.

While it may be premature to organize an ongoing era in the manner that I have for previous eras above, identifying practices and texts and nominating a gray champion for this seemingly secular crisis seems worth any risk (and might be kind of fun). Although few practices have yet established themselves as iconically Millennial, I offer three that could match that profile. The first is MASS Design Group (2009), which strives to produce "exceptional buildings and infrastructure [that] can actually address the health, economic, and social challenges the world faces *today*," and underscores that "architecture is more than just a building."[49] Their participation in creating the National Memorial for Peace and Justice, which engages the deep social concern about racial inequality, may make it the Millennial generation's first monument.[50] Another practice is Latent Design (2010), a Chicago-based design firm "working at the intersection of architecture and community development," which provides resource- and budget-conscious solutions to participatory approaches that "directly generate project opportunities to create social, economic and environmental impact beyond the building."[51] A third is the nonprofit collective Project H Design (2008), which focuses on developing design initiatives for K–12 students and their teachers using "rigorous design iteration, tinkering, applied arts and sciences, and vocational building skills" to engage in projects that connect people and attend to real social problems.[52] Surely, others will join this list, and the chances are great that they will share one common characteristic that emphasizes Millennial team orientation: few will resort to previous generations' age-old custom of using a principal's name in the practice's masthead.

Identifying a canonical Millennial text is much harder. If environmental sustainability warrants a call to action to which architects need to respond, one might consider William McDonough's *Cradle to Cradle* (written with Michael Braungart) from 2002 as a candidate. McDonough's practice was the first "green firm," and while the book set the tone for understanding architecture according to the life cycle of materials used in its making, by 2008 some came to question McDonough's credibility as a leader in the sustainable architecture movement.[53] Another might be the Parametricist Manifesto of Patrik Schumacher, a partner at Zaha Hadid Architects. Distributed in Millennial style in various forms from YouTube to volumes of hardbound books, the manifesto argues that a digitally enabled parametricism is the great new style after modernism, with relevance at all scales from interiors to urbanism. Yet its intent is largely formalist and wrapped in the theoretical jargon of a previous era, with scant acknowledgment of sustainability.[54] A third Millennial text would be the MoMA *Rising Currents* exhibition and catalog of 2010. And while it may perhaps seem a knee-jerk response to the precedents of the *International Style* and *Deconstructivist Architecture* shows, the numerous correlations with the Millennial ethos make the catalog a worthy candidate as an epochal text. Instead of chronicling existing work like its two predecessor efforts, it asked five interdisciplinary teams to take on an expansive future scope, reckoning with the sustainability of New York Harbor and issues related to the newly recognized concern of resiliency. The show and publication touched on the Millennial characteristics of confidence to look to the future, teamwork, and curatorial leadership with a civic purpose, with the entire undertaking digitally enabled.[55] While the geographic limitations of *Rising Currents* may render it ineligible as the definitive Millennial-directed text, it bears many of the attributes of what could be one.[56]

To answer the question of who will play the role of an architectural gray champion according to the Strauss-Howe script, two elder statesman candidates come immediately to mind: Peter Eisenman and Frank Gehry. Each has significantly influenced the profession over the course of his career. That both were showcased in the epochal text of the previous era, *Deconstructivist Architecture*, strengthens their candidacy. Like Wright before him, Eisenman maintained an idealistic, protean, and cantankerous persona that influenced many around the world. Gehry, while quieter in demeanor, focused more on built work than the dense theoretical treatises that Eisenman circulated, doing more to establish a parametric architecture transformed by the digital revolution. But environmental sustainability may be the focus of the next crisis, and neither Eisenman or Gehry has ever made it a primary component of his architecture. And if one applies a strict Strauss-Howe timeline, their pre-1943 birth years makes them members of the Silent generation and not Boomers. According to Strauss and Howe, gray champions of patriarch status must have "had previously been young adults during an era of spiritual *Awakening*."[57]

Better candidates may be the protégés of Eisenman and Gehry: Rem Koolhaas and Thom Mayne, respectively. Both are Pritzker prizewinners and both seem to have qualities that Millennials may relate to. Apprenticing at the Institute for Architecture and Urban Studies while Eisenman directed it, Koolhaas used New York as a laboratory of modernism to draft *Delirious New York*, his "retroactive manifesto." In it, he argues that a culture of congestion evolved (for better or worse) into the prevalent urban design practice of the developing world. Throughout his career, his work has been highly collaborative and has consistently ventured beyond the traditional boundaries of architecture. Parallel to Koolhaas, Mayne emerged from the fertile and fresh-thinking design world of 1970s Los Angeles that Gehry fostered. And although his early work seemed formally driven, following an esoteric Eisenmanesque script, it has evolved into a technically focused architecture that is cost-conscious yet built with formal assuredness in the civic realm. Both have recently turned to environmental sustainability as driving forces in their form making: Mayne by producing large, naturally cooled civic buildings and Koolhaas by becoming involved with resilient design through the Rebuild by Design competition. Since both were born in 1944, they fall into the lead edge of the Boomer generation using Strauss and Howe's dates. And each applies a proto-Millennial approach of leaving his name out of the masthead of his practice: Koolhaas with the Office for Metropolitan Architecture (OMA) and Mayne with Morphosis.

Moving Forward

Following the synchronizations of this chapter returns us to the rhetorical question of the last: How can one reasonably apply Strauss and Howe to academic scholarship? A supplement to the hedging strategy previously recommended is to move forward provisionally, treating their theory as background, as a form of cultural common sense, in the same way one might understand our world—especially our recent past—according to, say, Shakespearean or Jungian archetypes. To borrow from Timothy Snyder, using Strauss and Howe more as instructional guidance and less as practical directive allows one to take a step back and benefit from Strauss and Howe's insight while remaining vigilant that intuition treated as formula does not result in hubris. Probably the best lesson learned in applying Strauss-Howe generational theory to the last hundred years of architectural history is in reconciling its inconsistencies: this compels one to better understand Stern's grouping in the quote that begins this chapter and to dwell less on trying to explain a single generation and more on comprehending the rich interactions between neophytes, nomadic free agents, and elders in a generational constellation. Much of the writing on Millennials places great emphasis on the behavior of that cohort while de-emphasizing the actions of their elders. The remainder of this book attempts to rebalance attention between all these groups.

Challenges, Benefits, Vulnerabilities

CHAPTER 6

Generational Alignment Strategies
Millennials, Generation X, Boomers, Silents

Every moment of time is therefore in reality more than a point-like event—it is a temporal volume having more than one dimension, because it is always experienced by several generations at various stages of development.

KARL MANNHEIM

Part Two of this book discusses how the architectural community can benefit from understanding the impact of Millennials. A comprehensive catalog of key Millennial traits, defined from various sources, will prompt an examination of whether these traits lead to an alignment with the discipline of architecture or expose its vulnerabilities. Following a longitudinal method of contextualization that is the standard of sociological writing on generations, Chapter 5 established each distinct architectural cohort in a chronological narrative. Forthcoming chapters follow a case study format to survey generational characteristics related to a specific period, with an emphasis on whether or not architecture has been in the generational vanguard. While there is much in architecture's recent history that has been anticipatory and proto-Millennial and has allowed for a special rapport with the generation, there is an equal amount in its practices that can alienate and lose the brightest and most talented to other pursuits beyond architecture, a concern examined in this book's third and last part.

This chapter's catalog of Millennial characteristics has the added benefit of serving as a foil to better understand predecessor generations. Discussing three self-reflective texts of the last two decades will unveil the generational forces at play and how these might affect Millennials. Using this information to probe the interrelationship of all the generations that are active in contemporary architecture's practice and academy will provide a better understanding of the opportunities and challenges at hand. In the coming decades, only by recognizing and respecting generational values can we strengthen the bonds between each. In the analysis of these texts, and in other chapters in this book, I sometimes cite the generational affiliation of individuals involved to underscore the dynamics at play. My intent here is not to "out" someone's undisclosed or unidentified identity but rather to remind the reader that the values being set forth by those individuals are resonant (or dissonant) with a larger societal ethos.

Let me begin with outing my own affiliation: I was born in 1961 and have always considered myself as part of Generation X. While Pew Research and other demographers would identify me as a Boomer by birth year, like Barack Obama, I have seldom considered myself a Boomer, and this distinction leads me to favor Strauss and Howe's generational birth years over others. There have been times in my life, however, when I have found myself allied with Boomer values. This may give credence to both Nicole Borges's observations that I am a "Cuspar" and Jean Twenge's conclusion that generations smear into one another rather than change abruptly. It may also be consistent with Strauss and Howe's characterization of me as a dutiful Boomer "helpmate," or that I am even postseasonal. While a definitive resolution as to my true generational affiliation may never be conclusive, this does not absolve me from rising to the responsibility all generations must take on: to respect the values of those that both precede and follow us.

In this regard, I wholly endorse a basic Strauss-Howe precept that I believe is largely self-evident: the tone of a given era is formed by its young adults, with the corollary that society is best served when older generations adapt themselves to lead according to a younger cohort's profile. To explain this more fully, let me use the White/Gray debates recounted in Part One as an example. While the conflict was emblematic of the rancor of the Boomer-influenced era, by age, all who led the debate were members of the Silent generation. These architects offered design leadership that responded to the competing Boomer-driven values of the time, not the other way around. In this same regard, a primary motive of this book is to incent older generations to respond to Millennial-driven values, as I am convinced that these will become society's values as the century progresses. The sooner the architecture profession and academy as a whole can put these values into effect, the better off they will be.

The Millennial Age

Dominant generations set an era's tone: Boomers influenced the "sixties" (which lasted well into the seventies) and GIs influenced the Depression and World War II era. By presiding over important course-changing events, dominant generations recruit intervening recessive generations to continue the momentum until events precipitated by the next dominant generation eclipse it. If Millennials first arrived in the early 1980s, and only began impacting their own signature era after electing Obama in 2008, or with the beginning of the Great Recession, their influence as the dominant generation may carry forward well into the 2030s. And if their successor "Homeland" or "Generation Z" cohort are indeed recessive and act as helpmates, a Millennial influence may push past midcentury. Whether it extends for another decade or half a century, and given the momentum of disruption already occurring, looking back from some point in the future, the Millennials' impact will more than likely be as significant as that of the Boomers and GIs. To recognize this as of this writing, and also as a provisional shorthand to refer to our current era, I will refer henceforth to the "Millennial Age." How long it may last is anyone's guess.

Provisional Recommendations

In this book's second half, the provisional recommendations for the Millennial Age emanate from the findings of the first half. Primary among these is that Millennials' distinctions have drawn the attention of many, and other disciplines have begun to organize around them as leaders and change agents, which identifies them as disruptors. While the architectural community has been late to take notice, this should not deter it from doing so now. Millennials are increasingly becoming an active voice in architecture, and in the not too distant future, they will lead it. Elder generations have the responsibility to prepare them for this mantle. Whether writers see the generation's characteristics and behaviors in a positive light or not, most recognize their distinction. No matter what name we choose to refer to them, epochal influences—both technological and social—have formed Millennials. These are a combination of their being the first digital generation, the unprecedented scope of their upbringings, and the equally unprecedented scrutiny under which they have lived their lives. These societal forces have forged a group trending toward practicality, team orientation, and outward focus in a way that is both tolerant and civic-minded. And an overarching digital imprint affects all these attributes. I try to discern—as many writers on generations have done—the differences between Millennials and their predecessors by parsing the literature of the empiricists, many of whom use the ever-increasing abundance of data to validate or dispute claims, and contrasting it with the writing by historians who, like Strauss and Howe, sense patterns in the past that are now scheduled to repeat. Part One's generational historiography of the last century's architecture, when combined with the empirical findings that are emerging with increasing regularity, presents the architectural community with a provisional framework to better understand and contend with future generational challenges.

Within offices and schools of architecture at the beginning of the Millennial Age, as many as three distinct generations join the Millennials. When communication flows freely within this grouping, knowledge passes down and societies advance. Given the generational disruptions to other disciplines and industries in the last decade that are now affecting architectural practice and education, the risk seems great for a disruption in the transfer of architectural knowledge. It remains anyone's guess whether this will be limited to a response to the "drastic changes to pedagogy, licensure, and firm management"[1] that *Architect* magazine anticipates, or perhaps becomes a more significant rupture that will further devalue architecture's agency. If one goes so far as to accept Strauss and Howe's theoretical prediction of a future "secular crisis" that will reorder every institution, this rupture may indeed be substantial. Whether minor or major, the risk of this disruption warrants a reappraisal according to the best information available—even if, like that of Strauss and Howe and Twenge, it is controversial or conflicting—to better understand the core nature of each generation involved in both transferring and receiving information. After what has been a precarious period for many thanks to the Great Recession and continuing through the Trump era of unpredictability, this reexamination seems well worth any hazard associated with it. A new and large generation is about to take the reins of the profession at the time when an equally large one lets go. Recognizing the strengths and vulnerabilities of each participant group involved in this changeover best ensures a beneficial generational relationship rather than a toxic one.

Advantages and Disadvantages

Compared to other segments of society, the architectural community enters this transitional period with some strategic advantages. In the last century, the professional and educational practices of architecture showed their vanguardism, and later consistently exhibited Millennial characteristics before they manifested in the general population. Prominent among its advantages, the architectural profession digitized over two decades ago and consequently has suffered less the shocks that later stunned business sectors such as the music and publishing worlds. This gave an older generation the time to develop digital practices to later teach Millennials. Those graduating into the profession during this period maintained proficiency in computer languages more sophisticated than those found in other disciplines, becoming digitally proficient well before others during the same years. The 1996 Boyer report reaffirmed architectural education's roots in practice-based, experiential learning and collaboration, writing that "the design studio is a model that many other disciplines on campus, as well as elementary and secondary schools, could well profit from."[2] The design studio offers the very same pedagogy that Millennials across many disciplines would indicate a strong preference for several years later.

These same early advantages, however, may have inadvertently caused other disadvantages. Its forerunner tendencies may have desensitized architecture to the larger demographic changes that other professions were being made acutely aware of in the early 2000s. As a result, while architectural education may have been attuned to some significant Millennial tendencies, it was late to adopt others. For example, few architecture schools welcomed the distance learning methods that mathematics programs pioneered, despite the presence of calculation-based technical courses in their curricula. Architecture also stood by and allowed mostly business disciplines to scoop them and apply architecture-style studio teaching to new disciplines to meet demand, thus largely ignoring the 1996 Boyer Report recommendation to expand its teaching modes to other disciplines. And because architecture schools and practices have not spent the last decade grappling with the challenge of meeting Millennials' desires—such as their goal of a balanced life and their disdain for large lecture classes in education—not only have enrollments dropped, but the most talented may be going elsewhere. It is the goal of a balanced life that may be the most delicate for architecture to handle, as it challenges the slow iterations of an age-old work ethic with the pace of the digital age.

Offices and schools can still recognize the broader demographic changes occurring and adapt accordingly. A critical first step for architecture will be to assess the effectiveness on Millennials of contemporary leadership practices in the profession and pedagogical delivery methods in schools.

From the beginning of my inquiry, I have relied on the guidance of Richard Sweeney, the university librarian at my university, the New Jersey Institute of Technology (NJIT). Since he first began noticing them in 2003, Richard has observed firsthand how Millennials work and learn in a university setting. They first caught Richard's attention when he began seeing distinctly different chair arrangements in the university library, a pattern he later correlated with emerging attitudes of collaboration and team learning. From that time, Richard has closely observed how Millennials learn and interact, all the while examining and cataloging the growing body of literature that focuses on them. His efforts led to the *Chronicle of Higher Education* featuring him in a 2005 article discussing Millennials. Richard has used his encyclopedic knowledge to lecture widely and to conduct over one hundred focus groups from Yale to Cairo to test the validity of his findings.[3] The document that Richard created to accompany these focus groups identifies fourteen Millennial behaviors. Online as a white paper since 2007, it represents a clearinghouse for other research and has been cited over one hundred times in scholarly articles. Richard and I copresented our combined findings on Millennials and architectural education at the centennial meeting of the Association of Collegiate Schools of Architecture (ACSA) in 2012 with his Millennial accounting as a baseline. That paper launched this book.

Richard and I later decided to conduct our own poll to test that paper in advance of a presentation on Millennial research at New York's Center for Architecture in early 2016. Working closely with Dr. Perry Deess, NJIT's director of institutional research, we prepared a twelve-question online poll and asked the leadership of the American Institute of Architecture Students (AIAS) to solicit responses. We also asked the American Institute of Architects New York chapter and the Architects Foundation to query architects of all generations. This request sought to reveal any differences between Millennials and older architects, although we were aware that older groups might have provided different answers if they had been asked the same questions when they were younger. We organized questions into two groups. The first measured if architects responded differently to questions previously asked by Pew Research in telephone interviews in 2010 and 2014, using a methodology as close as possible to the original. The second query focused on current students' concerns and asked those who had already graduated to recall their education. The re-creation of the Pew poll of Millennials drew responses from young architects that were within ten percentage points of similarity to the original results regarding self-identification as a generation, parenting, home ownership, a desire to be famous, and prioritizing environmental sustainability. Millennial architects diverged from the general population by ten percentage points or more in responses regarding marriage, helping others, salary goals, and desiring lots of free time. Notably, having a successful marriage, helping others in need, and being successful in a high-paying career were listed as priorities among Millennial architects at levels three times higher in percentage than among non-architect Millennials.

The education section of our questions connected enrollment declines to salary expectations and found that one in three Millennials considered their curricula to be too theoretical and their schooling to have exhibited a severe, unhealthy imbalance between work and non-work. Responses differed by less than ten percentage points between all architectural generations, suggesting that older architects felt the same or had aligned themselves with their Millennial colleagues, although without a longitudinal perspective, which reasoning remains difficult to determine. Through subsequent focus groups of Millennial students and older managers, Richard and I probed for explanations as to why responses of students or practitioners of architecture differed from the general population. In the chapters that follow, I use the poll results in the discussion. These findings remain an important local reference point to the consolidated list of Millennial behaviors and characteristics that follows.

Millennial Behaviors and Characteristics

To establish a rubric with which to understand Millennials in Part Two, I blend Richard Sweeney's white paper list of behaviors with those tabulated by others. In our 2012 paper, we also included the personality traits developed by Nicole Borges and her colleagues in surveying medical students many years apart. For this book, I have added features identified by Strauss and Howe, Pew Research, and Jean Twenge. I list each separately below, followed by a consolidation of how those categories affect architecture.

MILLENNIAL BEHAVIORS (RICHARD SWEENEY, 2006)[4]

1. selective and option focused
2. experiential and exploratory learners
3. flexible and convenience driven
4. desiring personalization and customization
5. impatient

6. practical, results-oriented
7. multitaskers
8. digital natives
9. gamers
10. nomadic in their communication style
11. media/format agnostic
12. collaborative and respecting intelligence
13. focused on a balanced life
14. less inclined to read

MILLENNIAL PERSONALITY TRAITS (NICOLE BORGES, 2006)[5]

1. warm and outgoing   (warmth)
2. more abstract than concrete   (reasoning)
3. adaptive and mature   (emotional stability)
4. dutiful   (rule consciousness)
5. socially bold and adventuresome   (social boldness)
6. sensitive and sentimental   (sensitivity)
7. self-doubting and worried   (apprehension)
8. open to change and experimenting   (openness to change)
9. organized and self-disciplined   (perfectionism)
10. less solitary and individualistic   (lacking self-reliance)

MILLENNIAL TRENDS (PEW RESEARCH, 2010, 2014)[6]

1. confident
2. connected
3. open to change
4. networked with friends
5. unmoored from institutions

CORE MILLENNIAL TRAITS (STRAUSS AND HOWE, 2007)[7]

1. special
2. sheltered
3. confident
4. team-oriented
5. conventional
6. pressured
7. achieving

GENERATIONAL DIFFERENCES BETWEEN BOOMERS AND
GENERATION X/MILLENNIALS (TWENGE, 2012)[8]

1. increase in extrinsic values (money, image, fame)
2. decrease in intrinsic values (self-acceptance, affiliation, community)
3. decline in concern for others (e.g., empathy for outgroups, charity donations, the importance of having a job worthwhile to society)
4. increase in community service*
5. decline in civic orientation (e.g., interest in social problems, political participation, trust in government, taking action to help the environment and save energy)
6. decline in taking action to help the environment

*increase cited because of high school graduation requirements

While these many attributes may seem overwhelming and contradictory, I list these here as avatars for more in-depth descriptions provided in the following chapters. For the purposes of a rubric that guides the observations and recommendations to follow, I consolidate all the attributes into three overarching categories. These fall along a range between those supporting and aligning with architectural practice and education and those exposing vulnerability. As one might expect, this range also mirrors which studies find attributes to be positive or negative and which remain inconclusive. For example, I list the Strauss-Howe qualifier "special" in both the alignments and vulnerabilities categories. The consolidation that becomes the organizational structure for Part Two is as follows:

MILLENNIAL BEHAVIORS AND ARCHITECTURE: ALIGNMENTS

- experiential and exploratory learners (Sweeney); practical, results-oriented (Sweeney)
- collaborative and respecting intelligence (Sweeney); team-oriented (Strauss and Howe); connected (Pew Research)
- warm and outgoing (Borges)
- more abstract than concrete (Borges)
- socially bold and adventuresome (Borges); adaptive and mature (Borges); confident (Strauss and Howe); open to change and experimenting (Borges); open to change (Pew Research)
- organized and self-disciplined (Borges); achieving (Strauss and Howe); special (Strauss and Howe)
- increased community service (Twenge)

MILLENNIAL BEHAVIORS AND ARCHITECTURE:
ALIGNMENTS AND/OR VULNERABILITIES?

- selective and option focused (Sweeney); flexible and convenience driven (Sweeney)
- desiring personalization and customization (Sweeney); networked with friends (Pew Research)
- multitaskers (Sweeney)
- digital natives (Sweeney); gamers (Sweeney); nomadic communication style (Sweeney)
- media/format agnostic (Sweeney)
- dutiful (Borges)
- sensitive and sentimental (Borges)
- less solitary and individualistic (Borges); conventional (Strauss and Howe)

MILLENNIAL BEHAVIORS AND ARCHITECTURE: VULNERABILITIES

- impatient (Sweeney)
- focused on balanced life (Sweeney)
- less inclined to read (Sweeney)
- self-doubting and worried (Borges); sheltered (Strauss and Howe); pressured (Strauss and Howe)
- special (Strauss and Howe)
- unmoored from institutions (Pew Research)
- increased interest in money, image, fame (Twenge); decreased self-acceptance, affiliation, community (Twenge)
- decline in empathy for others (Twenge); decline in charitable donations (Twenge)
- less desire to have a job worthwhile to society (Twenge)
- decreased interest in social problems (Twenge); decreased political participation (Twenge)
- decreased trust in government (Twenge)
- decreased action to help the environment (Twenge)

On the positive side rest the values at the core of architectural education that Millennials seem to prefer: an emphasis on practical strategies, collaboration, and outward focus. These practical values combine with other preseasonal advantages that the architectural practice and teaching have benefitted from for over two decades. Primary among these is computing.

Since 1990, architecture's digital awareness has grown from 2-D drafting with computers to complex 3-D models that predict both aesthetic and technological possibilities. In the 2000s, this momentum expanded to include robotic milling and 3-D printing and continues to explore the potential for the direct connection of architecture and powerful computing through both the Internet of Things (IoT) and artificial intelligence (AI), also referred to as machine learning. The future offers the possibility of a built environment increasingly becoming an extension of the powerful devices in everyone's pocket, a hegemony led by Millennials. At the same time, architecture schools continue the expansion of projects with a civic focus, and practices are expanding their pro bono work, both sensibilities that began in the late 1960s. This expansion allies with Millennials' own outward focus. Based on these commonalities, architecture and its academies can confidently rely on each of these strategic assets to establish a special rapport with Millennials.

At the opposite extreme lie the challenging attributes that concern many. These include Millennials' tendency toward distraction, demand (often impetuous) for professional and instructional methods that suit their needs, and their quest for a balanced life. Critics of Millennials regularly list these as negatives, associating them with a common generational lack of focus, direction, and commitment. Accompanying this is the overarching complaint by many, largely unwarranted, that Millennials are just plain spoiled. These critics urge remedial action, while others suggest more adaptive strategies. Any adaptive strategy will need to dwell on how to balance the instantaneous qualities of digital technology with traditional architectural methods rooted in the haptic experiences of drawing and model building. How practitioners and educators equipoise a digitally enabled Millennial desire for real and immediate experience with abstract thinking in a slow, iterative process of trial and error may make all the difference in keeping the best and brightest Millennials interested in architecture.

In the middle list I place the attributes that are a toss-up: ones that adaptive strategists might use to their advantage but naysayers group with those needing remediation. These, too, center on the many things digital in the Millennial portfolio, including online courses, social networks, and video games. While in their preference for experiential learning, Millennials may favor the desk-side critique, their steady if begrudging gravitation toward online learning—whether because of preference or convenience alone—foretells that some combination of adaptive or hybrid learning may soon become unavoidable, driven both by cost and preference. The professional version of the same experience may increasingly be working online within distributed networks of freelance collaborators. This may radically challenge the physical nature of the office while spawning new opportunities for integrated production. While many in the profession and academy fail to see any purpose to social media, it is evolving into a new form of connectivity that will bind together various networks of collaborators. And while many in architecture might also consider digital games the ultimate distraction, other disciplines have been developing a pedagogy based on gaming for almost two decades. The possibility of using the building aspects of games such as *The Sims* and *Minecraft* is an option architecture has only begun to explore.

Generational Interaction in Contemporary Architecture

While maintaining an objective rubric of Millennial behaviors, characteristics, and values is an essential part of this inquiry, equally important is examining all the generations involved in the current environment. Struggles between the old and young have marked transitional periods in architectural practice and education before, and the Millennial Age will likely be no exception. Conflicts flared in the 1930s, when modern functionalism supplanted the Beaux-Arts, and in the late 1960s, when grassroots, value-driven approaches displaced a top-down technocratic regime. Interpreting these transitions according to the generational profiles outlined in Part One provides an alternative understanding of the state of architecture leading up to the beginning of the Millennial Age. Examining from a generational perspective three assessments of the state of architecture, one initiated jointly by the profession and academy, another from within the academy, and a third from a European professional magazine with global readership, uncovers both alignment and tension.

The last comprehensive and formal assessment of the state of architectural practice and its academies began in the mid-1980s, when a consortium from the architectural academy and profession approached Dr. Ernest Boyer, then president of the Carnegie Foundation for the Advancement of Teaching, to begin an independent examination of its discipline.[9] This initiative came at a time when America found itself fraught with anxiety. In 1983, a national commission had released "A Nation at Risk: The Imperative for Educational Reform," which focused on problems with youth and K–12 education, and which was followed by the dire reporting (and surprising best-selling success) of Allan Bloom's *The Closing of the American Mind*, a 1987 critique of American higher education. By the late 1980s, a steep recession began to counter the economic expansion of the Reagan years and bring on a national mood of wariness. When the Carnegie Foundation eventually published its findings in a 1996 report entitled *Building Community: A New Future for Architecture Education and Practice*, it chose an optimistic if guarded tone, privileging the possibilities of architecture over its problems. The constructive tone is in part due to the outlook of Boyer, whom his writing partner, Lee Mitgang, describes as a positive peacemaker who alone could have encouraged "the often fractious worlds of architecture education and practice to join forces to make the study possible."[10] But it is Boyer's astuteness in recognizing the emerging influence of computers, as well as the dormant but reemerging values of practical service and public focus in architecture, that forms the optimistic, forward-thinking core of the fittingly named *Building Community* report.

Eventually referred to by all as the Boyer report, the examination makes clear, however, that as the team observed on their many visits to schools, all was not well with architecture: "Repeatedly in our travels, we witnessed the estrangement of the academy and the profession, the isolation and stress of student life, the disconnection of architecture from other disciplines, and the inflexibility of the curriculum on many campuses." They cite a reputation on campuses of the architectural field as "splintered and disputatious," and describe sometimes encountering an autocratic, one-way communication in studio juries. They also encountered studios that were "more about personalities than principles, a place where the ideology of the instructor became the true curriculum."[11]

The Boyer report's concerns echo those of Bloom and the Nation at Risk commission from a decade earlier. Seen through a generational schema, the Boyer study began just as the tone set by a Boomer-driven era was transitioning to one of Generation X dominance. To project a positive future at this time of uncertainty, the Boyer report offers seven separate but interlocking priorities to renew architectural education and practice that address the needs of each generation. Beginning in a positive spirit, they recommend continuing the value-driven initiatives promoted by Boomers, among them maintaining architecture's focus on aesthetics, historic preservation, and urbanism, and they recommend the field's expansion toward considering the social values of health and happiness. They also reaffirm the Boomer imperatives to increase gender and racial diversity. In critique, the report echoes the concerns of other educational writers of the time, recommending the reinstatement of some form of standards. Perhaps to appease a Boomer aversion to top-down ordering, the study qualifies these somewhat paradoxically as "standards without standardization."[12]

The report seemed to second the sentiment of the time that the open-ended debate on values characteristic of the Boomer awakening era had crossed into the territory of being "splintered and disputatious." This rancor needed to be reined in to return to some form of common principle. Leading that recommendation were faculty leaders of the older Silent generation, who had come of age amidst a high degree of standardization and conformity. Indeed, the license the architectural community gave to the nonarchitect Ernest Boyer to critique its own practices may have been due as much to his esteemed resume as to his being a member of the conciliatory and practical-minded Silent generation. Endorsing this priority were many Boomers entering middle age who were then in faculty leadership positions. This endorsement came from a generation who had once patently rejected standardization but now saw a need for its restoration. Those who once declaimed "don't trust anyone over thirty" had become those over thirty. Yet neither Boomers nor Silents seemed to then trust that the emerging Generation X (those *under* thirty), whom writers and policy makers had recently labeled "wild," could handle the idealistic soul-searching associated with Boomers since the upheavals begun in the late 1960s. To recommend an optimistic return to somewhat pragmatic norms, the Boyer Report suggests doing so within a supportive environment, one both connected and unified. They conclude with a final priority: a call to prepare future architects for lives of civic engagement and service to the nation.[13] This last priority seems a throwback to the orderliness of the Silent generation and anathema to the Boomer credo that had expressed open scorn for the government and the nation. Yet a return to pragmatic norms, connectivity, and unity instead of fracture and dispute, all within a supportive environment, are priorities that would later become hallmarks of the Millennial generation. One can consider the prescient recommendations by the Boyer Report in the 1990s as another indicator of architecture's tendencies toward anticipating the values of coming generations. And as maligned as they might have seemed, it was the embrace by younger Generation X faculty of the computer—combined with their renewed interest in action over speculation through enterprises such as the design-build initiatives that the Boyer report acknowledges and applauds—that began the transition.

The most recent encapsulation of the state of the architectural academy is the 2012 compendium *Architecture School: Three Centuries of Educating Architects in North America*. This history, curated by the Association of Collegiate Schools of Architecture (ACSA), commemorates the centennial of ACSA's founding a hundred years prior. While written primarily by and for educators, the history also brings practice into its orbit. The project's editor, Joan Ockman, organizes it according to a bipartite structure: a grouping of six chapters into a chronological overview going back to before the American Revolution, followed by another twenty-nine chapters. The latter chapters, a "thematic lexicon," chronicle the many aspects of architecture education from its emergence into the early twenty-first century. The overall editorial approach is one of balance, with differing contributing authors asked not to over-privilege any school. And to avoid any suggestion of hierarchy, the editors organized the lexicon alphabetically. Notably present among its topics are the issues championed by the many Boomer writers involved: community engagement, ethics, gender issues, race and diversity, and sustainability. Ockman apologizes for any omissions in this lexicon, making special mention of the absence of any comparison between architectural education and other forms of professional and graduate education, which "regrettably did not make it into the book,"[14] as if to suggest that while many might find this topic pertinent, it remains too controversial for consideration at the time. I introduce this issue in Chapter 11 as a response to the call made by *Architect* for "drastic changes to pedagogy, licensure and firm management" in response to Millennials.

Ockman organizes part one into six sequential chapters of a "periodizing framework," which trace the development of architectural training from its earliest beginnings in the eighteenth century. This serial trajectory intends to offer enough momentum for the contemporary reader to rethink "[architecture's] assumptions and inevitability in the future."[15] The last four of these periodizing chapters are the ones I synchronize with generationally influenced eras in my previous chapter. In these, Ockman avoids setting hard dates to delimit a period, instead allowing writers to identify the significant events of each to describe both their emergence and overlap into years associated with another period. Ockman's editorial structure seems to align with Wilhelm Pinder's concept of generational entelechy, that the social and emotional center of gravity marks a particular age, not its boundaries.[16] Her first chapter, simply titled "Before 1860," alludes to the temporal entelechy of the looming Civil War crisis then about to reach crescendo. This period includes the practical flurries of formative activity, such as the chartering of the American Institute of Architects and its subsequent initiative to formalize architectural education following an objective German polytechnic model. Chapter 2 continues by describing the reform era's generational upheaval surrounding the polytechnic's eclipse by a French-led Beaux-Arts curriculum focused on aesthetics and the subsequent need to form the ACSA. Reading Ockman's "periodizing framework" of chapters, beginning with this shift in the nineteenth century, one thinks of a pendulum swinging several times, following an almost left-brain to right-brain polarity between objectivity and aestheticism as one generation's values supplant another.

Architecture School seems to sense that at the time of its publication, the pendulum had reached an apex and it anticipates another descent. By providing a basis for rethinking architectural education's future "assumptions and inevitability," Ockman emphasizes in her introduction that Architecture School is not a rearguard canonical history meant to control, promote, or oppose change, but is instead a forward-thinking enterprise seeking to "open up as many avenues as possible for future inquiry."[17] In the final history chapter, fittingly entitled "The Future That is Now," Stan Allen writes of a twenty-year interval of self-described generational change and ends with a guarded future prognosis. In several instances, Allen alludes to the birth years of those he writes about, or when they were educated, to underscore that they are all of a distinct cohort. He goes so far as to list in footnotes the individuals, like himself (most are members of Generation X), in leadership positions at schools, also noting their genders and global diversity. Allen proceeds to write of the many debates of this era: between analog and digital, theory and practice, and the role of collaborative initiatives in the global city.[18] He ends the chronology on a cautious note consistent with the end of an unravelling era and the skepticism of a Generation X mindset, describing how the debates of the generational period he covers "brought to light a deeper anxiety about the changing role of the architect in society."[19] Paraphrasing Rem Koolhaas, he finds the role of architects in a state of disruptive flux, no longer effective in many areas traditionally seen as their domain although potentially powerful in others unanticipated. Complicating a search for "new arenas and capacities," Allen describes a climate of increasing pluralism consistent with Generation X, exacerbated by the "leveling effect of new technologies and the tension between the global and local."[20] To address these anxieties in a constructive sense, he ends the chapter by invoking the political philosopher Kwame Anthony Appiah, who advocates establishing a form of transitional cosmopolitanism that, as Allen describes, pays "close attention to the necessary hybridity of a contemporary culture that works with elements of history and tradition at the same time as it takes advantage of new technologies and the opportunities of global exchange."[21] Appiah's words convey both the uncertainty and possibility affecting the period of time the chronology of *Architecture School* closes with, as if sensing the rough waters of some form of upheaval ahead might also bring opportunity.

A third appraisal through which one can discern generational layers is the Big Rethink campaign launched by *The Architectural Review* in 2011. The campaign focuses the *Review*'s readership—both European and North American—on challenges posed to architectural practice and education by ongoing global economic and environmental crises. At the campaign's core, *The Architectural Review* asked the architect and critic Peter Buchanan to write a series of monthly essays for the yearlong project. Central to Buchanan's writing is that we are facing a "looming crisis" that seems to resonate with Strauss and Howe's portent. Buchanan opens by stating, "we are in the throes of comprehensive systemic collapse. Along with other potent forces for change, this suggests these are times of major transition—times in which to rethink almost everything, including architecture and the design of the larger environment."[22] Without mentioning generations by name, Buchanan acknowledges "the association of particular epochs and their mindsets with particular cultural values and even personality characteristics."[23] Like Boyer, Buchanan (b. 1942) is a member of the Silent generation, yet he seems to lack Boyer's "positive peacemaker" temperament and instead unleashes a series of attacks against contemporary architectural practice and teaching more in line with Boomer combativeness. Buchanan writes based on a lifelong career in Britain and its commonwealth countries, set amidst a pattern of generational change parallel to what was happening in America: he came of age in the systematized curricula of a postwar standardization, saw firsthand the revolution that groups like Archigram began during the 1960s awakenings, and then presided over the decline of that momentum throughout the unraveling era that followed.

Buchanan aims his critique at academia in part nine of the campaign with his essay "Rethinking Architectural Education." Published in late 2012 with the subtitle "Detached from the ferment of epochal change, the groves of academe are failing to engage with current critical realities," the essay begins with the observation that:

to visit many architectural schools is to enter a time warp where the "any-thing goes" postmodern relativism of the 1980s persists, and tutors and lecturers pursue their own interests regardless of any larger relevance. Indeed, it almost seems that the more overwhelmingly urgent the looming crises provoked by systemic collapse of interdependent aspects of our global civilisation, the more frivolous the pursuits of academe.[24]

As one can glean from the reference to "tutors and lecturers," Buchanan is referring to British schools, yet similar versions of his critique have been voiced globally.[25] Buchanan himself complains that little has changed since he began writing about the relative ineffectiveness of architectural education in 1989,[26] contemporary to when the Boyer initiative also noticed studios where personal ideologies prevailed over principles.

Buchanan's rant singles out many entrenched Boomer characteristics, identifying the root cause of the current crisis as the postmodernist relativism he finds so dominant in architectural practice and education, a discourse with an inability to prioritize that considers all forms of reality as equivalent arbitrary constructs. For Buchanan, lingering postmodernism has become a major block in dealing with urgent issues of epochal change; he describes it as "like a vaccine inoculating against the many new currents of thought." In the architectural profession, Buchanan lays blame on the world-traveling "starchitects" and their overemphasis on capriciously chosen concepts removed from larger realities. Their professional example filters down to the academy's design studios, where students succumb to pressure to produce a concept early in the design process rather than allowing it to emerge from research or design development. Following this pedagogy, one concept is as good as another; the only defining distinction, Buchanan finds, is a demand for "startling originality, no matter how spurious." Supporting this practice is the disproportionate influence of architectural theory courses, which Buchanan complains "tend to be more concerned with such things as literary theory and French philosophy than anything to do with architecture and mistake obfuscation for profundity, dressing up the most banal of observations in obscure language."[27] Seemingly oblivious to the epochal change occurring all around, this malady of relativism and its purposeless intellectual pursuits is, says Buchanan, "exactly analogous to scholasticism at the end of the Middle Ages, which in its obsession with arguing over the number of angels on the head of a pin did not notice the Renaissance burgeoning all around."[28]

Despite his many tirades against Boomer-embraced postmodernism, Buchanan recognizes its original necessity, conceding that its initial multiple viewpoints were an essential strategy in breaking "the grip of modernity's too narrow certainties." Among the benefits Buchanan recognizes are the attention paid to the previously repressed voices of women and minorities and the rejection of modern architecture's contextual insensitivity. He even admits the initial usefulness of postmodern theory "in broadening discourse and drawing attention to the semiotic dimensions of architecture."[29] Despite these caveats, Buchanan concludes that the postmodernist initiative served its purpose, but now two full generations later has grown malignant and in need of reform: "Like modernity, postmodernity has hung on too long and the benefits it brought are now outweighed by its toxic downsides."[30]

If architecture is to address the epochal changes that Buchanan identifies, Boomer postmodernity having "hung on too long" remains a great challenge in creating a working relationship of generations, and establishing a harmonious relationship among generations will be useful albeit painful. Like the Silent and Lost recessive generations before them, Generation X will be challenged to turn against the Boomer tendencies that they themselves abetted, often in the dominating presence of an elder generation who may be blind to anything being amiss. In this respect, Generation X serves as the helpmate cohort, whose conflicted archetypal role is to continue the momentum of a dominant generation, but then change allegiances and embrace the countervailing initiative associated with the succeeding generation—in this case, the Millennials. This archetypal situation makes clear why some writers call the nomad-type a "hinge" generation. Strauss and Howe predict that a majority of Boomers will resist change, arguing that Generation X will perceive them as "pompous, authoritarian and (in power) more than a little dangerous" (parentheses theirs).[31] But if Boomers understand the larger schema, as Strauss and Howe write, they "can best serve civilization by restraining themselves (or by letting themselves be restrained by others) until their twilight years, when their spiritual energy would find expression not in midlife leadership, but in elder stewardship" (parentheses theirs).[32] For a successful generational transition to occur, select members of Generation X will also need to rise above the stereotype of being a "wild, soulless, and 'bad' generation"[33] (epithets perpetuated by Boomers) to help pass the baton.

The Generational Constellation

Together, Boomer and Generation X members make up a majority of architectural professionals and academics as of 2018, with smaller groups of
elder Silents and rising Millennials on the margins. A successful transfer
of knowledge will rely on collegiality and a cooperative relationship within
this contemporary generational constellation. This may be a challenge,
especially for the largest two groups. In the general population, the relationship between Boomers and Generation X has seldom been warm. Boomers
continue to malign Generation X and their nihilistic tendencies as another
lost generation, a rebuke that began just as the oldest were maturing thanks
to the publishing of Allan Bloom's *The Closing of the American Mind* and the
Nation at Risk initiative. In reaction, Generation X writers like Jeff Gordinier
still stereotype Boomers as a group lost in a cycle of solipsistic introspec-
tion and quarrelling, seemingly incapable of producing tangible outcomes[34]
and opting to take the easier option of "talkitecture." According to Strauss
and Howe's broad historical portrait, this finger-pointing is entirely familiar.
The following passage, parts of which are excerpted above, is worth quoting at length in order to compare it with the observations on contemporary
practice by William Saunders later in this chapter.

> Throughout American History, the nastiest one-apart generational feuds
> have been between midlife Idealists and rising Reactives. This has hap-
> pened every time—between Puritans and Cavaliers; Awakeners and Lib-
> erty; Transcendentals and Gilded; Missionaries and Lost. Idealists invari-
> ably come to look upon younger Reactives as a wild, soulless, and "bad"
> generation—while Reactives see older Idealists as pompous, authoritarian
> and (in power) more than a little dangerous. . . . The last skirmish between
> these two oil-and-water types arose just before World War I, grew mean
> after the Armistice, and contributed mightily to the "roar" of the 1920s.[35]

Here the dominant generation, Boomers, are the *idealists*, a group who set
in motion a cultural revolution focused on reshaping inner values. Following
them, Generation X (the recessive nomad-types) are the *reactives*, who have
continued this revolution toward a projected crisis. As chaos ensues, blame
for the discord flows in both directions. This tension between Boomers and
Generation X remains as discernable in 2018 as when Bloom and Gordinier
described it. It is also present in architecture schools and practice if one
looks carefully enough.

In architecture, the front line of this generational conflict is a digital one. The profession and academy transitioned to digital practices just as Generation X was entering or starting firms and joining the professoriate. Through the 1990s, the first wave of this generation pushed the parallel rules that Boomers learned off the drawing tables to make way for computers. As the decade progressed, X-Acto blades and straight edges increasingly became secondary to laser cutters for model making, with computer-controlled (CNC) milling machines and 3-D printers proliferating soon after. Generation X has exploited the computer to employ formal and scalar possibilities that were previously unimaginable. With firms like SHoP in the vanguard, Generation X's digitally empowered "get it done" attitude has sidestepped the traditional separation between design and production to form new types of design-build, trending toward mass customization. While Boomers have largely acquiesced to the digital revolution, their previous all-or-nothing debate between modernism and historicism, drowned out amidst the many formal choices available in an era of ever-expanding Generation X pluralism, still has its holdouts who keep the rancor fresh. The Boomer historian Witold Rybczynski contends that cutting-edge architects are "enemies of humanism [promoting] chaos and inhuman order."[36] Other Boomers still find trendiness and vacuity in this pluralism, which they see in sharp contrast to a Boomer-led deep inquiry into the *why* of architecture. Generation X's collective response seems to be: *why not?*

While some Boomers pioneered digital design, beginning with punch cards in the 1970s, and other older faculty understand its principles, a Boomer emphasis on process and an individualized "poetic" vision organized around foundational values or concepts still prevails. For many, whether these values or concepts bear relevance is less important than that they simply exist. Several often-used terms harken back to generations-old conflicts initiated by Boomers: one still hears the term "intervention" used to refer to an architectural project, as if conflict is a precursor to design and the role of architecture is to somehow mediate between belligerents. In this way, the quarrel between the "Whites" and "Grays" still goes on, although the values initially fought over have changed or have simply been forgotten. Critics still exhort designers to practice an "architecture of resistance," as originally expressed by Silent generation historian Kenneth Frampton and cataloged by him and other writers (including Joan Ockman) in the generationally consistent journal topically named *Oppositions*. This journal, which began publishing in 1973, sought to advance architectural theory through countering both the forces of mass-media culture and free-market capital-ism. The object of this resistance has blurred over the years, yet for many, especially Boomers, the call for opposition remains strong.

In response, a group of architects closely matching Generation X char-acteristics picked their own nasty "one-apart generational feud" with the midlife idealist Boomers. Chronicling this friction in the introduction to his edited volume, *The New Architectural Pragmatism*, William Saunders writes that by the mid-1990s:

> many highly intelligent young architects and architectural intellectuals were getting fed up with [their elders'] detachment, theoretical abstrac-tion, and helplessness. They wanted to (and could with an improved economy) get to work on real projects, real conditions, real places; they wanted to be ambitious without being dreamy, to improve bits of the world without self-aggrandizing delusions. . . . Their intellectual elders struck them as overly serious, overly self-important, overly righteous, and "pure."[37]

The provocateur of this self-described "cabal," Robert Somol (Saunders refers to him as "the consummate Bad Boy") began to take on the righteous piety of his elders. These older academics had progressively formed a self-defining monastic seclusion. Attired in all black and insulating themselves behind jargon-filled language, these high priests and priestesses of archi-tectural scholasticism willingly suffered the *difficult* contemplation of what architecture should be, believing that anyone taking themselves seriously must do the same. Somol and his cohort wanted none of this, writing: "Archi-tecture doesn't have to hurt."[38] The feud escalated as Sanford Kwinter, tak-ing the position of the old-guard nomenklatura, warned against "arguments for the easy,"[39] furthering a case he had made earlier: "Without constant contact with the culture and ethos of *difficulty* we are hard pressed to make ourselves better than dilettantes" (italics mine).[40] As part of this dispute, So-mol chose the occasion of the closing of the journal *Assemblage*[41] to dispel fake and righteous seriousness with a blast of candor: "I never subscribed to Assemblage . . . out of the 240-odd items published, I read about 12 all the way through. No shit. *Five percent*. Three of those were mine . . . the simple fact—one that we should celebrate rather than hide—is that *criticism isn't necessary*" (italics mine). It is notable that that public battle took place in the early 2000s just as a new guard of mostly Generation X academics were taking on leadership positions in North American schools, with the first Millennials in attendance.[42] Also notable is how their self-description as a "criminal pack" aligns with the generalized profile of their generation: "We hang out, play cards, drink until closing, escape conferences, plot futures, compete with laughter, and fight with conviction." With the stridency of Generation X's free agency, they formed a generational cohort, a "criminal pack [that] calls for action more than observation, privileges speculation over erudition and aims wildly at getting something going."[43]

With heads hot on both sides, it may seem difficult to resurrect what actually still binds the two generations together, or to imagine that Generation X were once "helpmates" to Boomers. Yet common ground prevails, perhaps less stridently in the rhetoric of high academe than in the core philosophy of individual architects. The first example is Generation X's continued mission of sustainability, which was begun by Boomers. In celebrating the first Earth Day in 1970, Boomers laid out the ethical and moral argument for environmental awareness as an affront to then-prevalent government and corporate irresponsibility. Generation X has joined this cause by applying digital imaging and modeling to produce evidence-based designs aimed at sustainable solutions. A second commonality is a focus on community design. Organized around grassroots operations begun in the 1960s, community design—and especially those practices focused on design-build for disadvantaged communities—has continued to blossom. Generation X turned the antiestablishment fervor of Boomers into a build-it-yourself free agency, one that mobilizes student work details to empower communities directly, often skirting entrenched agency and construction industry hierarchies. A third commonality is a continued commitment to an overarching work ethic associated with designing. While Generation X digital production capabilities far exceed what many sleepless nights of Boomer drafting could produce, the manic charrette culture in studios both academic and professional seems to have not abated. Instead, it has intensified to the point of exploitation by project managers and studio critics alike.[44]

These commonalities can provide the necessary points of agreement between Boomers and Generation X practitioners and faculty if both camps put other differences aside. More importantly, two of the three—sustainability and the civic purpose of community-focused design—are values that Millennials also share, making them the common threads that can unite a harmonious generational grouping. It is concern over work ethic that has emerged as a distinct point of difference between Millennials and their more senior generational cohorts. In a proclamation that announced their arrival on the scene in 2002, the AIAS Studio Culture Task Force declared emphatically, in manifesto-like fashion, that "STUDENTS SHOULD LEAD BALANCED LIVES" (all caps theirs). In doing so, they nailed to the door of the academy a long list of studio work ethic myths perpetuated by Boomers and their Generation X accomplices that Millennial students would no longer abide. (I dwell on this document's discontent in Chapter 9 and its less shrill recommendations in Chapter 7.)[45]

If Boomers and Generation X are allied through a common work ethic, among other accords, the digital foundation that Generation X and Millennials share offers a similar thread of unity, although they will need to deal with challenges. One is by the Boomer historian Harry Francis Mallgrave, who contends that embracing the digital and departing from the haptic skills of drawing and physical modeling may ultimately atrophy the part of the brain associated with design creativity.[46] By contrast, the Generation X architect Greg Lynn, arguing at a 2012 Yale conference that rhetorically asked the question "Is Drawing Dead?" advocates to his analog holdouts: "The rest of you proudly hold up your pens and pencils, but I would hold up my mouse."[47] Despite their digital nativism, Millennials seem to still straddle this divide. A 2006 survey of second-year design students showed a strong preference for hand drawing over computer rendering, claiming that "hand drawings are more successful in reflecting authorship, one's ability, and warmth in terms of artistic expression."[48] The Millennial Age will likely be marked by a careful renegotiation between the digital and analog before a digitally dominant practice takes over, if it ever fully does.

While some schools have already adopted a working balance between analog and digital design tools and at others it is a lively debate, for many schools the disagreement is toxic. And while the Great Recession eliminated virtually all nondigital firms, many practitioners recognize the need for analog education in order to become a designer. At the same 2012 Yale conference, the Generation X architect Marion Weiss offered a hybridized counterpoint to Greg Lynn, describing a "loose toggling" between media, a "strange conflation" of charcoal sketching, thinking in section, and parametric modeling in her own work.[49] To achieve harmonious generational fellowship, Generation X and Millennial faculty will need to reconcile with Boomer digital holdouts over this and other points. How seriously schools move to establish a working harmony depends on their view of the future and the role generations play. If a school views the downturn in enrollment as cyclical, with numbers eventually rising, they may see little risk in wait-ing for the discord to resolve, and if Boomers are indeed the cause, they will one day retire. Given the pace at which academia changes, this may be the likely default option at most schools. But for those schools looking for a competitive advantage in the face of a possible dramatic disruption, anticipating the hybridized digital leanings of a rising generation seems to be an educated wager with very little to lose.

The remaining chapters of Part Two include a further study of the compi-lation of Millennial behaviors and characteristics according to whether they support architecture, challenge it, or fall in between. I close each of these chapters by delving into the background of a subject as a "generational case study" that pinpoints transitional periods to develop an oscillation according to generational rhythms. These subjects include experiential learning and design thinking (Chapter 7), student-centered academic models (Chapter 8), and the parallel development of architecture and design tradi-tions (Chapter 9). Comprehending the cyclical sine curve of the long tail of each helps clarify Ockman's "assumptions and inevitabilities" beyond the present. Examining three contemporary texts to uncover the generational layers in each, and applying that assessment to contemporary practice and academia, will reveal in the next chapters both what binds and separates generations. How a generation's values express themselves in the future will be borne out by the contemporary interplay between older and younger cohorts as architecture seeks to advance its agency in the Millennial Age.

CHAPTER 7

Collaboration
Millennial Values and the Work of Architecture

Design is what keeps architecture from slipping into a cloud of heterogeneity.

ROBERT SOMOL AND SARAH WHITING

As they came of age at the beginning of the twenty-first century, Millennials found many of their values aligning with the study and practice of architecture. The generation's youthful, team-centered experiences prepared them for architecture's increasing collaboration and interdisciplinarity, their practical nature embraced a pendulum swing in architecture from the theoretical toward the pragmatic, and their civic focus aligned with a profession and academy yearning to increase their agency in the public realm. That these generational alignments preceded those of other disciplines and professions, such as music and journalism, spared architecture some of the disruptive shock that rocked these and other sectors in the 2000s. If recognized and acted on, architecture's proto-Millennial qualities position it to benefit rather than suffer from the waves of disruptive generational change that will likely continue through the first half of the twenty-first century. Both locally and globally, Millennials are projected to be disruptors who bring about dramatic urban change, with a growing number of them as architectural professionals. In 2002, the first wave of Millennial students produced a document on studio culture, declaring their specific values regarding the design studio, the primary vehicle for architectural education for past generations.[1] The document underscores their preference for experiential learning, a teaching philosophy with an equally long legacy. Design thinking, as taught at institutions such as Stanford's d.school, offers one example of a possible alignment between Millennial values and architectural education and a tantalizing preview of experiential learning migrating into professional practice. The emergence of design thinking—a pedagogical model Millennials naturally gravitate toward and one architectural schools have a long history of offering—provides a rich opportunity to fully embrace design in the way that Robert Somol and Sarah Whiting suggest in the quote that opens this chapter.

Research has identified the positive Millennial characteristics associated with teamwork, practicality, and outward focus. All of the analyses used in this book—by Pew Research, William Strauss and Neil Howe, Nicole Borges, and Richard Sweeney—find Millennials to be confident. Borges's study adds the character traits of warmth, outgoingness, organization, self-discipline, and maturity. While data also finds Millennials to be practical and results-oriented, this does not preclude them from being exploratory (Sweeney), experimental, socially bold, adventuresome (Borges), and, as almost all agree, open to change. A collaborative and team-oriented personality rounds out this profile. That Millennials respect both intelligence (Sweeney) and leadership (Pew)—and are often motivated by public purpose—further binds the generation. Jean Twenge contests almost all of these virtues, especially compared to other generations, yet she concedes a Millennial attachment to community service, although questioning the motive.

Urbanization

Many sources indicate that these Millennial characteristics will play out against a backdrop of growing urbanization, which will account for the greatest changes to the physical environment in the Millennial Age. The Millennial population is driving urban growth, and its architects will be called upon to innovate for the coming disruption, propelling digital networks to create "smart cities." According to a 2014 survey by Nielsen, 62 percent of Millennials prefer urban communities over suburban or rural ones. With a particular preference for mixed-use neighborhoods adjacent to transit, amenities, and places of employment, Millennials in 2014 were living in urban areas at a higher rate than any other generation. This has caused growth in US cities to outpace other locales for the first time since the 1920s.[2] The Millennial migration to cities builds upon the shift toward urban living that began when young-adult Boomers recast themselves as yuppies (young urban professionals) in the late 1970s. If economic expansion continues through the late 2010s, the number of Millennials still living at home (42 percent of whom were male and 32 percent female per a 2014 poll) will likely join the rest of their cohort in cities if their incomes increase and Nielsen's preference data holds. The Millennials' desire to live in cities parallels the zeal with which the GI generation migrated to suburbia, a trend that presented itself before World War II and that the federal government facilitated afterward, in part to prevent a war-energized economy from falling into recession. Whether the federal government acts in a similar way to facilitate Millennial desires will modulate the rapidity of twenty-first century urban growth.

While the yuppie urbanizing momentum in the US in the late twentieth century occurred predominately in what the Urban Land Institute calls "24-hour cities" (New York, San Francisco, Los Angeles, Washington, DC, etc.), they suggest that Millennial Age urban expansion will extend to the midsize "18-hour cities," such as Houston, Nashville, Charlotte, and Austin. These cities are more affordable, host high-paying jobs, and offer the quality-of-life amenities that Millennials indicate they expect.[3] As of 2015 (with the exception of Washington, DC), southern and western cities held the largest concentrations of Millennials, while Boomers remained highly clustered at almost twice the numbers in east-coast cities.[4]

Austin has emerged as first among the 18-hour cities, holding the highest concentration of Millennials. Despite the Great Recession, the city has shown high employment growth by leveraging its adjacency to the flagship campus of the University of Texas, which has remained flush through the recession with oil revenues from technological advances in drilling.[5] Austin combines urban convenience with amenities that include a progressive art and music scene showcased annually through its South by Southwest festival (SxSW). In a second evolution, SxSW has added a technological aspect, making it a debut location for innovative technology. As Austin's Millennials cluster near its walkable core, the progressive city stands in stark physical and demographic contrast to the suburban neighborhoods and conservative politics of other parts of Texas.

Millennial-induced disruptions have already affected the physical fabric of twenty-first-century American cities. As the economy improves, developers find that prerecession real estate formulas no longer apply, with market-rate versus affordable-unit ratios in flux and the balance between residential and commercial square footages varying as a sizeable amount of retail leaves the storefront for the internet. A notable change is Millennials overwhelmingly opting to rent rather than buy property. A number of factors drive this trend: insufficient income, the deferment of starting families, and an overriding desire to remain flexible. For Millennials, home ownership may not be the blue-chip investment it once was, as many remain "spooked by what happened to [their] home-owning parents."[6] To adapt, both private developers and municipal boosters find themselves constantly inventing new amenities to keep Millennials from moving to different apartments or decamping entirely for another city.

Choice in transportation represents another urban trend as Millennials lead a surge in transit ridership. In 2014, this hit a fifty-year US high. In traditional cities, Millennials report riding transit at least once a week, three times the rate of older generations (43 percent of Millennials versus 12 percent of those 30–60).[7] As a corollary to choosing transit, Millennials drive less; the measurement of the cohort's vehicle miles traveled (VMT) shows a 21 percent decrease over Generation X's at the same age fifteen years prior.[8] Over the same period, the percentage of high school seniors with driver's licenses declined from 85 to 73 percent.[9] This decrease in driving renders existing surface parking—especially in cities without a strong tradition of public transportation—as prime locations for new development. This disruption drives Millennial Age cities to be denser and better connected through transit, places where both public and private sectors furiously innovate new amenities to remain competitive.

A parallel disruption has occurred in the Millennial Age workplace, where new technology startups set the pace for postrecession growth, often locating their offices in transit-served areas of high density near where employees live.[10] The previous era's pattern of edge city development, with automobile-based office parks locating at the intersections of arterial highways, often near the suburban homes of upper management, peaked in the late 1990s, with vacancy rates increasingly outpacing those in urban areas through the 2000s.[11] Instead, twenty-first-century businesses locate in mixed-use downtowns of all scales, where the digital underpinnings of the new office allow for higher concentrations of employees using less square footage; from a high in the 2000s, postrecession office space per worker declined by some 25 percent.[12] Despite the decrease in gross area, these high-concentration offices still provide a wide variety of spaces and amenities, each designed for interactivity, efficiency, productivity, and creativity.[13] Within urban clusters, different businesses share customers, employees, infrastructure, suppliers, and knowledge within so-called innovation districts. Often adjacent to universities and featuring flexible co-working spaces, these areas support a roving network of freelance employees with many telecommuting. This peripateticism leaves some businesses of the Millennial Age city entirely nomadic, with no fixed address at all.

Market researchers have become acutely aware of Millennials' increasing economic impact and speculate that expenditures may increase from approximately $600 billion annually in 2015 to $1.4 trillion by 2020, which is almost one tenth of the US GDP.[14] A number of factors will determine in what markets these amounts will be spent and whether these figures will hold. Coming of age in a turbulent economy has added thriftiness and risk aversion to the list of Millennial characteristics. As of 2014, Millennials held more than half of their assets in cash (52 percent) and less than one-third of their assets in equities (28 percent), directly counter to the traditional long-term investment strategies of older generations.[15] Considerable student loan debt is a major contributor to their economic conservatism: by 2018, nationwide student loan debt hit $1.5 trillion, doubling what it was just ten years prior.[16] Nonetheless, as the economic community seeks to unleash Millennials' disposable income to boost the reviving economy, businesses are very much aware of Millennials' potential growth and its urban trajectory, as Standard & Poor's Ratings Services economist, Beth Ann Bovino, writes:

> However you look at it, [Millennials'] influence over the US—including our economy, politics, social norms, and how and where we live and do business–is growing, and fast. This can be a difficult prospect for prior generations, given the unflattering (and, the evidence suggests, untrue) stereotypes that often dog Millennials. Still, Millennials' propensity to marry and have children late, to rent instead of buy homes, and to live in cities without cars and other big-ticket trappings of suburban life, all has the potential to disrupt the consumption-based U.S. economy at a time when its recovery has been relatively lackluster.[17]

The release of Millennial-held dollars hinges on whether the US federal government will choose to stimulate the economy and unleash spending or continue its historic pattern of disinvestment in infrastructure. Throughout the 2010s, the American Society of Civil Engineers graded the country's infrastructure each year as dismal (as of this writing (2017), the ASCE's grade was a D+ with a projected investment of $3.4 trillion required to restore the country's systems to good working order).[18] As the Great Recession began, the federal government attempted to address this through the American Recovery and Reinvestment Act (ARRA). While this "stimulus package" looked directly to the infrastructure investments of the Roosevelt administration as a precedent, it eventually met with a frugal and intransigent Republican congress that caused it to fall woefully short. Future demographic trends may cause this mindset to shift as Republican voters age out of the electorate. In 2015, while more Silents identified or leaned Republican (47 percent) than Democrat (43 percent), all younger generations skewed Democratic: Boomers 47 percent to 41 percent and Generation X 49 percent to 38 percent. For Millennials, the spread was even greater, with 51 percent trending Democratic versus 35 percent Republican.[19]

While the 2016 elections showed that party identification and voting do not always align, as older voters age out of the electorate it remains highly likely that Millennial voters, who directly benefit from infrastructure spending, will open federal purses for reinvestment regardless of which party controls the government. As of 2010, 53 percent of Millennials believed that the "government should do more to solve problems." While that percentage had dropped in half by 2015, Millennials still remained nearly twice as likely to have faith in the government as Boomers.[20] As opposition numbers progressively decrease, Millennial voters and increasingly Millennial political leaders will likely spur a new infrastructure-building age with a major emphasis on supporting the Millennial Age city, and given current trends, its stridency will match or even exceed that which occurred in the middle of the last century. The question, really, is when.

Millennial Age Architectural Practice

The collaborative, practical, and civic-focused characteristics of Millennials—whose digital acumen sharpens each asset considerably—will be essential traits for architectural practices for innovation in the Millennial-Age city. If the architectural profession recognizes that the Millennials who are inducing the changes of this era and the architects who will increasingly play a role in administering those changes share the same values, it can expand its agency into areas the current disruption has yet to define. Working together with Generation X practitioners—who possess an innate understanding of how computers and digital networks can apply to urban issues at all scales—Millennials can combine their digital nativism with their elder cohort's experience. The pioneering interdisciplinary practice of landscape urbanism can become the operational template for new forms of collaboration with wholly new sectors, all under the umbrella of sustainability. The ingenuity of architects in creating urban amenities, and their understanding of the public and sometimes charitable nature of their services, can incent Millennials as they reinvent the twenty-first-century city.

The generation's established propensity for collaboration is prime for expansion in the Millennial Age. Kathi Vian, who directs the annual Ten-Year Forecast program at the Institute for the Future in Palo Alto, California, projects seven future economies as part of the Millennial Age, which she refers to mnemonically as the "the seven Cs."[21] Vian projects that by 2025, as much as half the total workforce will be freelance and fully embedded in one of the Cs: the collaborative economy. According to Vian, collaboration will expand far beyond just individuals working together toward a common end, to utilize aspects of what has come to be known as the "sharing economy," the foundation of trust that allows the ride-hailing companies Uber and Lyft and the home-sharing company, Airbnb, to thrive. In office practices, architectural or otherwise, the sharing economy will create a multivalence to allow the 2025 freelance worker the ability to commoditize what they can provide more efficiently, and also to seek out their needs, such as expertise, workspace, computing power, vehicles, etc., in order to meet objectives. The infrastructure of this collaborative economy will build a "rich ecosystem of peer-to-peer channels to set in motion a virtuous cycle that lets both distributors and freelancers prosper."[22]

The future Vian describes is consistent with Thomas Fisher's 2014 expansive projection for a postrecession architecture profession that will "cast aside some of our old practices and assumptions about what architecture entails and recognize the vast new array of design opportunities that the new economy has created."[23] As Fisher describes, Millennial Age architecture practices will be urban and especially smart city–focused, capable of addressing growing cities and their disruptions. Many will be public-interest design firms that use technology to develop practical, low-cost, culturally appropriate solutions for a global client base. Others will grow "polycultures" of disciplines to diversify the design-dominant nature of some firms, cultivating "a richer and more diverse ecology of staff and consultants from a wider range of backgrounds and fields." In Fisher's forecast, all will be digitally nimble and nuclear, supported by a distributed network of freelance collaborators. If the profession adopts these values, many of which align with those of Millennials, he projects that "we will see no end to the work we have to do."[24]

This employee-based, bottom-up vision of collaboration contrasts with the trend of firms building collaborative strength through mergers and acquisitions. During the Great Recession, several design firms took advantage of the prevalent twentieth-century practice of scaling up (what business jargon calls a "rollup") to form one corporate entity capable of delivering a full range of services to clients. With approximately 87,000 employees in over 150 countries, AECOM has emerged as the world's largest general architectural and engineering design firm, as measured by 2017 revenue.[25] Catalyzed by its 2007 IPO, AECOM has now rolled up over fifty firms, with each satisfying a certain disciplinary niche.[26] Diverse and notable AECOM acquisitions during the recession include the architecture firm Ellerbe Becket, the landscape architects EDAW, and the Tishman Construction Corporation. Whether firms such as AECOM continue to acquire as the recession recedes will be an indicator of which future model will prevail: the nimble digital practice forecast by Fisher or the conglomerated twentieth-century juggernaut recast in a Millennial Age form.

The popular image of the Millennial Age office, so common as to be lampooned on the HBO series *Silicon Valley*, is one of self-conscious yet casual organization, a place ornamented with juice bars and Ping-Pong tables. While cliché, these spaces nonetheless convey the in-between nature of the collaborative economy, functioning more like lobbies for multitaskers, open to the comings and goings of workers, clients, suppliers, etc. The physical space of architectural practices also follows this trend. Fading away are the post–WWII offices of the GI generation made iconic on the set of the Netflix series *Mad Men*. In the architectural office of this period, one entered through a minimal, austere lobby, where a sentry-like secretary sat at a desk amidst the requisite collection of Mies van der Rohe furniture. This room typically opened to a gallery of singular images of the office's oeuvre, a promenade meant to screen the sweatshop nature of the architectural practice beyond. The Millennial Age replacement for these formal lobbies immediately exposes the entrant to the studio, humming with a combination of design frenzy and collaborative chatter. One noteworthy example is the office of Snøhetta (also particularly collaborative for not including partners' names in the masthead), a design practice that integrates architecture, landscape, interiors, furniture, and graphic and brand design. Founded in 1989—and fortunate to have early-on won signature competitions with designs that were eventually constructed—the firm's Generation X partners, like those of contemporary firms such as SHoP, work in a space that reflects their own maverick free agency. As described by founding partner Craig Dykers, Snøhetta attempts to retain the small touches that keep it true to its collaborative and casual origins, such as the beer tap off the lobby, which transmits what he describes as the "the strange informality of our group." Within this grouping, different members of one creative discipline can immerse themselves in the practices of another to better understand their own. Dykers describes this immersion as similar to method acting.[27]

The media prominence of the "starchitect" may also be fading as quickly as the austere lobby, another vestige of Boomer-era postmodernism. Scorn for expressions of the starchitect's singular artistic vision has replaced praise as the Great Recession has receded. Outcries regarding impracticality, willfulness, and budgetary excesses indicate that starchitect values have become misaligned with those of the Millennial Age. For example, critics attacked the Boomer architect Zaha Hadid (who died in 2017), adding alleged labor practice violations to the list of other starchitect sins. True to the combative Boomer stereotype, Hadid immediately responded with a lawsuit.[28] *New York Times* art critic Holland Cotter complained in 2015 that the museum of the twenty-first century had yet to appear, citing Frank Gehry's 2014 Louis Vuitton Foundation as a continuation of a "love of gigantism," a lingering product of the "Arrogant Age" of the late twentieth century.[29] Pritzker-winner Richard Meier's 2018 professional demise for Me Too harassment offenses was heightened by his starchitect prominence. And singled out from all the rest, Boomer architect Santiago Calatrava has been universally pilloried for his excesses, especially for his bird-shaped terminal at New York's World Trade Center, for which even prominent architects have publicly reviled and mocked him. At a 2012 symposium, the Silent generation architect Michael Graves chose to use the occasion to attack the starchitect: "Cala-fucking-trava! What a waste." Graves continued to mock with his best Calatrava impression: "I will make wings for you and this subway station will cost four billion dollars." Fellow Silent Peter Eisenman joined in by recounting how Calatrava once came to lecture at Yale, only to spend the entire hour onstage drawing to music without saying a word. To this story, Graves replied: "Such a bore."[30] Once allied with Boomers after the White/Gray disputes, by the twenty-first century these Silent generation architects had turned on one of the younger generation's most prominent architects.

It may fall to Generation X architects to help in the transition toward a new form of leadership in the Millennial Age. Like other vanguards, Generation X's innovations appear to have come from across the Atlantic, where in the Netherlands, a new form of architectural pragmatism, first described as "projectivism," initially incubated. With varying degrees of connection to Rem Koolhaas's practice (if only geographical), firms such as UNStudio, MVRDV, ONL, and NOX Architekten began privileging the "how" of architecture, leaving the "what" and "why" undefined. These architects predict a Millennial Age pragmatism: "By systematically researching reality as found with the help of diagrams and other analytical measures, all kinds of latent beauties, forces, and possibilities can, projective architects maintain, be brought to the surface."[31] Taking a cue from his Dutch neighbors, the Danish-born architect Bjarke Ingels, founder of the firm BIG (Bjarke Ingels Group), also uses a projectivist, diagrammatic approach that weaves the practical with the fantastical. Founding his practice in 2005, Ingels expanded to New York in 2011, where he quickly ascended to replace the starchitect Norman Foster as the architect of the 2 World Trade Center building. Ingels carries the charm and celebrity of the starchitect with less swagger. In 2011, the *Wall Street Journal* named Ingels Innovator of the Year for architecture, and like Koolhaas, he is a winner of the Rebuild by Design competition, entrusted with designing levies for Manhattan. As a late member of Generation X (eight years away from being a Millennial, and with a boyishness that leads many to think that he is one), Ingels represents perhaps the best example as a forerunner of what a leading architect of the Millennial Age can be.

That Ingels's presence is spread across continents emphasizes the global nature of twenty-first-century practice. If urbanization will be the signal disruption of the Millennial Age in the US, that scope pales when compared to the level projected to take place worldwide. Able to accelerate through the use of building information modelling (BIM), US architecture practices have advanced globally, with many keeping offices on several continents. In many cases, overseas work kept firms whole through the recession.[32] In most Asian cities, where the sophistication of infrastructure arguably surpasses that in the US, and with governments continually stimulating their economies through the recession, urban growth has only accelerated. The UN expects this to continue, projecting the world's urban population to increase from 3.9 billion in 2014 to 6.3 billion by 2050. By this date, the Asian urban population will have increased by 61 percent and that of Africa will have tripled, meaning almost three quarters of the world's city dwellers will be living on those two continents.

While the migration of Millennials to US cities may be driven by preference, their movement to cities across the world may be more from necessity, and the changes will be far more dramatic. By contrast, the US urban growth rate for the same period is projected at only 7 percent, as the US urban population is already considered high by the UN at 81 percent (the UN counts both cities *and* suburbs in tabulating what constitutes the urban). Thus while the Urban Land Institute and PricewaterhouseCoopers might consider this trend worthy of a mindset shift in the US, its magnitude is but a fraction of the double- and triple-digit urban growth projected elsewhere globally. While mobilizing to deal with Millennial disruptions to American cities might prepare American architects to design for global urban disruption, the scale of change will be many factors greater.

These Asian and African urban disruptions will be vast enough, but even the most conservative climate change prediction expands their impact into the unknown. A 2015 World Bank report expects climate change to force 100 million into poverty by 2030.[33] Many will likely seek refuge in cities or in the growing archipelago of refugee camps that will likely form, which will each quickly grow to city size. After reaching saturation, refugees will seek to migrate to other countries and continents to begin a similar cycle. The refugee migration to Europe that began in the summer of 2015 and the subsequent disruptions it caused may be a small harbinger of what will come. Recent studies indicating that climate change catalyzed the Syrian civil war suggest that human conflict will become a byproduct of environmental degradation.[34] Alarming predictions, such as the assertion that simply being outdoors in parts of the Middle East for all but short periods will prove fatal by 2100,[35] or the idea that the warming of the Indian Ocean may disrupt the monsoon season and deny rain for multiple years to billions of south Asians, may expand the predicted refugee crisis dramatically.[36] In this context, disruptive innovation that creates the next cool phone app will seem frivolous when innovation will be a matter of survival.

The architectural profession may be called upon to innovate for this multipronged crisis, or it can remain within the comfortable confines of its discipline and leave the initiative to others. Yet examples of architects leading innovation abound. A government-led example is the Rebuild by Design competition, for which architects such as Ingels and Koolhaas are joined by universities such as MIT and UPenn, forming teams with many disciplines. At the sole-practitioner level, the remarkable and inspiring work of the Generation X architect Shigeru Ban, who uses humble, inexpensive, and easily deployable materials to create elegant and efficient dwellings for refugees, is another. Combining the drive of Millennials, the tactical leadership of Generation X, and the strategic idealism of Boomers offers the best possible generational alignment to meet these coming challenges.

Architectural Academies in the Millennial Age

By the beginning of the twenty-first century, the Millennial proclivities for collaboration, practicality, and civic focus had become as evident in architectural schools as in the profession, with clear linkages forming between them. The National Architectural Accrediting Board (NAAB) had maintained collaboration to be an essential accreditation requirement, and in 2003 revised its conditions to include a comprehensive design requirement, obliging students to demonstrate the incorporation of practical knowledge into a coordinated architecture project. The civic redirection of the profession drew parallels in schools, with many programs devoting time and resources to public works. A notable example of all three Millennial traits in play is the University of Oregon's Sustainable City Year program, begun in 2007. Coordinated through its College of Design (originally the School of Architecture and Allied Arts), the program deploys more than five hundred students operating across disciplines in over thirty courses working with a single city each year. The *Chronicle of Higher Education* described it as "one of higher education's most successful and comprehensive service-learning programs."[37]

Each Millennial inclination described above was emergent in schools in the 1990s, well before the first Millennial enrolled. Again, while this may indicate architecture's inherent vanguardism, if viewed according to a cycling generational framework, the characteristics Millennials possess today have oscillated through American architectural education from its formation in the mid-nineteenth century. Since its beginning, the studio has been the primary medium for teamwork, practicality, and public purpose, and while the organization of each has varied under different generational leadership, the studio has accrued great benefit from this long period of critical refinement. Millennials have indicated a strong preference for the hands-on, experiential learning methods that studios offer. Millennials learn by doing, engaging through experiences such as case studies, hands-on work, and increasingly, games and simulations. These activities speed learning and maintain interest, as if those participating were personally tutored. As with the video games that many Millennials play, their interest increases when these experiences are goal-oriented and collaborative. As the examples

presented later in this chapter prove, Millennials seem drawn to the cama-
raderie formed in close-knit environments like design studios cultivate, with
a special appreciation for peer-to-peer, just-in-time collaborative learning,
especially when it involves technology that they can flaunt.[38]

The Redesign of Studio Culture, a report issued by the American Institute
of Architecture Students in late 2002, heralded the arrival of Millennials
in architecture schools and affirmed for the coming age the importance of
studios. This self-reflexive document is evidence of an early and effective
collaboration of generations, as it was written largely by late-wave Generation X recent graduates, guided by Boomer faculty advisers, and supported
in numbers by both a task force and audience of first-wave Millennials. That
its themes are clearly Millennial, although it was produced by students
who had attended school in the late 1990s and are generally considered to
still be part of Generation X, shows yet again that architecture is slightly
ahead-of-phase with the prevailing cohort. The report focuses almost ex-
clusively on the studio rather than on architectural education as a whole,
underscoring the common importance of the studio to both architectural
pedagogy and Millennials. It opens with a statement of how studio culture
is so ingrained within architectural pedagogy to be almost taken for granted
and resist codification: "aspects [of the studio] are not usually written into
the curriculum or even the design assignments, but they are likely the most
memorable and influential."[39] Framed as a design problem, the document
builds toward an expression of values that follows a critique (at times searing) of existing conditions. (I focus on the darker aspects of the report in
Chapter 9.) The essential values expressed in the document as cultures of
optimism, respect, sharing, engagement, and innovation each align with the
positive character profile of Millennials described throughout this chapter.

Paul Taylor's *The Next America* cites optimism as an overarching Millennial characteristic, and Norman Foster states emphatically that it would
be impossible to be an architect without it.[40] Correlated with confidence,
optimism is a characteristic that almost all survey-takers identify in Millennials. While one might consider promoting optimism in a report advocating
reform to be stating the obvious, announcing a shift from the "downcast era"
pessimism of the previous unraveling era adhering to Generation X values
announces an important change of mood. The report exhorts schools to
take to heart Foster's comment by pointing out that the "idea that good
design has tremendous power to impact human life positively is an incred-
ibly optimistic view."[41] This is prefaced by the statement that as "the

designers of human environments, architects are inherently responsibility [*sic*] to produce spaces that uplift spirits, address social issues, protect the environment, provide safety, and improve the quality of life."⁴² As another example of the document's generational harmony, and anticipating the Millennial architect's optimism, confidence, and team orientation in the future profession, the report quotes then AIA president Thompson Penney: "If we want professionals to be confident, contributing leaders in society, we should take every care in making sure that the educational system encourages confidence (not defensiveness), empathy (not self-centeredness), and teamwork (not a star mentality)."⁴³

Penney's call for empathy and teamwork and the report's essential values of respect, sharing, and engagement anticipate the sharing and collaborative economy that Vian and Fisher predict later in the century, one that will underpin the Millennial Age. The Millennials' upbringing under Boomer parents uniquely positions them for this new economy. After growing up collaborating in schools, day care, teams, orchestras, peer-to-peer networks, games, and other programmed activities, Millennials came to higher education in the 2000s with the knowledge of how and when to work effectively with others. Even those who do not prefer collaboration typically take part if they think it gives them a practical advantage. Because of their collaborative upbringing, Millennials respect merit systems over others such as seniority. Continually working together from an early age has inculcated a natural tendency to divide labors according to proven skills and knowledge. A corollary to this is that Millennials appreciate intelligence and education, overall believing that it is "cool to be smart," and as a result, are electing to go on to college and graduate work in far greater numbers than did previous generations.⁴⁴

In an increasingly complex world, the AIAS report recognizes that contemporary issues can only be addressed by emphasizing collaboration instead of rivalry, stating that "students would be better served by learning about the value of collaboration and the negative effects of competition." It stops short of advocating for a fully noncompetitive environment, recognizing that while hierarchies can be difficult to establish and administer, they are nonetheless necessary to get work done. In doing so, the report self-diagnoses the need for a generation of "trophy kids," brought up in an ethos where no one loses, to accept that they eventually must abide by the organizational pyramids of a professional world. Throughout, the report supports increased collaboration without sacrificing individual student development, signifying that collaboration allows individuals to self-identify their skills, allowing a student to "find what they are good at." In this way, complementarity prevails over competition, with the identification and promotion of respected complementary skills anticipating both Vian's and Fisher's forecasts of an environment where most workers network as digitally nimble, freelance collaborators within a distributed sharing economy.

The *Studio Culture* report recommends collaboration not only among architecture students but also beyond the field, suggesting that architectural education "would be well served to make connection with programs on campus such as sociology, business, English, art, public policy, political science, and social work." This directive not only supports disciplinary expansion, it also cites the strategically practical benefit of "interacting with those who will someday serve as future clients." Strong recommendations for practical engagement of this kind pervade the document, emboldening students to complement the experience in the studio with visits to construction sites and design offices to fully embrace issues associated with clients, finance, and above all else, operating within the practical realities of designing with constraints. Nowhere does the document mention theory, the overarching academic preoccupation of the previous two generations.

The highest level of practical engagement the report recommends is in the civic realm, stating, "We are convinced that the value of architectural education and the profession will increase by engaging students within the community."[45] The report strongly recommends immersing studios in practical applications that offer design services in real collaboration with citizens and community organizations, a process that can ultimately yield visionary ideas. The goal of these efforts is to prepare students to serve as leaders and, primarily, good citizens who can affect change for the betterment of society. The task force recognizes design-build and community design courses that apply these methods and the recent increase in offerings of this kind, making specific mention of Samuel Mockbee, the leader of Auburn University's Rural Studio. Within several years, Millennial students would heed this call to apply their resourcefulness in response to the environmental catastrophes of Hurricane Katrina and later Sandy, and to the urban struggles of Detroit and locales suffering similar degradation. Many of these would be cataloged in the anthologies *From the Studio to the Streets: Service-Learning in Planning and Architecture* (2006), *Service-Learning in Design and Planning: Educating at the Boundaries* (2011), and *Architecture Live Projects: Pedagogy into Practice* (2014) as evidence of the practical, results-oriented preferences of Millennials in architectural education.

The final expressed goal of the report is to support a culture of innovation. Written in 2002, the report mentions the term well before it became a buzzword later in the decade, anticipating the renewed ethos of trial and error that would later be the battle cry of disruptive culture. The task force recognizes architecture as a discipline of innovation whose very essence is to design the new and unique, yet it cautions that innovation must also lead to improvement. Unlike innovative improvements later in the decade, its recommendations focus less on promoting technological ingenuity than on the embrace of risk. Finding that students often blindly follow faculty suggestions, the report dares students to take chances. This presents another example of the document's self-reflexivity, this time recognizing that helicopter parenting may have caused their generation to be risk-averse. The call to take on more risk may also be a commentary on the profession of architecture, which has shielded itself from much of the risk associated with design, and as a result, its effectiveness has decreased.

Although the task force's report coincided with the first disruptions of the early 2000s, it surprisingly makes little mention of the role of digital technology in the studio, yet another example of how architectural schools had, without fanfare or drama, steadily integrated the computer into everyday practices throughout the 1990s. By 2002, the academic debate had shifted from *if* the computer should be integrated into design education to *when* in the educational sequence it should be introduced. The task force matter-of-factly states the pros ("Digital technology offers exciting new opportunities in graphic representation, visualization, and construction methods") and cons ("We fear that computers may devalue the art and craft of architecture, decrease collaboration, isolate students, and emphasize product over process").[46] But without specifically mentioning the digital revolution happening all around, the 2002 report anticipates what will be required of an emerging generation in a deeply networked environment:

> We live in an increasingly non-linear world in which everything is connected. Twenty-first century architectural problems are complex, demanding multi-disciplinary responses and attention. If architects are to remain the generalist leaders of design teams, they need to be able to understand the language of multiple disciplines and of particular areas of expertise. Education needs to offer students a broader base of ideas from which to draw, different ways of knowing, different methods of research and analysis, and different approaches and attitudes.[47]

Generational Case Study: Experiential Learning Toward Design Thinking

The 2002 AIAS Studio Culture Task Force document underscores the importance of the studio to both architectural education and Millennials. Whether they studied design education or other disciplines, as Millennials entered college in the 2000s they gravitated toward the educational model fundamental to the architectural studio: experiential learning. Synonymous or closely related to constructivist, project-based, or service learning, experiential learning is the educational model with which Millennials grew up. By the early 2000s, writers on education began recommending that universities adapt to the emergent Millennial preferences by offering "communal learning in diverse, tacit, situated experiences" as opposed to the "solo integration of divergent, explicit information sources" prevalent in the traditional "talk and chalk" courses. By providing "active learning based on experience (real and simulated) that includes frequent opportunities for reflection," schools should impart knowledge "distributed across a community and a context as well as within an individual."[48]

This Millennial preference for experiential learning, the same teaching protocol at the core of the architectural studio that the AIAS report so values, is fortuitous for the architectural academy. But the benefit can only occur if architecture, as the Boyer report explicitly recommends, can "profit" from its mastery. Architectural studio education has a long and rich tradition in the US, but so, too, does experiential learning as being fundamental to American secondary education. Upon closer inspection, both emerged in their modern form at about the same time in the middle of the nineteenth century and both experienced periods of renewal consistent with a generational oscillation between objectivity and aestheticism. Tracing back their parallel development reveals essential similarities, while an awareness of how methods migrated laterally during fertile periods provides a strategic advantage when forging a contemporary union of values. If this is not opportunity enough, the relatively recent migration of the core components of experiential learning into a professional environment, which the d.school teaches as design thinking, may be one of the great leaps forward of the Millennial Age, the realization in a work environment of what Jeremy Rifkin calls "deep play." For the remainder of this chapter, I trace the parallel developments of architectural and secondary education to understand their connections and to tease out the abstractions that now inform the innovation platform of design thinking.

The architectural studio had evolved from a prehistory of medieval apprenticeships into institutionally based training in Europe by the beginning of the Enlightenment. Studio teaching crossed the Atlantic by the mid-nineteenth century, after which cycles of generational change have shaped it. The current Millennial Age triad of pragmatism, collaboration, and outward focus echoes a Bauhaus-inspired pedagogy of similar themes during the previous crisis era of the 1930s. This was preceded by the establishment of the first American architectural schools based on similar values following the polytechnic model (with its basis in another German innovation) around the time of the Civil War. Occurring at the counterpoised periods of aestheticism, the Beaux-Arts's overriding emphasis on artistic mastery eclipsed the practical professional range of the polytechnic model by the turn of the twentieth century, and postmodernism later displaced the collaborative and stagnating status quo with the persona of the architect as singular artist. The stereotypical starchitect of singular vision falling from his pedestal—as a wave of consensus-driven pragmatism ushers in the Millennial Age—effectively closes another generational cycle. Yet despite these wide fluctuations of attitude (summarized here and in previous chapters), the studio model itself—some dozen students working under the close guidance of a mentor over a sustained period, punctuated by a feedback loop of critique—has stood up to time's test and become more refined since the 1850s.

The studio model and its attitudinal oscillations parallel broader educational initiatives in American secondary education. These also trace their origins to the formalization of the mid-nineteenth century and form the heritage for the experiential learning Millennials came to know growing up. Beginning in the 1850s, through the efforts of Horace Mann, American education made a clean break with prior church-based education. Like architectural educators, Mann imported a German model of rigid standards taught in a communal learning format open to all citizens. To ensure a common pedagogy, Mann went so far as to develop specialty schools to educate teachers called normal schools, referencing the "norms" educators themselves would need to learn before imparting them to others. The classroom as a physical space, with chairs attached to writing surfaces, all facing a large desk with a teacher behind it, is a legacy of this era. While the motive for this formalization was to train workers for America's burgeoning Industrial Revolution, it is the small-town, one-room schoolhouse that remains a foundation myth of the beginnings of American public education. With its own bell on a pole or in a humble tower, the schoolhouse became a secular church, often located in such a proximity to compete directly with a town's religious structures. With all grade levels gathered in one class, learning became a collective and collaborative effort, with older students gradually joining the teacher to help bring the younger along. As regimented as it was, this teaching format was deeply experiential. However enduring this image is, America's rapid expansion as the nineteenth century progressed soon forced the same basic cell to stack vertically for multiple grades into rationalized brick boxes, a preview of the factories in which many of its students would one day work.[49]

While the next generation of educators accepted the secular nature of the communal classroom, they questioned the regimented norms of the initial system. These educators promoted a model that valued the "experience" involved in a student's learning as much as the subject matter taught. Beginning with John Dewey's Laboratory School in Chicago in 1896, progressives experimented with a new form of education that stressed creativity and critical thinking to allow children to grow mentally, physically, and socially. This experimentation brought the first studio-based learning to US secondary schools. Dewey advocated for student-centered arts education that could expand an authentic perception of the world, leading to higher understanding and action. Parallel overtures occurred with William Wirt's "platoon system" at Horace Mann High School in Gary, Indiana, and a curriculum formed by Quincy, Massachusetts, school superintendent Francis W. Parker. The "Quincy system" integrated a curriculum of learning-by-doing scenarios with artistic expression, featuring long-term projects culminating in exhibitions.[50]

Interior arrangements reflected these progressive era changes. Desks were unbolted from floors, allowing more freedom to arrange experiential learning environments. Closet space to store different experiential apparatus became an important design consideration, and specialty studios for non-traditional subjects, such as music and the industrial arts, first appeared. A subtle but important distinction occurred in this reorganization of interior educational spaces and furniture: students became the center of their own educational universe, displacing the teacher from his or her altar-like desk. In the same way that the Beaux-Arts had eclipsed the polytechnic, the vision of individual experiential learning had eclipsed the collective tendencies of normalized education.

While the interiors of progressive-era schools transformed considerably, the outer factory-like structure changed little, except to acquire additional accretions of Victorian-era decoration of whatever architectural style. One writer on school design describes the spiritless qualities of this type of structure as "a brick box with holes for windows in a style that can only be described as neutered."[51] This changed with the construction of a school that embodied the values of the next oscillation after the progressive era: Crow Island Elementary School in Winnetka, Illinois, built by Perkins+Will in 1940. This low-slung, suburban school furthered many of the experiential learning innovations of the previous era. Its L-shaped rooms allowed space for individualized and collaborative learning. A garden in the crook of each "L" allowed classroom experiences to expand into defined outdoor spaces, literally evoking Friedrich Froebel's nineteenth-century vision of a school as a "garden for children." The building was scaled to the child, with lowered ceilings, windowsills, and light switches, all set amidst a cozy environment that included fireplaces. The Crow Island School deliberately lacks the exalted spaces of the progressive era school; instead, thanks to an extended collaborative consultation with educators, designers, and other stakeholders, it is a humble and practical structure focused on children in a collective setting as its primary users. As part of the outreach that formed its spaces, a creative activities teacher suggested:

> The building must not be too beautiful, lest it be a place for children to keep and not one for them to use. The materials must be those not easily marred, and permitting of some abuse. The finish and settings must form a harmonious background [to] honest child effort and creation, not one which will make children's work seem crude. Above all, the school must be child-like, not what adults think of children. . . . It must be warm, personal, and intimate, that it shall be to thousands of children through the years "my school."[52]

The description renders an image of collective comfort where the well-being of the student is paramount, and one senses an echo of the *Studio Culture* report's call for a balanced life. If the Millennial Age is an archetypal echo of the era that built the Crow Island School, understanding the relationship between the school's physical qualities and the progressive values that built it offers a comparison to the physical learning environments organized for design thinking in the twenty-first century.

Crow Island became the template for the postwar school in which Baby

Boomers were educated. During the Boomer-led societal awakening, educators furthered John Dewey's initiatives to probe the values at the core of experiential learning and develop comprehensive theories for its deployment in schools for their Millennial children. Formalizing in the 1970s as the Association for Experiential Education, this initiative launched an accreditation system and journal, prompting writers to delve deeper into the educational method's mechanics. Prominent among these is David Kolb, who writes of an experiential learning philosophy that anticipates the appreciation Millennials share for the method. Emphasizing a student-focused, collaborative, and problem-solving approach, Kolb's experiential learning theory updates Dewey by integrating the findings of child psychologist Jean Piaget and organizational psychologist Kurt Lewin.

Kolb's four-step experiential learning model (ELM) begins with (1) *concrete experience*, when the learner assesses what he or she already knows and how it relates to a given context. A period of (2) *reflective observation* follows, when the student considers what works (or not) in a certain contextual situation. During (3) *abstract conceptualization*, a learner considers how to improve, and this is followed by a final stage: (4) *active experimentation*. Completion of the cycle begins a new one in a feedback loop continued until mastery is achieved, although according to Kolb, mastery should never lead to complacency. This echoes a common Boomer-era precept, with Kolb writing that "learning is best conceived as a process, not in terms of outcomes." His ELM is also infused with the Boomer ideal of egalitarianism, in which all experience is valued and should never be erased: "Everyone enters every learning situation with more or less articulate ideas about the topic at hand. We are all psychologists, historians, and atomic physicists. It is just that some of our theories are more crude and more incorrect than others." The other end of the cycle is similarly open-ended; while a learner might attain mastery, it must always be maintained in a continual process.[53]

Kolb's theory as applied to Millennial education has many alignments with contemporary architectural instruction. His paradigmatic teacher, who applies experiential learning techniques, is like a studio critic, less a disseminator and more a coach or facilitator. Kolb also identifies how each individual has a natural bias toward one of the four experiential learning steps, a latent expertise that lends itself to Millennial collaboration. These biases lead to roles: *diverger* (concrete experience); *assimilator* (reflective observation); *accommodator* (abstract conceptualization); and *converger* (active experimentation). This subdivision suggests that teams organized around the recognition of complementary learning styles—with each member respecting the advanced skill of another—can become a powerful tool to combine the abilities of freelance collaborators in the emergent sharing economy.

The Boomer ambition to seek equity in education gave new momentum to a struggle for school desegregation that still continues in the twenty-first century. As part of this struggle, Boomers sought to ensure that all children receive a proper education regardless of race, special needs, aptitude, etc. As a result, by the time Millennials reached grade school, public school education in the US had become highly variegated, with entirely autonomous programs for those with special needs bracketed by equally separate curricula for advanced students. Amid this pluralist segmentation, other specialty schools began to calve off as alternative or charter schools, some with a defined experiential and paraprofessional focus. New programs added considerable cost, and as public sector funding began to dwindle, those students in the middle, especially those in urban school districts, found themselves in overcrowded classrooms with a teacher at the front of the room often serving as little more than a caretaker. Nationwide concern over the failings in education, prompted by examinations such as the 1983 Nation at Risk report, caused parents to become highly involved in their children's education. As a result, student-centered, experiential learning became a gold standard that helicopter parents militantly fought for (the placement of the student at the center of his or her own educational eco-system—especially when augmented by technology—is a major theme of the next chapter). For families wealthy enough to opt out of the public school system entirely, private schools offered small classes to better facilitate learning, and many of the academic after-school programs or summer camps that many Millennials attended were based on experiential models.

Experiential Learning Becomes Design Thinking

When the d.school opened in a garage-like studio on Stanford's Palo Alto campus in 2005—its space described as looking "like a preschool playroom for grown-ups: Colorful furniture, open spaces and neon Post-it Notes abound[ing]"[54]—it brought experiential learning to higher education outside of traditional arts-based programs such as architecture. The first wave of Millennial adults would encounter experiential learning under a new banner: design thinking. In its mission statement, the d.school seems to fully anticipate Millennial preferences, offering "spectacularly transformative learning experiences" that compel students to "develop a process for producing creative solutions." Its global and team-based focus applies a public purpose, with a stated charge of taking on the world's messy problems by deploying human values at the "heart of a collaborative approach." Describing itself as a "hub for innovators," the school draws students and faculty from an interdisciplinary pool: engineering, medicine, business, law, the humanities, sciences, and education. By defining its own generational grouping as ranging from kindergarteners to senior executives, it seeks to create a "deliberate mash-up of industry, academia and the big world beyond campus [as] key to our continuing evolution." The d.school is thematically dedicated toward each Millennial value described in this book, and while never identifying the cohort except generically, it maintains that its "primary responsibility is to help prepare a generation of students to rise with the challenges of our times."[55]

For its version of experiential learning, the d.school incorporated the term "design thinking," which after 2000 became widely associated with disruption and innovation. Typically taught in university business schools and departments, design thinking introduces creativity into more traditional business or product development models that are more typically rooted in analytical, inductive, or deductive reasoning. Through an expansive brainstorming process, design thinking uses creative invention to spawn products, services, and systems that can serve a specific future human need.[56] Stanford professor Rolf Faste describes it as "ambidextrous thinking," applying a metaphor for how someone using both hands equally well, integrating one side of the brain's analytic functions with the opposite's creativity.[57]

Varying descriptions of design thinking abound.[58] All include problem definition and some sort of conclusive result, between which several stages expand or constrict activity to focus on a variety of applications. The stages of design thinking have strong correlations with Kolb's experiential learning theory. To compare to Kolb's ELM, I use the 2006 definition of design thinking generalized by the staff writers at *Fast Company* magazine.[59] In both its print and online versions, *Fast Company* has become a prominent twenty-first-century reporter on innovation and disruption. Its writers describe design thinking (whether in an academic or professional setting) as a four-stage, goal-oriented process best practiced in groups. Stage (1) defines a problem and then closely scrutinizes all aspects associated with it. This scrutiny implies leaving one's comfort zone to perform an exhaustive inquiry. Defining a problem requires a suspension of judgment and a redefinition of language used for discussion. A team enters stage (2) once a design thinking problem is determined. An initial goal of this stage is to create as many solutions as possible, no matter how obvious or naïve each may seem, articulating all the solutions in a similar manner that invites comparison, with special care taken not to default to prior methods or to solve each problem in the same way. During this brainstorming period, designers must remain vigilant against prejudices or filters that can cloud inventiveness. Ultimately, opportunities will present themselves, and the challenge is in identifying them. This is the stage where the multiple perspectives available through a team structure offer the greatest benefit, to debate which solution has the most promise. This is also the stage where 2-D and 3-D simulations using computers can transcend words to reveal prospects. Stage (3) commences with the refinement of designated solutions. At this point, teams must champion and nurture the promising results, while also warding off the "evil idea killers" that prejudices can bring. New ideas can often be fragile in their infancy, and it becomes imperative to create an environment conducive to growth, although this should not preclude experimentation and pushing toward failure. This is the point at which options may also merge. Before the process concludes in a fourth stage, *Fast Company* suggests a stage (3.5), which repeats the second and third steps until the right answer surfaces. Whether through successive iteration or on the first try, stage four selects a winning solution and commits resources to begin testing and prototyping. And at this conclusion, the team designates any tangential or unique ideas for future development as part of a separate process. With the initially identified problem declared solved and the opportunity fully uncovered, a new disruptive technology launches to seek investors.

At the end of their article, as if to summarize their somewhat verbose description with a statement prefaced by "in other words," *Fast Company* defaults to Wikipedia, which succinctly describes how this is different from previous methods:

> Design thinking is, then, always linked to an improved future. Unlike critical thinking, which is a process of analysis and is associated with the "breaking down" of ideas, design thinking is a creative process based around the "building up" of ideas. There are no judgments in design thinking. This eliminates the fear of failure and encourages maximum input and participation. Wild ideas are welcome, since these often lead to the most creative solutions. Everyone is a designer, and design thinking is a way to apply design methodologies to any of life's situations.[60]

Despite the obvious similarities in the sequential organization of both Kolb's theory and design thinking, a critical generational distinction forms to consider them both generationally and biologically. Generationally, Kolb's stages suggest an endless process in the Boomer search for value—once completed, begin again at the beginning. And while design thinking allows some cycling through a process mode in stage 3.5, its protocols are overwhelmingly focused on the Millennial practical end of bringing ideas to market—if the market says no, move on to something different. Through this generational lens, Wikipedia's specific choice of words describes the Boomers' continual search for values when it associates critical thinking with the "breaking down" of ideas, as a kind of deconstruction or unraveling. This Boomer way of thinking stands in stark contrast to design thinking as a creative process committed to the "building up" of ideas by seeking consensus and forming coalitions, leading to an optimistic Millennial "improved future."

From a biological point of view, Kolb's ELM differs from design thinking in that it caters more to secondary-school learners who are still immature and more prone to being traumatized by failure. A d.school design thinking pedagogy that was specifically crafted for K–12 education slightly changes its graduate-level stages to fit younger learners: understand, observe, point-of-view, ideate, prototype, and test.[61] The added *point-of-view* stage gently builds participants' confidence, and the process ends with *testing*, far short of the adult-world threshold. By contrast, design thinking as taught at Stanford audaciously embarks to "seek venture capital" after a process of rigorous inquiry performed by fully formed adults. In this regard, design thinking programs, especially at the graduate level, apply a fun-loving overlay to fit younger learners in order to mask the weaning from the "everyone wins," gentle world of experiential learning, all within a refined rubric of "helicopter educating."

Otherwise, design thinking falls thematically into step with many aspects of experiential learning's evolution going back to Horace Mann. The greatest commonalities may be with two of Kolb's stages that are naturally complementary and examples of ambidextrous thinking. The first is Kolb's *divergent* step, which corresponds to the expansive analytical thinking of *Fast Company*'s stage two period of multi-solution production. The second is his *convergent* synthetic stage, which corresponds to the refinement and solution-directed period that begins *Fast Company*'s stage three. In team settings, these stages can be a dialogue between those leaning toward divergence and those toward convergence, which is an example of a powerful and potentially advantageous division of labor for Vian's sharing, collaborative economy.

Design thinking's generational adaptation of experiential learning has evolved from protocols to a global credo in full alignment with Millennial values. In 2011, the d.school's sister institute in Germany published a commandment-like creed which governs the design thinking sensibility: (1) the human rule—all design activity is ultimately social in nature; (2) the ambiguity rule—design thinkers must preserve ambiguity; (3) the re-design rule—all design is re-design; and (4) the tangibility rule—making ideas tangible always facilitates communication.[62] The instruction to embrace ambiguity suggests an abiding Millennial confidence and optimism; the social rule speaks to collaborative values; and the tangibility rule implies both an eminent practical and public purpose.

Design thinking emerged as a coherent pedagogy contemporaneous with the development of Apple products, which Millennials know well and at least grudgingly respect. As Apple's facilitator, Steve Jobs led experiential teams of Kolb divergers and convergers armed with design thinking protocols to comprehensively consider every aspect of their work in terms of anticipating future Millennial needs. This process brought to market a series of products that fostered waves of disruption. Jobs knew the importance not only of creative thinking but also of the need for aesthetic refinement that accompanies it. He references this in his 2005 commencement address at Stanford:

[At Reed College] I decided to take a calligraphy class. . . . I learned about serif and sans serif typefaces, about varying the amount of space between different letter combinations, about what makes great typography great. It was beautiful, historical, artistically subtle in a way that science can't capture, and I found it fascinating. None of this had even a hope of any practical application in my life. But 10 years later, when we were designing the first Macintosh computer, it all came back to me. And we designed it all into the Mac. It was the first computer with beautiful typography.[63]

As Jobs gave that early Millennial class at Stanford his blessing in 2005, he also happened to be offering convocation to its first d.school class. This cohort of lead-edge Millennials would soon learn design thinking as a strategy for innovation and make it a standard of professional innovators.

Jobs's remarks underscore the importance of aesthetics as a critical differentiator in a time of rapid technological disruption. Architecture's generations-long integration of aesthetics into professional practice gives it an advantage held by few other disciplines. The convergence of innovation and capital graced by Apple's aesthetics, which emerged from Stanford and the surrounding Silicon Valley as Millennials became adults, forms a design sensibility that reverberates around the world. As the disruptions of the Millennial Age continue, architecture stands well-positioned to profit, but as I explain at the end of Chapter 9, it may also be highly vulnerable if it chooses another direction.

A generational framework going back to before the Civil War reveals how closely architectural education and experiential learning have intertwined, and an examination of a succession of their course corrections provides the historical context to understand the emergence of design thinking as a twenty-first-century business practice. Experiential learning's popularity with Millennials offers great advantages for architectural education to benefit. The issuance of the AIAS Studio Culture Task Force report by the first wave of Millennials expresses their specific values for the design studio, also underscoring their preference for experiential learning, which resides at its core. Emerging from the Great Recession, the professional architectural community has shifted toward an economy that is more sharing, collaborative, and civic-minded, which are all values that align with those of Millennials that have emerged through experiential learning. As the world urbanizes, multiple disruptions will challenge Millennial architects to rise to the better nature of their profession. In many arenas, the Millennial Age offers alignments aplenty between the generation's values and the architectural profession and academies of which to take advantage. In the next chapter, I describe specific advantages and disadvantages associated with the Millennials' prominent digital birthright and its many manifestations. How the architecture community responds will have a bearing on which side of the disruptive divide it finds itself later this century.

CHAPTER 8

Anytime, Anywhere
Digital Natives and Nomads

Nomadicity is an emerging fact of life, the needs of which are real, whose issues are fascinating, whose payoffs can be huge, and which makes all the problems we face in computing and communications harder.

LEONARD KLEINROCK

The nomadic tendencies of digitally native Millennials present the greatest variable affecting future architectural practice and teaching. While the positives of aligning with Millennial characteristics may be obvious, and the negatives equally self-evident, the attributes associated with Millennial nomadicity divide the architecture profession and academy, who question whether they are an asset or an impairment. While adaptive strategists in the profession might be eager to build upon the "anywhere, anytime" computing of nomadism, a countervailing naysayer adds nomadicity's effects to the growing list of Millennial liabilities emanating from their digital birthright. These critics dread the progressive undermining of architecture's physical and organizational structures that nomadicity may bring. Digital nomadism in the academy accelerates the long arc of ceding more responsibility to the student in the form of student-centered learning that begins with John Dewey. Adding online learning, social media, and digital games to its toolbox forces the academy to draw a line between focused work and a Millennial fusion of convenience and pleasure. Examining three academies focused on student-centered learning through a generational lens, one predigital, another that crossed the divide, and the third a fully digital product of the Millennial Age, places nomadism in a broader context.

Richard Sweeney identifies different Millennial behaviors associated with nomadicity, each in some way a result of the generation being digital natives. Sweeney categorizes how Millennials prioritize a nomadic communication style that is media and format agnostic, one following a path of greatest convenience. Pew Research writes that this communication style, whether through phone, tablet, or computer or via the platforms of Facebook, Instagram, or Snapchat—or whatever emerges next—weaves a Millennial network of friends distinct from older generations' social organization. This behavior sets a nomadic standard for the Millennials' emerging academic and professional relationships. Nomadicity's untethering from organizational structures informs other Millennial preferences: these Sweeney lists as being selective and option-focused, flexible and convenience-driven, prioritizing personalization and customization over traditional standards. Interchangeable activities clustered together and layered in the same time frame form the notorious Millennial behavior of multitasking. Digital games, which Millennials have grown up playing, often occupy one of these temporal layers. While in the abstract some have begun to identify the benefits of multitasking and how it parallels digital applications as well as the feedback loops of gaming, it remains a behavior so vexing to older generations that I deal with it more directly among the more extreme vulnerabilities discussed in the next chapter. The issues of architecture associated with nomadicity are many and all trace back to the beginnings of architectural computing.

While architecture adopted digital media earlier than many disciplines, its precocity may have led to complacency. New technology startups outside of architecture, such as Nest, have joined the race toward applying the Internet of Things, and the maker movement may outpace architecture's pioneering lead in 3-D printing. The profession has yet to fully reckon with how technology is disaggregating the office and stretching the workday across the globe, let alone anticipate what the Millennials' role will be in this transformation. In the academy, schools have been hesitant or reluctant to integrate online or "distance" learning, social media, and gamification, ceding advances using these methods to other departments. The professional version of "distance" working may form distributed social networks of freelance collaborators increasingly working online in new manners of integrated production, and might even incorporate some form of gaming. Any of these applications potentially threatens the physical nature of the traditional architect's office.

Nomadicity in the Profession

The arrival of adult Millennials into the computing world continues an evolution in computer technology with roots going back to World War II. The computer's widespread introduction in architecture coincided with the beginnings of digital nomadism, when the personal computer (soon shortened to simply PC) replaced the cumbersome and sequestered mainframes hidden in a windowless room to occupy desks out in the drafting room. This began a quiet but steady disruption of architectural practice that Phillip Bernstein, a former Autodesk vice president and faculty member at Yale University, organizes into three eras.[1] Bernstein calls the first disruption an era of *documentation*, when computer aided design (CAD) replaces manual 2-D drafting and when the nongraphical elements of an architectural project—the many tables, schedules, and specifications—are digitized. As 2-D evolves to 3-D rendering, documentation soon includes a realism spurred by parallel developments in film production and computer gaming. Millennial children would first experience the animated world of computer-generated imagery (CGI) in these virtual environments, a medium that soon became indiscernible from traditional still and motion photography.

In Bernstein's second era, one of *optimization*, building information modelling (BIM) emerges to drive representation and reorganize practice, its definition ranging from Finith Jernigan's expansive definition of "big BIM" as a "management of information and the complex relationships between the social and technical resources that represent the complexity, collaboration, and interrelationships of today's organizations and environment,"[2] to the National Institute of Building Sciences's (NIBS) terse description as simply "a digital representation of physical and functional characteristics of a facility."[3] What the facilities and interrelationships of the NIBS definition might be is left entirely open-ended. The arrival of BIM represents a dramatic conceptual shift in architecture. Before it, an architectural project existed inside the mind of lead designers, revealed progressively to the outside world as fragmentary physical information through drawings, scale models, and other media. BIM inverts this paradigm, relying on a single virtual model that "reports" back information on demand. This inversion can ultimately benefit the architect, as the time and effort distribution curve drawn by HOK's Patrick MacLeamy demonstrates (see Figure 8.1).

MacLeamy's curve shows how BIM favors a period of design when architects have the greatest control and when project changes are least expensive.[4] Using BIM, digital objects maintain an association with physical ones

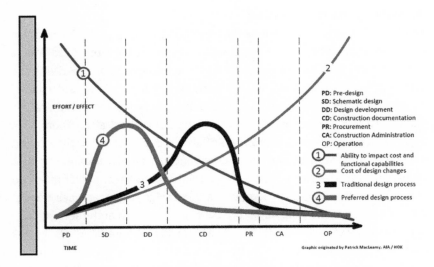

Figure 8.1. MacLeamy Curve. Patrick MacLeamy, AIA/HOK. From https://buildinginformationmanagement.files.wordpress.com/2012/08/macleamy-curve-2011.png, accessed October 9, 2016.

(whether planned or built), offering potential relationships with an almost infinite array of information that once resided in a nongraphic realm, or to use the now common term: "metadata." While this array represents another form of nomadism associated with information, it also implies a higher level of cohesion to maintain order amongst plenty. Whoever organizes this nomadic information retains control.

Much of the rhetoric associated with BIM focuses on an optimized practicality. It also emphasizes the collaboration required to replace traditional methods.[5] While Millennials played little if any role in initiating BIM, its digitally driven, practical, and collaborative attributes clearly align with their values. The platform also resonates with their preference for flexibility and control. Within a reorganized set of values regarding control, a Millennial embrace of BIM offers a new generational paradigm. Describing what it would replace, Bernstein writes how "questions (of control) derive from years of patterned behavior based on traditional AEC business models and are largely irrelevant in integrated, digitally based (BIM) projects where intention and execution are deeply connected."[6] In its stead, Bernstein envisions integrated teams working within a trusting and transparent environment based on a revolving agency of merit-based control, operating according to "collaborative models that combine responsibilities, risks, and rewards, and that provide open access to information, [in which] disputes over control give way to the issues of leadership: who is best suited to make a decision that benefits the project itself?"[7]

Bernstein's mention of patterned behavior refers to the division of labor between those involved in the abstract conception of design and the practical methods of construction, a division that has long bedeviled architects. For the last several generations, this division pitted parties against each other in a zero-sum conflict, creating classes of winners and losers. The aesthetic formalism so valued by Boomers and the following Generation X turned this division into a battle over control, a struggle architects too often lost over issues of cost or feasibility. BIM reorganizes the combatants in this conflict in a serendipitous alignment with the Millennial values of collaboration and practicality. If it can be applied successfully, the Millennial architect's embrace of BIM promises a new era of building on a more level playing field that favors the architect.

A new attitude of collaboration will lay the groundwork for Bernstein's third period, an era of *connection* to advance holistic representation and the interconnection of systems. Connectivity will enhance integrated project delivery (IPD),[8] the new business model that BIM has spawned, by taking advantage of billions of devices communicating with one another and with the Internet of Things. This enhanced connectivity will accompany a project from conception to construction and into its future. Like the tag sometimes applied to the Millennial generation for their unprecedented connectivity, these projects—from the moment of inception to well after demolition—will be "always on."

The entire history of digital computing falls within the four-generation cycle described in Chapter 5, beginning with the GI generation in the Great Depression and World War II crisis era (1929–1946). Consistent with this practical-minded period, digital computing evolved out of the military's need for improved ballistics and cryptography, among other purposes.[9] A Boomer-influenced period drove later advancements. In 1975, Charles M. (Chuck) Eastman describes a "building description system" that would act as a "design coordinator and analyzer, providing a single integrated data base for visual and quantitative analyses, for testing spatial conflicts and for drafting."[10] In the same year, Nicholas Negroponte, writing in *Soft Architecture Machines*, foresees a world consistent with a Boomer-driven concern for equity and values, one with the "possibility of everybody having the opportunity to live in a man-made environment that responds to and is 'meaningful' for him or her . . . provid[ing] to everyone a quality of architecture most closely approximated in indigenous architecture (architecture without architects)."[11] Then head of MIT's Media Lab, Negroponte anticipates three potentials for the computer based on the responsiveness he describes: (1) the computer as designer, (2) the computer as a partner to the novice with a self-interest, and (3) the computer as a physical environment that "knows me."[12] If the Millennial Age is an archetypal echo of the previous era that spawned digital computing, Millennials' practical mindedness, their unprecedented networking, and their reliance on all things digital can launch Eastman's and Negroponte's projections into a limitless connectivity to the billions of assets that Bernstein describes.

But the promise of connectivity comes with consequences yet unforeseen, ones that may profoundly disrupt many of architecture's traditions. Through sheer volume, twenty-first-century connectivity will induce a form of nomadicity that will cause disruption, with its double edge of innovation and obsolescence. While remaining largely neutral about its positive or negative effects, the computer scientists Erkki Patokorpi and Franck Tétard use the terms "ubiquity," "fluidity," and "metaspace" to describe nomadicity's impacts.[13] In their lexicon, an era of connectivity breeds ubiquity, the linkage of various distributed intelligent computing and heterogeneous communication units. This permits a fluidity that ruptures spatial and temporal contexts, creating "anywhere, anytime" situations that hold potential to be enriched by additional virtual layers accessible to multiple contextual factors. Ubiquity ultimately leads to the formation of metaspaces, the dominant yet transient reference points where "someone" is in "control of the relations between the different spaces of cyberspace."[14] As exciting as these abstractions may be to some, the chaos of ubiquity, rupture of context, and especially the question of who controls metaspaces unsettles others. Given their digital nature, Millennials are the likeliest to embrace if not accelerate this disruption, leaving others to catch up or be left behind. These abstractions of cyberspace correspond to the profound disruptions of the "electronic agora" depicted by William Mitchell, Negroponte's successor as director of the Media Lab. In his 1996 book, *City of Bits*, Mitchell describes the fragmentation implied in the double entendre of the title as inducing a nomadicity that "subverts, displaces, and radically redefines our notions of gathering place, community, and urban life"[15]; in other words, nomadicity will atomize the whole scope of architecture's domain.

The disruption of Millennial nomadicity will likely spread to all the spatial, temporal, and organizational elements of architectural practice, permanently antiquating the world of the gentleman professional presiding over his atelier. The natural progression of office transformations will lead to a point when firms (or whatever they will be called) will need to consider whether the office as physical space is necessary, optional, or simply irrelevant. This will generate many discussions as to whether the constant connectivity of social networks will ever replace the immediacy of office watercooler conversations, whether the nomadicity of Kathi Vian's recombinant freelancers will flatten the hierarchies of seniority, and if a web of online tutorials can ever replace the indelibility of teaching moments between young and old. Perhaps most disconcerting for digital immigrants is whether digital representation—which is capable of being projected anywhere at anytime—will replace the intimate iteration of communicating through hand drawing.

While any of these are warning enough, the possibility of another era beyond Bernstein's third may be soon on the horizon. While I save the bulk of my argument regarding an era of *automation* for Chapter 10, it bears describing here how Autodesk's Project Dreamcatcher, the software manufacturer's next generation of computational design, can formulate thousands of design options to satisfy specified objectives, including functional requirements, material type, manufacturability, performance criteria, cost restrictions, etc.[16] Another program, Modumate, was created by a Millennial-owned San Francisco startup that poses the question in its blog: "What would it feel like if you never had to draft again?"[17] Software such as Dreamcatcher and Modumate may become necessary tools for all Millennials, maximally defining what CAD, or computer *aided* design, effectively means. Using these tools will redefine design as selecting from multiple options, albeit options created by the architect's prompts. Dreamcatcher and Modumate may be the first steps of a digital encroachment on the architect's domain, when both the prompts and the decisions become automated, as Negroponte prophesied in 1975, and the computer becomes the designer.

Nomadicity in the Academy

The habits of Millennial digital nomads have disrupted the academy far more than the profession simply because Millennials have been present in academia longer. Whether nomadicity becomes a catalyst for innovation or an agent of obsolescence will depend largely on whether academic leaders can adapt. Given a Millennial presence in the academy for over a decade, advantage-seekers have already begun to apply methods that both correlate with Millennial values and anticipate their nomadic needs. These advances, however, have taken place in other units of the academy, not architecture. Millennial nomadism places the cohort at the center of a learning process wherein they expect the academy to serve them in a myriad of digitally enhanced ways on their own terms regarding place and time.

Richard Sweeney's characterization of Millennials as trending toward selectivity, flexibility, and convenience reveals different aspects of their desire to customize education. While Millennials express an overwhelming preference for experiential learning, which takes advantage of a long evolutionary arc that began with John Dewey, a tendency toward nomadism at times seem paradoxical. If Millennials prefer a teaching environment that involves groups of students collaborating on a project that progressively yields practical results, how can that be accomplished aspatially and asynchronously? How can common goals be achieved with everyone working nomadically?

Online Learning

Online learning rests at the core of Millennial Age educational nomadism. A digital transformation of the correspondence courses that evolved in the nineteenth century, online learning appeals to a Millennial desire for flexibility and convenience, and its enrollment continues to grow.[18] Yet despite its seeming popularity, if given the option, Millennials express in polls that they would choose another form of course delivery (if it is on their terms, of course). In response, many institutions offer a practice known as "convergence," which means providing the same material online as in the classroom. Taking a course of this type, a student can either view the lectures online or show up for the class, submitting course deliverables throughout. In convergence classes, as long as they perform well on tests, students can never physically attend class and still get an A.

Hybrid learning represents a compromise of sorts between the convenience of the online course and the immediacy of experiential learning. Often referred to as the "flipped classroom,"[19] this pedagogical model delivers course lectures online, reserving class time for the exercises and projects a student formerly did as homework. Given that students have had time to digest the material (and with the instructor able to verify that they've seen it), discussions held in the classroom are more interactive. Hybrid learning appeals directly to a Millennial preference for combining the practical and collaborative. Advanced forms of hybrid learning include assessment in the form of quizzes at the end of each online tutorial. Instructors are able to see whether online materials have been viewed, and based on overall performance, they can decide which subject matter needs to be focused on in class. An even more advanced form, known as "adaptive learning," analyzes student results to determine deficiencies and custom tailors future study by automatically reassigning failed modules with more remedial problem sets. Adaptive learning continues until a learner achieves an adequate level of competency. The hybrid model re-centers the classroom, displacing the instructor from the dominant position in the front to become more hands-on in a collaborative and project-oriented manner. It also compels students to be less passive, allowing them to take more responsibility for their own education with a greater impetus to experiment.[20]

The element of online learning that may prove to be more revolutionary has less to do with learning than with its assessment. Online "badges," akin to the merit badges of youth scouting programs, describe a learner's specific achievements through the use of detailed metadata. Associated with the accumulation of certain knowledge, a badge's metadata reveals relevant information: what organization issues the badge; what has to be accomplished to earn it; scores on tests, or the tests themselves; and it can also include a portfolio of classwork. A badge provides the date when a course was taken and can be programmed to expire. If new knowledge develops in a subject area, the badge can also require supplemental learning to remain current. While badges can assess offline accomplishments, assessments would have to be taken online to maintain objectivity and transparency.[21]

Badges stand poised to disrupt the credentialing through diplomas and transcripts that has been the monopoly of higher education. Kevin Carey writes how this system had become "so archaic and obscure that colleges themselves didn't trust what college diplomas and transcripts had to say . . . [Professional schools] required people with bachelor's degrees to take standardized multiple-choice tests as part of their application. A bunch of As on the transcript wasn't enough to grant you acceptance. Who really knew what they meant? Colleges also adopted a guilty-until-proven-innocent approach to credits earned from other colleges."[22]

Badges were first conceived by the open-source Mozilla Foundation, which developed the free web browser Firefox as an alternative to Microsoft's monopolistic Explorer browser. In the same libertarian spirit, Mozilla designed badges to be portals for an open-ended amount of data controlled by no central authority other than their owner. Once it established basic protocols, Mozilla sponsored a contest to see who could create the most interesting badges. Some universities participated, but most submissions came from organizations such as Disney-Pixar, Intel, the Smithsonian, and NASA, among others. To date, universities that have adopted badges include Carnegie Mellon for their computer science department and the University of California, Davis, for their interdisciplinary major in sustainable agriculture and food systems.[23]

Badges could have many applications in architectural education. They can provide evidence that a student is technically proficient, something accreditation teams struggle sometimes to find evidence of. Badges can provide the necessary proof that a student has the knowledge to design a certain kind of building. For example, if a studio focuses on a concrete building, an instructor could verify the knowledge of each student regarding relevant systems and assign other modules as required. Badges certify skills, whether in design technology or computer language. After graduation, they can become part of the exam process and continuing education. And in a manner similar to how LEED accredits professionals, badges can provide a way to distinguish oneself in a crowded marketplace.

In adopting online learning, a student can take advantage of the potential of badges to place them in control of their education and the certifications associated with proving experience. Kevin Carey describes how badges "will allow people to control and display information about themselves in new and powerful ways, by assembling credible evidence of knowledge and skills gained in a variety of contexts—in college, in the workforce, in life . . . The digital learning environments themselves will be built to make evidence of learning sophisticated and abundant instead of obscure. Educational identities will become deep, discoverable, mobile and secure."[24]

Social Networks

While most can accept online courses as a form of learning, the educational value of social networks leaves many deeply skeptical. Social networks represent yet another form of nomadism disrupting education. In the mainstream, they have expanded connectivity to establish entirely new or expanded forms of community. Although it has been widely adopted by older generations, social networking remains native to the Millennial mindset as the generation continually pioneers each new iteration, from Facebook to Instagram to Snapchat. As social networks have evolved, they have become ever more specific to behavior or purpose. For those seeking mates, social applications designed for portable devices cater to availability (Cupid), gender preference (Grindr), and even those seeking extramarital affairs (Ashley Madison). In the professional world, an active LinkedIn page is essential, and ResearchGate automatically informs academic colleagues in the sciences of common interests.

Education writer Roger McHaney describes how social networks influence education as a form of "connectivism." McHaney discusses connectivism in relation to constructivist learning, as described by David Kolb, Jean Piaget, and others, in which learners actively *construct* their understanding based on how new experiences test prior knowledge. Constructivist learning is often synonymous with the experiential learning that Millennials favor, as a constructivist learner's experience forms his or her core values. Connectivism accepts the innate nomadism of individual experiential learning as a discrete node; when networked with others, the learner is publicized to peers.[25] McHaney develops his ideas from those first articulated by George Siemens in 2004, just as Millennials were first graduating college. Notable among Siemens's connectivist principles are those aligning with Millennial values, such as (1) "learning and knowledge rests in diversity of opinions," (2) "nurturing and maintaining connections is needed to facilitate continual learning," and (3) the "ability to see connections between fields, ideas, and concepts is a core skill."[26] In the Millennial Age, Siemens considers connectivism a necessity and not an option. The vast amount of information the internet has made available requires a collective effort to absorb it. While traditional methods may have sufficed when information was scarce or finite, in a rapidly changing world, "decision-making is itself a learning process. Choosing what to learn and the meaning of incoming information is seen through the lens of a shifting reality."[27]

Within architectural education, social networks remain an unexploited resource and can provide a virtual extension of the classroom and studio with information organized according to topic, project, need, etc.[28] A Millennial tendency toward collaboration amidst the self-enforcing trust of an online presence makes social networks' application open-ended. I have observed my Millennial teaching colleague, Simon McGown, using Slack, a cloud-based, collaborative software that serves as an organization and information gathering tool. Slack allows nomadism to augment the in-person studio through social media behaviors such as publicly adding a "reaction" (not unlike Facebook's "like" option or the emojis of Instagram), to "comment" on content posted by fellow peers and professors alike, or to communicate privately via "direct messages." As an advanced form of student-centered learning, McHaney advocates that students form their own personal learning networks (PLNs), which provide a persistent and relevant network of community learning that reaches interested people and shares information outside the classroom. Students can initially become PLN consumers by linking to and using existing information, and as they become stronger and their expertise grows, they become PLN producers by creating and sharing new knowledge.[29] Following the progression of learning from traditional methods to connectivism, McHaney describes the changing role of the educator. In this progression, *instructivism* first values the teacher as an expert and lecturer, *constructivism* later shifts the teacher's role to guide and facilitator, and *connectivism* casts the teacher as a combination of master artist, network administrator, and curator.[30]

Games

A penchant for digital games is a hallmark of tech-savvy Millennials. For the youngest, playing a video game may have been a first memory. Games appeal to the Millennial desires for experience, collaboration, and a stimulating way to flex their confidence. During his many focus group sessions, Richard Sweeney would anecdotally describe his own observation that the only time Millennials suspend their multitasking is when playing a digital game. No text message or phone call could distract them from the chase, or being chased, or from building a new city.

The application of gaming to education and business coincided with the first Millennials graduating high school. With his 2001 book, *Digital Game-Based Learning*, Marc Prensky (who coined the term "digital native" the same year) launched a publishing career in advocating for gaming for Millennials based on his own combined experiences in education and business.[31] Digital games grow out of an extensive tradition of experiential learning, again going back to Dewey but also with the strong influence of Piaget.[32] In an educational environment, games provide a kind of "stealth learning," where focus is on the game while the ultimate yield is self-knowledge through experience.[33] Games also mirror good pedagogy, offering opportunities to progressively solve problems without the bite of real-life consequences, something game educators refer to as "scaffolded learning."[34] Overall, games respond to the Millennials' mandate to become engaged and active participants in their educational process.[35] Games have evolved to a level of consistent protocols known as the MDA framework: a game's *mechanics* are the rules that govern at the level of data representation and algorithms, its *dynamics* describe the system of player inputs and outputs over time affecting mechanics, and its *aesthetics* make it fun, promoting desirable emotional responses that encourage player interaction with the game system.[36]

Communication and education scholar Deborah Lieberman describes the learning benefits of digital games,[37] many of which align with Millennial characteristics. Like their analog antecedents, digital games are by definition experiential, an activity that encourages learning by doing. Computer games are participatory and engaging, with customized, rapid feedback that wards off distraction and makes one pay close attention. A game's consequences are not abstract or hypothetical but represented in the game directly. When played with others, games are collaborative, becoming a social medium. By giving positive feedback like awarding points, power, or rank for thoughtful planning and decision-making, games can build confidence; one gains self-assurance in order to succeed (and survive). Lieberman goes so far as to argue that even when players interact with virtual personae, a player's ego and self-image are so invested in the experience that game characters can serve as role models for players, their simulated interactions and emotional responses providing a form of social training.[38]

As they have evolved, digital games have not only become increasingly sophisticated in their use of virtual space, the formation of space has become the primary challenge among a popular subgenre known as "city-building games," also known as construction and management simulations (CMS). In these challenges, instead of vanquishing an enemy, a player's goal is to build within the context of an ongoing process. As their understanding and ability to control the process increases, players achieve more success, with periodic crises, such as fires or earthquakes, continually testing their skills. While other games' success hinge on high-speed action or violence, CMS games appeal to a broad audience precisely because action and violence are *not* principal components.[39] While the stalwart among CMS games is *SimCity*, first developed in 1989, competitors have emerged, some aimed at specific audiences: *Fortnite* is survival-themed, *Clockwork Empires* appeals to the hybrid nostalgia aesthetic of steampunk, and *Dwarf Fortress* mines a seemingly constant cultural obsession with the elfin world.[40] Microsoft's purchase of *Minecraft*—the city-building game enormously popular with children—in 2014 for $2.5 billion indicates how profitable and pervasive games focused on building have become.[41]

It is within the context of this fertile environment of digital game development, which has specific applicability to the built world in the Millennial Age, that it seems rather surprising that so little of gaming has migrated to architectural education. While some inroads have been made—the book *Space Time Play: Computer Games, Architecture and Urbanism: The Next Level* was published in 2007,[42] the Savannah College of Art and Design received a $40,000 award from NCARB to develop interactive games for its professional practice curriculum in 2012,[43] and the University of Portsmouth School of Architecture in the UK developed an online scenario-based game to teach practice management in 2014[44]—the incorporation of gaming into architecture has been minor despite continual chatter at academic conferences.[45]

The slow penetration of architectural education by the nomadic trends of online learning, social media, and digital games indicates how inattentive the academy has been to Millennial tendencies despite the early advantage in the use of digital technology that architecture once held. The reasons for this are perplexing, and there may be many causes. The association of online courses with for-profit online universities, some of dubious distinction, has been difficult to expunge, even after elite schools began offering content online.[46] Another may be online education's linkage to the traditional correspondence courses it grew out of, a course delivery method never taken seriously by architecture because of the perceived difficulty of applying it to studio work. The crude products of early web-based education may also have caused many to ignore more recent examples that have benefitted from bandwidth increases and other improvements. The end result is that other professional programs far outpace architecture in online opportunities: as of 2018, online engineering programs numbered 2,072 and business 5,215, while architecture counted only 36, with only 4 offering professional degrees.[47] The architectural academy's related nonacceptance of social media and gamification may be from a desire to insulate the all-or-nothing charrette environment from the addictive procrastination social media and games have caused in the general population.[48]

Unencumbered by any prior prejudice, and having only experienced the practical benefits of online learning, social media, and digital gaming, Millennials will follow a path of greatest convenience to expand their use of these technologies. Treated as innovation, architecture's adaptation of these disruptive nomadic technologies can begin an iterative process toward its ultimate potential benefit. Gravitating toward a hybrid and adaptive transformation of the ancillary courses of architectural education—technology, history, and practice—with some even taught through games, can focus resources on a studio enhanced by a connectivism linking it more directly to knowledge learned as well as the billions of assets of the internet. A laissez-faire approach, or outright resistance, leaves a pedagogy that will only grow increasingly unaffordable and less flexible. In a student-centered world where knowledge can be effectively transferred outside traditional methods, Millennials may even find the detour of convenience that leads outside the physical academy. California and New York, the two states with the highest numbers of registered architects, still allow licensure without an accredited degree. The first Millennial architect of prodigious talent with a libertarian streak, one who self-teaches online and makes a name for herself, may incent others to follow this shunpike and avoid the toll road of accredited architectural education entirely.

Generational Case Study: Student-Centered Academic Models

In the previous chapter, I used a generational framework to trace experiential learning from the course corrections beginning in the transcendental era, when Horace Mann liberated students from the pews of religious education, up through its contemporary embrace by Millennials. Within that timeline, John Dewey placed students at the center of their own education, a baby step toward the nomadism that digital media in the twenty-first century now affords. Next I will discuss Black Mountain College and Goddard College, two schools that formed during the dual crises of the Depression and World War II, applying Dewey's principles on student-centered early learning to higher education. I follow this with a description of Minerva, an online university that embodies a resurgence of those values at the beginning of the Millennial Age. Minerva's embrace of digital nomadism offers an example of what a future nomadic school of architecture can be.

Using the term "nomadic" to describe Millennial student-centeredness exposes an ambiguity regarding the term. One of the signals of Paul Taylor's "aha" moment, when a new generation becomes recognizable, occurs upon expression of their distinguishing characteristics, which separate them from the previous cohort. Given this thinking, how can Millennials be nomadic and at the same time reject the values of their archetypally nomadic Generation X predecessors? Many writers on generations, such as Jean Twenge, argue that generations gradually transition, and while Strauss and Howe claim the transition to be more abrupt, they concede that certain strands of one generation carry forth into the next and that this may make it seem gradual. Nomadicity, especially as enhanced by digital culture, is one of those strands. The distinction goes like this: if the Millennial is tagged as the "good kid," distinct from the Generation X "bad kid," and the former's collective tendencies counter the latter's grunge-era free agency, Millennials and Generation X can still share an allegiance to the hyperpractical ethos of nomadic computing. This, in part, unifies the two generations against the value-driven conflicts of Boomers still mired in the trenches of culture wars and partisan gridlock. If Millennials are digital natives, then Generation X are first-wave digital immigrants, both cohorts availing themselves of the selectivity, flexibility, convenience, and customization that nomadicity offers. A subtle distinction may be that while Generation X nomads are the true go-it-alone "lone wolves" that Jeff Gordinier describes, Millennial nomads are more tribal, hunter-gatherer types, operating as individuals yet still tethered to their "pack" by social media.

Black Mountain

Black Mountain College was the concept of John A. Rice, a brilliant, mercurial, and peripatetic scholar who stormed off from the conservative Rollins College in 1933 to use John Dewey's principles of progressive education to form Black Mountain. Rice's application of Dewey foreshadows the contemporary Millennial values of collaboration, practicality, and public purpose.[49] Its opening coincided with the rise of Adolf Hitler, the closing of the Bauhaus, and the subsequent persecution of artists and intellectuals across Europe. Rice was fortunate to lure many of them—outcasts, like himself—to a valley deep in the Appalachian Mountains to incubate a new form of pedagogy that blurred the distinction between faculty and student. Two of Rice's first refugee hires were Anni and Josef Albers, who applied a version of Bauhaus pedagogy inflected by Deweyan principles. And although they did not know it at the time of its founding, Black Mountain provided nomads like the Albers shelter from the growing chaos that would soon envelope the world.

Black Mountain's seclusion fostered a strong sense of individualism and creative intensity that imprinted on its students. Its pedagogy stressed that the study and practice of art was an indispensable aspect of a student's general liberal arts education and hence his or her identity. Its self-reliance—it was owned, operated, and democratically governed by the faculty—served as an example for students. All members of the community, faculty and students alike, participated in its operation, including farmwork, construction projects, and kitchen duty. It was within this sequestration that architect A. Lawrence Kocher and Bauhaus student Howard Dearstyne conceptualized a radically interdisciplinary "architectural center" in 1943. Kocher would later design Black Mountain's Bauhaus-inspired building based on a Walter Gropius and Marcel Breuer collaboration that had previously been rejected because of cost.

Black Mountain fostered an environment that attracted an extraordinarily diverse group of faculty and created maverick spirits, many who would be extremely influential later in the century. These included African American painter Jacob Lawrence, who went on to create a cycle of paintings that memorialized the black diaspora from the American South, and Willem de Kooning, who later helped launch the abstract expressionist movement. Also drawn to Black Mountain's ethos, composer John Cage and his life-long partner and collaborator, Merce Cunningham, went on to profoundly impact music and dance, respectively. Two students, the painters Robert Rauschenberg and Cy Twombly, would have influential careers, in part by distancing themselves from the generation of abstract expressionists during the upheavals of the 1960s. Many others, including Kenneth Noland, Ben Shahn, Franz Kline, Arthur Penn, and Dorothea Rockburne, as well as those not-so-famous, carried Black Mountain's predigital badge to impact the world in important ways.[50]

Significant to twentieth-century architectural history, it was at Black Mountain in 1949 that the first large-scale prototype of the now famous geodesic dome was created. Buckminster Fuller, working with students in a practical, collaborative spirit toward a broader purpose, iterated its form first using venetian blind scraps and later aluminum tubing.[51] In the fertile environment of divergent but supporting disciplinary leaders such as Cage, Cunningham, and de Koonig, and assisted by future artists such as Irving Penn, Fuller could incubate an idea that had been in his mind for years.

Despite successes such as Fuller's, the school could not sustain itself, and after twenty-seven years of operation, Black Mountain closed for financial reasons in 1956. It seemed almost to be the singular flare of a generation, one commemorated in a museum in nearby Asheville.

Goddard

An institution with values similar to those of Black Mountain, Goddard College has not only survived a succession of upheavals, but continues to gain momentum as it transitions through the current one. Located in Plainfield,

Vermont, Goddard was originally founded as a Universalist secondary school "seminary" in 1863 but by the time of the Great Depression faced financial hardship. Under the leadership of Royce (Tim) Pitkin, Goddard reorganized according to a Deweyan model similar to Black Mountain's. Alarmed by European fascism, Pitkin fused the liberal values of the seminary with Dewey's belief that interactive, self-directed education could help build civil, democratic societies.[52] When it opened in 1938, the school stressed experiential learning, prioritizing discussion in classrooms, incorporating practical work, and developing a system of student self-governance. The school placed an emphasis on using a student's full experiences to personalize a curriculum, beginning with each student being asked the question: What do you want to know?[53] In search of a more elemental education, Goddard had no grades, written exams, required courses, credits, or any of the trappings of traditional colleges of the time.[54]

As the consciousness-raising of the 1960s began another period of transition, the school pivoted for the new era in two ways that would later prove significant. The first was the establishment of a "low-residency" adult-education program in 1963 under the direction of Evalyn Bates, Goddard's director of adult education and community services. Bates applied her master's thesis from the University of Chicago to create a program, the first of its kind in the US, in which students would study at home and then come to campus for one intense weeklong period.[55] The next year, Pitkin launched the second significant initiative, a conference held at Goddard to instigate the creation of the Union for Research and Experimentation in Higher Education, which eventually grew to include twenty-two institutions including Bard, Antioch, and Sarah Lawrence. This consortium focused on nontraditional students and on the era's penchant for socially relevant research conducted in an interdisciplinary manner. It was also a vehicle for Goddard to export its low-residency model to other institutions.[56]

Both initiatives fostered a new form of interaction between student and academy, propelling Goddard to prominence. Relevant to architecture, David Sellers brought his experience as one of the first students to participate in the Yale Building Project to leading Goddard's design and construction program from 1969 to 1977.[57] One of the first in the US, the program added three student-built structures to the campus. While Black Mountain drew influential figures in the visual arts, Goddard attracted literary talent, with the novelists Raymond Carver, Richard Ford, and John Irving all spending time there. Amid this fertile experiential environment, Goddard graduates from this period achieved acclaim in the literary and performing arts included the playwright David Mamet, the novelist Walter Mosley, the actor William H. Macy, and the guitarist for the rock band Phish, Trey Anastasio.

By the late 1990s, Goddard's low-residency programs continued to expand with the advent of online education, but its more mainstream degree offerings began to see enrollment declines. To increase its residential class size, the college discounted tuition and decreased its selectivity, but this proved no remedy. With decreased funds, and because the constant occupancy of the popular low-residency programs allowed no downtime, Goddard lacked the time more than the resources to maintain the campus. As a result, Goddard's physical campus frayed, and two of the buildings constructed under Sellers's initiative fell into disrepair, eventually becoming uninhabitable. Facing deep financial uncertainty, Goddard's board voted in 2002 to close the residential college and focus undivided attention and resources on its still vital low-residency programs.

Critics declared the Goddard experiment dead; to some, it was a victim of hippie excess and lack of rigor. The ruins of the design-build program standing in evidence seemed to symbolize the plight of the college: erected with youthful exuberance out of whatever materials, but with little follow-through. To the surprise of many, Goddard's bold turnaround strategy proved skeptics wrong, and by 2010 it returned to solvency based on the strength of its low-residency programs. Goddard went on to expand its operations far afield, first to an old military facility in Port Townsend, Washington, and then in 2011 to the highly diverse Seattle neighborhood of Columbia City, where it offers instruction bilingually.

Minerva

Minerva is a four-year undergraduate college that admitted its first class in 2014 and is referred to euphemistically as the "online Ivy." It is the brainchild of Ben Nelson, who sold his web-based company, Snapfish, to start the college following principles that radically criticize the traditional university. Minerva caters to Millennials' nomadic tendencies to build on their collaborative and broadly purposeful desires.

At Minerva there is no campus per se; students take all classes online while living in cities around the world. Students in classes of less than twenty synchronously join online using video in intense and fast-paced sessions that include quizzes, projects, and discussions to keep them fully engaged. Minerva faculty employ a carefully designed curriculum for students to master lifelong skills rather than subjects. All Minerva students initially take four "cornerstone courses" that cut across the sciences and humanities to introduce core concepts and alternative ways of thinking. Afterwards they choose to join one of Minerva's five virtual colleges: social sciences, natural sciences, computational sciences, arts and humanities, and business, to develop discipline-specific critical thinking skills. Minerva's advanced software platform is highly adaptive, allowing a professor to pivot discussion based on responses or innate skills and custom-build seminar groups or project teams. Minerva intentionally recruits students who are "uneven," meaning really good at one thing, to maximize the potential for peer-to-peer learning. Minerva's software evaluates teaching methods and adjusts throughout a semester. It even restricts the instructor from droning on.[58]

Minerva enrolled its first class of seventy students in the fall of 2014 from 2,500 applicants (an acceptance rate of 2.8, lower than both Harvard and Stanford; several enrolling students declined admission to Ivy League schools).[59] Students spend their first year in San Francisco, followed by a rotation around the world: Buenos Aires and Berlin in the second year, followed by Bangalore, Seoul, Istanbul, and London for the final two. Living together in leased residence halls in those cities, students cook for themselves. For their seminars, they meet in libraries, museums, or parks (although communal attendance is not required) for a limited period, leaving them time to explore the host city. Exposure to global culture is essential to the experience, both through different locations and classmates. Minerva's student body is highly international: its first two classes hail from thirty-five countries, with only 10 percent from the US.[60]

By definition, Minerva is both physically and digitally nomadic. Like a hiker leaving for a long trip, everything it "holds" is carefully considered, leaving it lean and supple. Without any of the appurtenances of traditional universities such as buildings, sports teams, and tenured faculty, Minerva keeps its costs per student below $23,000 per year, including tuition and housing (but not travel). All a student needs to participate is broadband access and a computer enabled with audio and video. From a pedagogical standpoint, Minerva encourages students to rely on free web-delivered coursework such as MOOCs. Despite its wandering to different countries, Minerva offers no language training; those courses can be taken online from other providers.

Minerva is an educational experiment that places the student at the center of his or her own educational sphere, albeit in a highly controlled environment. While in some ways, the school's watchfulness seems like a continuation of the helicopter parenting of Millennials, Minerva does not coddle. Its teaching platform, carefully developed by a founding dean Stephen Kosslyn, a cognitive psychologist and neuroscientist previously from Harvard and Stanford, provides multiple opportunities for students to excel. But if they fail to perform to Minerva's standards, they are asked to leave. The Minerva system is designed to coax out the highest level of critical thinking skills necessary to be successful in the twenty-first century. Its critics have denounced it, predicting that Minerva's business model is unsustainable and that it will go the way of other online programs. Minerva indeed dipped into its venture capital funding to subsidize its inaugural class, pledging to pay every admitted student's tuition for four years, as well as free housing in San Francisco for the first year. Skeptics question whether it can sustain itself after its initial generosity. Others like the *Atlantic*'s Graeme Wood ponder the consequences of the opposite outcome:

> If Minerva fails, it will lay off its staff and sell its office furniture and never be heard from again. If it succeeds, it could inspire a legion of entrepreneurs, and a whole category of legacy institutions might have to liquidate. One imagines tumbleweeds rolling through abandoned quads and wrecking balls smashing through the windows of classrooms left empty by students who have plugged into new online platforms.[61]

Black Mountain, Goddard, and Minerva share a spirit of experimentation in challenging the status quo of their time. In their own way, each espouses the self-reliance of nomads. The values of practicality, collaboration, and public purpose join the schools archetypally across generations; Black Mountain created an artistic environment for fertile collaboration with a broad impact, Goddard stayed true to its original student-centered mission while at the same time enriching itself through adaptation during two generational course corrections, and Minerva has created a bold new format that responds to technological change in how it provides for the critical needs of its students. Each institution offers a template for how architectural education can absorb the impact of nomadism to its ultimate benefit. Its many successes aside, Black Mountain's may ultimately be a cautionary message of how generational disquiet can lead to undoing. Goddard's low-residency educational legacy[62] provides a predigital history rich for examination as online education evolves, its programs in creative writing and fine arts paving the way for the Boston Architectural College's Master of Architecture program, the first primarily online program in the country to be accredited by the National Architectural Accrediting Board. With the continual advancement of distance-learning formats, especially those that blend some form of concentrated experiential learning in assorted contexts, it is a matter of time before a school takes full advantage of the physically and digitally nomadic precedent that Minerva sets to teach architecture. The question remains less which school it will be, but whether it is a school that once taught architecture along traditional lines.

The three academies examined here all emphasize student-centered learning, which, through a generational lens, places nomadism in a broad historical context. This provides contemporary insight into how the nomadic tendencies of digitally native Millennials will affect future architectural practice and teaching. The adaptive strategists in the profession who apply the "anywhere, anytime" computing of nomadism will likely encounter a countervailing resistance seeking to preserve architecture's traditional physical and organization legacy. A parallel digital nomadism in the academy will seek to advance student-centered learning through online learning, social media, and digital games, indulging a Millennial blend of convenience and pleasure that challenges a longstanding tradition of focused work. Many positive Millennial characteristics naturally agree with those of architecture. And while some in architecture are adapting to the generation's digital nomadic tendencies, others remain hesitant or outright resistant, despite architecture's historic early embrace of computing. The next chapter dwells on those Millennial characteristics that prompt widespread concern, especially for architecture, given that those tendencies leave its practice and teaching highly vulnerable. Applying a generational historiography reveals a challenger to architecture that seems to not share the same vulnerabilities, a challenger that is very close and has been around for a very long time.

CHAPTER 9

An Accelerated Tempo
Millennial Time and Territory

> The children now love luxury; they have bad manners,
> contempt for authority; they show disrespect for elders
> and love chatter in place of exercise. . . . They contra-
> dict their parents, chatter before company, gobble up
> dainties at the table, cross their legs, and tyrannize
> their teachers.
>
> **HISTORICALLY MISATTRIBUTED TO SOCRATES**

The Millennial generation treats time in an unprecedented manner that renders vulnerable the architectural profession and academy. Their accelerated, restructured, and overlapped use of time creates tension with employers and educators alike. Since Millennials became adults, numerous studies have examined the origins and degrees of their accelerated expectations, the cohort's reappraisal of work and leisure, and the growing phenomenon of multitasking. Previously I described the positive aspects of the AIAS Studio Culture Task Force document; here I summarize the report's darker critiques and its proposition for how to balance concerns about Millennials with architecture's traditions. By establishing curricula aligned with Millennials' preferences, institutions such as Stanford's d.school and Olin College of Engineering teach design thinking skills that may embolden professionals to challenge architecture's traditional turf. Tracing design thinking's development according to generational dynamics uncovers catalytic moments that are relevant to understanding contemporary disruptions. This discipline's antecedents once posed a significant challenge to architecture's domain. In the Millennial Age, its descendants are again poised to encroach on architecture's traditional territory.

An Accelerated Tempo

Millennials bring their expectations for an accelerated tempo of interaction to their work environments. Conditioned by frequent and often positive support from parents, teachers, and coaches, Millennials typically anticipate professional performance feedback that is as frequent and encouraging. Many also expect these reviews to lead to regular and sustained professional advancement. These expectations parallel the world of social networks with constant feedback loops allowing only "likes" and no "dislikes." With these fast-paced expectations, typical young professionals find the pace of traditional promotion tracks punctuated by annual reviews excruciatingly slow: "Millennials don't want annual reviews—they want ongoing conversations."[1] Reared on explicit directions and grading rubrics, the generation that Ron Alsop once called "trophy kids" has grown into "checklist kids," who prefer a clearly defined and scripted work life ordered by step-by-step directions and short-term deadlines.[2] Along with frequent feedback, Millennials also expect their work environments to meet the standards set in their previous internships or professional exposure programs, which often offered an overlapping range of experiences, including outside engagement through forms of community service.

Many Millennials parcel time between work and leisure based on several factors of their upbringing. With their parents telling them they can do anything they put their minds to, Millennials carefully delineate both their career and lifestyles. Having also seen their parents and relatives work long hours, endure frequent layoffs, and experience a historically high rate of divorce, many instead choose "making a life" over "making a living."[3] Reluctant to work significant overtime, even for higher pay, Millennials overwhelmingly strive to protect their quality of life. In 2010, Pew Research found that many more Millennials ranked "being a good parent" (52 percent) and "having a successful marriage" (30 percent) as higher priorities than "having a high-paying career" (15 percent) or "becoming famous" (1 percent).[4] "Making a life" also has Millennials gravitating toward meaningful work; a 2008 study by PricewaterhouseCoopers found that 88 percent of Millennials indicated they would seek an employer whose corporate social responsibility values matched their own.[5] While Millennial employees consistently request structure and direction in assignments, enabled by untethered technology, they also prefer the flexibility to complete tasks at a time and place of their choosing. While early writers on Millennials describe this preference for flexibility, more recent studies find

Millennials to be more accepting of traditional schedules, perhaps due to experiencing difficulty in finding work.

The overlap of time involving media, commonly referred to as multitasking, is a phenomenon Millennials came of age with and is endemic to their generation. In 2010, Millennials (eight to eighteen years of age) in one study spent 7.5 hours per day on media, almost an entire workday. More remarkable, they squeezed a total of ten hours and forty-five minutes of content into that same 7.5 hours, meaning that for approximately a third of that time, they absorbed content from more than one source.[6] All media—including TV, music/audio, computer, video games, print, and movies—are not alike, and the impact of multitasking on all forms of performance varies based on many factors. While researchers since the 1950s have consistently found that the ability to successfully undertake simultaneous tasks is limited, these capacities may be changing for Millennials, especially as students. Research in the 2000s began finding that multitasking did not always interfere with comprehension. In one study, researchers found that taking a written test while a video played in the background did not necessarily hinder subjects' overall cognition.[7] Another 2005 study reports Millennials claiming that multitasking actually helps them concentrate.[8] An ability to multitask may come with being a digital native, because, as Gary Small and Gigi Vorgan write, "the bombardment of digital stimulation on developing minds has taught [Millennials] to respond faster . . . they encode information differently than the older minds do."[9]

Vulnerability of Time: The Profession

Millennials' attitude toward time—whether it is accelerated, parceled, or overlapped—has been nothing short of radical, causing other generations to either stand by dumbfounded or protest loudly. Whether it is the cause or a symptom of a larger phenomenon, the Millennial approach to time usage has disrupted the workforce. Indeed, the first publications regarding Millennials emerging in the 2000s came from the business world, offering guidance about how to accommodate their largely unanticipated behaviors, and much of the debate on the validity of the Millennial profile comes from academic disciplines associated with management, such as psychology and sociology. Large strategy firms like Ernst & Young and Pricewaterhouse-Coopers have joined this fray, understanding the essential nature of workforce performance. While some employers have shrugged off any negative associations and others have seized upon Millennials' digital provenance to use them to "up-mentor" other employees, many others dwell on the potential damage to businesses and even entire occupations that Millennials' time usage will cause. Fueled by the sociological tendency to find fault with rising generations, many sanction Millennials by seeking to curtail their time-altering tendencies. Whether this faulting is valid or not, failure to either accept or adapt to these changes in attitude will have significant implications on professional practices such as architecture.

The confidence and outlook Millennials bring to the workplace often accompany expectations derived from their upbringing and education. Frequent interaction, when combined with Millennials' expectation of positive feedback that strongly indicates advancement, requires a significant investment on the part of those who manage them. And many managers may be reluctant to provide oversight at a level consistent with that of a helicopter parent. Whether all Millennials exhibit this behavior or it is exaggerated is irrelevant; for the most written about and studied generation in history, their reputation for having a sense of entitlement is something that all who deal with Millennials must evaluate in a broader context. The larger question is whether entitlement is something every emerging adult feels, which gives them the license to make their mark. Or has Millennial entitlement crossed a historical pathological line toward narcissism?

Since Millennials emerged as young adults in the early 2000s, Jean Twenge has questioned their exceptionalism. In recent coauthored books, she and her colleagues have escalated that skepticism to allegations of narcissism. Discounting Strauss and Howe and others as empirically unverified and thus unscientific, Twenge has sought to prove that differences between Millennials and their predecessors are not what other writers claim, and in most cases are the polar opposite. Twenge finds an overwhelmingly extrinsic rather than intrinsic generational priority among Millennials. (In Twenge's usage, extrinsic values refer to money, image, and fame, and intrinsic values are self-acceptance, affiliation, and community.)[10] The survey data Twenge accesses is a consistent series of questions asked of American teenagers going back to the 1970s. Rebuttals to Twenge focus on this age limitation, arguing that all adolescents of any generation will show narcissistic tendencies.[11] The 2012 study by Kali Trzesniewski and Brent Donnellan attempting to replicate Twenge's methods found little difference among teenagers from various generations and little correlation of the data to the Millennial countertrends that Twenge cites. The replicated study disputes the narcissist tag, and the null findings also suggest that late adolescence may be too early to discern generational characteristics that only consolidate later. Opening their academic paper with the misattributed Socrates quote that begins this chapter, the authors also introduce other biases that older generations may have in seeking to explain this inconsistency in findings.[12]

Polling organizations such as Pew Research have taken Twenge's counterpoint seriously and seem to have tested some of her assertions in more recent polls, revealing a shift that might be read as aligning closer to her concerns. For example, in 2010 Pew found 28 percent of Millennials to be trusting of others; by 2014 the number had dropped to 19 percent.[13] And at each year it was measured, the percentage was lower than older generations' results, suggesting the trusting, "good kid" persona of Millennials that was popularized by Strauss and Howe may have been misapplied. Yet in Pew's 2014 poll, a majority of Millennials (53 percent) supported a "bigger government providing more services," a result that was ten percentage points higher than Generation X respondents and over twenty points higher than Boomers, conveying that while they may be less trustful of individuals, Millennials support the collective.[14] In 2014, Pew also found that Millennials gave a lower priority to environmental issues than older generations, although the inclusion of gay rights and other newly added issues may have affected the answers.[15] Our own 2016 AIAS poll yielded similar results, although students in focus groups (who answered in similar percentages to the students in straw polls) offered an explanation: they claimed that environmental awareness was almost universal among their peers and always has been, but because gay rights was then an extremely topical issue, it was foremost in their minds. This caused them to prioritize it when answering, but they argued that in no way did it diminish their concerns for global climate change. Some also thought the question was confusingly worded and biased.

The shift occurring between the 2010 and 2014 Pew studies may also support Strauss and Howe's claim that generational profiles modulate when a parental majority shifts. While ambiguous or conflicting results may dull the sharpness of some Millennial characteristics, they seldom refute the distinctness of the generation as a whole. It should also come as little surprise that a generation that is the best educated and most driven by parental expectation, with prodigious digital skills and full of optimism, would find critics among older generations. And this bias could compel elders to look for labels to lessen Millennials' importance, or to seek any data discrepancy as proof that their entire generational characterization is without merit. When studying generations, one must remember that they are never monolithic, and as Karl Mannheim and his followers argue, are less a homogenous group and more a collection of distinct cohorts of the same age bound together in a conflict over issues. To better understand generational dynamics among architects, one must work through any interference that bias brings to be able to identify alignments and opportunities. Simultaneously, one must also be able to recognize those innate or perceived Millennial vulnerabilities that might compromise architecture if all the generations do not agree on future professional values.

Richard Sweeney has identified impatience among Millennials as largely driven by the tempo of the twenty-first century, with the instantaneousness of the internet outclassing other responses that move at the speed of analog culture. Millennials have grown to expect instant gratification and, by their own admission, have little tolerance for delays like waiting in line or dealing with other unproductive processes that are more than an inconvenience. In the workplace, Millennial impatience often results from their inflated expectations regarding pay and advancement. In a 2010 study, two-thirds of Millennials surveyed expected a promotion within fifteen months on their first job. They also anticipated an increase in salary averaging 63 percent over five years (compared to a standard average salary increase of less than 15 percent over the same time). The study also finds Millennials indicating "opportunities for advancement" as their foremost priority when deciding on an employer.[16] When they do not advance, Millennials become furious and feel they are wasting their time; they are typically accustomed to a constant progression of learning new skills quickly and moving on.

Moving on is the actualization of impatient behavior that most concerns professions such as architecture. A 2016 Gallup study finds that 21 percent of Millennials report changing jobs within the previous year, three times the rate of other generations. Gallup estimates this turnover costs the US economy $30.5 billion annually, and reports that 55 percent of Millennials are not engaged at work, which can also be damaging.[17] Ron Alsop describes how Millennials target firms where they can refine as many marketable skills as possible to then use as leverage to seek employment elsewhere. They cite these skills on application materials similar to the way "badges" are used, and have no issue listing multiple jobs during the same year on their resumes, something that would have been a red flag for previous generations. Millennial architects, like their larger cohort, seek as diverse an experience as possible. Their expectations include a trajectory for rapid advancement, flexible work routines, frequent positive performance feedback, and opportunities to engage in interesting or community-oriented work. Focus group respondents have cited failure of employers to satisfy these desires as reasons for job-hopping. And if finding themselves pigeonholed as a CAD operator, assigned to work on only one building or space type, or, perhaps most insidious, indentured within a culture of overtime work with a sweatshop mentality, a Millennial employee will often depart as soon as a better opportunity arises.

It is the culture of overtime that violates a Millennial's need to parcel aside time for nonwork pursuits. Millennials' focus on quality of life rejects the workaholic tendencies of their Boomer/Generation X parents. Excessive time demands encroach on Millennials' closeness to family and comparatively larger network of friends. It also impedes upon their opportunities to work in the community or to enjoy the "play as a reward for hard work" ethos they were brought up with. And for the oldest Millennials, a culture of overtime takes away from their greatest stated priority according to Pew: to be good parents and have a successful family. Female architects are particularly vulnerable to family pressures, which may be a major reason why many leave the profession. A 2015 survey found that while women make up 42 percent of graduates from accredited architecture programs, only 28 percent are on staff at the firms polled.[18] The life priorities expressed by Millennial architects in our 2016 AIAS survey reveal quality-of-life concerns greater than those found by Pew in the rest of the generation. Millennial architects ranked "being a good parent" a slightly higher priority than Millennials in general (AIAS: 55 percent; Pew: 52 percent), but "having a successful marriage" scored a remarkable forty percentage points higher (AIAS: 70 percent; Pew: 30 percent). And that the older architects surveyed prioritized these values at even higher percentages than did their Millennial colleagues may be a cohort effect, indicating how dear all architects hold a family life that is so challenged by the demands of the profession. Older architects listed "being a good parent" as a slightly higher priority than Millennials overall (57 percent to 55 percent) and "having a successful marriage" as thirteen percentage points higher (83 percent to 70 percent). That Millennial AIAS respondents also gave a much higher priority than Pew's Millennials to "having a high-paying career" (AIAS: 40 percent; Pew: 15 percent) may be a similar indication that they desire more what they expect not to have. Given the comparatively low pay of architects compared to other professions, that older architects indicated a similar prioritization suggests that a desire for what one lacks is endemic to the profession.

To firm managers, Millennials' aversion to overtime, when combined with their prevailing impatience, suggests an unwillingness to put in the time it takes to design effectively. Their propensity to overlap their time by multitasking only compounds these misgivings, as multitaskers seem to be prone to distraction, unfocused, and shallow. For many in architecture, allowing this form of behavior in a profession so detail oriented is of great concern. Accompanying the criticism of multitasking, one increasingly finds correlation between it and the rise and treatment of attention deficit hyperactivity disorder (ADHD), which like narcissism, superficially seems like a Millennial-related affliction.[19]

Impatience, commitment, and distraction are frontline issues of an immense cultural shift occurring, which Nicholas Carr describes in his book *The Shallows: What the Internet Is Doing to Our Brains*: how "calm, focused, undistracted, the linear mind is being pushed aside by a new kind of mind that wants and needs to take it in and dole out information in short, disjointed, often overlapping bursts—the faster, the better."[20] Yet, as Carr was writing his book in 2009, the National Endowment for the Arts showed an increase in literary reading, with the most significant growth by Millennials (ages 18–24 in 2008), who had gone from a 20 percent decline in 2002 to a 21 percent increase by 2008.[21] That this finding came at the same time that Millennial reading of newspapers had declined suggests a far more complicated transition. Undoubtedly, the shift Carr describes will take time and will not be a zero-sum struggle in which the new fully supplants the old. Some hybrid of the linear mind enhanced by the juggling thinker will likely emerge. The identification of any perceived vulnerabilities will be better addressed through accommodation, adaptation, and acceptance rather than more draconian measures to police the professional environment of all multitasking by forbidding technology use, as some academics have tried to do.[22] In competitive academic and professional environments, that certain Millennials self-medicate, without medical oversight, for their perceived ADHD crosses a line into the dystopian. This should prompt the broader architectural community to question the expectations that might drive such behavior.[23]

Vulnerability of Time: The Academy

The 2002 Studio Culture Task Force report allowed the first wave of Millennials to announce their positive and optimistic values, which I outline in Chapter 7. Here I dwell on the less rosy part of that document: the generation's indictment of the darker side to the architectural academy that perpetuates myths leading to "emotional, physical, and cultural deprivation."[24] The task force issued the report in memory of one of its own who died colliding with a truck after leaving a studio sleep-deprived, and compares architectural education to a fraternity. In declaring that its hazing rituals (which it alleges *every* school practices) had gone too far, the task force argues that the myth that hazing somehow binds a brotherhood together should join the "ideas of the past." The report stresses that these sorts of myths form behaviors and patterns, described below, which make students prone to abuses that will perpetuate throughout their careers.

By emphatically claiming that students should live balanced lives, the 2002 task force predates the Millennial emphasis on parceling and structuring time that management writers were then just beginning to fixate on. The report seeks this life balance by creating a new demarcation specific to architecture between "making a life" and "making a living." It stridently rejects myths that "students should not have a life outside of architecture school" and that "architectural education should require personal and physical sacrifice," ultimately undermining the fraternal condition that "students must devote themselves to studio in order to belong to the architecture community." In undermining the foundation of a culture of expected overtime, it rejects the myths that "the best design ideas only come in the middle of the night," that "creative energy only comes from the pressure of deadlines," and that "it is more important to finish a few extra drawings than sleep or mentally prepare for the design review." The report also challenges the long-perpetuated myth of the architect as solo auteur, rejecting the belief that "the creation of architecture should be a solo, artistic struggle" and its corollary that "collaboration with other students means giving up the best ideas."[25]

As much as architecture students may naturally follow a Millennial preference for experiential learning, the task force seeks to restructure the time associated with it in accordance with a different set of values. It calls for a reversal of the temporal vortex that the architecture studio had become by negating the false assumptions that: (1) "it is *impossible* to be a successful architect unless you excel in the design studio," (2) "the *best* students are those who spend the most hours in studio," and (3) "success in architecture school is only attained by *investing all of your energy* in studio" (italics mine). It goes further in seeking to partition the studio's curricular dominance, stating that studio should no longer be "more important than other architecture or liberal arts courses," because it is impossible "to learn about complex social and cultural issues while spending the majority of time sitting at a studio desk." The studio task force report represents an early example of Millennials heeding their parents, who told them they could do anything they put their minds to, by emphatically claiming that they *do* have "the power to make changes within architecture programs [and] the design studio."[26]

While architectural educators may have become accustomed to giving criticism in the presence of multiple screens of video, text messages, and other media competing with computer drawings and renderings, and may also interact frequently with students using various forms of technology outside of class time, the challenge to the sanctity of the design process taught in studio courses still leaves many in the academy feeling vulnerable. It is thus no surprise that academics who endured the strenuous educational model that Millennials patently reject would think them to be entitled, if not arrogant, for rejecting it. After all, these upstarts attack the slow and iterative dogma proclaimed by Le Corbusier in his book *Creation Is a Patient Search*. According to this dogma, for architects to perform well, design must take all the time that is available, despite the fact that computing has replaced many of the drafting and model-building routines that once took so long. On the surface, the architectural academy seemed to have taken the studio culture report seriously, with the NAAB as of 2004 requiring schools to prominently post on their website a statement describing their position on studio culture and the AIAS issuing an amended document in 2008. However, the conditions leading to the emotional, physical, and cultural deprivation first identified in 2002 persist. In our AIAS poll, in response to the question "regarding the balance between life in studio and life outside of studio," 38 percent of Millennials surveyed reported a "severe unhealthy imbalance" while 68 percent acknowledged that an imbalance existed, but with the caveat that it was manageable. Only 4 percent reported they "didn't think any imbalance existed."

To have more than half the Millennials surveyed describe the studio system as imbalanced, whether it is manageable or not, suggests a festering problem. One might imagine how older generations of educators would view the complaints about studio as an entitled effort to diminish the rigors endured by those who came before them. This viewpoint implies that Millennials have little patience for the slow pace of the design process and instead impetuously demand instant production that frees time for other pursuits.

This may also be a stereotype and false dichotomy; the studio culture report states emphatically quite the opposite, that the "DESIGN PROCESS IS AS IMPORTANT AS PRODUCT" (all caps theirs), continuing with the insight that an "ability to view design as a process serves a graduate for a lifetime and withstands changes in architectural styles, materials, construction methods, and technology." They write instead that by rewarding the "best looking" projects, faculty fall prey to easy judgment of work that meets the standards of aesthetic formalism that older generations hold so high. This habit does collateral damage by marginalizing those students whose efforts, while not as visually appealing, still exhibit strong design-process ideas and skills, attributes that if nurtured and not unnoticed could allow them to successfully serve architecture in their own way. True to Millennial values, the task force seeks to protect the team from the repercussions of an undo idolization of the individual.[27]

The report acknowledges the new opportunities digital technology offers in graphic representation, visualization, and construction methods, but instead of following stereotype and advocating for the use of digital tools as an excuse to liberate time, the writers express concern that computers may make design too easy and devalue the art and craft of architecture. Consistent with protecting the Millennial team, the writers also express concern that computers will isolate students and decrease collaboration. Instead of expressing the impertinence one might expect from the portrait painted of Millennials, the task force urges educators and students to work together and deal with the wide range of implications that generational change and digital technology will bring.

Rather than insisting on strict temporal segregation, the studio culture report openly recommends evolving adaptive strategies that hybridize and balance the accelerated expectations of digital technology with traditional methods rooted in the haptic experience of drawing and model building. As one of these strategies, one can imagine adapting a kind of game-based coursework to invent pedagogy that accelerates cognition through excitement. Rather than view the Millennial insistence on parceling work and leisure as a shirking of responsibility, another strategy would argue for protecting and respecting outside opportunities for enrichment. Architecture traditionally draws inspiration from other disciplines, but if students are always working, when is interaction with those disciplines supposed to occur? Paul Taylor describes Millennials as ambling on a "slow walk to adulthood." Part of the rationale for the upward extension of adolescence to twenty-four years is because society is more urbanized, mobile, and globally networked than ever before.[28] Rather than dawdling, why not consider it as an expanded training in preparation for this age complicated by convolution, digital technology, and communication?

Architecture has always celebrated the generalist who can connect to other disciplines and keep multiple consultants focused. By embracing curiosity, the generalist architect is already a multitasker, and building information modeling is a software platform that overlaps and integrates many tasks for the new breed of time juggler. If, as research suggests, multitasking is becoming ingrained in the thinking patterns of current and future generations, then blending this phenomenon with methods of practice may be a distinct opportunity to explore. How practitioners and educators will take the abstract thinking of the slow, iterative process of trial and error in which they were trained and equipoise it with the digitally enabled Millennial desire for real and immediate experience may make all the difference in keeping the best and brightest Millennials interested in architecture and thereby protecting, if not expanding, its territory.

Vulnerability of Territory

While engineers, lawyers, and developers have increasingly encroached upon their domain, architects may find some comfort in knowing that as long as there is public demand for creative innovation, they will always retain some degree of control. Yet in an era of Millennial disruption, the greatest threat may come from what is now commonly known as the design profession, a sister discipline on the same side of qualitative/quantitative divide that many regard as interchangeable with architecture. Whether one calls it industrial design, product design, branding, or the result of any of the current wave of design thinking pedagogies, design has found renewed vigor in the twenty-first century by aligning with Millennial values. Exemplified by Apple's great success, design has left its mark on the physical accompaniments of the digital revolution in alignment with the Millennial digital birthright and appeals to both the generation's aesthetic and practical creed. The embrasure of assembly line design and production held together by the glue of branding—exactly the opposite of architecture's use of a temporary muster of consultants to create a one-off building—may appeal to Millennials' team orientation. And if a good part of architectural thinking in the future becomes automated, the mass production associated with design's time- and cost-saving nature would appeal to Millennials' practical tendencies.

Those in the product design disciplines have the proven experience to know where to begin this transition to automation. Additionally, the directness of design thinking as a series of protocols leading toward innovation may have greater appeal to Millennials than architecture's gradual and poky ways, causing architecture to be even more vulnerable. For Millennials to comprehend process from beginning to end, not as some open-ended spiral of discovery that engulfs all available time, is the first step toward fulfilling their quest for increased quality of life.

In advocating for greater integration between architecture and other disciplines, the 1996 Boyer report made the prescient statement regarding the design studio that I have isolated phrases from several times. Here I include it in longer form:

> The good news is that architecture, by nature and tradition, holds vast potential as a model for the integration and application of learning, largely because of its most distinctive feature—*the design studio.* The integrative possibilities of studio extend far beyond architecture. . . . Beyond question, the design studio is a model that many other disciplines on campus, as well as elementary and secondary schools, could well profit from.[29]

When Stanford launched its d.school in 2005, deploying design think-ing in a studio setting, it seemed to endorse the report's recommendation. Yet while Ernest Boyer and Lee Mitgang may have correctly predicted the future potential of the studio as a model in the twenty-first century, they did not anticipate that those profiting from the model would not come from architecture.

Territorial Vulnerability: Design Curricula

Within ten years of the Boyer report's recommendation, the d.school opened at Stanford in full anticipation of Millennials' experiential learning upbring-ing. Conceived in 2004 by Stanford mechanical engineering professor David Kelley, the d.school is in many ways an academic extension of Kelley's design firm IDEO.[30] Kelley formed IDEO in 1991 when he merged his own firm with three other design practices: Mike Nuttall's Matrix Product Design and two firms founded by Bill Moggridge, ID Two and Moggridge Associates (using generational bracketing, all are Boomers). IDEO pioneered innova-tion consulting, guiding public and private entities toward complementing technical innovation with "human-centered" services in order to launch fully integrated brands.[31] Buoyed by what Kelley refers to as "creative optimism," it is this culture that he, his partners, and staff, many of whom also teach at the d.school, practice at IDEO. IDEO helped forge the design ethos associated with Apple products that Millennials know and respect, ultimately causing an overlap of innovation and capital to hover over Stanford and its surrounding Silicon Valley to form an aesthetic sensibility that became worldwide. The unification of skills, unleashed on Millennial-driven emerging markets, allowed some businesses to become wildly successful. In response, by 2014 some sixty schools of higher education in the US offered some form of design thinking integrated with more traditional twentieth-century curricula.[32]

Other disciplines outside the arts have applied design thinking in a manner similar to the d.school. The Franklin W. Olin College of Engineering in Needham, Massachusetts, near Boston, applies design thinking to engineering education in a studio setting. Olin also had the institutional foresight to open just as the first Millennials entered college in 2002. Like the d.school, it, too, responds to Millennial values, stressing creativity, teamwork, and entrepreneurial practicality. Its stated goal is to transcend the stereotype of the engineer as rigidly analytical. As Olin president Richard K. Miller stresses, the college seeks to mold engineers to be "comfortable as citizens and not just calculating machines." Miller extends the Millennial characteristic of confidence to a call for courage: "I don't see how you can make a positive difference in the world if you're not motivated to take a tough stand and do the right thing."[33]

The school came into existence after the Olin Foundation leadership, which had historically given large individual gifts to schools, grew frustrated with the ineffectiveness of its philanthropy in bettering engineering education. Instead of broadening engineering's appeal, the Olin Foundation's beneficiaries increasingly focused on specialized study. After consulting with the National Science Foundation, the Olin Foundation decided to divert funds from schools it had previously sponsored and spend $480 million to start its own. Creating an institution to prompt learning through inquiry and discovery using an interdisciplinary, experiential approach, Olin sought to remedy the default condition in engineering education of "too much note-taking in the classroom and not enough hands-on learning." Even more so than at the d.school, Olin students learn in a studio-like environment that "looks like a hybrid of dot-com office and arts classroom. Bright collages with diagrams and equations fill the white walls, and piles of paper, markers,

Lego blocks, tools, laptops, and iPods clutter six big wooden tables."[34] Olin's interdisciplinarity extends beyond campus, with articulated agreements with neighboring Babson, Wellesley and Brandeis. There, Olin students complement their engineering education with business, humanities, and life-sciences classes.

Recruited from a deanship at another engineering college, Miller launched Olin in 2001 by first enlisting faculty and then inviting thirty Millennial students for a "partner year" to help create and test a project-based learning curriculum. Olin's student-centeredness prioritizes Millennials' demand for quality of life, to which an early event in its history pays homage: one month into the first semester, students complained that faculty had underestimated the time needed to complete team-based studio problems, and students were staying up all night. In response, Miller declared a moratorium on classes, and like a Boomer parent jazzing up a Millennial birthday party, rented an inflatable bouncy castle for everyone to blow off steam.

Olin's impact has rippled through higher education. The Princeton Review wrote in 2007 that Olin "may well be the most dynamic undergraduate institution in the country." Constance M. Bowe, writing for Harvard Macy Institute (a Harvard Medical School affiliate), developed a case study of Olin, describing Olin's methods as trying to create students who were more like stem cells, capable of becoming any other kind of cell. In 2015, Harvard Medical School instituted its own reforms; in addition to introducing hospital clinical rotations a year earlier, it moved lectures online to reserve classroom time for studio-like problem-solving in groups, interviewing patients, and thinking through complex situations that might arise in practice.[35]

Olin and the d.school anticipated Millennial educational preferences by offering design thinking pedagogies instilled with Millennial values, and easily accommodated Millennial characteristics that others disparaged. Attracting and educating Millennials according to their preferences represents an opening the architectural academy and profession may have initially missed. If the academy loses potential students to more adaptive pedagogies, and designers educated in other disciplines encroach upon the profession, architecture leaves itself doubly vulnerable.

Generational Case Study: Design Paralleling Architecture
Using a generational framework to examine experiential learning reveals how a succession of developments during societal course-corrections ultimately led to a learning strategy that closely fits with Millennials' characteristics.

The migration of its abstract underpinnings to the business practice of design thinking, as pioneered by IDEO, warrants a similar exploration. A closer look reveals that design thinking has a long heritage, with institutional roots arguably as deep as or even deeper than architecture's. During the last crisis era, which spawned modernism, industrial design seriously challenged architecture. In 1939, the prominent architectural trade journal, *Pencil Points*, warned that industrial designers are "pioneering ahead of us, and making us rapidly obsolete."[36] In the Millennial Age, design thinking's challenge to architecture echoes aspects of the previous upheaval.

In 1979, Ada Louise Huxtable described industrial design as a "curious amalgam of promotion, marketing, technology, and taste invented by the 20th century to serve and shape a consumer economy."[37] While industrial design as a label only came into common usage after the US patent office recognized the title in 1913, the term "industrial" connects its traditions to machine production beginning in the Industrial Revolution. And tracing industry's origins in handmade practices leads even further into the past. By the beginning of World War II, industrial design broadly engaged all aspects of the physical world, from products to graphics and motion pictures, all forms of transportation—automobiles, aircraft, and ocean liners—buildings, interior finishes and new synthetic materials, and entire coordinated advertising campaigns. In its twenty-first-century iteration as design thinking, the discipline has expanded from its nucleus of physical design into the systematized, conceptual, and virtual realms. Having largely shed any pairing with the word "industrial," design now typically stands alone as a single word to describe a vast array of undertakings, of which architecture is often seen as a subset.

Like architecture, this amorphous discipline traces its roots in Western culture to the prehistory of medieval guilds. Early professional recognition of decorative production dates back to fifteenth-century English royal court patents related to stained glass.[38] State-sponsored French design education followed in 1648 with the conjoining of the Gobelins Manufactory and the French Royal Academy of Painting and Sculpture (Académie Royale de Peinture et de Sculpture) in Paris, both under the direction of Charles Le Brun (a noted painter, Le Brun designed the interiors at Versailles). By contrast, the Royal Academy of Architecture (Académie Royale d'Architecture) would not open until 1671. The Gobelins facility trained craft artists to state-certify all areas of the "decorative arts." Pierre L'Enfant, the designer of the baroque plan for Washington, DC, who also helped complete Federal Hall, the early republic's first capitol in New York, is a product of this French decorative pedagogy. L'Enfant learned how to design cities and buildings not through formal architectural training, but through an art school education that taught him about cities and buildings only to enable him to accurately depict them on decorative tapestries.[39]

In America, mechanically enabled decorative and utilitarian production advanced significantly before the Civil War, with "mechanics institutes" opening in New York, Philadelphia, Boston, and Baltimore. The year 1826 proved especially significant: in that year, the National Academy of Design opened in New York with Samuel F. B. Morse (who later developed Morse code) as its first president, Philadelphia's Franklin Institute began hosting exhibitions and awarding medals, and the first fully accredited, degree-granting arts college opened as the Maryland Institute for the Promotion of the Mechanic Arts, today's Maryland Institute College of Art (MICA).[40] By contrast, the American Institute of Architects did not charter until 1857 and MIT would not begin its degree programs until 1868.

Through the nineteenth century, many expositions in Europe and America presented objects both decorative and industrial. While American designers often felt unsophisticated among this competition, admiration in Europe grew for what came to be known as an "American system" of manufacturing distinctly utilitarian objects, an esteem best exemplified by Cyrus Mc-Cormick's reaper receiving the gold medal at the 1851 Great Exhibition in London's Crystal Palace. It took the 1925 International Exhibition of Modern Decorative and Industrial Arts in Paris to shock American design out its self-diagnosed inadequacy. Declining the invitation to participate, trade officials used the excuse that the US could not "contribute sufficiently varied design of unique character or of special expression in American artistry to warrant [participation]."[41] The Paris exhibition's success led to an American outcry to initiate parallel efforts to appeal to the American consumer,[42] which in turn mobilized American manufacturing to value design. Consumer manufacturing shrewdly used this cultural shaming as a way to boost sales by differentiating products in a saturated market. Rallying under the banner of "industrial design," American manufacturers separated themselves from their European counterparts and from one another by taking conscious pride in producing utilitarian objects styled loosely after their mechanical nature. Influenced by the emerging aircraft industry, this aestheticizing of the machine along vague aerodynamic principles came to be known as streamlining.[43]

The US automobile industry led this commercial shift in styling. After Chevrolet instituted annual model changes in 1926, sales doubled, and those of the Ford Model T—whose style had remained virtually unchanged since its dramatic 1913 introduction—dropped by 25 percent. The next year Ford's market share dropped to 15 percent from a high of 52 percent five years earlier, forcing it to take the drastic measure of closing its production line to retool and ultimately introduce its Model A.[44] Automobile styling brought design innovation to producers across the consumer industry. The sudden market appreciation for design compelled industrial designers to professionalize as the American Union of Decorative Artists and Craftsmen (AUDAC) in 1927 to fight off flagrant piracy among manufacturers.[45]

By the time the Great Depression began, American manufacturing under the banner of industrial design had become a well-organized and critical component of the economy with strong public recognition that would last well after World War II. Throughout the Depression, European advances influenced both design and architecture, with émigrés fleeing fascism in Europe joining both fields (many early AUDAC meetings were conducted in German). Both industrial design and architecture renounced their historical forms in favor of a machine aesthetic as an overriding expression of modernity, albeit in different ways. Industrial design's near-universal adoption of streamlining as both a formal and conceptual strategy bears similarity to how contemporary design thinking applies to management practices. In common usage, "streamlining" as a verb came to imply any process that increased economy and practicality. A national collectivizing fueled by Rockefeller funding marshaled teams working toward a new American style, despite the industries' many émigrés, that would atone for the embarrassment of the Paris exhibition.[46]

As with heroic architectural modernism, prominent figures would lead industrial design's ascendance: Walter Dorwin Teague, Norman Bel Geddes, Henry Dreyfuss, and Raymond Loewy. All but Loewy were American-born, and except for Dreyfuss, the rest were self-starting nomad-types from the Lost generation.[47] None had any formal training in anything related to manufacturing (industrial design education, as the term is applied in the twenty-first century, had yet to establish itself): Teague went to art school and came from advertising; Bel Geddes and Dreyfuss came from the theater; and Loewy, a bon vivant, by pure happenstance began his career in fashion.[48] By 1927, all four had established stand-alone businesses as industrial designers, and each played a critical if compartmentalized and collaborative role in defining the movement. Teague was the realist who established design as a business, whose "manner impressed manufacturers who feared the imagined vagaries of long-haired artists."[49] Helping to found the Society of Industrial Designers in 1944 and serving as its first president, Teague became known as the "dean of industrial design." Bel Geddes, regarded as the P. T. Barnum of design, became the field's promoter through his visionary and futuristic proposals, although little of his commercial work proved financially successful. Apprenticing for Bel Geddes, Dreyfuss was the youngest (a member of the GI generation) and focused primarily on design's human interface. He would become the Industrial Designers Society of America's first president in 1965. As streamlining's most prolific form-maker, Loewy also became its figurehead celebrity, known for trips to the country that included "the biggest white convertible and the most beautiful blondes." To the public, Loewy "looked like a designer."[50]

Industrial design's legitimacy grew from its remarkable financial success during the worst of the Great Depression. An industrial designer's influence on a product could boost sales from 25 to 900 percent.[51] A 1934 *Fortune* magazine article described the extraordinary fees industrial designers commanded, with retainers of $50,000 and rates of $50 per hour at a time when a typical corporate executive made $5,000 per year and laborers earned fifty cents per hour. The *Fortune* article both legitimized and popularized the new field,[52] and notable new curricula at the Pratt Institute, the University of Cincinnati, and the Carnegie Institute of Technology (later Carnegie Mellon), grew rapidly. As a private sector bright spot amid economic gloom, industrial design lured many unemployed architects. With visionary skills of promotion, Bel Geddes wrote: "In the perspective of fifty years hence, the historian will detect in the decade of 1930–1940 a period of tremendous significance . . . doubtless he will ponder that, in the midst of a world-wide melancholy owing to an economic depression, a new age dawned with invigorating conceptions and horizons lifted."[53]

A little over fifty years in the future, David Kelley, Bill Moggridge, and Mike Nuttall merged several firms to form IDEO in 1991, and whether they were heeding some cyclical call for "invigorating conceptions" or even respecting Bel Geddes's prediction, they nonetheless laid the groundwork for the coming Millennials' affinity with design by launching the d.school. IDEO would also become economically successful in large part by anticipating Millennials' consumer habits. By the time the d.school opened in 2005, IDEO's revenues exceeded $60 million, with 350 employees in six offices in America and Europe.[54] Like the Depression in the 1930s, the recession propelled the design sector's growth; by 2016, IDEO's revenues rose to an estimated $90 million.[55] As industrial design historian Carroll Gantz asserts, industrial design is traditionally recession-proof, because manufacturers have historically seized the opportunity of a downturn to innovate and pivot in order to build momentum for the next expansion.[56]

While architecture and design are often seen as interchangeable, a hidden tension exists between the two disciplines, one that at times has reached acrimony. While IDEO and the d.school might espouse a broad sense of interdisciplinarity appealing to Millennials, nowhere do they include architecture by name as a collaborator. The school's materials make no mention of architecture, and in a 2015 IDEO Fact Sheet of the six hundred-plus employees, the company officially lists none as hailing from architecture, although they account for sixteen other disciplines.[57] Whether this segregation is by intent or neglectful omission, it belies a division that began as industrial design emerged in the 1920s. An examination of this earlier division projects how twenty-first-century architecture's domain may be vulnerable along similar lines.

The omission of the US from the 1925 Paris show shocked America in different ways. Due to the historical American weakness for all things European, the show stunned the US's antiquarian sensibility into a new style that had been slowly maturing in Europe since before World War I. At the same time, the show awakened somnolent manufacturers to the realization that the pragmatic "American system" suddenly aligned with a newfound reverence for the machine. While on the surface the objects produced by this sudden revolution may have appeared similar to each other, significant differences separated architects from industrial designers. The many prewar architects who trained at the École des Beaux-Arts were receptive to anything European, while industrial designers instead favored an American streamlined aesthetic coming from the native automobile and aircraft industries. Class divisions also arose. Architects served clients who tended to be social elites driven by conspicuous consumption, and were primarily concerned with custom artisanship and the one-off piece. By contrast, industrial designers embraced mass production as inherently democratic, and appealed to the people directly through commercial venues such as department stores.[58]

The Depression exacerbated this class divide, elevating the industrial designer as one attuned to the masses while the architect became associated with the rich capitalists who many believed caused the Depression.

American institutions supported by capitalists only fueled this growing feud. Under the leadership of the Columbia-trained architect Richard F. Bach, New York's Metropolitan Museum of Art initiated an industrial arts program in 1918 to carry out "the application of arts to manufacture and practical life."[59] Bach's elitist manner, and his frequent uncertainty as to whether to embrace the new machine aesthetic or fall back on historicism, set him at odds with the emergent machine aesthetic and its proponents. When Bach launched the *Exhibition of Contemporary American Design* in 1929 to emulate the "ensemble" effect of the Paris show, its contradictory subtitle, *The Architect and the Industrial Arts*, revealed his bias. By favoring established architects over emerging designers, he infuriated AUDAC, which launched its own show in retaliation.[60] At the Century of Progress Exposition in Chicago in the summers of 1933 and 1934, it was architecture's turn for spite as it forced the cancellation of nine pavilion designs because their industrial designer creators were uncredentialed as architects.[61]

On another front, New York's Museum of Modern Art attacked industrial design's basis in streamlining as antifunctionalist. When Philip Johnson organized MoMA's *Machine Art* exhibit in 1934, he mostly deemed engineered objects as worthy of inclusion, consciously avoiding most of the commercially popular industrial designs of the day that exhibited any form of styling.[62] The few Johnson allowed—a Kodak camera and Taylor barometer, for example—one anti-streamlining critic dismissed as "among the more painful exhibits."[63] In its 1938 Bauhaus retrospective, MoMA committed itself to defining a historical and qualitative standard of modern design in the US based on the "best of Europe." Johnson's standards of excellence were purely aesthetic, Eurocentric, and elitist, with little regard for the grassroots foundation of US industrial design, its public acceptance, or its commercial success.[64]

The decade's conflict climaxed in 1939 with the opening of the New York World's Fair, with industrial design decisively upstaging architecture. The fair marked the high point of a remarkable ascension in a stunningly short period of time, during which industrial design went from an adjunct of advertising to having virtually complete design control over everything produced in America, from the most insignificant industrial products such as matchsticks to continental infrastructure.[65] Teague dissuaded the fair's board of design (mostly architects) from its highly unimaginative original plan to commemorate George Washington, instead convincing them to create a tableau for envisioning the future. Teague went on to design the

US pavilion as well as exhibitions for major companies including Ford, US Steel, and DuPont. This time no one challenged his or any other industrial designer's credentials.

The fair's greatest impact on the public was its projection of the expanded urbanism of the future. Each of the big four—Teague, Loewy, Dreyfuss, and Bel Geddes—produced scaled-down simulated cities that borrowed liberally from Ebenezer Howard, Le Corbusier, and Rockefeller Center. Teague designed a city of connected skyscrapers for US Steel, Loewy a rocket port that predicted a space age, Dreyfuss a garden city for one hundred years hence, and Bel Geddes created the remarkable Futurama for General Motors. In a great irony, Dreyfuss and Bel Geddes, the industrial designers, designed every aspect of how visitors experienced each of their future cities, including the buildings' form, circulation, and spaces, leaving the architects, Harrison & Fouilhoux and Albert Kahn, respectively, to design the exterior envelope essentially as packaging.

The visions presented at the World's Fair enthralled a generation who, after fighting the war, came back to reshape America following the fair's many prompts. Following the logistical prowess that won the war, a streamlined practicality greatly expanded the city for GIs in automobiles. The GI generation's characteristic attributes—practicality, teamwork, and outer focus—prefigure those of twenty-first-century Millennials and connect streamlining and design thinking across time by generational archetype. Embracing similar values, Millennials will preside over a twenty-first-century metropolitan transformation of an even greater scope. Apple, IDEO, and Google have set a twenty-first-century design and production standard, making a 1936 description of design's broad scope seem like it was written today:

Well-rounded design service embraces virtually every department of business, even including the legal aspects and labor problems. [It was] proving its power to sell not only articles of merchandise but such intangibles as service and company reputations. . . . But the soundest foundation on which design builds for the future is its unquestioned ability to determine what the public wants, to build products to meet those demands, to cut cost in the process.[66]

If a desire for civic cohesion manifests itself in the voting shifts projected for the late 2010s, or if Donald Trump fulfills his infrastructure building promise and the political will to begin an urban transformation emerges, adherents to design thinking are as well poised to lead it as were their pre-decessors. Architects found themselves sidelined in the 1930s; in an echo of that course correction, the profession may find itself again vulnerable to marginalization eighty years later.

Based on what later befell streamlining, a strict belief in generational cycles may bring architecture some comfort. Even before the World's Fair opened, industrial design's rival architects began efforts to win back popular appeal using MoMA as their conduit. At Christmastime in 1938, the museum initiated its "Useful Objects under $5" program to try to dispel a reputation for elitism and expensive taste.[67] The same year, consciously exhibited as an alternative to American curvilinear design, Alvar Aalto's furniture, lighting, and glassware included shapes inspired by the body and nature, rather than abstract interpretations of speed. As war began in Europe, MoMA organized a competition to "discover good designers and engage them in the task of creating a better environment for today's living," awarding top prizes to the architecturally trained Eero Saarinen and Charles Eames.[68] Each would influence a postwar design shift away from American streamlining toward European modernism, but with a distinct American warp and lilt. Later generations would bemoan streamlining's effect on cities, which to reduce the metaphorical friction on fast-moving cars, built highway cloverleafs that eroded the fine-grained prewar urban fabric. The only significant aspect of streamlining to linger was the styling of American automobiles. Having adopted the aerodynamics of military aircraft, vehicles with prominent but useless tail fins celebrated a daily victory parade on new American highways well into the 1960s.

The Boomer-driven social upheavals that began in the 1960s shocked the design professions arguably more than architecture. Public perception had switched since the 1930s; now industrial design found itself labeled elitist because of its cozy association with corporate America. The use of the word "industrial" in the term only reinforced the relationship.[69] The era's critics had awakened the public to "planned obsolescence," a practice that had been fundamental to industrial design since the 1930s, describing it as socially reprehensible. Once lauded as artists for the people during the Depression, by the 1960s, industrial designers found themselves blamed for enabling a commercialism that forced unnecessary and continual product changes on many who could better use their resources elsewhere. And as environmental awareness grew, they also bore responsibility for the ma-terial wastefulness of their practices. Criticism crescendoed with Victor

Papanek's 1973 book, *Design for the Real World*,[70] in which he argued, "It is about time that industrial design, as we have come to know it, should cease to exist . . . There are few professions more harmful." Preaching directly to antiestablishment youth and using their street language, Papanek accused industrial design of serving as a "pimp for big business interests."[71]

As recessions rolled through the economy in the 1970s, industrial design's association with consumerism had so damaged its reputation that many wrote its obituary, claiming it was "now becoming the subject of dissertations."[72] Once the stalwart of the design disciplines, the crafting of automobiles also began a steady decline. After a peak in popularity when stylists replaced superfluous tail fins with a combination of angularity and horsepower to produce the iconic "muscle cars" of the late 1960s, American automobile design lost leadership and market share to German and Japanese manufacturers. Ironically, these industries had been economically resuscitated by the US after WWII, although many of them had once produced war machines. These countries also proved fertile environments for domestically scaled consumer objects produced at manufacturers such as Germany's Braun and Japan's Panasonic and Sony. American car manufacturers seemed to ignore this competition, as well as their competitors' moves toward efficiency driven by environmental concern. Instead, US manufacturers promoted gigantism, first with the longest consumer automobiles ever made, commonly referred to as "boats," and later with bloated trucks that consumed enormous amounts of fuel. Naming these vehicles after the iconic locations of America's last frontiers, their branding satisfied a longing for pioneer nostalgia rather than inspiring a machine-age future. A distinct lack of product and design diversity left the American automobile industry highly vulnerable, and had the US government not financially rescued them during the Great Recession, General Motors and Chrysler would have gone out of business entirely.

The twenty-first century's design thinking movement eventually emerged from the disquiet of 1960s social upheaval. Parallel to architecture, postmodernism affected industrial design to sweep away the singular organizational structures that streamlining had once represented. With garish and irreverent designs, the Memphis group privileged surface aesthetics over function in an early volley against orthodoxy. This flamboyant opening was followed by a pluralistic imperative to rediscover the fundamentals of design: its utilitarian roots, its processes, and its audience. A renewed interest in ergonomics and semiotics focused on a product's relation to both the body and the mind that perceives it.[73] Carnegie Mellon psychologist Herbert Simon's 1969 book *The Sciences of the Artificial* began an inquiry into design decision-making and problem-solving processes that laid the groundwork for later design thinking ideology.[74] Industrial design also began to focus on environmental and social causes by looking carefully at the resources involved in production. Doing so revived its associations with industry, except now according to reset values. The design professions also reestablished their relationship with the public by showing that they cared about their welfare. As a young woman in her twenties, Patricia Moore traveled the US and Canada disguised as a woman in her eighties to learn firsthand the exclusions faced by the elderly in the physical environment.[75] Moore exemplified a heightened sense of public purpose and inclusion that would change laws and become a popular topic in design thinking pedagogies.

Contemporary Design and Millennial Alignment

By the turn of the Millennium, design had rehabilitated itself and was restored to a stature it had not held since the 1930s. It also reinstated many of the previous era's organizational structures. After a forced separation, it renewed its association with industry, with many companies again embracing design as a means toward market advantage. In the process it rekindled an adoring relationship with the press. Along with those at *Fast Company*, *Businessweek*'s editor, Bruce Nussbaum, would become a champion of design thinking, and the publication would sponsor the annual International Design Excellence Awards (IDEA) program in partnership with the revived Industrial Designers Society of America (IDSA). In early 2000, *Time* magazine published a cover announcing "The Rebirth of Design" with the tagline: "Function is out. Form is in. From radios to cars to toothbrushes, America is bowled over by style."[76] In the lead article, "The Redesigning of America," writers acknowledged the objects still functioned perfectly well; they heaped praise on how they seamlessly integrated function with a form derived from a careful consideration of ergonomics, material, color, and the populace they served. As in the 1930s, *Time* recognized a new "design economy" that was both popular and profitable.

Sensing new global competition, design leaders also revived 1930s-style nationalism. Apple products proudly claimed "Designed in California" (eliding the fact that they are *made* in China). As early as 1989, David Kelley (soon to be a founding partner at IDEO) commented that: "People are waking up to it [design] because they are scared to death of the Japanese and world competition in general."⁷⁷ Others took direct or more nuanced approaches to realign American design with a leadership that had left it. To absorb Braun's design insight, the American company Gillette simply bought it outright. IDEO's Bill Moggridge advised a more subtle approach. Rather than acquire, he argued that American design should emulate the Japanese Shinto values of conjoining the "forces of man, nature, and the cosmos . . . [to] strive for balance and harmony through simplicity of line and use of natural materials. The hallmark of this new design would be elegance in a quiet package."⁷⁸ Although with less emphasis on natural materials, Apple would Americanize the European and Japanese design sensibility of minimalist elegance through the 2000s to reap enormous profit.

Using a generational framework to trace the roots of design thinking back to the time of modernism's emergence reveals distinct interactions with architecture during catalytic periods. In these instances, each discipline responded to the conditions of the time, in some cases with synchronicity, in others allowing tensions to divide them. In this chapter on vulnerability, I emphasize more the strain than the unity, yet I wish to remind that there is much common ground between architecture and design, with a long tradition of successful collaboration and individuals straddling both disciplines. At the same time, the conditions of the twenty-first century are new and enormously challenging, and while architecture should address these with a collaborative spirit, appraising its own vulnerability is a necessary form of due diligence. Millennial-driven technological change is already blurring disciplinary boundaries. The appliances that traditionally fall within the domain of industrial design will weave themselves into buildings through the Internet of Things. As prefabrication becomes more prevalent in construction, industrial design's experience with assembly-line manufacturing gives it a distinct advantage. Future structures may become more like an extended web of premade components performing as integrated appliances, with the domain of architecture left unclear. And the grassroots "maker movement," combining traditional craft with 3-D printing, may form the foundation of Jeremy Rifkin's third industrial revolution, which also aligns more with design than architecture.

In the last crisis era, tensions flared as architecture experienced a significant challenge from industrial design. By projecting a progressive new style through a broad array of physical production organized around the aesthetics of streamlining, industrial design appealed to a young adult plurality seeking to distance themselves from the past. While architecture was experiencing a similar transition in style, its production methods connected it to the capitalist elite who many associated with causing the Great Depression. Whether valid or not, the elite association also connected architecture to bygone styles. By contrast, industrial design's association with emerging automobile technology and the formal fluidity associated with it provided a mandate to rethink urbanism entirely for a world based on the car. Twenty years prior, based on qualifications, this task would have fallen squarely within the domain of architecture.

In the current Millennial Age, the "elegance in a quiet package" credo of design thinking, which Millennials consider their house style, draws parallels with what happened in the 1930s. If urban issues will dominate the twenty-first century, design thinking may provide an attractive strategy for addressing them, despite the fact that, again, architects are more qualified. In the 1930s, industrial designers showed a distinct ability to communicate with a large audience by aligning a formal style with broad public purpose. In the 2020s, architecture's inability to offer comparable appeal may leave it again marginalized. If a parallel crisis-era confidence in industrial design, engaging all scales from object to urban, reemerges in the Millennial Age, it may be riding a wave of reaction to embarrassment like that felt early in the last century. America's shame after the 1925 Paris exhibition caused industrial design to bounce back with resolve to introduce streamlining as a coherent focus. After the upheavals of the 1960s accused it of being a "pimp to business," industrial design reexamined its values and entered the Millennial Age ascendant, its professional numbers increasing fourfold from 9,000, as reported in 1997, to 39,700 by 2016.[79]

The ascendance of design presents an impressive organizational challenge that renders the architectural academy and profession once again vulnerable in this century. A generational framework reveals formative periods when the design discipline grew, when mechanics institutes promoted a pragmatic "American system" of manufacturing, and later, when streamlining brought cohesion to take on architecture's dominance, and reexamination in the 1960s brought renewed public purpose. Each era provides a root system for the Millennial values that design aligns with today and for which the d.school and others have developed effective curricula to grow a new disciplinary tree. Making architecture vulnerable from within, the abuses enumerated in the 2002 Studio Culture Task Force report, if not corrected, could weaken the discipline. The report proposes mediations between traditional architectural practices and the Millennial predisposition for an accelerated, restructured, and overlapped usage of time, which has created friction with employers and educators alike. Millennial architects have high expectations and will follow a path of convenience to attain their aspirations. Given a great pending disruption, whether that path ultimately leads through architecture, as it eventually did for previous generations, is not guaranteed.

PART THREE

Disruption, Innovation, Continuity

CHAPTER 10

Medicine, Law, Architecture
Comparing the Professions

> To ask why societies incorporate their knowledge in the professions is thus not only to ask why societies have specialized, life-time experts, but also why they placed expertise in people rather than things or rules.

ANDREW ABBOTT

This book's first third introduces the Millennial generation and their characteristics, how they fit within a broader tableau of generational groups, and how various sociological viewpoints seek to understand Millennials and their interplay with other generations. Parsing recent architecture through a generational historiography provides valuable insight into significant past shifts in both the profession and the academy. The second part of the book enumerates the alignments and misalignments between Millennials and architecture. In equal measure these can both advance and inhibit architecture as it moves forward. How the profession and academy embrace the Millennials' technological predisposition presents the greatest variable.

This final book part serves as a third act in a traditional tripartite narrative that seeks to bring us to some resolution. The disruption foreshadowed in Chapter One stands to affect not only architecture but each profession. Understanding the features architecture shares with other professions reveals how it is in flux due to digital automation. Comparing architecture's organizational ascent to how its sister disciplines, medicine and the law, heightened their own status provides some direction. To bring this narrative to a close, I seek to answer the larger rhetorical question asked by *Architect* magazine that began my inquiry. In previous chapters I have used fragments of it; here I present the full query:

> How will the Millennials respond to the opportunities and challenges that they are inheriting—both in the profession and the world at large? How will they influence the practice of architecture? And perhaps most important, without drastic changes to pedagogy licensure and firm management, is the profession prepared to capitalize on what comes next?[1]

My conclusions as to "what comes next" in the next chapter synthesize the findings of this book. My goal, however, is that my findings spark a debate about how architecture can redesign its future to emerge reinvigorated from the coming period of profound disruption.

The Great Recession left the architecture profession significantly compromised, assaulted on many fronts, and increasingly unsustainable. As the economy recovers, some reordering has begun to deal with the profession's vulnerabilities. In academia, a similar reshuffling is afoot as the academic values emerging from the upheavals of the 1960s are finally giving way to those of successor generations. Both transitions carry a spirit of optimism that parallels (or may even be inspired by) that which characterizes Millennials. Tomas Rossant expresses this optimism about the profession of architecture in the twenty-first century by putting it in historical context, stating that "in the last century, the JD [the professional law degree] was the elastic degree; with it you could go into politics, run a corporation, or a non-profit. Then came the MBA, with it you no longer needed a degree in finance to run a company; the MBA could also take you to politics, or advertising. In this century, Millennials can use an architecture degree with the same elasticity." Applying a weaving metaphor often used in architecture, Rossant continues: "in the tartan grid of practice, the Millennial architect will be able to knit together many different disciplines; they will become the warp to the weft of the many stove-piped specializations." Rossant's attitude sets a leadership example for older generations consistent with a theme of this book: that our examination should be less a preoccupation with Millennials than a call for broader generational cooperation.[2]

The Disruption Around Us

In the 1980s, both Robert Gutman and Dana Cuff observed how the domain of architecture was being whittled away by others—financiers, engineers, lawyers, builders, and an ever-increasing phalanx of managers governing facilities, programs, and the value of design and construction.[3] It was as if the coalition of disciplines assembled after World War II to build infrastructure and expand the city was unraveling, and each profession was out for itself. Since Gutman and Cuff's observation, the erosion has increased to a critical point. From his perspective teaching professional practice at Yale School of Architecture for over two decades, Phillip Bernstein has watched the architect's influence wane. Bernstein argues that even though architecture is a critical component of the building sector, which in its entirety operates in large capital pools which create significant value, the architect gains less reward for services rendered than other participants. The reason for this is that clients have commodified the architect's responsibility, meaning that they will not pay beyond certain expectations. An increasing aversion to risk by the architectural profession has also played a significant role. Together these create downward pressure on compensation, furthering a vicious cycle leading to intense market competition. Vainly trying to remain profitable by lowering costs, architects cut salaries and services.[4] They also outsource, a practice the digitally connected global economy has made far easier. This cycle leaves differentiation through design quality as a sole defense against commodification. Left as a middleman, the architect is vulnerable to disruption, his or her services encroached upon by clients at one end and builders at the other. Without self-initiated innovation that reaffirms the value proposition architects offer, Bernstein sees the profession as significantly compromised.[5]

Understanding in the abstract how architecture is a profession helps to clarify both its domain and how commodification threatens it. In his seminal work on the professions, Andrew Abbott argues that each profession organizes its domain as *jurisdictions* around three distinct and serial phases: *diagnosis, inference,* and *treatment.* Using the medical practice as a paradigm, Abbott describes both diagnosis and treatment as phases in which standardized procedures, or "routines," are employed, sometimes by others. It is the inference phase that defines a profession's jurisdiction and holds the other phases, diagnosis and treatment, in its orbit. For example, in the inference phase, a doctor's decision stems from a diagnosis that may have relied on lab work by technicians and leads to effective treatment performed by therapists or other subordinates. Further protected through certification, inference becomes the inner keep of a profession's jurisdiction. Abbott also describes how medicine as a jurisdiction administers over entirely separate professions, such as pharmacy and nursing, in a practice he refers to as *subordination*.[6] Throughout this chapter and the next, I frequently use the terms *jurisdiction, diagnosis, inference, treatment*, and *subordination* as Abbott uses them. Maintaining a jurisdiction's abstract purpose and defending it in a constantly changing context is an ongoing campaign. As Abbott writes:

> The organizational formalities of professions are meaningless unless we understand the context. This context always relates back to the power of the professions' knowledge systems, their abstracting ability to define old problems in new ways. Abstraction enables survival.[7]

In parallel, the architect's design inference transforms a building program into instructions for construction. As Bernstein describes, architecture's professional domain has waned, its procedures and routines on the margins commodified or made subordinate to other domains. In the diagnosis stage, programming has devolved to owner-led entities, often employing specialists from the ever-growing domain of strategy firms. In the treatment phase, the architect's influence in the contract document and building administration phases has been encroached upon by a hybrid accountant-engineer, the so-called "value engineer." Growing incursions on the essential inference phase of architecture by other professions, such as engineering, accounting, and law, threaten to undermine its core tasks. Any future technological disruption will only serve to further wedge into these fractures. By understanding Abbott's abstract model, we can also recognize the architectural academy's culpability in failing to fortify the core jurisdiction against these incursions.

While architecture's early adoption of digital technology in the 1990s may have insulated it from the disruptions that affected other industries, its immunity may be over. As in other disrupted sectors, digital technology is also contributing to an erosion of the architect's control. In the profession, after production returned to prerecession levels, the increased billings returned only a fraction of jobs, suggesting that digitally enabled automation had already begun. While the automation of BIM has replaced lower-level drafting positions, it may also soon begin to work its way up the hierarchy as software like Autodesk's Dreamcatcher, Modumate, and others even more developed begin to leave their mark. As a result, a higher tier of human decision makers in the design process may soon become unnecessary. A cruel irony may be that, just prior to their replacement, machine learning will have stealthily absorbed a single architect or a firm's design sensibilities. If this comes to fruition, then only those specifying direction at the beginning of the design process, checking in at critical intervals, and certifying at the end of the sequence will remain. Given the downward pressure on fees, firms may choose to keep the savings associated with automation rather than use that capital to repurpose employees toward other ends. Those out of work, experiencing what in the 1930s John Maynard Keynes called "technological unemployment," will have to look elsewhere.

It is also ironic that architecture is being disrupted just as the public's overall appreciation of design is increasing. Design professions outside architecture captured the public's attention in the Great Depression, and the contemporary success of IDEO and the rise of design thinking programs outside the arts are strong evidence that this may be happening again. Then as now, architects may not be fully replaced, but their role diminished. In the 1939 World's Fair, Wallace Harrison and Albert Kahn still designed the fair's most important pavilions, but in a subordinate role to the industrial designers who controlled the overall process. Bohlin Cywinski Jackson's contemporary designs for Apple continue a similar subordination to a higher aesthetic authority. This lack of prestige, combined with the reputation of a grueling education and the prospect of low compensation, may be deflecting Millennials considering architecture as a career toward better opportunities.

While architecture will undoubtedly always attract students, the most talented and ambitious may go elsewhere. In his chronicling of the construction in the 1950s of the interstate highway system, the largest construction project in history, Tom Lewis describes how emerging aerospace and electronic technologies after World War II captured the imagination of the engineering profession and drew away the best engineers. When the call came to build the largest physical creation of their time, the design of the US system of highways was left to some of the least qualified civil engineers.[8] In a parallel circumstance, the excitement and lucrative compensation of the twenty-first-century technology sector may be luring away the most intelligent and talented from architecture at a time when the global expansion of cities will need them most. The lesson of Lewis's accounting is that if the architectural profession and academy do not rally to attract the talent necessary for Millennials to lead, the critical work of the coming decades may be done poorly and without imagination, or it will go to other disciplines with better-qualified staff.

If the prospect of architecture's disruption is unsettling, the realization that all professions are vulnerable only furthers concern. In their 2015 book *The Future of the Professions*, Richard and Daniel Susskind assert that automation and innovation will effectively dismantle every profession in the near future. These include medicine, law, architecture, and even the clergy. The Susskinds claim that "we are on the brink of a period of fundamental and irreversible change in the way that the expertise of these specialists is made available in society."[9] In their view, the current professions are antiquated, opaque, and no longer affordable, with the expertise of the best enjoyed only by the few. The Susskinds conclude that as humanity inevitably transitions from a "print-based industrial society" to a "technology-based Internet society," the "grand bargain" struck between the laity and the professions will eventually be terminally rescinded.[10]

As in other twenty-first-century disruptions, two parallel sets of changes will bring on the Susskinds' forecast. First, automation will streamline and optimize traditional ways of working through the application of technology. Second, innovation will transform the working professional using increasingly capable systems, giving birth to new ways of sharing practical expertise. It bears noting that the Susskinds focus less on the disruption to industry sectors that concerns Clayton Christensen and others who write about it, and dwell more on disruption's potential to liberate knowledge from those who hoard it. In doing so, they situate all professionals as a controlling elite in a class struggle with the public (Abbott refers to those who share this view of professionals as "monopolists"). The Susskinds' position is best articulated when they quote Stanley Fish, who writes that "professionalism wears a darker face, the face of manipulation and self aggrandizement . . . and stands for an activity in which a small and self-selected group conspires against the laity by claiming a superiority that is based finally on nothing more than the obfuscating jargon and the seized control of the machinery of production and distribution."[11] Given the meager contemporary compensation of architects, it seems yet another irony that they be identified by some as being on par with the higher paid professionals who the monopolists condemn.

Abbott's monopolists typically claim that every profession tries to create a mystique to protect its jurisdiction. Harold Laski describes this aura as "veneration not very different from that of the priest in primitive societies; for the plain man he, like the priest, exercises a mystery into which the uninitiated cannot enter."[12] As a profession's jurisdiction is threatened, its sense of mystery tends to expand. Both the architectural profession and academy seem to have fallen victim to this form of mystification in their language, custom, rhetoric, and even clothing, with their priest-like characteristics particularly unsettling: the vow of poverty, the autonomous liturgy, the tendency to marry within caste, and the obsessive wearing of black. Continuing these practices only makes the profession more vulnerable to those who might want to violate its jurisdiction: by simply pulling away the curtain behind the jargon and certifications, others may find little expertise worth paying for.

The incremental dismantling of each profession will begin with a "routinization" through automation of those aspects of the profession already commodified, eventually expanding over the fortified walls that protect Abbott's inference phase of service. The Susskinds claim that the undermining of a profession's jurisdiction will be enabled by an artificial intelligence using "brute force processing and massive storage capacity, rather than simulation of human thought processes."[13] They do concede that there will always remain a need in some sort of professional capacity for those critical junctures of human intervention when "we tend to want another human being to have reflected, and perhaps agonized, over decisions and advice that mattered to us."[14] Consistent with the monopolists, they predict a profession's demise as more opportunity than challenge: "We ask people to look beyond the professions to be open to alternative and better ways of handling [a] limited understanding of human beings. And from the recipient's perspective, crudely, if we can find more affordable, less forbidding, higher quality, and more transparent and empowering ways of helping people, then we should expect these to be warmly welcomed."[15]

Parallel to the Susskinds inquiry, a 2013 Oxford University study by the researchers Carl Frey and Michael Osborne examines the susceptibility to computerization of over seven hundred US occupations.[16] They estimate that 47 percent of total American employment is at high risk and could expect to be automated within the next two decades. While they estimate automation will be principally confined to low-skill and low-wage occupations, they also find that "algorithms for big data are now rapidly entering domains reliant upon pattern recognition and can readily substitute for labor in a wide range of non-routine cognitive tasks."[17] Without a specific timetable, Frey and Osborne set the probability of the computerization of architects at 1.8 percent and those of architectural drafters at 52 percent. This places architects in the low-risk category with doctors and engineers (mostly under 2 percent), and drafters in the medium-risk category along-side dental assistants (51 percent) and commercial pilots (55 percent).[18] The specific destinations for an architect's instructions in Abbott's treatment phase—Brickmasons (82 percent), Roofers (90 percent), and Cabinetmak-ers (92 percent)—Frey and Osborne predict will largely be automated. Despite the variability based on category, and the seeming immunity for higher-trained professionals, they stress that the effects will likely change the nature of work across entire industries and occupations.[19] These trans-formations will create new and gradually expanding breaches in the wall surrounding architecture's inference. Eliminating the need for one out of two drafters, which is the traditional entry-level position for architects, will significantly disrupt the path toward licensure. And if there are any disci-plines left in the treatment phase that are still subordinated to architecture, those tasks will be almost entirely be performed by machines.

Since Frey and Osborne's report, others have made similar forecasts. McKinsey Global Institute generally supports their finding that roughly half of jobs are at high risk and go into greater detail about the pace and extent of change they expect will affect $16 trillion in current wages in the global economy. While McKinsey predicts that less than 5 percent of human oc-cupations will be erased entirely, they speculate that about two-thirds of all occupations will have at least one-third of their activities automated. They assert that more occupations will change fundamentally than will be automated away.[20]

Whether one believes the future forecasts of Frey and Osborne or McKin-sey, the Susskinds seem to accurately describe a contemporary state of flux. In summarizing the current situation for specific participants from a genera-tional perspective, they portray those at the end of their careers (Boomers) as hoping to "keep transformation at bay until they hang up their boots." For those at the beginning (Millennials), the Susskinds expect them to have second thoughts about committing to any profession and caution them to be wary of their parents and advisers who are still fixated on the professions of the twentieth century. As for specific accomplices, the Susskinds contend that educators are "unsure what they are training the next generation of professionals to become," that insurers have "little grip on the new risks that are emerging from radically different work practices," and that regulators are "hesitant about what it is that they may soon be regulating," and as a result, are "steadfastly discouraging change." Leading strategists of each profession are either "exploring 'blue oceans,' while others are 'disrupting' their current ways of working" as "nobody wants to be dubbed a late adopter in the post professional society, so the laggards are now pleased to say (or rationalize) that they preferred to be a 'fast second.'"[21]

The disruption to the professions the Susskinds describe includes education and is consistent with the dramatic changes to higher education predicted by John Carey and John Hennessy described in Chapter One. The Susskinds contend that in addition to methods, the content taught in professional academies will also change dramatically. As I describe in the next chapter, the architectural profession, whether unconsciously or through intent, seems to be moving toward some form of reorganization. By most measures, on the other hand, the American architectural academy seems to be ignoring the disruption entirely. Despite a 22 percent decline in new students enrolled in accredited programs between 2009 and 2014,[22] accredited architecture programs continue to expand. At the lowest ebb of the recession in 2009, five wholly new accredited architecture programs sought candidacy;[23] by 2015, the number had grown to eighteen programs either seeking or in candidacy.[24] This expansion continued during the recession, even as almost half of those who had completed internships in the United States did not seek licensure.[25]

One of those unlicensed graduates, Casius Pealer, describes this as "represent[ing] a huge loss of energy, talent, diversity and strength for the profession of architecture. It's as if we have a pipeline that has been leaking 45% for over twenty years, and we just accept it. Some of our leaders even think it's a good thing, whether they are willing to say so publicly or not."[26] While the "good thing" Pealer may be referring to is the assertion that architectural education qualifies as a strong foundation for other professional endeavors, a position the AIA actively advertises and Tomas Rossant predicts, nonetheless, the oversupply creates significant downward pressure on salaries. And increasing the number of schools at a time when enrollment is in decline, the profession is arguably oversupplied, and, as the Susskinds argue, "educators are unsure what they are training the next generation of professionals to become" also seems imprudent. However, one motivation for new schools in the twenty-first century is for smaller universities to add a professional school to increase their ratings. Even with the high cost of studio teaching, architecture schools are still less expensive to start and run than those teaching law, medicine, or business. Others see codependence as a motive. Robert Gutman contends cynically that the profession secretly encourages schools to keep churning out more architects in order to keep labor costs low.[27] One might also argue that architecture schools have become more faculty-serving than student-serving, where faculty use teaching to experiment through their students, supplement their own low professional incomes, or secure health benefits. Given the highly cyclical nature of architecture's growth, the use of schools as safe havens to weather economic recessions also cannot be ruled out as a motivation for opening more.

The academy's failure to train for an effective inference stage has contributed to the American architectural profession's growing incapacitation. The root causes align with Buchanan's Big Rethink critique of 2011,[28] which faults schools still teaching seventies-era aesthetic formalism, propagating the myth of the solo designer instead of teaching a knowledge base necessary to fortify architecture's professional jurisdiction. And while some inroads have been made, the prevailing pedagogy still largely ignores the Millennial preference for practical purpose and collaboration. Earlier critiques, including those by Cuff and Gutman and the Boyer report, predate Buchanan's concern, and perhaps none is more comprehensive than Thomas Fisher's. In his 2000 book, *In the Scheme of Things*, Fisher criticizes a pedagogy that undervalues the importance of economics, finance, and management, thereby separating the aesthetic and analytic, overemphasizes drawings and models at the expense of the written and verbal communication necessary to collaborate with other professions and communicate with the public, and typically compels students to work autonomously in constant competition instead of sharing a common knowledge base in collaborative pursuits.[29] In their 2002 Studio Culture report, Millennials themselves voiced similar concerns.

The profession's weakness as described by Bernstein, the academy's inadequacy as outlined by Fisher, and the impotence felt by those without proper preparation leave the architectural community demoralized. Recent external forces have only magnified this sense of dejection. The Great Recession forced a third of practitioners to leave the profession and kept many prospects from entering, but as the economy moves toward recovery, architectural enrollments remain low and unemployment threatens as technological unemployment looms. The effects are serious and have been years in the making. In 1988, Robert Gutman observed the debilitating effect of architecture's disunity, noting that a "combination of diversity and fragmentation are major factors that help to explain why architecture is populated by a higher proportion of alienated and disappointed men and women than any major profession."[30] By 2012, architects were among the occupational groups most prone to suicide, with rates almost twice as high as medicine's and law's.[31]

If architecture is to emerge from disruption reinvigorated and no longer demoralized, it must reestablish its jurisdiction by recalibrating its gatekeeping strategy for degrees, internships, and licensure and reformulating its pedagogy relevant to the needs of the Millennial Age. Before I discuss each of these undertakings in the next chapter, it may be useful to reconsider the long arc of architecture's past reforms in the context of other professions. Applying a framework of generational rhythms helps to pinpoint the propitious past eras when substantive change occurred (or did not, and why) and the generational dynamics involved.

Comparing the Professions

The consideration of all professions as a group leads many to treat the most prestigious and best compensated of them as standards, namely medicine and law. The Susskinds began their research with law (Richard is a lawyer, Daniel an economist), and Abbott employs medical terminology in his abstract model of the professions. Dana Cuff reflects on how those who study architecture often make comparisons to medicine or law, from which she draws out several distinctions. Primary among them is that architecture, when considered as an art, maintains a high degree of cultural plurality. In contrast, expertise that resides in biological science or carefully documented legal precedent is less readily challenged. When one goes beyond the functional characteristics of architecture, which nonarchitects can also produce, its cultural value, in Cuff's words, is "not nearly as persuasive as the results of other professionals' neglect, which can be fatal or incarcerating."[32] Nonetheless, a long tradition exists of lateral comparison between architecture and other professions, and addressing the current disruption comprehensively requires a lateral analysis and also a longitudinal one. This becomes especially critical when many of those other professions, including engineering, accounting, and law, are invading architecture's jurisdiction. A longitudinal examination of each profession often reveals a long period of time—spanning many generations—before reform is fully enacted. Applying a generational framework to uncover fertile historical moments and see how the generational groups of that time initiated (or restricted) action helps clarify our own moment. As in other situations, this inquiry shows how timing can be everything.

Comparing the Professions: Medicine

The medical profession credits the 1910 Flexner report with the prestige, compensation, and rigor that the practice maintained through the twentieth century. Abraham Flexner, an educator without a direct connection to medicine, produced the document, which was commissioned by the American Medical Association with funding from the Carnegie Foundation. Upon the report's completion, the AMA quickly followed its recommendations for medical education reform that had long-lasting consequences for the profession. The sequence and requirements of medical education—the premed track, medical school, licensure, and residency—have remained largely intact based on Flexner's reforms.[33]

Flexner grounded his critique in the statistic that US medical education oversupplied doctors at a ratio five times greater than that of Germany, with many whom Flexner considered woefully ill-trained.[34] Flexner identified the cause as the proliferation of so-called "proprietary schools"—small, for-profit trade schools owned by one or more doctors that granted degrees after two years. These typically employed part-time, local doctors to provide instruction that was purely "didactic" and largely without clinical or laboratory exposure.[35] The cudgel that Flexner gave the AMA to eliminate the proprietary schools was the requirement that medical education follow a newly legitimized scientific method of university-based laboratory training in human physiology and biochemistry, all associated with a hospital for clinical training.[36] The financial burden of these requirements forced proprietary schools to either close or merge with other entities. Flexner also provided the template for how each state should sanction the creation of medical schools and regulate their size and for how the AMA should police their rigor.

Flexner's remarkable effectiveness caused many contemporary professions to consider a similar appraisal. What may not have been evident then was how Flexner's report culminated a legacy of responses to challenges to medicine's jurisdiction. These trace back to the era of Jacksonian populism when sectarianism and folk healing tested established orthodox medicine's exclusivity. Among these, homeopathy presented the greatest challenge to traditional medicine.[37] It was during this defensive period that an entrenched and orthodox profession sought legitimacy by founding the American Medical Association, which, within two years, charged a committee to set the standards for preliminary medical education. It also established a board to formally attack all sectarians, including homeopaths, and the patent medicines they prescribed. The struggle between orthodox medicine and homeopathy continued for much of the nineteenth century, with each claim-ing to be legitimate science. The conflict prevailed until the 1880s when a truce of sorts was achieved, with orthodox medicine absorbing some of its rival's attitude toward patient care, and homeopathy conceding some of its unproven philosophical positions. The arrival of European methods, with a track record of therapeutic success, found a professional medical community more receptive to unification, and in 1904, the AMA's Council on Medical Education called for national implementation of an "ideal" medical curriculum. This included two years of preliminary education requirements for entry into medical school, followed by two years of medical school–based training in laboratory sciences, then two more years involving clinical rota-tions in a teaching hospital.[38] This gave the basis in 1906 for the council to inspect all medical schools to classify them as "acceptable, doubtful, or unacceptable," thus laying the groundwork for Flexner's complete and thorough inspection several years later. In 1907, the AMA also expanded its jurisdiction by establishing a Council on Pharmacy and Chemistry to set standards for drug manufacturing and advertising to intensify its battle against patent medicines.[39]

In unifying and professionalizing medicine, the positive outcome of Flexner's reforms overshadows the significant collateral injuries. Armed with Flexner's report, to combat oversupply, the AMA successfully reduced the number of medical schools from a high of 160 in 1905 to 85 by 1920.[40] Flexner's medical school standards also successfully eliminated sects such as electropathy, cranial diagnosis, and hydrotherapy, most of which were associated with proprietary schools. Despite the accommodation it had previ-ously secured, homeopathy could not survive Flexner's purge, although os-teopathy, a related treatment method, did survive. It took many decades for homeopathy and other alternative practices, such as chiropractic medicine, to regain legitimacy. But to the AMA's discredit, it also adhered to Flexner's sexist and racist notions, curtailing advances by women and African Ameri-cans to become doctors.[41] Eventually Flexner's insensitivities would become footnotes, as Abbott describes medicine by the middle of the twentieth century as a profession that "had assumed a position of social prominence and power envied throughout the occupational world. Included in its vast organizational empire were a host of subordinate professional groups."[42]

Comparing the Professions: Law

Like medicine, the practice of law professionalized as the American Bar

Association (ABA) in the nineteenth century in response to Jacksonian populism, although almost two generations later than medicine did. This was in part due to law's largely local purview, but also because of its highly disorganized nature prior to the Civil War, especially regarding legal education through apprenticeships.[43] After its charter in 1878, the ABA's advocacy began slowly, and it was not until 1893 that it established a Section of Legal Education and Admissions to the Bar, followed in 1900 by the launch of the Association of American Law Schools (AALS). Both the ABA's Section of Legal Education's and the AALS's mission became to promote university-based law schools, in part to rein in the law's own unique heritage of proprietary schools that many in the profession blamed for an oversupply of unqualified lawyers.[44] Legal proprietary schools continued a long-standing tradition of apprenticeship and self-directed study, otherwise known as "reading" the law.[45]

As dean at Harvard Law School from 1870 to 1895, Christopher Langdell led the challenge of this proprietary heritage, and Harvard's school became the model to emulate. Under the patronage of the university's president, Charles Eliot, a biologist, Langdell reformed Harvard's curriculum, applying a scientific mindset to the law similar to that which paved the way for Flexner's reforms to medical education. Langdell believed that the student, guided carefully by a law professor, could draw out the principles of law through inductive, scientific reasoning. If law was a science, Langdell argued (with Eliot's unconditional support), then cases could be considered a form of data. In addition to this heavy emphasis on case law, Langdell brought new structure to Harvard's legal education. He required a bachelor's degree for entry, prescribed a given period of study (two years eventually became three), and established passage of yearly final examinations as a condition for advancement.[46] Langdell's case law–based pedagogy emerged as the norm in the twentieth century, albeit not without challenge, and Harvard's academic structure became the model many law schools adopted.

As legal education began to formalize, its education-focused bodies sought to resolve confusion regarding degree nomenclature. While Harvard's norm-setting program required an undergraduate degree for admission, the school still maintained the LLB (bachelor of laws), a degree it first granted in 1847, as a first (and then only) professional degree. By 1902 Harvard students grew envious of their medical colleagues' title of doctor and, joined by faculty, petitioned the university to award a JD (juris doctor), based on German precedent. While the Harvard Corporation declined this request, the newly formed University of Chicago Law School adopted the suggestion, using its undergraduate degree requirement for admission as rationale. However, when it later decided to admit law students without an undergraduate degree, Chicago granted them the LLB, a degree with essentially the same requirements as its JD.[47] The ABA's Section of Legal Education followed Chicago's lead and in 1906 adopted a resolution favoring the JD as the first professional degree, albeit only for those with a prior undergraduate education; those without would still receive the LLB. Many schools adopted the recommendation, and by 1926, 80 percent of university-based programs offered both degrees. Rather than settling anything, the failure to distinguish the curricula of both degrees created generations of dispute. Elite law schools (Harvard, Yale, and Columbia) argued persistently that if Langdell's pedagogy was the standard, and Harvard offered an undergraduate professional degree, then any school that called the same education a professional doctorate practiced a form of self-aggrandizement. This criticism took hold, and most schools stopped offering the JD, some only a few years after instituting it.[48] By 1960, the JD had all but vanished.[49]

Accompanying the debates on degree nomenclature, legal organizations continually attacked marginal education that was not to the standards pioneered by Langdell. These organizations were so impressed with Flexner's report that in 1913 they requested that the Carnegie Foundation perform a similar appraisal of US law schools. By the time Alfred Reed, writing for Carnegie, finally reported in 1921, he endorsed Langdell's education system, but rather than producing a Flexner-like mandate for a single scientific method for law, he concluded that legal cultures were too diverse and law schools too varied in their delivery for a single system to prevail.[50] And dashing legal organizations' hopes that Carnegie would advise them on how to restrict legal sectarianism taught through proprietary systems, Reed instead registered egalitarian sympathy for part-time programs, many of which were the continuation of the read-the-law tradition and more affordable than university-based schools, recommending that "the making and administration of the law shall be kept accessible to Lincoln's plain people."[51] Thus after making significant progress toward reform, the legal profession's headway stalled, its initial movement toward clarifying degrees reversed itself, and its attempts to establish academic rigor based on full-time education backfired. Unlike medicine, which staunchly maintained Flexner's pedagogical format and curricular rigor, the legal profession could not maintain unity.

The 1960s brought a sudden turnaround in the law degree debate. In 1964, the ABA's Section of Legal Education put forth essentially the same 1906 resolution, and by 1965, almost half of American law schools phased out the LLB in favor of the JD as the first professional degree; by 1971, the LLB ceased to exist. Changed circumstances led to the reversal. With the post-war expansion of higher education, most law school applicants by 1960 now held undergraduate degrees. Proponents of a single degree echoed Harvard students and faculty of the previous era, claiming the LLB "tends to impair the image of the legal profession. It also lessens the image of the law school in the minds of those who instruct the other divisions of the parent institution."[52] Wording of the resolution seconded this finding, stating: "There is a lack of uniformity among the law schools approved by The American Bar Association" and "confusion has arisen in the minds of the public as to the difference, if any, between the Bachelor of Laws (LL.B.) degree and the Juris Doctor (J.D.)."[53] The resolution also argued that the JD terminology more accurately described the relevant academic accomplishment at approved law schools.

As it did throughout the century, Harvard, joined now by Yale and Columbia, held steadfast to its defense of the LLB as the first professional degree, but ultimately the student activism of the era brought about change. In an era of ossified establishment thinking, the clamor of students (and alumni) against LLB holdouts became too great, ultimately causing the administrations of those schools to yield.[54] Concerns that eliminating the LLB would diminish the numbers of African Americans and women attending law school proved unwarranted: between 1971 and 2010 the percentage of African Americans enrolled almost doubled and women increased five-fold.[55] Instead, the clarification of the status of the JD put lawyers on par with medical practitioners in terms of professional salaries and prestige on campus, and this status helped lawyers to extend their influence from the courtroom to government bodies at all levels, as well as to corporate and institutional boards in the way that Tomas Rossant observes.[56]

The Great Recession seems, however, to have brought the expansion of the law profession and its academies to a halt. In 2015, only 60 percent of law graduates were employed full time in the legal industry ten months after graduation.[57] Between 2006 and 2015, the number of law school applicants in the US fell from 88,700 to 51,000.[58] Reasons vary; according to David Barnhizer, "virtually all law schools across the US pumped too many lawyers into a system that was already filled to the brim and now is overflowing."[59]

Former vice president Walter Mondale has noted that "people are turned off on legal education because of a lack of suitable paying jobs."[60] Angered over their inability to find work, some law graduates have successfully sued the schools for overstating their potential success in the job market when they applied. To make sense of this disruption, the American Bar Association enlisted a task force, which submitted a report and recommendations in 2014.[61] Those recommendations may not alter what Barnhizer claims: that the combined low employment and dropping enrollment are a "'transformative event,' not a cycle that will return to a familiar equilibrium."[62]

Comparing the Professions: Architecture

Dana Cuff's reservations that architecture is fundamentally different as a profession from both the law and medicine are valid. Nonetheless, enough parallel historical initiatives, including similar professional entities forming at the same time, exist to make a lateral assessment valuable. As it did for its legal students, Harvard began requiring an undergraduate degree for admission to its professional architecture programs in 1906,[63] ironically, not long after Frank Lloyd Wright spent five years interning under Louis Sullivan without any higher degree. A year after its charter in 1912, the Association of Collegiate Schools of Architecture (ACSA) also became intrigued by Flexner's impact on medicine, and, as occurred in the legal field, the ACSA would eventually commission Carnegie to perform a similar examination of architectural education. Like the AMA, the ACSA chose to first perform an internal review, and whether influenced by Flexner or feeling the need to also regularize education, they established "standard minima" curricular requirements as a result of that review.[64] The interruption of World War I delayed momentum, and it was not until 1930 that the ACSA renewed its effort to produce an independent study, which concluded in 1932. Although funded by Carnegie, the report was coauthored by two architectural educators, Francke Huntington Bosworth and Roy Childs Jones, causing it to lack Flexner's outsider viewpoint.[65]

If the ACSA's original interest in Flexner's report on medical education was to enact similar reforms for the architectural profession and to standardize its procedures, by the time Bosworth and Jones's *Study of Architectural Schools* appeared in 1932, its recommendations were completely the opposite. Rather than offer a deep critique, the authors found in American architecture schools a "fundamental vitality," and echoing Alfred Reed's Carnegie-funded recommendations to the ABA, the report endorsed degree diversity and recommended against standardization.[66] As a result the ACSA dropped its standard minima in favor of supporting pedagogical experimentation the same year the report was published, and until the establishment of the NAAB eight years later, architectural education would proceed without any common accreditation standards.[67] The diversity Bosworth and Jones identified was reflected in the eleven different degree types architecture maintained at the time. A 1927 report set out to remedy the "confusion and misunderstanding" regarding all these types by attempting to supply universal content and length-of-study standards, but by 1931, William Hudnut, one of its authors, reversed position, characterizing the diversity of degrees as lending "color," and opining that color could be more important than clarity.[68]

After World War II, the AIA took its turn and produced another Carnegie-underwritten study employing the architectural historian Turpin Bannister. The two-volume *Architect at Mid-Century: Evolution and Achievement* offers many recommendations, all while maintaining architecture's academy and profession as "inseparably interdependent." Bannister wrote that "the closest liaison" must be maintained between the two in order to "adjust content and method to the changing needs of practice."[69] In the rapid expansion of both the practice and the academy (enrollment had doubled since Bosworth's report), Bannister's recommendations led to little substantive change at a time when expansion, not reform, was the mood of the age. A third survey of architectural education released in 1967 by Princeton faculty members Robert Geddes and Bernard Spring (known subsequently as the Princeton report) instead caused an uproar of denunciation. While it ultimately also failed to lead to reform, the Princeton report came closest to proposing change as comprehensive as Flexner's in terms of the scope of architectural education and its relation to the profession. In recognizing a disciplinary range far beyond architecture, Geddes and Spring declared this new terrain as "environmental design" and devised a "modular jointed framework" that could potentially lead to over a thousand careers related to design. To create this framework, the authors culled prior literature and solicited the most progressive educational ideas from colleagues to propose six "interlocking" educational phases that could lead to many different courses of study with some flexibility. Although never explicitly stated, the report effectively proposes that professional education be at the graduate level, although without necessarily associating that instruction with architecture schools. Degrees granted using the framework could be in landscape, urban design, planning, etc.—any aspect of the environment in need of design attention.[70]

The 1996 Boyer report followed the Princeton report, and was the first Carnegie-funded examination led by nonarchitects. As outlined more thoroughly in Chapter Six, it reaffirmed what architects already did well in their service to society while also setting out to repair the frayed relationship between the academy and the profession. Although its authors avoid any discussion of curricular or degree reform, the number and type of degrees had become increasingly confused. Once moribund, PhDs had revived, and some schools had converted undergraduate to graduate degrees by shortening the elapsed time but keeping the same requirements. To remedy this, in 1991 architecture's five "collateral organizations" set a 2002 deadline for a single degree nomenclature.[71] The year came and went, and although additional discussion ensued, architecture in the twenty-first century finds itself no closer to a single degree and a systemized educational structure than when discussion first started at the beginning of the twentieth.

Comparing the Professions through Generations

Comparing the professional developments of American medicine, law, and architecture reveals common stages of development, from initial organization to established academic legitimacy, from the organization of degrees as a path to licensure to the creation of an ethics code that binds their jurisdiction and limits incursion by others. Beginning in the mid-nineteenth century, progression through these stages for each profession has taken considerable time, and if one accepts the basic concept of generations, many distinct generational cohorts have been involved.

All three professions experienced significant stirrings to clarify both their professional education and degree thresholds during the reform era, which straddled the turn of the last century. Beginning in the 1880s, propelled by the young adult momentum of American progressives, medicine successfully rode a scientific revolution emanating from Germany to usher in dramatic change to its profession. While these reforms did not fully take root until after the close of the time period, the initiative started by the AMA in the era's last years and continued by Flexner still took full advantage of the value-driven activism that defined the period. On the other hand, reforms to legal and architectural education, which began later, did not achieve the same success. When each finally compiled reports amid the unraveling ethos of the 1920s and 1930s respectively, those reports recommended preserving the status quo of the fields' fragmented disciplinary missions rather than unifying around reform. To attain the parity it had sought with medicine, law would have to wait for a period similar to the reform era, the consciousness-raising era of the 1960s. Architecture's Princeton report might have sought a similar parity, but it failed.

Emergent student activism seems to have characterized each archetypal era. Progressive law students began the movement to elevate their degrees in the reform era, an effort not completed until their archetypal successors, the Boomer generation, continued it several generational cycles later. By contrast, Geddes and Spring's proposal for architecture failed as wariness of top-down initiatives by Boomer students with slogans such as "question authority" prevailed in producing an entirely different outcome. For architecture, the failure of generations to agree doomed the initiative.

External events undoubtedly contribute as much as the mood of a particular era to precipitating change. Strauss and Howe would argue that an era's receptivity plays a critical role in its acceptance of change. According to their schema, major transformations occur primarily during so-called "social moments" that are either internal and value-driven or external and motivated by some significant test. Eras between social moments predominated over by recessive generations are more prone to maintaining status quo. Both the AMA and AIA organized professionally during the sectional unraveling that preceded the American Civil War. The AMA's was a defensive move in 1847 against homeopathy and other sectarian groups, and the AIA, while less defensive, was founded in 1857 amidst uncertainty after two false starts.[72] Both organizations would have to wait until the reform era to be on firm enough foundations to establish effective pedagogies. In a similar unraveling era at the end of the next century, the failure of architecture to fulfill its 1991 pledge to agree on a common degree exhibits a similar trend toward nonaction. The legal profession's ability to agree to a common degree during the value-driven period of change in the 1960s occurred because the conditions that previously prevented it—some applicants not having undergraduate degrees—no longer existed. One can speculate as to whether any external conditions prevented architecture from a similar ratification. While the answer may lie in acknowledging Cuff's and others' conclusion that architecture is altogether a different discipline, this disregards the significant parallel activities it encountered in establishing itself as a profession along with law and medicine.

An answer may lie in how architecture stands as a profession compared to its sisters. In his study, Andrew Abbott catalogs the many requirements other writers on professions use to describe a vocation's maturation, generally including its organization, teaching, licensure, and ethics as critical aspects of securing its jurisdiction. One writer, Magali Larson, adds an additional requirement; she argues that to reach its highest functional level, a profession needs to attain a "steady state," or elite status.[73] Medicine sought and attained elite status using Flexner's report, and law finally attained a parallel status by the 1970s. At the same time law was affirming its elite status, architecture rejected the Princeton report's argument for graduate-level professional education, emphatically distancing itself from any label of elitism this reform might bring. At a joint AIA-ACSA convention in 1968, where the report was reviewed and attacked, architecture chose instead to launch a campaign of inclusion, accepting the civil rights activist Whitney Young's admonition to increase sensitivity to those disadvantaged,[74] echoing, in a way, Reed's earlier recommendation for sustaining variegation in the law. With a presiding generation of Millennials—who are both the most diverse and tolerant generation in history—will a perceived elitism remain the external condition that prevents architecture from striving toward a professional status on par with its sister disciplines?

A longitudinal analysis of architecture compared to the professions of law and medicine reveals common eras of both activity and passivity. It also shows the varying successes of each at achieving a higher state of order. Understanding the interrelationship between generations offers awareness as to how architecture might adapt itself in the current Millennial Age. The Susskinds, Frey and Osborne, and the McKinsey institute forecast a combination of automation and liberating information disrupting all professions. This disturbance will find architecture already impaired, its professionals weak, and its academies miscalibrated and oversupplying the profession. When considering joining a discipline this dysfunctional and at odds with the needs of their time, Millennial students may instead be going elsewhere. Yet one group's disruption can be another's chance at bold initiative through innovation. It will be architecture's challenge to shift from disrupted to disruptor, from reactive to proactive. Accepting Millennials' values and seconding their optimism, as described in the next chapter, would represent a critical step toward making this shift.

CHAPTER 11

What's Next?
The Academy, Licensure, Practice

> **As with all historic tipping points, it seems inevitable in retrospect: Of course it was the young people . . .**
>
> **TIM KREIDER**

Emerging from the Great Recession, the architectural practice remains weakened, and if only a portion of the technological unemployment that is forecast occurs, the consequences will still be significant. The twenty-first-century trend of opening new architecture schools only contributes to oversupply and worsens an already tenuous situation. And incursions into architecture's inner domain, what Andrew Abbott calls inference, from the reinvigorated design discipline or from other rivals with a better understanding of automation and other technological developments, are other stressors. Managing oversupply from the academy into the profession will be a distinct trial, but the prospect of architectural practices and schools mobilizing Millennials—who intuitively grasp technology, have the confidence to innovate, seamlessly network in teams, and, without prompting, actively pursue a larger mission for the public good—can broaden architecture's jurisdiction to potentially absorb the academy's output. Removing the barriers to communication and cooperation between generations is a way to achieve this.

The early alignment between architectural and Millennial characteristics provides common principles by which to fully integrate the generation into the practice and education. While it may have been slow at first to recognize Millennials, architecture has become—to use a phrase borrowed from Richard and Daniel Susskind—a "fast second" in attempting to understanding the cohort as a distinct part of its culture. The architectural community has begun to answer *Architect* magazine's 2013 call for changes to practice, licensure, and pedagogy.[1] Later that year the AIA issued a forward-looking document that included the following description:

> The youngest generation of workers, children of both Baby Boomer and Gen X parents, have different work styles, preferences and expectations than their predecessors. Millennials are characterized as natural collaborators who integrate communication and work technologies deeply and seamlessly. They value quality of experience and learning opportunities over extrinsic rewards, and crave regular feedback and encouragement. . . . Many firms realize that their mid- to senior-level managers have difficulty leading the adoption of new technologies and look to their Millennial workers to drive adoption of advanced tools.[2]

The AIA has since made concrete efforts to support Millennials' priorities in other ways, including distributing a public awareness campaign about the value of architecture through various media that includes holding a film competition,[3] financially supporting design centers and their social impact missions, and promoting technological ways to advance the collaboration-driven platforms of building information modelling (BIM) and integrated project delivery (IPD). The National Council of Architectural Registration Boards (NCARB) has overhauled many aspects of licensure, rewriting the licensing exam to better reflect new modes of practice that include instant results, encouraging experimentation by schools to decrease the length of the internship requirement,[4] and improving its social media presence to demystify the internship and licensure process. Architecture schools have also begun to experiment with gamification and low-residency degrees. And to better understand future students, the Association of Collegiate Schools of Architecture (ACSA) retained a consultant to better position architecture in the higher education marketplace based on the preferences of Millennial students.[5] So if the profession and academy are already naturally absorbing Millennials, why should any further accommodations be made? While adopting a laissez-faire attitude may ultimately effectively blend Millennials with the architectural community, doing so still ignores the gravity of the current disruption and the shock of automation that is yet to come. It also ignores the opportunity to turn the disruption into an advantage.

Innovate/Disrupt: The Profession

The arrival of Millennials can be advantageous to architecture if Millennial architects' technological predisposition can innovate around the incursions on jurisdiction in both Abbott's diagnosis and treatment phases of practice. In the diagnosis phase—what many architects call the front end—applying innovative and measurable data analysis, or any form of physical or conceptual organization, in anticipation of potential building can expand the architect's purview. Expanding the use of BIM and moving the bulge of Patrick MacLeamy's curve increasingly to the left can further empower the architect's domain. While strategy firms such as McKinsey Global Institute and PricewaterhouseCoopers exert considerable contemporary influence in how businesses organize themselves, the architectural profession can build a new level of integrated service by combining data control with its own proprietary design inference to advise businesses about physical need. In this way, architecture can extend a data stream to inform later design phases, something strategy firms may lack the combination of creativity and interdisciplinary skill to accomplish. In Abbott's treatment phase—also known in architecture as the back end—IPD and parametric manufacturing offer similar opportunities to continue data-driven engagement beyond construction into the postoccupancy phase. Consolidating these findings offers new possibilities. First, the tremendous amount of data emitted by buildings, now commonly referred to as "data exhaust," can cycle back and fertilize Abbott's diagnosis stage in a continuous feedback loop. In this scenario, architects will be able to warranty buildings to draw additional fees if their performance meets expectations. While this treads into an area of risk that architects have traditionally been averse to, Thomas Fisher argues that since investment banks have used transparent data as a way for their clients to understand and manage risk, the architecture profession can emulate them to similar advantage.[6] Finding fees less commodified than other traditional services, some architectural firms have already expanded into both the front and back ends of practice, but other disciplines, led by the strategy firms, have also entered this domain. By establishing proprietary control over the feedback loop of a single data stream, the architecture profession can radically restate its value to the public and best these rivals.

The future success or failure of the architectural profession may depend on how Millennials distinguish themselves in Abbott's inference phase. The professional dismantling that the Susskinds predict, however severe, will occur incrementally throughout the Millennial generation's professional career. Advances in software will undoubtedly affect the labor structure of architectural offices, perhaps affirming Carl Frey and Michael Osborne's prediction that the role of the drafter will be significantly computerized. And if machine learning begins to automate certain aspects of design in the inference phase, many professionally trained architects may find themselves technologically unemployed. How Millennials anticipate and integrate this automation will be critical to their future. While the architectural profession might see automation as an incursion on its jurisdiction, society at large, as the Susskinds contend, may instead see it as democratization with a significant cost savings. Clients will expect to draw on some of automation's cost savings related to design fees, as will the software provider through licensing. The remainder will go to the software's operator, who achieves expectations. This leaves no guarantee of what the architect's share will be, if any. The sooner the profession begins to experiment with some form of automation, organizing Millennials and their innate technological skill at the controls, the better chance it will have of claiming its fair share of this savings. And the reinvestment of those profits may be able to right the ship of what is now a failing business model. Substantiating an equitable fee structure can bolster architecture's jurisdiction and also make the case for its expansion. Sustainable profits directed toward maintaining a living wage can also begin to lure back those leaving the architectural practice over quality-of-life issues.

The emergence of an entirely new intellectual property, a data-driven, semiautomated design enterprise, raises many questions, as tantalizing as they are unnerving. Who controls the data and with whom it can be shared becomes an issue of monetization, with risk reorganized according to a new rubric. If machine learning applies a particular style, say "prairie school" or "critical regionalist," who claims any royalties? Perhaps more importantly, what does this say about the art of architecture? What becomes of its artistry when technology takes control? (Musicians disrupted by their industry's upheavals may have a great deal to say about this.) This will be a question resonating in architectural practice and schools as the disruption continues. While the Susskinds acknowledge the need for a human to "agonize" over a decision, and for some clientele, aesthetic human intervention will undoubtedly remain a necessity, that person, too, will increasingly look to data as a basis for his or her decision making. It is the cultivation and continued growth of aesthetic sensibility that may be most challenged and will require the vigilance of many in its defense.

Generational theorists may offer guidance regarding the stridency of a counterpoint and how long it must be sustained. Karl Mannheim and José Ortega y Gasset suggest that every generation maintains those who are for and against in a continual battle of wills. As a generation's dominance shifts, so, too, does that balance. A minority opposition in one generation will set the tone for those who will lead in the next. William Strauss and Neil Howe's theory postulates that dominant generations build so significant a momentum that it transfers to successors with only minor correction. In architecture, one can use this in understanding how dominant heroic modernists, after World War II as part of the GI generation, passed momentum on to those who Robert Stern calls "refiners" and demographers refer to as the Silent generation. If this pattern holds for Millennials, the effect of their disruption may carry through to the next generations, and according to a close reading of Strauss and Howe, it will be the Millennials' children, abetted by a minority opposition among the generation that follows them, who will finally challenge them. If the Millennials' primary innovative thrust will be technological, they could eventually become technocratic, and as happened with modernism, their challengers will be those invested in architecture's aesthetic values. That rebuttal may arrive in an era of professional dissolution, although the candle of that critique will begin to burn during the current disruption, and a distinct but resolute minority will likely keep its flame burning.

Innovate/Disrupt: The Academy

The protection and cultivation of architecture's core values from technological automation will be even more important to the academy than to the profession. At the same time, architectural educators will have to recalibrate pedagogy to respond effectively to computerization as well as other threats to the profession's jurisdiction. While these challenges are significant, they are attainable, and architectural educators, knowingly or not, have been building toward addressing them for decades. Recognizing the alignment between Millennials and architecture can further this end. Architecture's steady embrace of computers beginning in the 1980s has provided a platform for the digitally native mindset of Millennials to accelerate from, but students will need to transcend software competence and be able to master its code. Mastery will allow them to take command of future artificial intelligence organized around BIM, effectively utilizing its built-in collaborative possibilities to advance IPD and break disciplinary silos. To take on outside strategy firms, architectural pedagogy will need to fully embrace the practical importance of economics, finance, and management. It will also need to complement architects' graphic skills by better teaching of verbal and written communication. And if architecture can overcome its overemphasis on working individually and competitively, it can leverage Millennials' propensity to work collectively, thereby sharing a common professional knowledge base that can expand architecture's jurisdiction.

Augmenting an architect's education will be difficult to accomplish within the confines of an undergraduate professional degree. If the present duplicate system continues, those holding only the undergraduate professional degree may be the first to become technologically unemployed. Frey and Osborne maintain that educational attainment exhibits a strong negative relationship with an occupation's probability of computerization.[7] Undergraduate curricula that lead to graduate professional degrees have been in use in architecture for over a century. Following the Princeton report's implied directive and making a graduate degree the exclusive degree, as in medicine and law, comes with advantages and disadvantages.[8] Given the prior frustration in trying to accomplish this, one wonders if architecture has the stamina. But if the coming disruption is as severe as the Susskinds expect, every option for the discipline's survival should be revisited. A professional degree at the graduate level offers many advantages if collectively the architectural community accounts for its negative effects. Architecture's sister professions also debated degree reform, and while it took generations before reform succeeded, it was often a change in external context or generational dynamics that made the difference.

The emergence of the scientific measurability that precipitated Flexner's reforms in the field of medicine invites comparison to the contemporary rise in quantifiable data in the built environment, the so-called data exhaust that the Internet of Things will increasingly produce. For architects to effectively apply this data will require additional preparation. While oversupply from schools into the profession was a major motivator for medicine's reforms, empowering doctors to practice using the emerging scientific method was equally important. The required training raised academic standards, which forced the closure of those schools incapable of complying and compelled local jurisdictions to certify a minimum level of preparation. While the outcome stemmed the oversupply, it also raised the demand for health care overall, its effect simultaneously restricting and expanding its market.[9] In Magali Larson's terms, medicine achieved its steady-state, elite status, but the public perception was that the status had been earned. In architecture, the elitist label has represented a significant hurdle to an elevated single professional degree since the 1960s. Claims that it will deter those with socioeconomic disadvantages from entering the profession persist, even though similar concerns voiced among lawyers proved unwarranted. Those in architecture who wish to invalidate any comparison need to go no further than Flexner's notorious racism and sexism, or the AMA's puritanical zeal to purge sects that later proved worthy, although to do so ignores medicine's highly effective value proposition to the public and the widespread respect it garners. Another hurdle is the claim that architecture's inherent subjectivity and diversity of outlook inhibits a common pedagogy and a single degree. This ignores how the law ultimately overcame Reed's claim that its diverse methods and constituencies necessitated multiple pedagogies and degrees. While these arguments against degree reform represented obstacles for older generations, Millennials may encounter them differently in the face of the coming disruption. The common educational foundation necessary for architecture to leverage quantifiable data offers an opportunity similar to the one that medicine used to unify and vastly expand its jurisdiction. A generation that tends to seek consensus and is propelled by practicality might recognize this opportunity. As the most diverse and tolerant generation, Millennials may be able to problem-solve their way past these hurdles with equality and unity.

In architecture's century-long path toward curricular and degree reform, the 1967 Princeton report offers an organizational logic that previous generations disregarded. It lays a foundation for professional education while simultaneously broadening the umbrella for the widest range of careers in "environmental design" at all levels, including undergraduate education.[10] Many of its five strategies, solicited from other educators and studies, read as if written for today with Millennials in mind. These include the use of "sophisticated gaming techniques," "stored teaching programs [on computers]," and "field stations for advocacy planning and design in disadvantaged communities."[11] Similar to the medical school sequence formulated by Flexner, professional environmental design education includes initial general instruction with some preprofessional focus akin to premed, professional schooling, both didactic and clinical, and internship phases of residency and specialization.[12] Learning organizes around two-year modules with more variability in sequence than medicine, with any subset requiring licensure—architecture, landscape, planning, etc.—at the graduate level. The authors anticipate students attaining certification at the end of any two-year interval, acknowledging that some of the thousand possible environmental design careers may not require a professional degree. For those undecided on a career, the junction between intervals provides an opportunity to select from a choice of future programs that best match a student's aptitude and motivations.[13] The Princeton report recommends expansion on many axes including time, endorsing design education at the elementary and high school levels as well as for those in higher education who are not specifically studying design. The report's overall breadth allows for a common educational foundation at a national scale for professionals in multiple professions, the subordinates of each, and for the general public served.

A contemporary adaptation of the Princeton report, elevating professional architectural education to the graduate level, may actually increase the breadth of undergraduate design education rather than limit it. And if well deployed, this might reverse enrollment declines in many architecture departments. If architecture and design can fully unify, at least at the undergraduate level, in the manner that orthodox medicine and homeopathy achieved in the 1880s (but absent the later betrayal), colleges can become a crossroads of degree paths for Millennials, a generation already predisposed to design. Enrollees can range from those seeking technical or vocational training to students seeking a fast track to professional degrees, with many others in between.[14] A design-centric blend of technical and humanist learning oriented toward a data-driven future can serve as a common foundation program to draw students who are otherwise enrolling in the design thinking curricula offered in non-design departments such as business, engineering, and computing. It can also function as a sampler for those considering design education, or for those pursuing other degrees who have a secondary interest in it.[15] Rather than requiring freshman studios as a form of "boot camp," a prearchitecture design curriculum can ramp up to the more demanding coursework required for graduate school admission. Shed of its negative image of continual manic production in studio, design can become the default stand-by major, rather than business, communications, or psychology, for those Millennials undecided on a career.

For all the opportunities a contemporary application of the Princeton report offers, focus groups nonetheless indicate that Millennials—especially those saddled with high student loan debt—cannot fathom the prospect of paying for additional education. Our AIAS poll, however, reflects a different aspiration: 39 percent of Millennials who are either enrolled in a bachelor of architecture program or hold the degree replied that they plan to return for graduate work in architecture, and 28 percent reported planning for a master's or PhD in another discipline. If over 60 percent of architecture students see value in graduate-level training, education reform that extends the period of study may be more attainable than many think, especially if it leads to a better chance for employment at a higher salary. In focus groups, students also complain about confusing degrees and how changing career course added years to their undergraduate education. Many also blame low salaries for why architects leave the profession, which they say no one warned them about. Greater clarity regarding students' expectations may save many of them time and money overall. If enrollment continues to decline, market forces may cause schools to close, which has already begun to happen in legal education.[16] And given the high unemployment rate after graduation and high student loan debt, one cannot rule out the prospect that students will take a cue from their law colleagues to sue their educators, alleging false promises. None of these complaints are new, and the current gloomy prospects echo the alienation Robert Gutman described thirty years ago.[17]

To turn gloom to optimism, the architectural academy will need to reappraise itself in concert with the organizations that administer to the practice and licensure. Uncovering its own previous reform history in parallel to those of its sister professions will show how changing contexts offer opportunity for later generations. The legal profession's 1906 arguments were successfully repurposed in 1964; the Princeton report may be equally valuable fifty years later. Any reappraisal of architecture must foreground Millennials, as they will preside over architecture's sustained technological transformation and, if prepared, can reinvent the discipline consistent with their values. An overriding Millennial optimism may be the best remedy to the profession's gloom. Reappraisal will also require resolute, respectful, and progressive leadership across generations. As architecture enters a technologically driven era, its leadership must maintain a high regard for creativity and also be able to candidly discuss oversupply, its consequences, and potential remedies. While raising the bar for licensure might limit supply, it also offers the best path toward the professional stature required to increase demand for services, a demand that can be fulfilled by employing technological prowess and interdisciplinary collaboration. The prospect of an enhanced and expanded profession after a strategic reappraisal will help Millennials leap the hurdles that have thwarted previous generations of architects.

Innovate/Disrupt: Internship and Licensure

The architectural internship may be the educational phase most affected by the computerization of drafting. The drafter has traditionally been the apprentice position in offices, a position in which architects hone their craft. The obsolescence of drafting may deter private firms from taking on the responsibility of training interns.[18] As a result, the obligation for training interns may fall back upon the schools. This trend has already begun with NCARB's Integrated Path to Architectural Licensure program, the first to emerge of many similar proposals that are modeled on the medical residency.[19] That architecture schools lack the revenue of teaching hospitals, which benefit from significant public subsidies and steady insurance company revenues, will remain a significant obstacle to expanding this form of residency. However, if over time architecture can emulate medicine's increase in public value after Flexner's reforms, residency funding may emerge from both public and private sources.[20] Residency locations can expand beyond schools to the many design centers that have opened in cities, public and private research centers, institutions that typically keep architects on staff such as universities, and a final place that might evolve as the "teaching office." While remaining private, teaching offices could be incented by external funding. Another inhibitor is the fear that interns will lose the hands-on experience that comes from working in a professional architectural practice. Medical residencies have addressed this issue by allowing doctors to perform various regulated paraprofessional activities as residents under careful supervision.

The Princeton report's allusion to medical residency could provide the basis for its contemporary adaptation to architecture. The report's initial "organized internship" phase involves a period of professional activity supervised jointly by schools and the profession and covering the widest possible range of professional responsibilities. In a second "professional internship" phase, an intern works independently in a specific area of design, earns a respectable salary, and makes an economic contribution to the host organization. Together, the two phases recommended in the Princeton report would correspond to what has become the residency phase of graduate medical education.[21] Blending the propositions of the Princeton report with the model of the contemporary medical residency would prepare architects for general practice, and it could also steer them toward specialization. Current graduate medical education includes an optional postresidency fellowship intended for the pursuit of the board certification that deems a doctor qualified to provide quality patient care in a given specialty. Although it is voluntary, a majority of physicians choose to become board certified.[22] Given the potential specializations in architecture that the incorporation of data will drive, future architectural internships that include board certification could reside within a variety of organizational entities. The rigor and duration of these internships would correlate with their complexity.[23] As these specializations broaden architecture's jurisdiction, some portion of additional fees charged in the practice would loop back and support the internship programs. If architecture can demonstrate a value proposition comparable to that of medicine, it might also expect the same public and private support in the future that university hospitals receive.

In order to thrive, the architectural profession must expand at both its front and back ends, and architectural education could grow following similar trajectories. A residency program at the back end could extend continuing education to last the course of a professional career, with digital badges continually credentialing expertise in specific areas. The specialty boards that might form outside of traditional architectural practice to maintain this branch of pedagogy could also be beachheads into other jurisdictions. The postgraduate layering of responsibility provides an opportunity to resolve the long-standing and sometimes petty conflict over who can refer to themselves as architects. At the end of medical school, graduates call themselves doctors and hold the title MD, although they cannot practice until they fulfill their residency requirement. In the same way, architects will be allowed to use the title upon graduation, but will need to attain a higher certification through residency and/or fellowship based on different tracks in order to practice. Those tracks with the highest responsibility—health, safety, and welfare—could be on par with that of a surgeon. Others will be able to achieve licensure as general practitioners. This degree structure would provide the disciplinary elasticity that Tomas Rossant believes architects should aspire toward without lowering any standards. Architectural education can also expand in the other direction, as the Princeton report suggests, into high school and even grammar school programs. Efforts here could sow seeds for a variety of careers in architecture later on, allowing the practice to influence design education at an earlier level and potentially drawing in more Millennials and the following generation with a predisposition to design.[24]

Titles and Jurisdictions

At the 2016 AIA convention in Philadelphia, Rem Koolhaas complained that the computer industry had taken over architecture's metaphors. While Dana Cuff writes of the proverbial disconnect between what architects say they do (and how the public imagines they operate) and how they perform,[25] other disciplines have appropriated the root term "architect," less as a reference to the stereotype of the master builder with a singular vision, and more as any individual who deals with highly complex issues in an ever-changing context.

The 2012 publication of Doug Patt's book, *How to Architect*, raised hackles online as to whether or not "architect" can be used as a verb. Some argue that because John Keats first used the verb form in 1810 (according to the Oxford English Dictionary), Patt's was an allowable usage. Others caution that, while "design" and "engineer" maintain dual usage, "lawyer" does not, and "to doctor" means to falsify and is considered a pejorative. The caution implies that "to architect" might eventually attract similar negative connotations. What also emerges among this prattle is that the computer industry has completely absorbed the word and has used it as both noun and verb since its earliest days. In the realm of technology, the term "computer architecture" fills a descriptive void that neither computer science nor computer engineering can satisfy. While its exact definition is difficult to pin down, "architecture" used in a computing context implies the specific interaction between software and hardware to form a system compatible with other technologies. It also refers to how creatively a system's logic and standards relate to users. Computer architecture has no scale: it can be micro or macro.[26]

If architecture as a discipline must incorporate many aspects of computerization as it transforms itself and expands in the Millennial Age, it seems appropriate that it return the gesture Koolhaas complains of and appropriate some of the computer industry's metaphors. Three computer science aphorisms and practices seemed particularly relevant to mention here. One is the two-part ninety-ninety rule (a.k.a. the rule of credibility). The rule's first part postulates that 90 percent of software development time accounts for preparation, while only 10 percent applies to actually writing it. The second part claims that of the time taken to write code, less than 10 percent has to do with the ostensible purpose of the system; the remaining 90 percent of the time deals with the less critical but still necessary responsibilities of maintenance and housekeeping.[27] When applied to data-enhanced architectural design, 90 percent of the project's time must be devoted to the diagnostic phase on the front end, and another 90 percent is devoted to the treatment phase on the back end. The total amount of time thus required stands as an appropriate metaphor for the considerable opportunities available in expanding architecture's jurisdiction.

A second metaphor worthy of appropriation is a form of business practice that architects are already beginning to emulate. "Agile" software development emphasizes close collaboration between a development team and business stakeholders that involves the frequent delivery of business value, working in tight, self-organizing teams, and using smart methods to craft, confirm, and deliver code. First circulated in 2001 as the Agile Manifesto, the concept encourages rapid and flexible response to change.[28] A third appropriation is of a cluster of metaphors: *objects*, *aspects*, and *advice*. An *object* is an element of software that contains either data or code, while an *aspect* adds additional behavior to existing code without affecting the code itself. The modularity that the existing behavior allows for is called the *advice*. Taken together, this strategy allows behavior not central to a code's logic to be included in a program in a manner that does not clutter its core function with unnecessary lines of script.[29] How these elements work together could describe how future forms of collaboration between specialties can be organized with specificity and efficiency.

Journalists also use the word "architect" outside the context of building. For example, in a 2016 *New York Times* magazine article about Barack Obama's economic legacy, Andrew Ross Sorkin uses the word "architect" three times. He refers to Timothy Geithner (who would later become treasury secretary) as the "architect" of Obama's bank bailout and to Barney Frank as "one of the major legislative architects of Obama's economic program." These individuals performed near-Herculean tasks in dealing with embattled parties under tense circumstances in order to earn the title of architect. It may be equally important to note that Sorkin uses the term a third time to describe those who also applied considerable skill, but instead were driven by avarice and *caused* the economic crisis.[30] In the public lexicon, use of the words "architect" and "architecture" expand the imagination far beyond the craft of building, the protection of health, safety, and welfare, and the otherwise constrained world of the contemporary architectural practice.

In the Millennial Age, the term architecture thus describes a highly complex system managed by those under pressure who respond to an ever-changing context. But this description is at odds with the reality of the current profession with its diminished jurisdiction. What if, instead, architects could leap out of their humdrum world of limited power to fulfill the persona the public has applied to them? While this might seem a fantasy, the way a profession refers to itself in context establishes its existential organizational formality and jurisdiction, as Abbott describes. And this context relates back to the power of a profession's knowledge system and "its abstracting ability to define old problems in new ways."[31] In this sense, what the word architecture means resides at the abstract heart of its jurisdiction. In 1936, when Joseph Hudnut unified three major design professions—architecture, urban planning, and landscape architecture—under the masthead of the Harvard Graduate School of Design, his intentions may have been magnanimous, but he inadvertently subordinated architecture within the larger dominion of design.[32] While design had no formal jurisdiction in the sense that Abbott uses to define expert professions, architecture nonetheless found itself one of three bubbles within a larger Venn diagram labeled "design." With the addition of urban design in 1960, there were four. More self-subordination would follow, with William Wurster clearing architecture from the masthead of the school at UC Berkeley in favor of environmental design and Robert Geddes and Bernard Spring's use of the same term in the Princeton report. In the twenty-first century, architecture is still considered one of the design professions as these pioneers foresaw, but with design again challenging architecture's jurisdiction, the relationship is rendered ambiguous. Is architecture subordinate, or is it autonomous and in direct competition? While the discussion of a profession's name as having anything to do with its stature might seem like nothing more than wordplay, if the struggle over degree nomenclature teaches anything, it is that the titles chosen to describe what one does and the clarity of purpose that surrounds them have great bearing on how society treats the profession.

The answer may lie in abstracting, in Abbott's sense of the word, the public's perception of the architect as one who administers over a complex system in an ever-changing context. This could apply to a range of pursuits, whether they be object-oriented, spatial, organizational, virtual, etc. Each of these falls within the larger realm of design, something that Robert Geddes claims as our birthright when he exclaims "We are all designers."[33] If one can imagine a third dimension to this Venn diagram's organization, architecture could represent the shared higher organizational responsibilities that hover above each of these pursuits. With this in mind, it can perhaps apply a titling system borrowed from a sister discipline: engineering. To define a specialization, engineering simply applies the term civil, chemical, mechanical, etc., before it. If architecture moves to a form of residency-style credentialed specialization that clarifies its jurisdictions, it can apply a similar method to designate specialty certification. Architects certifying construction-readiness could be executive architects, those specializing in infrastructure, civil architects, those applied to strategy, organizational architects, and so forth.[34] And those who develop dual skills in the actual and virtual can share a Venn diagram with their sister professionals as computer architects.

In examining the "tradition of self-examination" the Boyer report describes, it bears noting that reports by Bosworth (1932), Bannister (1954), Geddes (1967), and Boyer (1996) have consistently been generational in their timing, with each reflecting the generational dynamics of its time. The time that has elapsed since the Boyer report now approaches the length of a typical generation, suggesting that a formal reexamination is now due, and the post–Great Recession uncertainty in the academy and profession certainly makes the need seem critical. Yet one might also ask the legitimate question: how effective have these reports really been? While the Boyer report led to a limited rapprochement between the academy and the profession, Geddes's work, as forward thinking as it may have been, went mocked and unheeded. Bannister's and Bosworth's were mostly self-congratulatory and ultimately ineffectual. When understood according to a generational framework, it comes as no surprise that these efforts failed to build traction. In retrospect, for two academics in 1967 tied to an elite university, trying to preach for systematic reorganization to a constituency euphoric in an antiestablishment spiritual awakening, at a time when social values held more priority than educational systems, the Princeton report would seem doomed from the start. And in 1932, for another pair of academics to find any sense of unity auditing schools at the end of a long societal unraveling also seems too much to expect.

But if one accepts the basic understanding of generations—that the young adults are the primary influence on particular eras—then perhaps these top-down undertakings were all misguided. As architecture reexamines itself yet again, this time why not drive the inquiry from contemporary architecture's rank-and-file: its Millennials. Instead of circling the country to interrogate schools about what is going wrong, with all the nail-biting anxiety that accompanies an accreditation visit, why not mobilize Millennials in both the practice and in school to investigate, disrupt, and innovate from within; in contemporary parlance, let them "hack" architecture. While it may seem unimaginable to hand over the keys to a generation in which many have little confidence, with its gift of being consistently in the vanguard, architecture may already have started this process. In its 2015 Foresight report, the AIA highlights its participation in the AEC (Architecture, Engineering, Construction) Hackathons, creative events that team technologists with stakeholders to shape the future of the built environment. Hackathons cultivate an iconoclastic spirit in which participants seek to "break things" and rebuild them from the ground up. In the same way that Geddes and Spring scoured the country for good ideas about teaching and practicing architecture to fuel their report, design-specific Hackathons could be disruptive events that set out to rebuild specific ideas about practice and education. These ideas could then rise to consideration by the larger community. In the same way that NCARB encourages schools to foster new ideas for internships, its sister affiliates, AIA, AIAS, and ACSA, could incent individual practices and schools to nurture ideas that emerge from Hackathon rounds. Each can rally its members to provide in-kind support in the form of design know-how.

Hackathons across the US could cull the best ideas about practice and teaching using the same studio learning that design thinking curricula have applied so well (except they call it brainstorming). Technologies such as social networks, online learning, and gaming can offer transformative new strategies. Each Hackathon could also provide a forum to identify vulnerabilities and dispel any myths, replacing them with a ready catalog of generational alignments between previously estranged age groups. The memory of the Great Recession is still fresh in many minds, and many firms and schools found creative ways to endure it. Many also experienced or observed the unnecessary suffering of those who left the profession. Governments and institutions after the Great Depression found innovative ways to lessen casualties; the architectural profession can do the same after this recent downturn, leveraging Millennials' technological aptitude and can-do attitude to mash together different scenarios and solutions. Contending with the coming disruption and emerging transformed is a design problem that all generations engaged in architecture can set out to solve, with Millennials in the lead.

Let me give an example of how this might work, using my own personal experience and knowledge to mash together a proposition. At one of these

Hackathons, I would share and contextualize the story of Juster Pope Frazier, a small partnership practicing in the western Massachusetts town of Shelburne Falls. Learning early on how hard it was to bring design talent to a remote community and keep it, the firm set aside a portion of profits to retain staff when commissions dried up. To wait out these cyclical downturns, staff would stay busy with research, systems upgrades, and pro bono work. What Juster Pope Frazier essentially did was self-insure.[35] If it were scaled up and institutionalized, an insurance fund of this type could prevent the house-clearing that is so common to architecture and one of the demoralizing aspects of the profession that is keeping Millennials away. If firms self-insured, recessions could be times when design centers mobilize to see the pro bono work they have been cultivating get built. The Great Recession introduced the phrase "shovel-ready" to common language. I know from my years of teaching about infrastructure that shovel-ready is a condition long known to infrastructure builders, who first learned it in the Great Depression. In this earlier crisis, the federal government stimulated the economy, capital rates were low, and contractors bid competitively. Since then, every forward-thinking transportation bureaucrat learned to keep several shovel-ready projects on a shelf. With the same foresight, every design center could keep the same inventory of projects and work with a firm, like Juster Pope Frazier, that has staff waiting to participate in rallying the profession and the community at a time when each need it most.

The propositions I make to close this book seek to prime the discussion about how to use the accelerating disruption as an opportunity to innovate. I hope that this will prompt others to make similar proposals based on the information I've presented. As other professions are encountering the technological change the Susskinds describe, architecture stands now in a less-than-healthy state. The choice seems clear: architecture can continue the status quo and slide toward uncertainty, or it can regroup to establish an identity and stature it has long sought. By applying a generational understanding to their own profession's history and that of other professions, architects can build a strong basis for beginning to reaffirm their field's identity and the jurisdiction that comes with it. Mobilizing the Millennial generation, whose technological skill and other characteristics in many ways predispose them to help, will be critical to accomplishing this. Overcoming the misalignments between Millennials and other generations' expectations will be equally important. The Millennial Age will be a time when every aspect of society will undergo creative reappraisal, and enabling the inner designer in the larger population will be a task that Millennial architects will lead. As Robert Geddes writes, this may have a payoff:

> We are all designers. Every day, we organize things to accomplish goals, from the shape of the table for a peace conference to the strategic development program for a business. Perhaps, like Winston Churchill, we might even be called the "architect of victory."[36]

Millennials in Architecture Survey

Survey Methodology

Results for the 2016 Millennials in Architecture Survey are based on an online poll using Survey Monkey taken between December 28, 2015, and January 20, 2016. The survey was announced at the American Institute of Architecture Students Annual Forum on December 28, 2015, in San Francisco. Subsequent announcements through social media, the American Institute of Architecture Students (AIAS), the American Institute of Architects New York Chapter (AIANY), and the American Institute of Architecture Foundation (AIAF) drew respondents who self-identified as Millennials and others who either identified as older generations or chose not to self-identify. Of twelve questions, three requested basic information on age, gender, and generational identification, two questions asked about educational attainment, two questions probed values using wording similar to Pew Research Trust surveys in 2010 and 2014, two questions delved into employment, and three into educational experience. Darius Sollohub and Richard Sweeney, NJIT university librarian, wrote the questions with guidance from Dr. Eugene Perry Deess, director of institutional research, planning, and assessment at NJIT. The survey was approved by the NJIT Institutional Review Board in December of 2015.[1] The sampling error of the survey, or margin of error, is plus or minus 4 percent.

Survey findings were presented at the AIA New York Center for Architecture on January 22, 2016, by Darius Sollohub and Richard Sweeney, who followed up with two focus groups at the center in the spring of 2016.

Question 1

In what year were you born? (enter four-digit birth year; for example, 1976)
Answered: 472   Skipped: 16

2000	—	1990	30	1980	5	1970	1
1999	—	1989	21	1979	4	1969	2
1998	—	1988	31	1978	2	1968	5
1997	5	1987	10	1977	3	1967	2
1996	7	1986	10	1976	4	1966	1
1995	35	1985	18	1975	6	1965	1
1994	39	1984	18	1974	1	1964	5
1993	48	1983	3	1973	1	1963	2
1992	53	1982	14	1972	2	1962	—
1991	38	1981	13	1971	4	1961	2

1960	2	1950	—	1940	—
1959	1	1949	1	1939	—
1958	2	1948	—	1938	—
1957	2	1947	1	1937	2
1956	—	1946	2	1936	—
1955	2	1945	—	1935	1
1954	2	1944	3	1934	1
1953	1	1943	—	1933	—
1952	1	1942	—	1932	—
1951	2	1941	1	1931	—

Question 2

Are you . . . (male, female, or other)

Answered: 488   Skipped: 1

ALL

ANSWER CHOICES	RESPONSES	
Male	48.46%	236
Female	51.13%	249
Other	0.41%	2
TOTAL	**Answered**	**487**

MILLENNIAL (excludes those not identifying with a generation)

ANSWER CHOICES	RESPONSES	
Male	44.09%	138
Female	55.91%	175
Other	0.00%	0
TOTAL		**313**

ALL OTHER ARCHITECTS (excludes those not identifying with a generation)

ANSWER CHOICES	RESPONSES	
Male	72.00%	54
Female	28.00%	21
Other	0.00%	0
TOTAL		**75**

Question 3

Which of the following generations do you identify with?

Answered: 487   Skipped: 1

ANSWER CHOICES	RESPONSES	
Millennial (includes Generation Y)	64.27%	313
Generation X	11.29%	55
Boomer	3.08%	15
Silent (born before end of WWII)	1.03%	5
I really don't identify with a generation	20.33%	99
TOTAL		**487**

Question 4

Which degree do you currently hold? If you do not yet have a degree, choose "None of the above" and proceed to the next question.

Answered: 487   Skipped: 1

ALL

ANSWER CHOICES	RESPONSES	
BArch	34.29%	167
BArch with a post-professional master's	5.13%	25
MArch	17.86%	87
MArch with non-architecture bachelor's	5.75%	28
PhD	0.00%	0
None of the above	36.96%	180
TOTAL		**487**

MILLENNIAL (excludes those not identifying with a generation)

ANSWER CHOICES	RESPONSES	
BArch	37.70%	118
BArch with a post-professional master's	4.79%	15
MArch	13.42%	42
MArch with non-architecture bachelor's	3.83%	12
PhD	0.00%	0
None of the above	40.26%	126
TOTAL		**313**

ALL OTHER ARCHITECTS (excludes those not identifying with a generation)

ANSWER CHOICES	RESPONSES	
BArch	40.00%	30
BArch with a post-professional master's	6.67%	5
MArch	24.00%	18
MArch with non-architecture bachelor's	8.00%	6
PhD	0.00%	0
None of the above	21.33%	16
TOTAL		**75**

Question 5

If you are still in school, or plan to return to school, what is the highest degree you plan to attain? If you are out of school and do not plan to pursue other degrees, select N/A.

Answered: 482   Skipped: 6

ALL

ANSWER CHOICES	RESPONSES	
BArch	9.75%	47
MArch	28.01%	135
Post-professional master's in architecture	3.53%	17
PhD in architecture	1.45%	7
Bachelor's in another field	1.66%	8
Master's in another field	14.73%	71
PhD in another field	3.32%	16
N/A	37.55%	181
TOTAL		**482**

MILLENNIAL (excludes those not identifying with a generation)

ANSWER CHOICES	RESPONSES	
BArch	10.93%	34
MArch	34.41%	107
Post-professional master's in architecture	4.82%	15
PhD in architecture	1.29%	4
Bachelor's in another field	1.93%	6
Master's in another field	17.36%	54
PhD in another field	3.86%	12
N/A	25.40%	79
TOTAL		**311**

ALL OTHER ARCHITECTS (excludes those not identifying with a generation)

ANSWER CHOICES	RESPONSES	
BArch	5.56%	4
MArch	12.50%	9
Post-professional master's in architecture	1.39%	1
PhD in architecture	0.00%	0
Bachelor's in another field	1.39%	1
Master's in another field	4.17%	3
PhD in another field	1.39%	1
N/A	73.61%	53
TOTAL		**72**

Question 6

Which three of the following do you value most? Pick only three.
Answered: 486   Skipped: 2

ALL

ANSWER CHOICES	RESPONSES	
Having a high-paying career	41.77%	203
Having a successful marriage	72.02%	350
Living a very religious life	7.82%	38
Being a good parent	55.97%	272
Having lots of free time	23.25%	113
Becoming famous	5.56%	27
Helping others in need	60.49%	294
Owning your own home	27.98%	136
	Answered	**486**

MILLENNIAL (excludes those not identifying with a generation)

ANSWER CHOICES	RESPONSES	
Having a high-paying career	43.59%	136
Having a successful marriage	70.51%	220
Living a very religious life	7.37%	23
Being a good parent	53.53%	167
Having lots of free time	25.00%	78
Becoming famous	5.45%	17
Helping others in need	63.14%	197
Owning your own home	27.56%	86
	Answered	**312**

ALL OTHER ARCHITECTS (excludes those not identifying with a generation)

ANSWER CHOICES	RESPONSES	
Having a high-paying career	42.67%	32
Having a successful marriage	81.33%	61
Living a very religious life	9.33%	7
Being a good parent	56.00%	42
Having lots of free time	17.33%	13
Becoming famous	8.00%	6
Helping others in need	54.67%	41
Owning your own home	25.33%	19
	Answered	**486**

Question 6 comparison to Pew Research Trust and others.

The AIAS/AIANY poll asked questions regarding the same eight values previously polled by Pew Research Trust. Because of limitations with online survey methods, the AIAS/AIANY question format differed. It asked: "Which three of the following do you value most? Pick only three." Pew Research, using telephone interviews, asked respondents to rank according to whether the value was "one of the most important things in your life, very important but not the most, somewhat important, or not important."[2]

Pew Research Trust survey (January 2010). Life's priorities: percentage saying each is one of the most important things in their lives

MILLENNIAL (18–29 years of age)

ANSWER CHOICES	RESPONSES	
Having a high-paying career	15%	NA
Having a successful marriage	30%	NA
Living a very religious life	15%	NA
Being a good parent	52%	NA
Having lots of free time	9%	NA
Becoming famous	1%	NA
Helping others in need	21%	NA
Owning your own home	20%	NA

OTHER GENERATIONS (Generation X, Boomer, Silent)

ANSWER CHOICES	RESPONSES	
Having a high-paying career	7%	NA
Having a successful marriage	35%	NA
Living a very religious life	21%	NA
Being a good parent	50%	NA
Having lots of free time	10%	NA
Becoming famous	1%	NA
Helping others in need	20%	NA
Owning your own home	21%	NA

Question 7

Please indicate on a scale from "1" to "10" how well each of the following phrases describes you. For example, a "10" describes you very well and a "1" does not describe you at all. If you feel that you fall somewhere in between, you can choose any number between "1" and "10."
Answered: 488   Skipped: 0

ALL

ANSWER CHOICES	RESPONSES	AVERAGE
A religious person	488	43%
An environmentalist	488	68%
A supporter of gay rights	485	75%
A patriotic person	487	61%
TOTAL	**Answered**	**488**

MILLENNIAL (excludes those not identifying with a generation)

ANSWER CHOICES	RESPONSES	AVERAGE
A religious person	313	43%
An environmentalist	313	68%
A supporter of gay rights	313	76%
A patriotic person	312	60%
TOTAL	**Answered**	**313**

ALL OTHER ARCHITECTS (excludes those not identifying with a generation)

ANSWER CHOICES	RESPONSES	AVERAGE
A religious person	75	49%
An environmentalist	75	70%
A supporter of gay rights	73	73%
A patriotic person	75	71%
TOTAL	**Answered**	**75**

Question 7 comparison to Pew Research Trust and others.

The AIAS/AIANY poll asked questions regarding identification similar to those previously polled by Pew Research Trust. Because of limitations with online survey methods, the AIAS/AIANY question format differed. It asked: "Please indicate on a scale from '1' to '10' how well each of the following phrases describes you. For example, a '10' describes you very well and a '1' does not describe you at all. If you feel that you fall somewhere in between, you can choose any number between '1' and '10.'" Pew Research, using telephone interviews, asked respondents, "Please use a scale from 1 to 10, where '10' represents a description that is PERFECT for you, and '1' represents a description that is TOTALLY WRONG for you."[3]

Pew Research Trust survey (February 2014). The way adults describe themselves

MILLENNIAL

ANSWER CHOICES	RESPONSES	PERCENTAGE
A religious person	NA	36%
An environmentalist	NA	32%
A supporter of gay rights	NA	37%
A patriotic person	NA	49%

GENERATION X

ANSWER CHOICES	RESPONSES	PERCENTAGE
A religious person	NA	52%
An environmentalist	NA	42%
A supporter of gay rights	NA	37%
A patriotic person	NA	64%

BOOMER

ANSWER CHOICES	RESPONSES	PERCENTAGE
A religious person	NA	55%
An environmentalist	NA	42%
A supporter of gay rights	NA	33%
A patriotic person	NA	75%

SILENT

ANSWER CHOICES	RESPONSES	PERCENTAGE
A religious person	NA	61%
An environmentalist	NA	44%
A supporter of gay rights	NA	32%
A patriotic person	NA	81%

Question 8

Which of the following will you (or did you) consider most important in choosing an employer?

Answered: 486   Skipped: 2

ALL

ANSWER CHOICES	RESPONSES	
Opportunities for career progression	38.68%	188
Good benefits packages including pensions, healthcare, and other benefits	7.61%	37
Flexible work arrangements	12.14%	59
High salary	3.91%	19
Corporate values that match yours	20.37%	99
A company's reputation for good ethical practices	13.37%	65
None of the above	3.91%	19
	Answered	**486**

MILLENNIAL (excludes those not identifying with a generation)

ANSWER CHOICES	RESPONSES	
Opportunities for career progression	38.14%	119
Good benefits packages including pensions, healthcare, and other benefits	6.09%	19
Flexible work arrangements	14.10%	44
High salary	4.49%	14
Corporate values that match yours	20.83%	65
A company's reputation for good ethical practices	12.50%	39
None of the above	3.85%	12
	Answered	**312**

ALL OTHER ARCHITECTS (excludes those not identifying with a generation)

ANSWER CHOICES	RESPONSES	
Opportunities for career progression	41.33%	31
Good benefits packages including pensions, healthcare, and other benefits	5.33%	4
Flexible work arrangements	5.33%	4
High salary	4.00%	3
Corporate values that match yours	21.33%	16
A company's reputation for good ethical practices	17.33%	13
None of the above	5.33%	4
	Answered	**75**

Question 9

When you graduate (or graduated) from college, your primary goal will be (was) . . .

Answered: 488   Skipped: 0

ALL

ANSWER CHOICES	RESPONSES	
To become a licensed architect	46.52%	227
To be involved in a creative field	23.36%	114
To work in a field that improves the conditions of the world	26.84%	131
None of the above	3.28%	16
TOTAL	**Answered**	**488**

MILLENNIAL (excludes those not identifying with a generation)

ANSWER CHOICES	RESPONSES	
To become a licensed architect	44.41%	139
To be involved in a creative field	24.28%	76
To work in a field that improves the conditions of the world	30.03%	94
None of the above	1.28%	4
TOTAL	**Answered**	**313**

ALL OTHER ARCHITECTS (excludes those not identifying with a generation)

ANSWER CHOICES	RESPONSES	
To become a licensed architect	53.33%	40
To be involved in a creative field	20.00%	15
To work in a field that improves the conditions of the world	18.67%	14
None of the above	8.00%	6
TOTAL	**Answered**	**75**

Question 10

Do you (did you) think that your design education is (was) . . .
Answered: 484   Skipped: 4

ALL

ANSWER CHOICES	RESPONSES	
too practical; not theoretical enough	8.06%	39
too theoretical; not practical enough	33.88%	164
well balanced in teaching theoretical and practical knowledge	58.06%	281
TOTAL	**Answered**	**484**

MILLENNIAL (excludes those not identifying with a generation)

ANSWER CHOICES	RESPONSES	
too practical; not theoretical enough	8.36%	26
too theoretical; not practical enough	31.83%	99
well balanced in teaching theoretical and practical knowledge	59.81%	186
TOTAL	**Answered**	**311**

ALL OTHER ARCHITECTS (excludes those not identifying with a generation)

ANSWER CHOICES	RESPONSES	
too practical; not theoretical enough	6.85%	5
too theoretical; not practical enough	41.10%	30
well balanced in teaching theoretical and practical knowledge	52.05%	38
TOTAL	**Answered**	**73**

Question 11

Architecture schools nationally have recently experienced a decline in enrollments. Which one of the following do you think is the primary cause:
Answered: 486   Skipped: 2

ALL

ANSWER CHOICES	RESPONSES	
Perception of poor employment prospects upon graduation	34.77%	169
The path to graduation and licensure is too long and strenuous	16.26%	79
The prospect of a career that will cut into free time and family time	10.49%	51
Low expectations about salary over a lifetime	26.13%	127
Other design-related fields are more attractive	12.35%	60
TOTAL	**Answered**	**486**

MILLENNIAL (excludes those not identifying with a generation)

ANSWER CHOICES	RESPONSES	
Perception of poor employment prospects upon graduation	34.82%	109
The path to graduation and licensure is too long and strenuous	19.17%	60
The prospect of a career that will cut into free time and family time	10.54%	33
Low expectations about salary over a lifetime	23.32%	73
Other design-related fields are more attractive	12.14%	38
TOTAL	**Answered**	**313**

ALL OTHER ARCHITECTS (excludes those not identifying with a generation)

ANSWER CHOICES	RESPONSES	
Perception of poor employment prospects upon graduation	35.14%	26
The path to graduation and licensure is too long and strenuous	9.46%	7
The prospect of a career that will cut into free time and family time	4.05%	3
Low expectations about salary over a lifetime	36.49%	27
Other design-related fields are more attractive	14.86%	11
TOTAL	**Answered**	**74**

Question 12

Regarding the balance between life in studio and life outside of studio, whether recent or years past, which one statement describes your experience with studio in school:
Answered: 483   Skipped: 5

ALL

ANSWER CHOICES	RESPONSES	
A severe unhealthy imbalance existed in school.	37.27%	180
An imbalance existed, but it was manageable.	57.14%	276
I didn't think any imbalance existed.	5.59%	27
TOTAL	**Answered**	**483**

MILLENNIAL (excludes those not identifying with a generation)

ANSWER CHOICES	RESPONSES	
A severe unhealthy imbalance existed in school.	37.50%	117
An imbalance existed, but it was manageable.	58.01%	181
I didn't think any imbalance existed.	4.49%	14
TOTAL	**Answered**	**312**

ALL OTHER ARCHITECTS (excludes those not identifying with a generation)

ANSWER CHOICES	RESPONSES	
A severe unhealthy imbalance existed in school.	31.51%	23
An imbalance existed, but it was manageable.	61.64%	45
I didn't think any imbalance existed.	6.85%	5
TOTAL	**Answered**	**73**

NAAB-Accredited Program Enrollments 2007–2017

Academic Year	Source(s)	Total Enrollment	Nonresident Alien	First-time Enrollment
2007–2008		29,133	NA	NA
	2008 NAAB Report on Accreditation in Architecture Education			
	(Washington: National Architectural Accrediting Board, 2008), 7.			
	www.naab.org/wp-content/uploads /2008-Report-on-Accreditation-in -Architecture-Education.pdf			
2008–2009		25,707	1,652	NA
	2009 Report on Accreditation in Architecture Education			
	(Washington: National Architectural Accrediting Board, 2009), 11, 19.			
	www.naab.org/wp-content/uploads /2009-Report-on-Accreditation-in -Architecture-Education.pdf			
2009–2010		27,852	2,992	8,553
	2010 Report on Accreditation in Architecture Education			
	(Washington: National Architectural Accrediting Board, 2010), 12, 14, 19.			
	www.naab.org/wp-content/uploads/2010 -Report-on-Accreditation-in-Architecture -Education.pdf			

Academic Year	Source(s)	Total Enrollment	Nonresident Alien	First-time Enrollment
2010–2011		24,478	2,288	8,307
	2011 Report on Accreditation in Architecture Education			
	(Washington: National Architectural Accrediting Board, 2011), 15, 17, 21.			
	www.naab.org/wp-content/uploads/2011-Report-on-Accreditation-in-Architecture-Education.pdf			
2011–2012		26,850	2,732	8,120
	2012 Report on Accreditation in Architecture Education			
	(Washington: National Architectural Accrediting Board, 2012), 15, 17, 21.			
	www.naab.org/wp-content/uploads/2012-Report-on-Accreditation-in-Architecture-Education.pdf			
2012–2013		25,958	3,200	7,169
	2013 Annual Report from the National Architectural Accrediting Board			
	(Washington: National Architectural Accrediting Board, 2013), 18, 20, 24.			
	www.naab.org/accreditation/publications/			
2013–2014		24,989	3,765	6,597
	2014 Annual Report from the National Architectural Accrediting Board			
	(Washington: National Architectural Accrediting Board, 2014), 10, 12, 16.			
	www.naab.org/accreditation/publications/			
2014–2015		24,208	4,283	7,052
	2015 Annual Report National Architectural Accrediting Board, Part I			
	(Washington: National Architectural Accrediting Board, 2015), 9, 12.			
	www.naab.org/accreditation/publications/			

Academic Year	Source(s)	Total Enrollment	Nonresident Alien	First-time Enrollment
2015–2016		24,456	4,560	7,368
	2016 Annual Report National Architectural Accrediting Board, Part I			
	(Washington: National Architectural Accrediting Board, 2016), 9, 10, 12.			
	www.naab.org/wp-content/uploads /NAAB_2016AnnualReport_Part1.pdf			
2016–2017		24,109	NA	6,982
	For total enrollment and first-time enrollment, see "Education" in 2018 NCARB by the Numbers (website) (Washington: National Council of Architectural Registration Boards, 2018), www.ncarb.org /nbtn2018/education.			

Net change in total enrollment 2007–2017: -17.2%
Nonresident alien enrollment as a percentage of total enrollment in 2008: +6.4%
Nonresident alien enrollment as a percentage of total enrollment in 2016: +18.6%
Net change in nonresident alien enrollment 2008–2016: +276%
Net change in first-time enrollment 2009–2017: -18.4%

Acknowledgments

This book began after I stepped up to administer the school of architecture at NJIT in 2010. The dean at the time, Urs Gauchat, periodically encouraged faculty to take time out to reexamine pedagogy to ensure our effectiveness. The next year, I organized a colloquium of fellow faculty to take on such a task. As part of our program, we invited Richard Sweeney, our university librarian, to discuss his research on Millennials. Richard had spent much of the previous decade reading every article he could find on the generation and had by then conducted focus groups at over sixty institutions. What he conveyed to us came both from deep data and experience. I was amazed that I had heard little about this. My faculty colleagues also scratched their heads. Afterward I asked him if we could give a paper together on his findings specific to architectural education. We gave that paper at the 100th ACSA Annual Meeting in Boston in 2012. Later, when I asked him if he would consider writing a book together, he said no. "I will be retiring soon, but you can use all my research," he said. I took six heavy boxes of photocopied articles to an offline computer lab on his library's fourth floor and spent the summer reading the content of those boxes to begin this book.

Along the way, many individuals and groups offered assistance. Prominent among these were the ranks of Millennials in the American Institute of Architecture Students (AIAS) chapters. Many mustered respondents for focus groups and surveys. NJIT's AIAS chapter under the leadership of Mona Patel, Lizza Medina, and John Cassidy helped me convene sessions at our school and at conferences away. Danielle Mitchell of the national organization promoted a survey that Richard and I had written. With her campaigning, it went viral. Joel Pominville also helped spread the message. The recently graduated Alex Alaimo invited me to the AIA and AIAS national conferences to discuss my research and has consistently provided guidance. At one of those panels, my longtime colleague Frank Mruk introduced me to the seminal work of Andrew Abbott.

My initial intent had been to write about Millennials in the context of design pedagogy, but early reactions from publishers and from the many professionals I engaged with urged me to consider the broader discipline of architecture. Through the leadership of Tomas Rossant, then chapter president of AIA New York, the chapter convened a panel at New York's Center for Architecture to present the findings from our survey. I thank Tomas, Danielle Mitchell, Justin Mihalik, George Miller, and Pascal Sablan for their spirited discussion and the center's Suzanne Mecs for hosting and promoting the survey. I also thank Sherry-Lea Bloodworth Botop for promoting the survey through social media at the AIA Foundation. A later interview with Tomas Rossant helped focus the conclusions of my book. Subsequently, the offices of Gensler, Perkins Eastman, Ennead, and Arup also invited me to present findings, with the ensuing discussions always illuminating. A follow-up interview with Arup's Leo Argiris led me to understand how the profession could adapt to Millennials. My former coworkers, Suzie Rodriguez and Susan Strauss, read chapters and offered direction. A day spent interviewing my old boss, dean, and life mentor Jim Polshek gave my ideas deep longitudinal breadth.

As an architecture school administrator, I would use the conferences I traveled to as a sounding board with my peers. Thomas Fisher, who chaired the panel in Boston where Richard and I first presented, has given continual encouragement. I don't think I would have had the courage to write this book without Tom's example and support. At other conferences I interviewed ACSA's Michael Monti and Georgia Tech's Michelle Rinehart. These led to phone interviews with NCARB's Michael Armstrong and Yale's Phil Bernstein and Amy Wrzesniewski. I am grateful to LSU's Jori Erdman for inviting me to the 2014 ACSA Administrators Conference to share my findings. I also greatly value the after-session conversations on ideas in the book with Hawaii's Dan Friedman, Roger Williams's Steve White, Tulane's Ken Schwartz, and Mississippi's Greg Hall. Outside architecture, Antioch's Donna Mellen provided insights on the chapter discussing American K-12 education.

Faculty and students at NJIT's College of Architecture and Design played a critical role in incubating ideas. The seasoned authors Zeynep Çelik, Karen Franck, and Gabrielle Esperdy guided me through this, my first book. The late Michael Mostoller (who had been my undergrad professor) enthusiastically read chapters. Our incredible architecture librarian, Maya Gervits, and her assistant, Danielle Reay, helped secure seemingly unattainable resources. And Mark Bess put my findings into practice, insisting I lecture in his professional practice courses, and had the courage to apply gaming to a class. As the writing progressed, I would work ideas from the book into my teaching, and as a result, many students, too many to name here, would offer critical advice and, with classic Millennial impatience, demand to know when it would be published. The independent study seminar on Millennials I held with students Nidhip Mehta, Carmel Pratt, and Maya Barreto offered me unparalleled perception. And I am thankful to Nidhip for later inviting me to address a conference on the future of education in New Delhi. I am also indebted to the fine architect Jak Inglese and Habitat's Peter Waldt and Jeff Farrel for helping provide the epiphany that caused me to recognize the Millennial generation.

I was trained to be an architect. Writing a book has required a major midcareer recalibration, which I could not have done without the help of those more professionally talented. Joan Gaurdanella, through her editing, taught me the craft of prose, while literary agent Liza Dawson showed me how a book gets put together. Jerry Fuller guided me through many ups, downs, and distractions. Professor Tom Heinzen brought focus to the writing and helped me with a title. My old high school buddy, professor Michael Calabrese, reminded me that writing has to have punch, and my college roommate, Dr. Gideon Besson, put the medical profession into context for Chapter Ten.

I consider it a stroke of providence to have found myself at the University of Texas Press, to which I was directed by my colleague Alex Marshall. Robert Devens, the press's editor-in-chief, has guided the project with encouragement and sometimes tough love, and he has put together a strong team to whom I am extremely grateful, including Sarah McGavick, Lynne Ferguson Chapman, Derek George, Leyla Aksu, and Samantha Allison Hoffman.

In the book, I describe the odd but well-recorded phenomenon of up-mentoring, when a Millennial teaches older colleagues about technology and social change. Throughout the writing of this book, I have been powerfully up-mentored by many: Nate Roberts taught me the power of technological innovation. Eric Bieber showed me unbridled Millennial fortitude, and We-Work's Jacob Reidel (although technically Generation X) has demonstrated Millennial agency. My academic colleague Simon McGown has reinvigorated my teaching in ways I would never have done myself. His reading of my chapters came with surgically precise edits. Tyler Tourville and Liz Opper have taught me lessons on Millennial values. In this category I place my Millennial children, Isabel and Louisa, who have both taught me a great deal about Millennial social standards, technological advancement, memes, and the power and beauty of digital games. And many times they have quickly corrected their dad (with classic eye-rolling) on any misrepresentations of their generation I may have made.

An axiom of the generational theory this book examines proposes that while an era's tone is set by its young adults, each generation alive also plays a critical role. This so-called generational constellation, I would argue, covers every complex initiative, like writing a book. In this project, my wife Kelley, a fellow member of Generation X, has helped me to successfully navigate the temporal passage between two powerful generations: the Millennials ahead of us (our kids) and the Boomers whose shadow we fall within. And in our efforts, Kelley and I have been guided by her mother Arlene, a member of the Silent generation (who is not afraid to speak), and my late mother Izabella, a WWII partisan fighter and the primary touchpoint in my family to what has been called the greatest generation.

Amongst other members of my generational constellation, my colleague and interim dean Tony Schuman, an unreconstructed Boomer, has continually held high his generation's values and has provided commentary in many car rides home. Perhaps the wisest guide of this constellation has been Robert Geddes, Princeton dean emeritus. His thoughts and writing inspire this book's conclusion. These were annealed on a remarkable summer day in 2016, when we spent the morning together discussing Millennials and his 1967 Princeton report, and the afternoon at Princeton's Institute for Advanced Studies, in a building Geddes designed, within an institution founded by Abraham Flexner, who figures prominently in Chapter Ten.

Richard Sweeney died on May 20, 2016. A commuter rushing to work did not see him in the crosswalk. Richard was crossing the street on his way to campus, carrying cartons of bottled water for a staff meeting. Generational theory describes a unique figure who leads at a critical transition point when the influence of older generations give way to the order of the new. Many, like Franklin Roosevelt, did not live to see the results of their leadership. In this endeavor, Richard was such a champion. Every minute I spent in his office—my eyes glued to the pictures of his children pinned up on the wall behind him—my conceptions improved. After he died, I finished the manuscript by often reconstructing that scene in my mind: of a wise Baby Boomer counseling a skeptical and wary Generation Xer as I stared up at the Millennial faces on the wall staring back at me.

Notes

Preface

The epigraph is from Elwood Carlson, "20th-Century U.S. Generations," *Population Bulletin* 64, no. 1 (2009): 5.

1. Rohan Mascarenhas, "NJIT students work with Habitat for Humanity to design Newark homes," *Star Ledger*, December 2, 2009.

2. Elizabeth Evitts Dickinson, "The Millennials: Children of the Revolution," *Architect*, January 2013, 110.

3. David Welch and Elisabeth Behrmann, "Who's Winning the Self-Driving Car Race?" *Bloomberg*, May 7, 2018, https://www.bloomberg.com/news/features/2018-05-07/who-s -winning-the-self-driving-car-race.

1. Introduction

The epigraph is from Martin Heidegger, *Sein und Zeit* (*Jahrbuch für Philosophie und phanomenologische Forschung*, 1927) 8, 384, quoted in Karl Mannheim, "The Problem of Generations," in *Essays on the Sociology of Knowledge*, ed. P. Kecskemeti, trans. Edith Schwarzschild and Paul Kecskemeti (London: Routledge & Kegan Paul, 1952), 282.

1. United Nations, Department of Economic and Social Affairs, Population Division, *World Urbanization Prospects: The 2014 Revision, Highlights* (New York: United Nations, 2014), 2–4, accessed September 23, 2015, https://esa.un.org/Unpd/Wup /Publications/Files/WUP2014-Highlights.pdf.esa.un.org/unpd/wup/Highlights /WUP2014-Highlights.pdf.

2. Marc Prensky, "Digital Natives, Digital Immigrants," *On the Horizon* 9, no. 5 (October 2001): 1–6, accessed May 7, 2015, http://www.marcprensky.com/writing/Prensky%20-%20 Digital%20Natives,%20Digital%20Immigrants%20-%20Part1.pdf.

3. Pew Research Center, *Millennials Will Benefit and Suffer Due to Their Hyperconnected Lives*, Janna Anderson and Lee Rainie, eds., Pew Internet & American Life Project, February 29, 2012, 27-28, http://www.pewinternet.org/~/media//Files/Reports/2012/PIP _Future_of_Internet_2012_Young_brains_PDF.pdf.

4. David Hambling, "Game Controllers Driving Drones, Nukes," *Wired*, July 19, 2008, http://www.wired.com/2008/07/wargames/.

5. Jingjing Jiang, "Millennials Stand Out for Their Technology Use, but Older Generations Also Embrace Digital Life," Pew Research Center, May 2, 2018, http://www .pewresearch.org/fact-tank/2018/05/02/millennials-stand-out-for-their-technology-use -but-older-generations-also-embrace-digital-life/.

6. Pew Research Center, *Millennials: Confident. Connected. Open to Change*, Paul Taylor and Scott Keeter, eds., February 2010, 25-32, http://pewsocialtrends.org/assets /pdf/millennials-confident-connected-open-to-change.pdf.

7. Pew Research Center, *Teens, Social Media & Technology Overview 2015*, Amanda Lenhart, ed., April 9, 2015, 2, http://www.pewresearch.org/wp-content/uploads/sites/9 /2015/04/PI_TeensandTech_Update2015_0409151.pdf. By 2018, Pew reported that 95 percent of teens had a smartphone or access to one and 45 percent said they are online on a near-constant basis. See Jiang, "Millennials Stand Out for Their Technology Use, http:// www.pewresearch.org/fact-tank/2018/05/02/millennials-stand-out-for-their -technology-use-but-older-generations-also-embrace-digital-life/.

8. Jiang, "Millennials Stand Out for Their Technology Use."

9. Pew, *Millennials: Confident. Connected. Open to Change*, 34.

10. Neil Howe and William Strauss, *Millennials Rising* (NY: Vintage Books, 2000), 36.

11. Elwood Carlson, "20th-Century U.S. Generations," *Population Bulletin* 64, no. 1 (2009): 5.

12. Carlson, "20th-Century U.S. Generations," 5. Carlson refers to Millenials under ten as "New Boomers."

13. Frank Hobbs and Nicole Stoops, *Demographic Trends in the 20th Century*, US Census Bureau, Census 2000 Special Reports, Series CENSR-4 (Washington, DC: US Government Printing Office, 2002), 143.

14. Foster Cline and Jim Fay, *Parenting with Love and Logic: Teaching Children Responsibility* (Colorado Springs: NavPress, 1990). Although its popularity is associated with the 2000s, the term "helicopter parent" was first used in print by Cline and Fay in 1990.

15. Taylor and Keeter, "Millennials," 2–4.

16. Taylor and Keeter, 71, 84; see also Eric Greenberg and Karl Weber, *Generation We: How Millennial Youth are Taking Over America and Changing Our World Forever* (Emeryville, CA: Pachatusan, 2008), 29–32.

17. William Strauss and Neil Howe, *Millennials Go to College* (Washington, DC: Life-Course Associates, 2007), 77; Howe and Strauss, *Millennials Rising*, 162–166. See also Lawrence C. Stedman, *The NAEP Long-Term Trend Assessment: A Review of its Transformation, Use, and Findings* (Washington, DC: National Assessment Governing Board, 2009), 12, http://www.nagb.org/content/nagb/assets/documents/who-we-are/20-anniversary/stedman -long-term-formatted.pdf. The author refers to the rise guardedly as "stable achievement."

18. Madeline Goodman et al., *America's Skills Challenge: Millennials and the Future* (Princeton, NJ: Educational Testing Service, 2015), 4–5, http://www.ets.org/s/research /30079/asc-millennials-and-the-future.pdf.

19. Arthur Levine and Diane R. Dean, *Generation on a Tightrope: A Portrait of Today's College Student* (San Francisco, CA: Jossey-Bass, 2012), 79–93.

20. Richard Sweeney, "Millennial Behaviors & Demographics" (working paper, New Jersey Institute of Technology, revised December 22, 2006), http://unbtls.ca/teachingtips /pdfs/sew/Millennial-Behaviors.pdf.

21. Pew Research Center, *The Boomerang Generation: Feeling OK about Living with Mom and Dad*, Kim Parker, ed., 2012, 1–4, http://assets.pewresearch.org/wp-content /uploads/sites/3/2012/03/PewSocialTrends-2012-BoomerangGeneration.pdf.

22. Joel Stein, "Millennials: The Me Me Me Generation," *Time*, May 20, 2013. Stein's observation of Millennial narcissism references Frederick S. Stinson et al., "Prevalence, Correlates, Disability, and Comorbidity of DSM-IV Narcissistic Personality Disorder," *Journal of Clinical Psychiatry* 69, no. 7 (July 2008): 1033–1045. Others have disputed this claim, arguing that age, and not generation, is the cause. See B. W. Roberts, G. E. Edmonds, and E. Grijalva, "It Is Developmental Me Not Generation Me: Developmental Changes Are More Important than Generational Changes In Narcissism," *Perspectives in Psychological Science* 5 (2010): 97–102.

23. Paul Taylor, *The Next America: Boomers, Millennials, and the Looming Generational Showdown* (New York: Public Affairs, 2014), 18–20, 227.

24. Susan M. Sawyer et. al., "The Age of Adolescence," *Lancet Child & Adolescent Health* 2, no. 3 (March 2018): 223–228.

25. *Stress in America: Paying With Our Health* (Washington, DC: American Psychological Association, 2015), 5, https://www.apa.org/news/press/releases/stress/2014/stress -report.pdf. Millennials are not the only stressed generation; Generation X respondents reported roughly the same stress levels in the same study.

26. Taylor, *The Next America*, 20.

27. David Goldman, "Music's Lost Decade: Sales Cut in Half In 2000s," *CNN Money*, February 2, 2010, http://money.cnn.com/2010/02/02/news/companies/napster_music _industry/. While the music industry tried in vain to fight off what it saw as a flagrant violation of copyright policy driven by an amoral "law of the commons" mentality, the shock nonetheless forced a complete reformulation of the industry's revenue model. Recent sales have rebounded but remain a fraction of those of the previous decade.

28. Amy Mitchell and Katerina Eva Matsa, "The Declining Value of U.S. Newspapers," *Fact Tank* (blog), Pew Research Center, May 22, 2015, www.pewresearch.org/fact-tank /2015/05/22/the-declining-value-of-u-s-newspapers/.

29. Sam Tanenhaus, "The Millennials Are Generation Nice," *New York Times*, August 15, 2014.

30. Pew, *Millennials: Confident. Connected. Open to Change*, 110–138.

31. Pew Research Center, *Millennials in Adulthood: Detached from Institutions, Networked with Friends*, Paul Taylor et al., eds., March 7, 2014, 4–6, http://assets .pewresearch.org/wp-content/uploads/sites/3/2014/03/2014-03-07_generations-report -version-for-web.pdf.

32. Michael Dimock, "Defining Generations: Where Millennials End and Post-Millennials Begin," Pew Research Center, March 1, 2018, http://www.pewresearch.org/fact -tank/2018/03/01/defining-generations-where-millennials-end-and-post-millennials-begin/.

33. Nicole J. Borges et al., "Comparing Millennial and Generation X Medical Students at One Medical School," *Academic Medicine* 81, no. 6 (2006): 571–576. Borges defines Gen-

eration Xers as born between 1965 and 1980 and Millennials as born from 1981 to 1999. Her research finds that Cuspars, born 1975 to 1980, share traits with both generations.

34. William Strauss and Neil Howe, *The Fourth Turning* (New York: Broadway Books, 1998), 97–98.

35. Michael Lind, "Generation Gaps," *New York Times*, January 26, 1997, http://www.nytimes.com/books/97/01/26/reviews/970126.26lindlt.html.

36. Michael Wilson and Leslie E. Gerber, "How Generational Theory Can Improve Teaching: Strategies for Working with the Millennials," *Currents in Teaching and Learning* 1, no. 1 (Fall 2008): 30.

37. For a summary of the Millennial debate and Strauss and Howe's role in it, see Eric Hoover, "The Millennial Muddle: How Stereotyping Students Became a Thriving Industry and a Bundle of Contradictions," *Chronicle of Higher Education*, October 11, 2009, http://chronicle.com/article/The-Millennial-Muddle-How/48772/.

38. Eliana Johnson and Eli Stokols, "What Steve Bannon Wants You to Read," *Politico*, February 7, 2017, www.politico.com/magazine/story/2017/02/steve-bannon-books-reading-list-214745; David Kaiser, "What's Next for Steve Bannon and the Crisis in American Life," *Time*, February 3, 2017, http://time.com/4659390/howe-strauss-steve-bannon/.

39. TechCrunch Disrupt events are organized by CrunchBase, a self-described leading platform for discovering innovative companies. See their website for more information at https://about.crunchbase.com/about-us/.

40. Alicia Di Rado, "A Degree in Disruption," *USC Trojan: A Magazine of the University of Southern California*, Autumn 2013, accessed October 10, 2015, https://news.usc.edu/trojan-family/a-degree-in-disruption/.

41. Josh Linkner, *The Road to Reinvention: How to Drive Disruption and Accelerate Transformation* (San Francisco, CA: Jossey-Bass, 2014).

42. Walter Isaacson, *Steve Jobs* (New York: Simon & Schuster, 2011), 308–309, 473–475.

43. Karen W. Arenson, "Columbia's Internet Concern Will Soon Go Out of Business," *New York Times*, January 7, 2003, http://www.nytimes.com/2003/01/07/education/07COLU.html. Columbia's illustrious list of partners included the London School of Economics and Political Science, Cambridge University Press, the British Library, the Smithsonian Institution's National Museum of Natural History, the New York Public Library, the University of Chicago, the American Film Institute, the RAND Corporation, the Woods Hole Oceanographic Institution, the UK Natural History and Science museums, the Victoria and Albert Museum, and the University of Michigan.

44. Jill Lepore, "The Disruption Machine: What the Gospel of Innovation Gets Wrong," *New Yorker*, June 23, 2014, http://www.newyorker.com/magazine/2014/06/23/the-disruption-machine.

45. Clayton M. Christensen, *The Innovator's Dilemma: When New Technologies Cause Great Firms to Fail* (Boston, MA: Harvard Business School Press, 1997).

46. Taylor, *The Next America*, 183–197.

47. Standard & Poor's Ratings Services, *Millennials Are Creating Unsafe Conditions On U.S. Roads—But Not In The Way You Might Think*, RatingsDirect (New York: McGraw Hill Financial, October 19, 2015), 4–5, http://static.politico.com/09/d0/99397d434c759a290ae11a8af620/standard-and-poors-report-on-millennials-impact-on-infrastructure.pdf.

48. Peter Grier, "The Year of Disruption," *Christian Science Monitor*, December 26, 2016, 31–36.

49. Polly Mosendz, "What This Election Taught Us About Millennial Voters," *Bloomberg News*, November 9, 2016, https://www.bloomberg.com/news/articles/2016-11-09/what-this -election-taught-us-about-millennial-voters. See also Clara Hendrickson and William A. Galston, "How Millennials Voted This Election," *Brookings*, November 21, 2016, www .brookings.edu/blog/fixgov/2016/11/21/how-millennials-voted/.

50. "The Parties on the Eve of the 2016 Election: Two Coalitions, Moving Further Apart," Pew Research Center, September 13, 2016, http://www.people-press.org/2016/09/13/the -parties-on-the-eve-of-the-2016-election-two-coalitions-moving-further-apart/.

51. Charles M. Blow, "The Power of Disruption," *New York Times*, February 3, 2017, www.nytimes.com/2017/02/13/opinion/the-power-of-disruption.html.

52. Kermit Baker And Jennifer Riskus, "What's Next: The Market, The Forecast," *Architect*, January 2014, 110–111. The Architecture Billings Index (ABI) is computed as a diffusion index, with the monthly score calculated as the percentage of firms reporting a significant increase plus half the percentage of firms reporting no change. Comparisons are always to the previous month.

53. 2012 AIA Survey Report on Firm Characteristics (Washington, DC: American Institute of Architects, 2012), 5.

54. 2010 AIA/NCARB Internship and Career Study: Quantitative Results, prepared by the Rickinson Group (Washington, DC: American Institute of Architects/National Council of Architectural Registration Boards, 2010), 7.

55. Anthony P. Carnevale, Ban Cheah, and Jeff Strohl, *Hard Times: College Majors, Unemployment and Earnings, Not All College Degrees Are Created Equal* (Washington, DC: Georgetown Center on Education and the Workforce, 2012), 7, http://files.eric.ed.gov /fulltext/ED528241.pdf.accessed June 25, 2012, http://cew.georgetown.edu/unemployment.

56. July 2014: Architecture Billings Index, *Architect*, September 2014, 46–46.

57. Thomas Fisher, "Architecture and the Third Industrial Revolution," *Architect*, January 2014, 101–103.

58. Jeremy Rifkin, *The Third Industrial Revolution* (New York: Palgrave Macmillan, 2011), 268–269.

59. The first-time enrollment of 8,553 in the academic year 2009–2010 fell to 6,597 in the 2013–2014 academic year. See Appendix II on page 263.

60. From a total enrollment of 29,133 in the 2007–2008 academic year, total NAAB-accredited program enrollment declined to 24,109 by the 2016–2017 academic year. See Appendix II on page 263.

61. "Trends in International Student Enrollment in Architectural Education," Association of Collegiate Schools of Architecture, December 2016, www.acsa-arch.org/resources /data-resources/international-students-in-architectural-education/. This evaluation includes candidate schools along with NAAB-accredited programs. An evaluation of only NAAB-accredited programs without candidate programs from 2009 finds the nonresident alien population to be 1,652 out of a total enrollment of 25,707, or 6.4 percent. See Appendix II on page 263.

62. Karin Fischer, "Colleges Are Wary of Global Economy's Effect on Foreign Enrollments," *Chronicle of Higher Education*, July 16, 2012, http://chronicle.com/article /Colleges-Are-Wary-of-Global/132875/.

63. Carnevale, Cheah, and Strohl, *Hard Times*, 7.

64. Anthony P. Carnevale and Ban Cheah, *From Hard Times to Better Times: College Majors, Unemployment, And Earnings* (Washington, DC: Georgetown Center on Education and the Workforce, 2015), 8, https://cew.georgetown.edu/wp-content/uploads /HardTimes2015-Report.pdf.

65. This represents an increase over average economic growth. *Occupational Outlook Handbook*, 2014–2015 ed., Bureau of Labor Statistics, US Department of Labor, s.v. "Architects," accessed May 30, 2015, http://www.bls.gov/ooh/architecture-and-engineering /architects.htm (site defaults to latest edition).

66. Ken Auletta, "Get Rich U.: There Are No Walls Between Stanford and Silicon Valley. Should There Be?" *New Yorker*, April 30, 2012, www.newyorker.com/reporting/2012/04/30 /120430fa_fact_auletta.

67. David Brooks, "The Campus Tsunami," *New York Times*, May 3, 2012, www.nytimes .com/2012/05/04/opinion/brooks-the-campus-tsunami.html.

68. Michelle Rinehart, "Changes in Higher Education Financial Models" (working paper, prepared for the National Architectural Accrediting Board, June 2012), https://docplayer .net/20057441-Changes-in-higher-education-financial-models.html. Rinehart's observations are based on Robert Zemsky, *Making Reform Work: The Case for Transforming American Higher Education* (New Brunswick, NJ: Rutgers University Press. 2009).

69. Eden Dahlstrom and Jacqueline Bichsel, *ECAR Study of Undergraduate Students and Information Technology, 2014* (Louisville, CO: ECAR, October 2014), 22, https://library .educause.edu/~/media/files/library/2014/10/ers1406-pdf.

70. Fiona M. Hollands and Devayani Tirthali, *MOOCs: Expectations and Reality*, Center for Benefit-Cost Studies of Education, Teachers College, Columbia University, May 2014, accessed May 7, 2015, https://www.researchgate.net/publication/271841177_MOOCs _Expectations_and_reality.

71. Tamar Lewin, "Universities Reshaping Education on the Web," *New York Times*, July 17, 2012, http://www.nytimes.com/2012/07/17/education/consortium-of-colleges-takes -online-education-to-new-level.html.

72. Lewin, "Universities Reshaping Education on the Web."

73. Kevin Carey, *The End of College: Creating the Future of Learning and the University of Everywhere* (New York: Riverhead, 2015), 72–73.

74. Elizabeth Evitts Dickinson, "The Millennials: Children of the Revolution," *Architect*, January 2013, 112.

2. Who Are the Millennials?

The epigraph is from Neil Howe and William Strauss, *Millennials Go to College* (Washington, DC: LifeCourse Associates, 2007), 3.

1. Pew Research Center, *Millennials: Confident. Connected. Open to Change*, Paul Taylor and Scott Keeter, eds., February 2010, 9, http://www.pewsocialtrends.org/files/2010/10 /millennials-confident-connected-open-to-change.pdf; Eric Greenberg and Karl Weber, *Generation We: How Millennial Youth Are Taking Over America and Changing Our World Forever* (Emeryville, CA: Pachatusan, 2008), 20.

2. Pew, *Millennials*, 10.

3. Howe and Strauss, *Millennials Go to College*, 77; Neil Howe and William Strauss, *Millennials Rising* (New York: Vintage Books, 2000), 162–166.

4. Pew, *Millennials*, 5.

5. Richard Sweeney, "Millennial Behaviors & Demographics" (working paper, New Jersey Institute of Technology, revised December 22, 2006), http://unbtls.ca/teachingtips /pdfs/sew/Millennial-Behaviors.pdf.

6. Pew, *Millennials*, 20–21.

7. Trip Gabriel, "Boomers: The 'Not As I Did' Parents," *New York Times*, November 30, 1995, http://www.nytimes.com/1995/11/30/garden/boomers-the-not-as-i-did-parents.html.

8. William Strauss and Neil Howe, *The Fourth Turning* (New York: Broadway Books, 1998), 243–248.

9. "Suicide Rate by Age, 2000–2010," American Foundation for Suicide Prevention, accessed September 10, 2013, http://www.afsp.org/understanding-suicide/facts-and-figures/. A 2018 report published by the Centers for Disease Control and Prevention raised an alarm that suicide was on the rise across the country. While it showed an increase of suicide among Millennials, those rates peaked around 2010–2011 and have since declined. Boomers and Generation X have the higher numbers of suicides. See "Suicide Rising Across the US," Centers for Disease Control and Prevention, updated June 11, 2018, https://www.cdc .gov/vitalsigns/suicide/index.html.

10. Howe and Strauss, *Millennials Go to College*, 64.

11. Pew, *Millennials*, 20.

12. Eric Hoover, "The Millennial Muddle: How Stereotyping Students Became a Thriving Industry and a Bundle of Contradictions," *Chronicle of Higher Education*, October 11, 2009, 22, http://chronicle.com/article/The-Millennial-Muddle-How/48772/. See also Fred A. Bonner II, Aretha F. Marbley, and Mary F. Howard-Hamilton, eds., *Diverse Millennial Students in College: Implications for Faculty and Student Affairs* (Sterling, VA: Stylus Publishing, 2011).

13. Nicole J. Borges et al., "Comparing Millennial and Generation X Medical Students at One Medical School," *Academic Medicine* 81, no. 6 (June 2006): 571–576.

14. Ron Alsop, *The Trophy Kids Grow Up: How the Millennial Generation Is Shaking Up the Workplace* (San Francisco: Jossey-Bass, 2008).

15. American Psychological Association, "Stress in America: Missing the Health Care Connection," February 7, 2013, 19.

16. Howe and Strauss, *Millennials Go to College*, 64.

17. Pew, *Millennials*, 13.

18. Jingjing Jiang, "Millennials Stand Out for Their Technology Use, but Older Generations Also Embrace Digital Life," Pew Research Center, May 2, 2018, http://www .pewresearch.org/fact-tank/2018/05/02/millennials-stand-out-for-their-technology-use -but-older-generations-also-embrace-digital-life/.

19. Marc Prensky, introduction to *From Digital Natives to Digital Wisdom* (Thousand Oaks, CA: Corwin, 2012), 2, http://marcprensky.com/writing/Prensky-Intro_to_From_DN_to _DW.pdf.

20. Ivor Tessell, "Reverse Mentoring Sees the Young Teach the Old," *The Globe and Mail*, June 11, 2012, https://www.theglobeandmail.com/report-on-business/small-business /sb-digital/web-strategy/reverse-mentoring-sees-the-young-teach-the-old/article4247172/. See also: Ron Alsop, "Young Mentors Teach 'Old Dogs' New Tricks," *BBC Capital*, March 12, 2014, http://www.bbc.com/capital/story/20140311-meet-your-mentor-hes-just-24.

21. Mark Bauerlein, *The Dumbest Generation: How the Digital Age Stupefies Young Americans and Jeopardizes Our Future* (New York: Tarcher/Penguin Books, 2008).

22. Howe and Strauss, *Millennials Go to College*, 66–67.

23. Pew, *Millennials*, 71. Millenials are significantly less critical of government than other generations.

24. Pew, *Millennials*, 83.

25. Pew, *Millennials*, 15.

26. Pew, *Millennials*, 78.

27. Pew, *Millennials*, 7.

28. Pew, *Millennials*, 15.

29. Howe and Strauss, *Millennials Go to College*, 70.

30. William Strauss, *Millennials and the Pop Culture* (Washington, DC: LifeCourse Associates, 2006), 88.

31. Donald F. Roberts, Ulla G. Foehr, and Victoria Rideout, *Generation M: Media in the Lives of 8-18 Year-Olds* (Menlo Park, CA: Kaiser Family Foundation, March 2005), 28–29. Study indicates percentage of seventh- through twelfth-graders who listen to recorded music in a typical day on CDs, tapes, or MP3 players.

32. Strauss, Howe, and Markiewicz, *Millennials and the Pop Culture*, 61.

33. Paul Taylor and Rich Morin, "Forty Years After Woodstock, a Gentler Generation Gap," Pew Research Center, August 12, 2009, www.pewsocialtrends.org/2009/08/12/forty -years-after-woodstockbra-gentler-generation-gap/.

34. Howe and Strauss, *Millennials Rising*, 185.

35. Howe and Strauss, *Millennials Go to College*, 68.

36. Jean M. Twenge et al., "Generational Differences in Young Adults' Life Goals, Concern for Others and Civic Orientation, 1966–2009," *Journal of Personality and Social Psychology* 102, no. 5 (2012): 1045–1062.

37. Greenberg and Weber, *Generation We*, 40–44.

38. Jean M. Twenge, *Generation Me: Why Today's Young Americans Are More Confident, Assertive, Entitled—and More Miserable than Ever Before* (New York: Simon and Schuster, 2006).

39. Joel Stein, "Millennials: The Me Me Me Generation," *Time*, May 20, 2013.

40. Kathleen Gibson, "Building Community 2.0: Millennials and the Changing Face of Design Education" (Interior Design Educators Conference, Baltimore, MD, 2012).

41. Elizabeth Evitts Dickinson, "The Millennials: Children of the Revolution," *Architect*, January 2013, 109–134.

42. Stan Allen, "The Future That Is Now," in *Architecture School: Three Centuries of Educating Architects in North America*, ed. Joan Ockman (Cambridge, MA: MIT Press, 2012), 216.

43. Finith Jernigan, *Big BIM Little BIM* (Salisbury, MD: 4 Site Press, 2007), 23.

44. Allen, "The Future That Is Now," 216.

45. Allen, "The Future That Is Now," 224. See also Charles Waldheim, ed., *The Landscape Urbanism Reader* (Princeton, NJ: Princeton Architectural Press, 2006).

46. For Millennial green interests, see Greenberg and Weber, *Generation We*, 40–44; for their migration to cities, see Christopher B. Leinberger, *The Option of Urbanism: Investing in a New American Dream* (Washington DC: Island Press, 2008), 86–112.

47. The Trust for Public Land. *2014 City Park Facts*, February 2014, 27, https://www.tpl .org/sites/default/files/files_upload/2014_CityParkFacts.pdf.

48. Walter Isaacson, *Steve Jobs* (New York: Simon & Schuster, 2011), 125–134, 375.

49. Ken Segall, *Insanely Simple: The Obsession That Drives Apple's Success* (New York: Penguin Books, 2012).

50. Stan Allen et al., "Stocktaking 2004: Questions about the Present and Future of Design," in *The New Architectural Pragmatism: A Harvard Design Magazine Reader*, ed. William S. Saunders (Minneapolis: University of Minnesota Press, 2007), 103.

51. Robert Somol and Sarah Whiting, "Notes Around the Doppler Effect and Other Moods of Modernism," *Perspecta* 33 (2002): 77.

52. Richard W. Hayes, "Design/Build: Learning by Constructing," in *Architecture School: Three Centuries of Educating Architects in North America*, ed. Joan Ockman (Cambridge, MA: MIT Press, 2012), 286.

53. John M. Cary Jr., ed., *The ACSA Sourcebook of Community Design Programs at Schools of Architecture in North America* (Washington, DC: ACSA Press, 2000).

54. John M. Cary Jr., *The Power of Pro Bono: 40 Stories About Design for the Public Good by Architects and Their Clients* (New York: Metropolis, 2010).

55. Anthony Schuman, "Community Engagement: Architecture's Evolving Social Vocation," in *Architecture School: Three Centuries of Educating Architects in North America*, ed. Joan Ockman (Cambridge, MA: MIT Press, 2012), 256.

56. John Cary and Courtney E. Martin, "Dignifying Design," *New York Times*, October 6, 2012, https://www.nytimes.com/2012/10/07/opinion/sunday/dignifying-design.html.

57. Rebecca Jacobson, "Architects, Engineers Compete to Save the New York Coastline," *PBS NewsHour*, June 18, 2014, https://www.pbs.org/newshour/science/crowdsourcing-prevent-future-hurricane-sandy.

58. From 2010 to 2016, Phillip Bernstein of the Yale School of Architecture and Amy Wrzesniewski of the Yale School of Management have applied the Vroom-Yetton Decision Making for Leaders (DMFL) test to students as they embark on the Yale design-build project at the end of the first graduate year. The instructors consistently found architecture students to be far more autocratic than collaborative compared to students' peers in the School of Management as well as adult business executives and military leaders. Phillip Bernstein, conversation with author, June 17, 2016; Amy Wrzesniewski, conversation with author, July 1, 2016.

3. Generations in Historical Context

The epigraph is from Julián Marías, *Generations: A Historical Method*, trans. Harold C. Raley (Mobile: University of Alabama Press, 1970), 106.

1. Karl Mannheim, "The Problem of Generations," in *Essays on the Sociology of Knowledge*, ed. Paul Kecskemeti (New York: Routledge, 1952), 276–320.

2. Mannheim, "Problem of Generations," 292.

3. William Strauss and Neil Howe, *Generations: The History of America's Future, 1584 to 2069* (New York: Harper, 1991), 64.

4. Wilhelm Pindar, *Problems of Generation in the History of European Art* (Berlin: Franfurter Verlags-Anstalt, 1926), cited in Marías, *Generations*, 114–117.

5. Mannheim, "Problem of Generations," 306–307.

6. José Ortega y Gasset, *The Modern Theme* (New York: Harper and Rowe, 1960), 15.

7. Julius Peterson, "Literary Generations," in *The Philosophy of Literary Science*, ed. Emil Ertmatinger (Berlin: Junker und Dünnhaupt, 1930), cited in Marías, *Generations*, 122. Peterson writes that the suppressed type "may choose to travel abandoned paths as his

nature would have him do: he may subordinate himself to the dominant tendency and renounce his own peculiarity, or he may simply withdraw and await the future."

8. Mannheim, "Problem of Generations," 308.

9. Emma Parry and Peter Urwin. "Generational Differences in Work Values: A Review of Theory and Evidence," *International Journal of Management Reviews* 13 (2011): 83–84.

10. B. W. Roberts, G. E. Edmonds, and E. Grijalva, "It Is Developmental Me, Not Generation Me: Developmental Changes Are More Important Than Generational Changes in Narcissism," *Perspectives in Psychological Science* 5, no. 1 (2010): 97–102.

11. Lisa Cameron, Nisvan Erkal, Lata Gangadharan, and Xin Meng, "Little Emperors: Behavioral Impacts of China's One-Child Policy," *Science* 339, no. 6122 (February 22, 2013): 953–957.

12. Paul Taylor, *The Next America: Boomers, Millennials, and the Looming Generational Showdown* (New York: Public Affairs, 2014), 18–20, 227.

13. Eric Greenberg and Karl Weber, *Generation We: How Millennial Youth Are Taking Over America and Changing Our World Forever* (Emeryville, CA: Pachatusan, 2008), 13.

14. Nicole J. Borges et al., "Comparing Millennial and Generation X Medical Students at One Medical School," *Academic Medicine* 81, no. 6 (June 2006): 571–576.

15. Eric Hoover, "The Millennial Muddle: How Stereotyping Students Became a Thriving Industry and a Bundle of Contradictions," *Chronicle of Higher Education*, October 11, 2009, 14, http://chronicle.com/article/The-Millennial-Muddle-How/48772/.

16. William Strauss and Neil Howe, *The Fourth Turning* (New York: Broadway Books, 1998), 68.

17. Barack Obama, *The Audacity of Hope: Thoughts on Reclaiming the American Dream* (New York: Crown Publishers, 2006), 36.

18. Kali H. Trzesniewski and M. Brent Donnellan, "Rethinking 'Generation Me': A Study of Cohort Effects from 1976–2006," *Perspectives on Psychological Science* 5, no. 1 (2010): 58–75. See also Kristin Dombek, *The Selfishness of Others: An Essay on the Fear of Narcissism* (New York: Farrar, Straus and Giroux, 2016).

19. Pew Research Center, *Millennials: Confident. Connected. Open to Change*, Paul Taylor and Scott Keeter, eds., February 2010, 4, http://www.pewsocialtrends.org/files/2010/10/millennials-confident-connected-open-to-change.pdf.

20. Neil Howe and William Strauss, *Millennials Rising* (New York: Vintage Books, 2000), 12.

21. Strauss and Howe, *The Fourth Turning*, 233–239.

22. "Economic Mobility: Is the American Dream Alive and Well?" (Washington, DC: Economic Mobility Project, Pew Charitable Trusts, 2007), 5.

23. William Strauss and Neil Howe, *Millennials and the Pop Culture* (Washington, DC: LifeCourse Associates, 2006), 61.

24. Douglas Coupland, *Generation X: Tales for an Accelerated Culture* (New York: St. Martin's Press, 1991). Coupland now rejects the claim that he named the generation. The term "Generation X" first emerged well before the cohort in 1950s counterculture, resurfacing in 1960s mod culture and again as the name of a 1970s punk band.

25. Strauss and Howe, *The Fourth Turning*, 238.

26. Strauss and Howe, *The Fourth Turning*, 194, 243.

27. Strauss and Howe, *The Fourth Turning*, 171.

28. Phillip Johnson and Mark Wigley, *Deconstructivist Architecture* (New York: The Museum of Modern Art, 1988), 7.

29. Sharon L. Nichols and Thomas L. Good, *America's Teenagers—Myths and Realities* (Mahwah, NJ: Lawrence Erlbaum, 2004), 3–9.

30. "Survey of Americans on Values," *Washington Post*/Harvard University/Kaiser Family Foundation study, July/August 1998, 18, https://kaiserfamilyfoundation.files.wordpress.com/1998/12/survey-of-americans-on-values-topline.pdf. In a 2011 analysis of the European Social Survey, respondents scored only a 1.87 out of a possible 4 when asked if "most people view people in their 20s as having high moral standards." Jeremy Leach, *The Poor Perception of Younger People in the UK* (London: Intergenerational Foundation, August 17, 2011).

31. Douglas Rushkoff, *The GenX Reader* (New York: Ballantine Books, 1994).

32. Jeff Gordinier, *X Saves the World: How Generation X Got the Shaft but Can Still Keep Everything from Sucking* (New York: Penguin, 2008).

33. M. J. Stephey, "Gen-X: The Ignored Generation?" *Time*, April 16, 2008, http://www.time.com/time/arts/article/0,8599,1731528,00.html#ixzz289iZLqW2.

34. Elwood Carlson, "20th-Century U.S. Generations," *Population Bulletin* 64, no. 1 (2009): 3.

35. Landon Jones, *Great Expectations: America and the Baby Boom Generation* (New York: Ballantine Books, 1980), 2.

36. Pew, *Millennials: Confident. Connected. Open to Change*, 13.

37. Herbert M. McLuhan, *Understanding Media: The Extensions of Man* (New York: McGraw-Hill, 1964), 8–9.

38. Herbert M. McLuhan, *Gutenberg Galaxy: The Making of Typographic Man* (Toronto: University of Toronto Press, 1962), 158.

39. McLuhan, *Gutenberg Galaxy*, 248.

40. Pew, *Millennials: Confident. Connected. Open to Change*, 6, 15, 51.

41. Pew, *Millennials: Confident. Connected. Open to Change*, 16.

42. Pew Research Center, *The Boomerang Generation: Feeling OK about Living with Mom and Dad*, Kim Parker, ed., 2012, 3, http://assets.pewresearch.org/wp-content/uploads/sites/3/2012/03/PewSocialTrends-2012-BoomerangGeneration.pdf.

43. Landon Jones, *Great Expectations: America and the Baby Boom Generation* (New York: Ballantine Books, 1980).

44. Mannheim, "Problem of Generations," 307.

45. Neil Howe and William Strauss, *Millennials Go to College* (Washington, DC: Life-Course Associates, 2007), 66–70.

46. Pew, *Millennials: Confident. Connected. Open to Change*, 104, 133.

47. Pew, *Millennials: Confident. Connected. Open to Change*, 7.

48. Pew Research Center, *Millennials in Adulthood: Detached from Institutions, Networked with Friends*, Paul Taylor et al., eds., March 7, 2014, 41, http://assets.pewresearch.org/wp-content/uploads/sites/3/2014/03/2014-03-07_generations-report-version-for-web.pdf.

49. Pew, *Millennials: Confident. Connected. Open to Change*, 8.

50. Mary Elizabeth Hughes and Angela M. O'Rand, *The Lives and Times of the Baby Boomers* (New York: Population Reference Bureau/Russell Sage Foundation, 2004).

51. Carlson, "20th-Century U.S. Generations," 3.

52. John Gertner, *The Idea Factory: Bell Labs and the Great Age of American Innovation* (New York: Penguin Press, 2012), 1, 4.

53. Strauss and Howe, *The Fourth Turning*, 148.
54. Malvina Reynolds, "Little Boxes," Schroder Music Company, 1962.
55. Lewis Mumford, *The City in History* (New York: Houghton Mifflin Harcourt, 1961), 486.
56. Carlson, "20th-Century U.S. Generations," 3.
57. Strauss and Howe, *The Fourth Turning*, 147.
58. Mannheim, "Problem of Generations," 319–320.

4. Working with Generational Theory

The epigraph is from Paul Taylor, *The Next America: Boomers, Millennials, and the Looming Generational Showdown* (New York: PublicAffairs, 2016), 1.

1. William Strauss and Neil Howe, *Generations: The History of America's Future, 1584 to 2069* (New York: Harper, 1991), 64.
2. Karl Mannheim, "The Problem of Generations," in *Essays on the Sociology of Knowledge*, ed. Paul Kecskemeti (New York: Routledge, 1952), 306–307.
3. José Ortega y Gasset, *The Modern Theme* (New York: Harper and Rowe, 1960), 15.
4. Julius Peterson, "Literary Generations," in *The Philosophy of Literary Science*, ed. Emil Ertmatinger (Berlin: Junker und Dünnhaupt, 1930), cited in Julián Marías, *Generations: A Historical Method*, trans. Harold C. Raley (Mobile: University of Alabama Press, 1970), 122.
5. William Strauss and Neil Howe, *The Fourth Turning* (New York: Broadway Books, 1998), 309.
6. Strauss and Howe make this argument most clearly in discussing the relationship of Millennial college students to their parents' generations in Neil Howe and William Strauss, *Millennials Go to College* (Washington, DC: LifeCourse Associates, 2007), 167–168.
7. Pew Research Center, *Millennials: Confident. Connected. Open to Change*, Paul Taylor and Scott Keeter, eds., February 2010, 63–64, http://www.pewsocialtrends.org/files/2010/10/millennials-confident-connected-open-to-change.pdf.
8. For multiple definitions of hipsters, see Urban Dictionary, s.v. "hipster," accessed September 14, 2013, http://www.urbandictionary.com/define.php?term=hipster.
9. Robert Craft and Igor Stravinsky, *Conversations with Igor Stravinsky* (Garden City, NY: Doubleday, 1959), quoted in William Strauss and Neil Howe, *The Fourth Turning* (New York: Broadway Books, 1998), 79.
10. Strauss and Howe, *The Fourth Turning*, 14, 25. "Saeculum" derives originally from Etruscan, with both the French "*siècle*" and English "century" descending linguistically from it.
11. Strauss and Howe, *The Fourth Turning*, 3.
12. Strauss and Howe, *The Fourth Turning*, 100.
13. Strauss and Howe, *Generations*, 71.
14. Strauss and Howe, *Generations*, 77–78.
15. Strauss and Howe, *Generations*, 77–78.
16. C. L. Seibel and M. Nel, "Generation X: Intergenerational Justice and the Renewal of the Traditioning Process," *Theological Studies* 66, no. 2 (2010): 876–883.
17. Strauss and Howe, *The Fourth Turning*, 115.
18. Strauss and Howe, *The Fourth Turning*, 100.
19. Strauss and Howe, *Generations*, 81.
20. Strauss and Howe, *Generations*, 90–92.

21. Strauss and Howe, *Generations*, 92.

22. Strauss and Howe, *Generations*, 78.

23. Strauss and Howe, *The Fourth Turning*, 283.

24. Strauss and Howe, *The Fourth Turning*, 274.

25. Timothy Snyder, *On Tyranny: Twenty Lessons from the Twentieth Century* (New York: Penguin, 2017), 9–13. The book formed from a series of cathartic Facebook posts written immediately after the 2016 election.

26. Bess Connolly Martell, "Yale Historian Shares 'Sobering' Analysis of the Past, and an Action Plan for the Present, in New Book," *YaleNews*, March 16, 2017, news.yale.edu/2017/03/16 /yale-historian-shares-sobering-analysis-past-and-action-plan-present-new-book.

27. Paul Blumenthal and J. M. Rieger, "Steve Bannon Believes the Apocalypse is Coming and War is Inevitable," *Huffington Post*, February 18, 2017, www.huffingtonpost.com /entry/steve-bannon-apocalypse_us_5898f02ee4b040613138a951. After Bannon's departure from the Trump administration, blog chatter about the validity of Strauss and Howe abated, but not before some speculated that Donald Trump might be the mysterious gray champion. But if this figure is meant to elicit the strong support of the young adult generation, as the GIs demonstrated for Roosevelt, Millennials' scant approval of Trump argues against the title. A 2018 poll found only 19 percent of Millennials approving of Trump and 63 percent disapproving, 46 percent of whom strongly disapproved ("January 2018 Toplines," NBC News/GenForward at the University of Chicago survey, January 3-16, 2018, http://genforwardsurvey.com/assets/uploads/2018/01/NBC-GenForward-Jan-2018-Toplines -1.pdf). If Bannon and others on the right honor Trump as their gray champion, their biases may be reading into Strauss-Howe theory what they wish to believe. An opposing view from the left might find the president not to be the gray champion at all, but part of the crisis itself.

28. Jeremy W. Peters, "Bannon's Views Can Be Traced to a Book That Warns, 'Winter Is Coming,'" *New York Times*, April 8, 2017, www.nytimes.com/2017/04/08/us/politics /stephen-bannon-book-fourth-turning.html.

29. The full title that appears on the cover of the 1998 paperback edition of Strauss and Howe's *The Fourth Turning* is: *The Fourth Turning, An American Prophecy: What the Cycles of History Tell Us About America's Next Rendezvous with Destiny.*

30. A University of Vermont survey found that of those Millennial students polled, 35 percent read all seven books, two-thirds at least some; 45 percent saw all of the movies and 86 percent at least some. See Anthony Gierzynski, *Harry Potter and the Millennials: Research Methods and the Politics of the Muggle Generation* (Baltimore, MA: Johns Hopkins University Press, 2013).

5. Architecture History by Generation

The epigraph is from Robert A. M. Stern, *New Directions in American Architecture* (New York: Braziller, 1969), 7.

1. To construct this four-part chronology, I rely on four successive chapters of *Architecture School: Three Centuries of Educating Architects in North America*. Published to commemorate the centennial of the Association of Collegiate Schools of Architecture's founding, the edited volume comprehensively describes interactions between the practice and the academy. See Joan Ockman, ed., *Architecture School: Three Centuries of Educating Architects in North America* (Cambridge, MA: MIT Press, 2012).

2. Spiro Kostof, *History of Architecture* (New York: Oxford University Press, 1985), 716.

3. Lois Craig et al., *The Federal Presence: Architecture Politics and Symbols in the United States Government Buildings* (Cambridge, MA: MIT Press, 1978), 298–403.

4. Raymond Hood, "The Design of Rockefeller Center," *Architectural Forum* 56 (January 1932): 1.

5. Rem Koolhaas, *Delirious New York* (New York: Oxford University Press, 1978), 150.

6. Anthony Alofsin, "American Modernism's Challenge to the Beaux-Arts," in Ockman, *Architecture School*, 102.

7. Alofsin, 102–104.

8. Alofsin, 95–100.

9. Terence Riley, *The International Style: Exhibition 15 and the Museum of Modern Art* (New York: Rizzoli, 1992).

10. Kenneth Frampton, *Modern Architecture: A Critical History* (New York: Oxford University Press, 1980), 8–10.

11. Nikolaus Pevsner, *Pioneers of Modern Design* (New York: Penguin, 1975), 27.

12. Clarence Stein, *Toward New Towns for America* (Cambridge, MA: MIT Press, 1951).

13. Dennis DeWitt, "Benjamin Thompson, FAIA (1918–2002)," accessed December 2, 2013, http://www.bta-architects.com/c/BenjaminThompsonFAIA.html.

14. Joan Ockman and Avigail Sachs, "Modernism Takes Command," in Ockman, *Architecture School*, 126.

15. Ockman and Sachs, "Modernism Takes Command," 141.

16. The term itself is attributed to José Luis Sert, who used it in the name of a conference at Harvard in 1956.

17. Ockman and Sachs, "Modernism Takes Command," 127–129. See also A. Lawrence Kocherand Howard Dearstyne, "The Architectural Center: An Organization to Coordinate Building Research, Planning, Design, and Construction," *New Pencil Points* (July 1943): 26–49.

18. Sigfried Giedion, *Space, Time and Architecture: The Growth of a New Tradition* (Cambridge: Harvard University Press, 1954), 5.

19. Giedion, *Space, Time and Architecture*, 22.

20. Sigfried Giedion, José Luis Sert, and Fernand Léger, "Nine Points on Monumentality" (1943), in *Architecture Culture 1943–1968: A Documentary Anthology*, ed. Joan Ockman (New York: Rizzoli, 1993), 29–30.

21. Roland Marchand, "The Designers Go to the Fair, II: Norman Bel Geddes, The General Motors 'Futurama,' and the Visit to the Factory Transformed," in *Design History: An Anthology*, ed. Dennis P. Doordan (Cambridge, MA: MIT Press, 1995), 105–121.

22. Mary McLeod, "The End of Innocence: From Political Activism to Postmodernism," in Ockman, *Architecture School*, 171.

23. McLeod, "The End of Innocence," 162–168. See also Alofsin, "American Modernism's Challenge to the Beaux-Arts," 148–157.

24. For a review of both positions, see Rosemarie Haag Bletter, "Five Architects. Eisenman, Graves, Gwathmey, Hejduk, Meier; Five on Five," *Journal of the Society of Architectural Historians* 38, no. 2 (May 1979): 205–207.

25. Heinrich Klotz, *The History of Postmodern Architecture* (Cambridge, MA: MIT Press, 1988), 325.

26. Robert Venturi, *Complexity and Contradiction in Architecture* (New York: MOMA, 1966), 22.

27. Alofsin, "American Modernism's Challenge to the Beaux-Arts," 117.

28. Simon Sadler, *Archigram: Architecture without Architecture* (Cambridge, MA: MIT Press, 2005), 7.

29. Stan Allen, "The Future That Is Now," in Ockman, *Architecture School*, 211.

30. McLeod, "The End of Innocence," 194.

31. Allen, "The Future That Is Now," 212.

32. Michael Meredith, as quoted in "11 Architects, 12 Conversations," *Praxis* 11/12 (June 2010): 5.

33. McLeod, "The End of Innocence," 190.

34. Olivier Boissière, "Ten California Architects," *Domus* 604 (March 1980): 17.

35. Phillip Johnson and Mark Wigley, *Deconstructivist Architecture* (New York: The Museum of Modern Art, 1988), 7.

36. William Strauss and Neil Howe, *Generations: The History of America's Future, 1584 to 2069* (New York: Harper, 1991), 71.

37. Strauss and Howe, *Generations*, 71.

38. Stern, *New Directions*, 8.

39. Charles Jencks, "2000 July: Jencks' Theory of Evolution, an Overview of 20th Century Architecture," *Architectural Review*, December 7, 2011. See also Charles Jencks, *Modern Movements in Architecture* (New York: Anchor, 1973), 28.

40. Alison Smithson and Peter Smithson, *The Heroic Period of Modern Architecture* (New York: Rizzoli, 1981), 5.

41. Strauss and Howe, *Generations*, 36.

42. Strauss and Howe, 37.

43. For more on Le Corbusier, see Charles Jencks, *Le Corbusier and the Tragic View of Architecture* (Cambridge, MA: Harvard University Press, 1974); for more on Mies van der Rohe, see Elaine S. Hochman, *Architects of Fortune: Mies van der Rohe and the Third Reich* (New York: Grove Press, 1989).

44. As to whether Strauss and Howe's generic description of the gray champion is praiseworthy enough, given Wright's well-documented egotism, see Brendan Gill, *Many Masks: A Life of Frank Lloyd Wright* (New York: G. P. Putnam, 1987).

45. Robert McCarter, *Frank Lloyd Wright* (New York: Phaidon, 1997), 123.

46. Intergovernmental Panel on Climate Change, *Climate Change 2014: Mitigation of Climate Change, Working Group III Contribution to Fifth Assessment Report of the Intergovernmental Panel on Climate Change* (Cambridge: Cambridge University Press, 2014), www.ipcc.ch/pdf/assessment-report/ar5/wg3/ipcc_wg3_ar5_full.pdf. The report shows "that global emissions of greenhouse gases have risen to unprecedented levels despite a growing number of policies to reduce climate change. Emissions grew more quickly between 2000 and 2010 than in each of the three previous decades . . . only major institutional and technological change will give a better than even chance that global warming will not exceed this threshold."

47. Elizabeth Evitts Dickinson, "The Millennials: Children of the Revolution," *Architect*, January 2013, 115.

48. Allen, "The Future That Is Now," 216.

49. MASS Design Group (website), accessed March 23, 2014, www.massdesigngroup.org. While many who were asked to name a Millennial firm suggested MASS Design Group, based on when Michael Murphy, executive director at MASS Design Group, attended col-

lege, he may be a few years short of qualifying as a Millennial according to Strauss-Howe birth years.

50. "The National Memorial for Peace and Justice," MASS Design Group, accessed June 4, 2018, massdesigngroup.org/work/design/memorial-peace-and-justice. The *Dallas News* called the memorial "the single greatest work of American architecture of the 21st century, and the most successful memorial design since the 1982 debut of Maya Lin's Vietnam Veterans Memorial in Washington, D.C." Mark Lamster, "The Single Greatest Work of 21st Century American Architecture Will Break Your Heart," *Dallas News*, August 29, 2018.

51. Latent Design (website), accessed September 23, 2018, www.latentdesign.net. Nominated by AIAS members.

52. Project H Design (website), accessed May 13, 2017, www.projecthdesign.org. Identified as a "new model of alternative practice" in Stan Allen, "The Future That Is Now," in Ockman, *Architecture School*, 226–227.

53. Danielle Sacks, "Green Guru Gone Wrong: William McDonough," *Fast Company*, November 1, 2008, http://www.fastcompany.com/1042475/green-guru-gone-wrong-william -mcdonough.

54. Patrik Schumacher, "Parametricism—A New Global Style for Architecture and Urban Design," *Architectural Design* 79, no. 4 (July/August 2009), accessed March 23, 2014, www.patrikschumacher.com/index.htm.

55. Barry Bergdoll, *Rising Currents: Projects for New York's Waterfront* (New York: MOMA, 2010).

56. These three selections were chosen early in the writing of this book with the hope that a more definitive text would emerge before publication. During that interval I unsystematically queried many individuals (mostly Millennials) hoping for a definitive answer, yet responses's varied widely. Some nominated Rem Koolhaas's *S,M,L,XL*, but this came out only a few years after *Deconstructivist Architecture* and is arguably too early to be canonical specific to Millennials. Others remembered that *Graphic Anatomy* by Atelier Bow Wow seemed to be on every studio desk in the late 2000s. Still others recommended (somewhat sardonically) *101 Things I Learned in Architecture School* because it had become a meme of studio culture. It became so popular that it was sold at the apparel store Urban Outfitters, with one nominator claiming "90% of your students have either had, read, or still have that book." While this may resonate with Marc Prensky's tag for "checklist kids" discussed in chapter 9, it lacks the gravitas of other generations' canonical texts—but that may be my own generational bias showing through. The majority of respondents did suggest that perhaps canonical books were a notion of analog culture and that as one respondent stated, "The most influential sources for some time now have been the websites archdaily and archinect." See Rem Koolhaas and Bruce Mau, *S,M,L,XL (Small, Medium, Large, Extra-Large)* (New York: Monacelli Press, 1995); Atelier Bow Wow, *Graphic Anatomy* (Tokyo: Toto, 2007); Matthew Frederick, *101 Things I Learned in Architecture School* (Cambridge: MIT Press, 2007); archdaily.com (website); and archinect.com (website).

57. Strauss and Howe, *Generations*, 81.

6. Generational Alignment Strategies

The epigraph is from Karl Mannheim, "The Problem of Generations," in *Essays on the Sociology of Knowledge*, ed. Paul Kecskemeti, trans. Edith Schwarzschild and Paul Kecskemeti (London: Routledge & Kegan Paul, 1952), 283. Here Mannheim paraphrases Wilhelm Pinder. See W. Pinder, "Kunstgeschichte nach Generationen," in *Zwischen Philosophie und Kunst: Johannes Volkelt zum 100. Lehrsemester dargebracht* (Leipzig: Pfeiffer, 1926), 20. Pinder, foremost an art historian who taught, among others, the architectural historian Nicholas Pevsner, often uses analogies to describe the relationship between generations during a given period. He describes these as "an accidental chord, an apparent harmony, produced by the vertical coincidence of notes which in fact owe a primary horizontal allegiance to the different parts (i.e. the generation-entelechies) of a fugue." Mannheim, "The Problem of Generations," 284.

1. Elizabeth Evitts Dickinson, "The Millennials: Children of the Revolution," *Architect*, January 2013, 112

2. Ernest L. Boyer and Lee D. Mitgang, *Building Community: A New Future for Architecture Education and Practice* (Princeton, NJ: Carnegie Foundation for the Advancement of Teaching, 1996), 85.

3. Scott Carlson, "The Net Generation Goes to College," *Chronicle of Higher Education* 52, no. 7 (October 7, 2005): A34, http://chronicle.com/article/The-Net-Generation-Goes-to /12307.

4. Richard Sweeney, "Millennial Behaviors & Demographics" (working paper, New Jersey Institute of Technology, revised December 22, 2006), http://unbtls.ca/teachingtips /pdfs/sew/Millennial-Behaviors.pdf.

5. Nicole J. Borges et al., "Comparing Millennial and Generation X Medical Students at One Medical School," *Academic Medicine* 81, no. 6 (2006): 571–576.

6. Pew Research Center, *Millennials: Confident. Connected. Open to Change*, Paul Taylor and Scott Keeter, eds., February 2010, http://www.pewsocialtrends.org/files/2010/10 /millennials-confident-connected-open-to-change.pdf.

7. Neil Howe and William Strauss, *Millennials Go to College* (Washington, DC: Life-Course Associates, 2007), 59–60.

8. Jean M. Twenge et al., "Generational Differences in Young Adults' Life Goals, Concern for Others, and Civic Orientation, 1966–2009," *Journal of Personality and Social Psychology* 102, no. 5 (2012): 1045–1062.

9. The Boyer report was commissioned as an independent study of the profession of architecture by the American Institute of Architecture and what are known as its collateral organizations: the American Institute of Architecture Students (AIAS), the National Conference of Architectural Registration Boards (NCARB), the National Architectural Accrediting Board (NAAB), and the Association of Collegiate Schools of Architecture (ACSA). See Boyer and Mitgang, *Building Community*, xii.

10. Boyer and Mitgang, xiv.

11. Boyer and Mitgang, 7–9, 87.

12. Boyer and Mitgang, 63–74.

13. Boyer and Mitgang, 26–28.

14. Joan Ockman, ed., *Architecture School: Three Centuries of Educating Architects in North America* (Cambridge, MA: MIT Press, 2012), 31–32.

15. Ockman, *Architecture School*, 32.

16. Wilhelm Pinder, *Problems of Generation in the History of European Art* (Berlin: Franfurter Verlags-Anstalt, 1926), cited in Julián Marías, *Generations: A Historical Method*, trans. Harold C. Raley (Mobile: University of Alabama Press, 1970), 114–117.

17. Ockman, *Architecture School*, 31.

18. From these debates, I extract a provisional synthesis in Chapter 2 to list as the pre-seasonal indicators of characteristics that Millennials have now embraced.

19. Stan Allen, "The Future That Is Now," in Ockman, *Architecture School*, 228.

20. Allen, 228.

21. Allen, 229.

22. Peter Buchanan, "The Big Rethink Part 1: Towards a Complete Architecture," *Architectural Review*, December 21, 2011, www.architectural-review.com/rethink/viewpoints/the-big-rethink-part-1towards-a-complete-architecture/8624049.fullarticle.

23. Peter Buchanan, "The Big Rethink Part 9: Rethinking Architectural Education," *Architectural Review*, September 28, 2012, www.architectural-review.com/today/the-big-rethink-part-9-rethinking-architectural-education/8636035.fullarticle.

24. Buchanan, "The Big Rethink Part 9."

25. Ashraf Salama, *New Trends in Architectural Education: Designing the Design Studio* (Raleigh, NC: Tailored Text, 1995), 3.

26. Peter Buchanan, "What Is Wrong with Architectural Education? Almost Everything," *Architectural Review*, July 1989, reprinted October 31, 2012, www.architectural-review.com/today/1989-july-whats-wrong-with-architectural-education-almost-everything/8637977.fullarticle.

27. Buchanan, "The Big Rethink Part 9."

28. Buchanan, "The Big Rethink Part 9."

29. Buchanan, "The Big Rethink Part 9."

30. Buchanan, "The Big Rethink Part 9."

31. William Strauss and Neil Howe, *Generations: The History of America's Future, 1584 to 2069* (New York: Harper, 1991), 409.

32. Strauss and Howe, *Generations*, 382.

33. Strauss and Howe, *Generations*, 409.

34. Jeff Gordinier, *X Saves The World: How Generation X Got the Shaft but Can Still Keep Everything from Sucking* (New York: Viking, 2008).

35. Strauss and Howe, *Generations*, 409.

36. *Architizer* Editors, "Interview: Witold Rybczynski On *How Architecture Works*," *Architizer* (blog), http://architizer.com/blog/practice/materials/interview-witold-rybczynski/, accessed January 2016. Criticizing cutting-edge architecture, Rybczynski, in promoting his book *How Architecture Works: A Humanist's Toolkit* (New York: Farrar, Straus and Giroux, 2013), attributes the phrase "the enemies of humanism to be chaos and inhuman order" to Geoffrey Scott, *The Architecture of Humanism: A Study in the History of Taste* (New York: Norton, 1999).

37. William S. Saunders, ed., *The New Architectural Pragmatism* (Minneapolis: University of Minnesota Press, 2007), viii–ix.

38. Robert E. Somol, "12 Reasons to Get Back in Shape," in *Content*, ed. Rem Koolhaas and Brendan McGetrick (Koln: Taschen, 2004), 86.

39. Sanford Kwinter, "Confessions of an Organicist," *Log*, no. 5, ed. Robert E. Somol and Sarah Whiting (Spring/Summer 2005): 107.

40. Sanford Kwinter, "Concepts: The Architecture of Hope," *Harvard Design Magazine* 19 (Fall 2003/Winter 2004): 37. Kwinter furthers his argument for difficulty in the same piece, writing: "It must not be forgotten the work of these practitioners [Schoenberg and

Picasso] is purposely and necessarily *difficult*—and it is this difficulty that we must find a way to celebrate today. . . . And it is arguable that dilettantism—whose many modern forms include parochialism, specialism, 'expertise'—represents a deeper and more menacing form of mediocrity in our present culture." Others have a different take on Kwinter's enthusiasm for the difficult. In response to a rhetorical question on the Archinect discussion forum, "Why is Sanford Kwinter so popular?" a respondent, Steven Ward, wrote with seeming candor (and avoiding capitalization) "i consider myself an ambitious reader of arch texts, but his are still mostly opaque to me—certainly not anything that can influence my thinking, since i only have a fuzzy idea of what's being proposed. i've tried one book, given up, only to buy another because i wasn't willing to accept that here was a celebrated architecture theorist from whom i could glean so little!" While others came to Kwinter's defense, most simply attributed his popularity to his hair. Steven Ward, reply to "Why is Sanford Kwinter so popular?" Archinect discussion forum, November 9, 2011, archinect .com/forum/thread/26681002/why-is-sanford-kwinter-so-popular/.

41. *Assemblage* had accepted the baton to promote high architectural theory after *Oppositions* stopped publishing in 1984.

42. Stan Allen, "The Future That Is Now," 225.

43. Robert E. Somol and Sarah Whiting, "Okay, Here's the Plan," *Log*, no. 5 (Spring/Summer 2005): 5.

44. Thomas R. Fisher, "Patterns of Exploitation," *Progressive Architecture*, May 1991, 9.

45. AIAS Studio Culture Task Force, *The Redesign of Studio Culture: A Report of the AIAS Studio Culture Task Force* (Washington, DC: American Institute of Architecture Students, 2002), 6, www.aias.org/wp-content/uploads/2016/08/Studio-Culture-Stories-and -Interpretations.pdf.

46. Harry F. Mallgrave, *The Architect's Brain: Neuroscience, Creativity and Architecture* (London: Wiley, 2010), 219.

47. Matt Shaw, "Is Drawing Dead? Yale Searches for an Answer," *Architects Newspaper*, February 15, 2012, blog.archpaper.com/2012/02/is-drawing-dead-yale-searches-for-an-answer/.

48. B. S. Apili and Y. Basa, "The Shifting Tides of Academe: Oscillation Between Hand and Computer in Architectural Education," *International Journal of Technology and Design Education* 16 (2006): 273–283.

49. As quoted in Richard W. Hayes, "Vital Signs: Is Drawing Dead?" *Constructs: Yale Architecture* 15, no. 1 (Fall 2012): 9.

7. Collaboration

The epigraph is from Robert Somol and Sarah Whiting, "Notes Around the Doppler Effect and Other Moods of Modernism," *Perspecta* 33 (2002), 75.

1. Aaron Koch et al., *The Redesign of Studio Culture: A Report of the AIAS Studio Culture Task Force* (Washington, DC: American Institute of Architecture Students, 2002).

2. "Millennials Prefer Cities to Suburbs, Subways to Driveways," *Newswire* (blog), Nielsen, March 4, 2014, www.nielsen.com/us/en/insights/news/2014/millennials-prefer-cities-to-suburbs-subways-to-driveways.html.

3. Hugh F. Kelly, *Emerging Trends in Real Estate: United States and Canada 2016*, (Washington, DC: PwC and Urban Land Institute, 2015), 6, http://uli.org/wp-content /uploads/ULI-Documents/Emerging-Trends-in-Real-Estate-United-States-and-Canada -2016.pdf.

4. "Millennials Prefer Cities to Suburbs," 2.

5. Amy Madden, "Texas Oil Boom Means More Money For UT, A&M," *Dallas Morning News*, November 22, 2013, www.dallasnews.com/news/texas/2013/11/22/texas-oil-boom-means-more-money-for-ut-am.

6. Patrick J. Kiger, "Moving to Where the Price Is Right," *Urban Land*, February 9, 2015, http://urbanland.uli.org/economy-markets-trends/moving-price-right/.

7. *Who's on Board: 2014 Mobility Attitudes Survey* (New York: TransitCenter, 2014), 16, transitcenter.org/wp-content/uploads/2014/08/WhosOnBoard2014-ForWeb.pdf.

8. *Beyond Traffic 2045: Trends and Choices* (Washington, DC: US Department of Transportation, 2014), 15–18, www.dot.gov/sites/dot.gov/files/docs/Draft_Beyond_Traffic_Framework.pdf.

9. Brian C. Tefft et al., *Timing of Driver's License Acquisition and Reasons for Delay among Young People in the United States, 2012* (Washington, DC: AAA Foundation for Traffic Safety, July 2013), 3, http://newsroom.aaa.com/wp-content/uploads/2013/07/Teens-Delay-Licensing-FTS-Report.pdf.

10. Paul R. Levy and Lauren M. Gilchrist, Philadelphia Center City District, *Downtown Rebirth: Documenting the Live-Work Dynamic in 21st Century U.S. Cities* (Philadelphia: International Downtown Association, 2014), http://definingdowntown.org/wp-content/uploads/docs/Defining_DowntownReport.pdf.

11. Victor Calanog, "Why Suburban Office Markets Will Continue to Flounder," *National Real Estate Investor*, December 14, 2010, http://nreionline.com/distress/why-suburban-office-markets-will-continue-flounder/. As the recession receded, the suburban office market also rebounded somewhat, but only in regions with downtown urban growth. See Peter Linneman, "Suburban Office: A Dying Breed?" (Princeton: NAI Global, 2013), http://www.naimiamiblog.com/wp-content/uploads/2013/11/Whitepaper-Suburban-Office-A-Dying-Breed.pdf.

12. Norm Miller cites this figure as 27 percent. See Norm G. Miller, "Workplace Trends in Office Space: Implications for Future Office Demand," *Journal of Corporate Real Estate* 16, no. 3 (September 2014): 159–181. The Regional Plan Association, citing data from the 2012 Global Coworking Survey, puts the figure at 33 percent. See Regional Plan Association, "The Future of Work: Fourth Regional Plan Roundtable," February 26, 2015, 14, http://library.rpa.org/pdf/RPA-4RP-Whitepaper-The-Future-of-Work.pdf. And the General Services Administration says it's 24 percent. See *Workspace Utilization and Allocation Benchmark* (Washington, DC: US General Services Administration Office of Governmentwide Policy, Office of Real Property Management Performance Measurement Division, July 2011), 11, https://www.gsa.gov/cdnstatic/Workspace_Utilization_Banchmark_July_2012_%281%29.pdf.

13. *Innovative Workplaces: Benefits and Best Practices* (Washington, DC: US General Services Administration Office of Governmentwide Policy, 2006), 9-18, http://www.gsa.gov/cdnstatic/Innovative_Workplaces-508_R2OD26_0Z5RDZ-i34K-pR.pdf.

14. Beth Ann Bovino, "Millennials and the U.S. Economy: The Kids Are All Right (or Soon Will Be)," Standard & Poor's Financial Services, April 29, 2015, 1, http://docplayer.net/49276647-Millennials-and-the-u-s-economy-the-kids-are-all-right-or-soon-will-be.html.

15. "Think you know the Next Gen investor? Think again," UBS Investor Watch, 1Q 2014, 5, www.ubs.com/content/dam/WealthManagementAmericas/documents/investor-watch-1Q2014-report.pdf.

16. Jillian Berman, "Student Debt Just Hit $1.5 Trillion," *MarketWatch*, May 12, 2018, www.marketwatch.com/story/student-debt-just-hit-15-trillion-2018-05-08.

17. Bovino, "Millennials and the U.S. Economy," 1.

18. *2017 Infrastructure Report Card* (Reston, VA: American Society of Civil Engineers, 2017), http://www.infrastructurereportcard.org/wp-content/uploads/2017/10/Full-2017-Report-Card-FINAL.pdf.

19. "A Deep Dive Into Party Affiliation," Pew Research Center, April 7, 2015, 9, http://assets.pewresearch.org/wp-content/uploads/sites/5/2015/04/4-7-2015-Party-ID-release.pdf.

20. Pew Research Center, *Millennials: Confident. Connected. Open to Change*, Paul Taylor and Scott Keeter, eds., February 2010, 63, http://www.pewsocialtrends.org/files/2010/10/millennials-confident-connected-open-to-change.pdf; see also Pew Research Center, *Beyond Distrust: How Americans View Their Government*, November 23, 2015, 24, http://www.people-press.org/files/2015/11/11-23-2015-Governance-release.pdf.

21. Kathi Vian, quoted in Allison Arieff and Eva Hagberg Fisher, "Roundtable: Work in 2025," *Dialogue* 28, 2015, 27, http://www.gensler.com/design-thinking/publications/dialogue/28/roundtable-work-in-2025; see also Kathi Vian and Carol Coletta, "5 Things You Need to Know About Our Economic Future," May 20, 2015, in *Knight Cities*, produced by the John S. and James L. Knight Foundation, podcast, http://www.iftf.org/future-now/article-detail/podcast-kathi-vian-talks-with-the-knight-foundation-about-the-seven-economy-future/. The seven "C" economies are: collaborative, creative, corporate, consumer, civil, criminal, and crypto.

22. Vian, in Arieff and Fisher, "Roundtable," 27.

23. Thomas Fisher, "Architecture and the Third Industrial Revolution," *Architect*, January 2014, 101–103.

24. Fisher, "Architecture," 101.

25. "ENR 2017 Top 150 Global Design Firms," Engineering News-Record, updated July 2017, www.enr.com/toplists/2017-Top-150-Global-Design-Firms-1; "History," About AECOM, AECOM (website), accessed May 28, 2018, www.aecom.com/about-aecom/history/.

26. Robin Amer, "AECOM is bigger. But is that better?" *Medill Reports Chicago*, March 13, 2014, accessed November 9, 2015, newsarchive.medill.northwestern.edu/chicago/news-228924.html (article no longer available online). See also John Gittelsohn and Matthew Winkler, "World's Biggest Engineering Firm Plans to Spend Billions to Become Biggest in Infrastructure," *Bloomberg*, March 6, 2017, http://www.bloomberg.com/news/articles/2017-03-06/aecom-seeks-purchases-in-bid-to-become-biggest-in-infrastructure.

27. Rob Alderson, "We Chat to Snøhetta About Designing Banknotes, Studio Rituals and the Problems with Civic Commissions," *It's Nice That*, October 6, 2015, www.itsnicethat.com/features/snohetta-interview.

28. Suzanne Stephens and Anna Fixsen, "Case Closed: Zaha Hadid v. *New York Review of Books* and Martin Filler," *Architectural Record*, January 23, 2015, http://www.architecturalrecord.com/articles/3311-case-closed-zaha-hadid-v-new-york-review-of-books-and-martin-filler.

29. Holland Cotter, "Toward a Museum of the 21st Century," *New York Times*, October 28, 2015, www.nytimes.com/2015/11/01/arts/design/toward-a-museum-of-the-21st-century.html. While most generational timelines would place Gehry among the Silent generation, his Bilbao Museum of 1997 remains one of the early built examples of starchitecture.

30. Karrie Jacobs, "Santiago Calatrava: The World's Most Hated Architect?" *Fast Company*, December 18, 2014, www.fastcodesign.com/3039658/santiago-calatrava-the-worlds-most-hated-architect/. For the video that Jacobs describes, see "A conversation with Peter Eisenman and Michael Graves," Architectural League NY, January 4, 2015, https://archleague.org/article/conversation-peter-eisenman-michael-graves/.

31. Roemer van Toorn, "No More Dreams?" in *The New Architectural Pragmatism*, ed. William S. Saunders (Minneapolis: University of Minnesota Press, 2007), 56.

32. Suzanne Stephens, "Where the Work Is," *Architectural Record*, November 2010, 79.

33. Stephane Hallegatte et al., *Shock Waves: Managing the Impacts of Climate Change on Poverty*, Climate Change and Development Series (Washington, DC: World Bank, 2016), xi, https://openknowledge.worldbank.org/bitstream/handle/10986/22787/9781464806735.pdf.

34. Bruce Campbell and Lisa Goddard, "Climate Change, Food Security and the Refugee Crisis: Connecting the Dots to Avoid Future Tragedy," *News blog*, Research Program on Climate Change, Agriculture and Food Security, October 27, 2015, https://ccafs.cgiar.org/blog/climate-change-food-security-and-refugee-crisis-connecting-dots-avoid-future-tragedy/.

35. John Schwartz, "Deadly Heat Is Forecast in Persian Gulf by 2100," *New York Times*, October 26, 2015.

36. Anders Levermann et al., "Basic Mechanism for Abrupt Monsoon Transitions," *Proceedings of the National Academy of Sciences* 106, no. 49 (December 8, 2009): 20572–20577, www.pnas.org/content/106/49/20572.full.

37. Scott Carlson, "10-Week Think Tanks," *Chronicle of Higher Education*, May 20, 2013.

38. Darius Sollohub and Richard Sweeney, "Millennials in Design Education," in *Proceedings of the 2012 100th ACSA Annual Meeting: Digital Aptitudes and Other Openings*, ed. Mark Goulthorpe and Amy Murphy (Washington, DC: Association of Collegiate Schools of Architecture, 2012), 469.

39. Aaron Koch et al., *The Redesign of Studio Culture: A Report of the AIAS Studio Culture Task Force* (Washington, DC: American Institute of Architecture Students, 2002), 3.

40. Paul Taylor, *The Next America: Boomers, Millennials, and the Looming Generational Showdown* (New York: Public Affairs, 2014), 20. For Foster's quote on optimism, see www.inspiringquotes.us/quotes/WI8x_70TOXa9D.

41. Koch, *Redesign of Studio Culture*, 20.

42. Koch, 20.

43. Koch, 12.

44. Sollohub and Sweeney, "Millennials in Design Education," 469.

45. Koch, *Redesign of Studio Culture*, 23.

46. Koch, 11.

47. Koch, 13.

48. Chris Dede, "Planning for Neomillennial Learning Styles: Implications for Investments in Technology and Faculty," Educause, August 2004, https://www.educause.edu/research-and-publications/books/educating-net-generation/planning-neomillennial-learning-styles-implications-investments-tech.

49. David C. Hutchison, *A Natural History of Place in Education* (New York: Teachers College Press, 2004), 49–52.

50. Julian Vasquez Heilig et al., "From Dewey to No Child Left Behind: The Evolution and Devolution of Public Arts Education," *Arts Education Policy Review* 111 (2010): 136-

145; see also David J. Hoff, "A Blueprint for Change," *Education Week* 18, no. 32 (1999): 37–43.

51. Ben E. Graves and Clifford A. Pearson, *School Ways: The Planning and Design of America's Schools* (New York: McGraw-Hill, 1993), 25.

52. Francis Presler, interview by Dwight Perkins and Eero Saarinen, in David C. Hutchison, *A Natural History of Place in Education* (New York: Teachers College Press, 2004), 53. See also Eleanor Nicholson, "The School Building as the Third Teacher," in *Children's Spaces*, ed. Mark Dudek (Oxford: Architectural Press, 2005), 53.

53. David A. Kolb, *Experiential Learning: Experience as the Source of Learning and Development* (Englewood Cliffs, NJ: Prentice Hall, 1984), 28. A metaphor often used to describe Kolb's pattern is the experience of learning to ride a bicycle. When first straddling a bike, one brings the concrete understanding of balance to the undertaking. After a succession of experiential learning cycles, using training wheels or having someone holding on, a rider can proceed unsupported with an increasing sense of confidence. And after reaching a certain confidence, while the adage that one "never forgets how to ride a bike" might apply, to rise to a higher level of mastery in a new context, say to be able to ride safely on a city street with complex traffic patterns, Kolb's steps must be repeated.

54. Melissa Korn and Rachel Emma Silverman, "Forget B-School, D-School Is Hot: 'Design Thinking' Concept Gains Traction as More Programs Offer the Problem-Solving Courses," *Wall Street Journal*, June 7, 2012, www.wsj.com/articles/SB10001424052702303 506404577446832178537716/.

55. "Our Point of View," Stanford University Institute of Design (website), accessed December 3, 2015, http://dschool.stanford.edu/our-point-of-view/ (page since deleted).

56. Hasso Plattner et al., eds., *Design Thinking: Understand, Improve, Apply* (Berlin/Heidelberg: Springer-Verlag, 2011), 4.

57. Rolf Faste, "Ambidextrous Thinking," in *Innovations in Mechanical Engineering Curricula for the 1990s* (New York: American Society of Mechanical Engineers, November 1994).

58. For excellent graphic depictions and short text descriptions of design thinking methods through 2005, see Hugh Dubberly, *How Do You Design: A Compendium of Models* (San Francisco: Dubberly Design Office, 2004), http://www.dubberly.com/wp-content /uploads/2008/06/ddo_designprocess.pdf.

59. "Design Thinking . . . What Is That?" *Fast Company*, March 20, 2006, www .fastcompany.com/919258/design-thinking-what/. I use this definition because it has consistently come up first in a Google search after those seeded by the d.school or its for-profit affiliates.

60. Due to the fluidity of the web, this succinct and eloquent definition is no longer part of Wikipedia's section on Design Thinking.

61. "Taking Design Thinking to Schools," Hasso Plattner Institute of Design, Stanford School of Education, 2009, web.stanford.edu/dept/SUSE/taking-design/presentations /Taking-design-to-school.pdf.

62. Plattner, *Design Thinking*, xiv–xvi.

63. Steve Jobs, "'You've Got to Find What You Love,' Jobs Says," transcript of commencement address (June 12, 2005), *Stanford News*, June 14, 2005, http://news.stanford .edu/news/2005/june15/jobs-061505.html.

8. Anytime, Anywhere

The epigraph is from Leonard Kleinrock, "Nomadic Computing," keynote address: International Conference on Mobile Computing and Networking (1995), 10, https://www.lk.cs.ucla.edu/data/files/Kleinrock/Nomadic%20Computing.pdf.

1. Phillip Bernstein is the former vice president for strategic industry relations and a longtime lecturer in professional practice at Yale University. The "three eras" are described in a presentation entitled "The Evolving Role of the Architect in the Era of Connection," live-streamed at ARCHITECT Live from the American Institute of Architects Convention on May 20, 2016.

2. Finith Jernigan, *Big BIM Little BIM* (Salisbury, MD: 4 Site Press, 2007), 23.

3. *National Building Information Modeling Standard* (Washington, DC: National Institute of Building Sciences, 2007), accessed September 5, 2016, www.wbdg.org/pdfs/NBIMSv1_p1.pdf (page since removed). The full definition also adds: "As such it serves as a shared knowledge resource for information about a facility forming a reliable basis for decisions during its lifecycle from inception onward."

4. Weisheng Lu et al., "Demystifying Construction Project Time–Effort Distribution Curves: BIM and Non-BIM Comparison," *Journal of Management in Engineering* 31, no. 6 (March 2015): 1.

5. See Howard W. Ashcraft, "Furthering Collaboration," in *Building (in) the Future*, ed. Peggy Deamer and Phillip G. Bernstein (New York: Princeton Architectural Press, 2010), 145–158.

6. Phillip Bernstein, "Models for Practice: Past, Present, Future," in Deamer and Bernstein, *Building (in) the Future*, 197.

7. Bernstein, "Models for Practice," 197.

8. "Integrated Project Delivery (IPD) is a project delivery approach that integrates people, systems, business structures and practices into a process that collaboratively harnesses the talents and insights of all participants to optimize project results, increase value to the owner, reduce waste, and maximize efficiency through all phases of design, fabrication, and construction." American Institute of Architects, *Integrated Project Delivery: A Guide*, version 1 (Washington, DC: American Institute of Architects, 2007), https://info.aia.org/SiteObjects/files/IPD_Guide_2007.pdf.

9. This is to distinguish computing using electronics from computing by hand, which had been a practice for centuries. For more on ballistics, see descriptions of the ENIAC (Electronic Numerical Integrator and Computer), considered widely to be the first electronic computer. ENIAC was devised to calculate artillery firing tables for the US Army Ballistic Research Laboratory. See John Mauchly, "The ENIAC," in *A History of Computing in the Twentieth Century*, ed. Nicholas Metropolis, J. Howlett, and Gian-Carlo Rota (New York: Academic Press, 1980), 541–550. For more on cryptography, see descriptions of Claude Shannon's "Mathematical Theory of Communication," which is credited as being the foundation document of binary code. See Jon Gertner, *The Idea Factory: Bell Labs and the Great Age of American Innovation* (New York: Penguin Press, 2013), 115–135.

10. Charles M. Eastman, "The Use of Computers Instead of Drawings," *AIA Journal* 63, no. 3 (March 1975): 50. While Eastman may have been prophetic regarding a prototype for BIM, he was less optimistic about 2-D CAD: "Only much later, after using this limited mode allows BDS (Building Description Systems) to become widely understood will any machine representation replace the drafting board."

11. Nicholas Negroponte, preface to *Soft Architecture Machines* (Cambridge, MA: MIT Press, 1975).

12. Negroponte, preface to *Soft Architecture Machines*.

13. Erkki Patokorpi and Franck Tétard, "From Mobility to True Nomadicity and Ubiquity: Discussing Fluidity, Metaspaces, Micromobility, and Multiple-Profiling," in *Global Mobile Commerce: Strategies, Implementation and Case Studies*, ed. Wayne Huang et al. (Hershey, PA: Information Science Reference, 2008), 1–17.

14. Patokorpi and Tétard, "From Mobility to True Nomadicity and Ubiquity," 1–17.

15. William Mitchell, *City of Bits: Space, Place, and the Infobahn* (Cambridge: MIT Press, 1996), 8. Mitchell continues: "The Net has a fundamentally different physical structure, and it operates under quite different rules from those that organize the action in the public places of traditional cities. It will play as crucial a role in twenty-first-century urbanity as the centrally located, spatially bounded, architecturally celebrated agora did (according to Aristotle's Politics) in the life of the Greek polis and in prototypical urban diagrams like that so lucidly traced out by the Milesians on their Ionian rock."

16. "Project Dreamcatcher," Projects, Autodesk Research, accessed September 26, 2016, autodeskresearch.com/projects/dreamcatcher.

17. Richman Neumann, "9 Reasons Architects Should Be Designing, Not Drafting," Modumate (blog), January 30, 2018, http://www.modumate.com/9-reasons-architects -should-be-designing-not-drafting/.

18. Ryan Craig, "A Brief History (And Future) of Online Degrees," *Forbes*, June 23, 2015, http://www.forbes.com/sites/ryancraig/2015/06/23/a-brief-history-and-future-of-online -degrees/#473873097e37/.

19. "7 Things You Should Know About Flipped Classrooms," 7 Things You Should Know About series, Educause Learning Initiative, Educause, February 2012, accessed August 28, 2016, http://library.educause.edu/resources/2012/2/7-things-you-should-know-about -flipped-classrooms.

20. "7 Things You Should Know About Flipped Classrooms."

21. Kevin Carey, *The End of College: Creating the Future of Learning and the University of Everywhere* (New York: Riverhead Books, 2015), 203–219; see also "7 Things You Should Know About Badges," 7 Things You Should Know About series, Educause Learning Initiative, Educause, June 2012, accessed August 28, 2016, http://library.educause.edu /resources/2012/6/7-things-you-should-know-about-badges.

22. Carey, *The End of College*, 206.

23. "Case Studies: Badges in Action," Reconnect Learning, accessed September 13, 2018, http://reconnectlearning.org/case-studies/. See also Lin Y. Muilenburg and Zane L. Berge, eds., *Digital Badges in Education: Trends, Issues, and Cases* (New York: Routledge, 2016).

24. Carey, *The End of College*, 218–219.

25. Roger McHaney, *The New Digital Shoreline: How Web 2.0 and Millennials are Revolutionizing Higher Education* (Sterling, VA: Stylus Publishing, 2011), 166–167, 186–189.

26. George Siemens, "Connectivism: A Learning Theory for the Digital Age," elearnspace, December 12, 2004, http://www.elearnspace.org/Articles/connectivism.htm.

27. Siemens, "Connectivism."

28. Marc Aurel Schnabel and Jeremy J. Ham, "A Framework for Social Networked Architectural Education," in *Open Systems: Proceedings of the 18th International Confer-*

ence on Computer-Aided Architectural Design Research in Asia," ed. Rudi Stouffs et al. (Singapore: CAADRIA, National University of Singapore, 2013), 313–322.

29. McHaney, *The New Digital Shoreline*, 188.

30. McHaney, 197.

31. Beginning in 1993, while at Bankers Trust Company, Prensky created Corporate Gameware, a game-based e-learning business to instruct on corporate compliance and how to employ financial derivatives. Prior, Prensky taught at the elementary school, high school, and college levels. See his resume on his website at http://www.marcprensky.com /about/Prensky-Resume.pdf.

32. Brian M. Winn, "The Design, Play, and Experience Framework," in *Handbook of Research on Effective Electronic Gaming in Education*, ed. R. Ferdig (Hershey, PA: IGI Global, 2009), 1010–1024.

33. Jenn Shreve, "Let the Games Begin: Entertainment Meets Education," *Edutopia*, March 23, 2005, 28–31, https://www.edutopia.org/video-games-classroom.

34. Winn, "The Design, Play, and Experience Framework," 1011.

35. Marilla. D. Svinicki, "New Directions in Learning and Motivation," *New Directions for Teaching and Learning* 1999, no. 80 (December 2002): 5–27.

36. Robin Hunicke et al., "MDA: A Formal Approach to Game Design and Game Research." (paper, Proceedings of the Challenges in Game AI Workshop, 19th National Conference on Artificial Intelligence, San Jose, CA, July 2004), https://aaai.org/Papers /Workshops/2004/WS-04-04/WS04-04-001.pdf.

37. D. A. Lieberman, "What Can We Learn From Playing Interactive Games?" in *Playing Video Games: Motives, Responses, and Consequences*, ed. P. Vorderer and J. Bryant (Mahwah, NJ: Lawrence Erlbaum Associates, 2006), 379–397.

38. Lieberman, "What Can We Learn From Playing Interactive Games?" 392.

39. Andrew Rollings and Ernest Adams, *Andrew Rollings and Ernest Adams on Game Design* (San Francisco: New Riders Publishing, 2003), 417–420.

40. Richard Moss, "From *SimCity* to, well, *SimCity*: The History of City-Building Games," *ArsTechnica*, November 11, 2015, http://arstechnica.com/gaming/2015/10/from -simcity-to-well-simcity-the-history-of-city-building-games/3/.

41. Matt Peckham, "Minecraft is Now Part of Microsoft, and it Only Cost $2.5 Billion," *Time*, September 15, 2014, http://time.com/3377886/microsoft-buys-mojang/.

42. Friedrich von Borries, Steffen P. Walz, and Matthias Böttger, eds., *Space Time Play: Computer Games, Architecture and Urbanism: The Next Level* (Basel, Switzerland: Birkhauser, 2007).

43. National Council of Architectural Registration Boards, "Three Architecture Programs to Receive 2012 NCARB Awards Totaling $75,000," press release, November 2, 2012, https://www.ncarb.org/press/three-architecture-programs-receive-2012-ncarb-awards -totaling-75000.

44. Paula Crat-Pegg, "Scenario Engine: Concepts of Play and Game Design in Architecture," *Portsmouth School of Architecture Yearbook 2015-16* (Portsmouth, UK: Portsmouth School of Architecture, 2016), 131, http://www2.port.ac.uk/media/contacts-and -departments/arch/downloads/UOP_Architecture_Yearbook_2016_Low-Res_DigitalVersion .pdf. Portsmouth collaborated with its School of Computing and Creative Technology and with the Dublin School of Architecture.

45. Francesc Valls et al., "Videogame Technology in Architecture Education," in

Human-Computer Interaction: Novel User Experiences, Proceedings, Part III, ed. Masaaki Kurosu (18th International Conference, HCI International 2016, Toronto, ON, July 17–22, 2016), 436–447. See also Kathryn Terzano and Victoria Morckel, "*SimCity* in the Community Planning Classroom: Effects on Student Knowledge, Interests, and Perceptions of the Discipline of Planning," *Journal of Planning Education and Research* 37, no. 1 (March 2017): 95–105.

46. Eric Kelderman, "Online Programs Face New Demands From Accreditors," *Chronicle of Higher Education*, November 6, 2011.

47. "List of Accredited Online Degree Programs," Guide to Online Schools, SR Education Group, accessed June 4, 2018, www.guidetoonlineschools.com/degrees. That art and design programs number 281 and architecture only thirty-six fails to justify the often-heard excuse among architecture academics that the artistic content of architecture defies online education.

48. Indeok Song et al., "Internet Gratifications and Internet Addiction: On the Uses and Abuses of New Media," *CyberPsychology & Behavior* 7, no. 4 (September 2004): 384–394.

49. Martin Duberman, *Black Mountain: An Exploration in Community* (Garden City, NY: Anchor Press/Doubleday, 1973), 24–40.

50. "Black Mountain College: A Brief Introduction," Black Mountain College Museum and Arts Center, accessed September 27, 2016, www.blackmountaincollege.org/history/.

51. Duberman, *Black Mountain*, 295–298.

52. "College History," About Goddard, Goddard College, accessed December 12, 2015, www.goddard.edu/about-goddard/goddard-difference/college-history/.

53. Scott Carlson, "Goddard College's Unconventional Path to Survival," *Chronicle of Higher Education*, September 4, 2011, http://chronicle.com/article/Goddard-Colleges /128876.

54. Pitkin organized Goddard around four principles: (1) thought should be tested by action; (2) we only learn what we can inwardly accept; (3) one matures by carrying responsibilities suited to one's capacities; and (4) college should provide educational opportunities for adults because learning should continue throughout life. Forest K. Davis, *Things Were Different in Royce's Day: Royce S. Pitkin as Progressive Educator, a Perspective from Goddard College, 1950–1967* (Adamant, VT: Adamant Press, 1996), 110–112.

55. Kelley Collar, "Getting to the Roots of Adult Education: A Conversation with Goddard's ADP Pioneer," *Clockworks: Goddard College's Semiannual Community Magazine*, Winter/Spring 2007, http://3xl39023n0uyvr5xx1gc1btk.wpengine.netdna-cdn.com/wp -content/uploads/2014/06/2007_Evalyn_Bates_article.pdf.

56. L. Barrett et al., "Report of a Visit to the University Without Walls by the Union for Experimenting Colleges and Universities" (Chicago: Commission on Institutions of Higher Education, North Central Association of Colleges and Secondary Schools, May 1972), http://eric.ed.gov/?id=ED083909.

57. Richard W. Hayes, *The Yale Building Project: The First 40 Years* (New Haven, CT: Yale University Press, 2007).

58. Carey, *The End of College*, 133–138; see also Alyson Krueger, "Readin', Writin', Revolution," *Pennsylvania Gazette*, February 18, 2016, thepenngazette.com/readin-writin -revolution/.

59. Carey, *The End of College*, 138.

60. Claire Cain Miller, "Extreme Study Abroad: The World Is Their Campus," *New York*

Times, October 30, 2015, www.nytimes.com/2015/11/01/education/edlife/extreme-study
-abroad-the-world-is-their-campus.html.

61. Graeme Wood, "The Future of College?" *Atlantic*, September 2014, www
.theatlantic.com/magazine/archive/2014/09/the-future-of-college/375071/.

62. Goddard's low-residency program has influenced over sixty other institutions, many part of the original Union for Research and Experimentation in Higher Education. Now based in Cincinnati, Union Institute & University is the descendent of the original consortium, recast as a for-profit, low-residency university in multiple locations.

9. An Accelerated Tempo

Long attributed to Socrates by Plato, the epigraph's true origins remain unclear. A portion of it is used as an epigraph to open Kali H. Trzesniewski and M. Brent Donnellan, "Rethinking 'Generation Me': A Study of Cohort Effects from 1976–2006," *Perspectives on Psychological Science* 5, no. 1 (2010): 58–75. The website Quote Investigator claims the passage is from a 1907 dissertation by Kenneth John Freeman and is the author's own summary of the complaints regarding young people in ancient Greece. The words were subsequently changed, misattributed to Socrates, and frequently used throughout the 1960s and 1970s, as well as more recently in writings debating whether or not Millennials are narcissists. According to Quote Investigator, Freeman's original phrase is: "Children began to be the tyrants, not the slaves, of their households. They no longer rose from their seats when an elder entered the room; they contradicted their parents, chattered before company, gobbled up the dainties at table, and committed various offences against Hellenic tastes, such as crossing their legs. They tyrannised over the paidagogoi and schoolmasters." See Garson O'Toole, "Misbehaving Children in Ancient Times," Quote Investigator, updated May 1, 2010, http://quoteinvestigator.com/2010/05/01/misbehaving
-children-in-ancient-times/.

1. Gallup, *How Millennials Want to Work and Live* (Washington, DC: Gallup, 2016), 3.

2. Ron Alsop, *The Trophy Kids Grow Up: How the Millennial Generation is Shaking Up the Workplace* (San Francisco: Jossey-Bass, 2008), 115–133.

3. E. S. Ng, L. Schweitzer, and S. T. Lyons, "New Generation, Great Expectations: A Field Study of the Millennial Generation," *Journal of Business and Psychology* 25, no. 2 (2010): 282.

4. Pew Research Center, *Millennials: Confident. Connected. Open to Change*, Paul Taylor and Scott Keeter, eds., February 2010, 18, http://www.pewsocialtrends.org/files/2010/10/millennials-confident-connected-open-to-change.pdf.

5. *Millennials at Work: Perspectives from a New Generation* (London: PriceWaterhouse-Coopers, 2008), 8, www.pwc.de/de/prozessoptimierung/assets/managing_tomorrows_people_millennials_at_work-perspectives_from_a_new_generation.pdf. The study also finds that 86 percent of Millennials would consider leaving an employer if its values no longer matched their expectations.

6. Victoria J. Rideout, Ulla G. Foehr, and Donald F. Roberts, *Generation M2: Media in the Lives of 8- to 18-Year-Olds* (Menlo Park, CA: Henry J. Kaiser Family Foundation, January 2010), www.kff.org/entmedia/8010.cfm.

7. Jennifer Lee, Lin Lin, and Tip Robertson, "The Impact of Media Multitasking on Learning," *Learning, Media and Technology* 37, no. 1 (March 2012): 94–104. This study compared one Millennial group who read and answered multiple-choice questions regard-

ing three articles without media distraction (silence) with two other groups given the same tested reading assignment but who also watched videos playing at the same time and later answered questions about both media. Of the two groups watching videos, one was told they could ignore the videos but were tested anyway (background), while the other was told that they would be tested on both the reading assignment and the video (test). There was no significant difference in reading comprehension scores among participants in the silence condition. Those in the test group did score lower than both the silence and background groups. See also Marc Prensky, *Don't Bother Me, Mom—I'm Learning! How Computer and Video Games are Preparing Your Kids for 21st Century Success and How You Can Help!* (New York: Paragon House, 2016), and H. Jenkins et al., *Confronting the Challenges of Participatory Culture: Media Education for the 21st Century* (Chicago: The John D. and Catherine T. MacArthur Foundation, 2006), 36.

8. Rideout, Foehr, and Roberts, *Generation M2*, 48. The study finds a slight correlation between self-reported grades and media exposure. Those reporting A and B grades spent one minute more exposed to media than those reporting B and C grades. Students that reported Cs, Ds, and below, however, spent forty-five minutes on average more with media, specifically with audio media and video games. See Table 7A, page 48.

9. G. Small and G. Vorgan, *iBrain: Surviving the Technological Alteration of the Modern Mind* (New York: HarperCollins, 2009), 25.

10. Jean M. Twenge et al., "Generational Differences in Young Adults' Life Goals, Concern for Others, and Civic Orientation, 1966–2009," *Journal of Personality and Social Psychology* 102, no. 5 (2012): 1045–1060.

11. B. W. Roberts, G. E. Edmonds, and E. Grijalva, "It Is Developmental Me Not Generation Me: Developmental Changes Are More Important than Generational Changes in Narcissism—Commentary on Trzesniewski & Donnellan (2010)," *Perspectives in Psychological Science* 5 (2010): 97–102.

12. Kali H. Trzesniewski and M. Brent Donnellan, "Rethinking 'Generation Me': A Study of Cohort Effects from 1976–2006," *Perspectives on Psychological Science* 5, no. 1 (2010): 58–75. See also Kristin Dombek, *The Selfishness of Others: An Essay on the Fear of Narcissism* (New York: Farrar, Straus and Giroux, 2016).

13. Pew, *Millennials: Confident. Connected. Open to Change*, 23; Pew Research Center, *Millennials in Adulthood: Detached from Institutions, Networked with Friends*, March 2014, 7, http://assets.pewresearch.org/wp-content/uploads/sites/3/2014/03/2014-03-07 _generations-report-version-for-web.pdf.

14. Pew, *Millennials in Adulthood*, 35.

15. Pew, *Millennials in Adulthood*, 45. Pew found that Millennials were less likely to identify themselves as "environmentalists" (32 percent) than Generation X in 1999 (42 percent). Boomers (42 percent) and Silents (44 percent) fell in the same range as Generation X. Pew asked participants to describe on a scale from 1 to 10 whether the descriptions "a religious person," "an environmentalist," "a supporter of gay rights," or "a patriotic person" were "PERFECT for you" (capitalization theirs). Focus-group participants claimed that this wording led them to prioritize.

16. Ng, Schweitzer, and Lyons, "New Generation, Great Expectations," 281–292.

17. Gallup, "How Millennials Want to Work and Live," 8.

18. Annelise Pitts et al., *Equity by Design: Knowledge, Discussion, Action!* (San Fran-

cisco: AIA San Francisco, 2015), 10, http://issuu.com/rsheng2/docs/equityinarch2014 _finalreport/. The poll was taken at firms owned by AIA members.

19. The condition may have long gone unnoticed until twentieth-century psychiatry identified it, although the rise in cases parallels the emergence of Millennials and may reflect a heightened awareness of the syndrome by both parents and psychiatrists alike. See Klaus W. Lange et al., "The History of Attention Deficit Hyperactivity Disorder," *Attention Deficit and Hyperactivity Disorders* 2, no.4 (December 2010): 241–255, www.ncbi.nlm. nih.gov/pmc/articles/PMC3000907/. See also Michael Wilson and Leslie E. Gerber, "How Generational Theory Can Improve Teaching: Strategies for Working with the Millennials," *Currents in Teaching and Learning* 1, no. 1 (Fall 2008): 35.

20. Nicholas Carr, *The Shallows: What the Internet Is Doing to Our Brains* (New York: Norton, 2011), 10.

21. *Reading on the Rise: A New Chapter in American Literacy* (Washington, DC: National Endowment for the Arts, January 2009), https://www.arts.gov/sites/default/files /ReadingonRise.pdf.

22. Stuart Green, "I'm Banning Laptops from My Classroom," *Wall Street Journal*, July 10, 2016, Opinion/Commentary, www.wsj.com/articles/im-banning-laptops-from-my -classroom-1468184264/.

23. While administrations cannot require students to medicate, the voluntary use by students of Ritalin, an ADHD treatment drug called the "study drug," is prevalent. See Daniel Ari Kapner, *Recreational Use of Ritalin on College Campuses* (Washington, DC: Higher Education Center for Alcohol and Other Drug Abuse and Violence Prevention, U.S. Department of Education, August 2008), http://files.eric.ed.gov/fulltext/ED537616.pdf.

24. AIAS Studio Culture Task Force, *The Redesign of Studio Culture: A Report of the AIAS Studio Culture Task Force* (Washington, DC: American Institute of Architecture Students, 2002), 6.

25. AIAS, *The Redesign of Studio Culture*, 6.

26. AIAS, 6.

27. AIAS, 11.

28. Susan M. Sawyer et al., "The Age of Adolescence," *The Lancet: Child and Adolescent Health* 2, no. 3 (March 2018): 225.

29. Ernest L. Boyer and Lee D. Mitgang, *Building Community: A New Future for Architecture Education and Practice* (Princeton, NJ: Carnegie Foundation for the Advancement of Teaching, 1996), 85.

30. The school's official name is the Hasso Plattner Institute of Design at Stanford University. Plattner, the co-founder of the software company SAP AG, donated $35 million to found the d.school after initially reading an article about the design firm IDEO.

31. Nuttall and Moggridge both studied industrial design in the UK, which complements Kelley's US degrees in electrical engineering and design. All three founding principals brought experience in designing physical products—Kelley had worked for Boeing and Moggridge is credited with designing the laptop.

32. Shelley Goldman et al., "Student Teams in Search of Design Thinking," in *Design Thinking Research: Building Innovation Eco-Systems*, ed. Hasso Plattner et al. (Berlin; Heidelberg: Springer-Verlag, 2014), 11.

33. John Schwartz, "Re-engineering Engineering," *New York Times*, September 30, 2007, www.nytimes.com/2007/09/30/magazine/30OLIN-t.html.

34. Erico Guizzo, "The Olin Experiment: Can a Tiny New College Reinvent Engineering Education?" *IEEE Spectrum Magazine*, May 1, 2006, http://spectrum.ieee.org/at-work /education/the-olin-experiment.

35. Laura Krantz, "Harvard Medical School Revamps Curriculum," *Boston Globe*, September 20, 2015, https://www.bostonglobe.com/metro/2015/09/19/harvard-medical -school-revamps-curriculum/CAwgolcZZKAMBsQiwBBfEL/story.html.

36. Eugene Raskin, editorial, *Pencil Points* (April 1939): 238, as quoted in Arthur J. Pulos, *The American Design Adventure, 1940-1975* (Cambridge, MA: MIT Press, 1988), 30. Raskin's full quote states that industrial designers "realize . . . that people use not only buildings, but furniture, autos, ships, trains, planes, clothes, canned goods, fountain pens—and so on through the whole list of material goods. . . . [Industrial designers] are out designing all these things, pioneering ahead of us, and making us rapidly obsolete."

37. Ada Louise Huxtable, "Industrial Design: Invented to Serve and Shape a 20th Century Consumer Economy," Design Notebook, *New York Times*, May 24, 1979, C10.

38. Carroll M. Gantz, *The Industrialization of Design: A History from the Steam Age to Today* (Jefferson, NC: McFarland, 2011), 10. The first attempt to state-sanction design as a proprietary practice occurred in 1449 through the establishment of documents called "letters patent" by the English King Henry VI. In order to install stained glass at Cambridge, a technology not previously used in England, Henry VI granted 20 years' exclusive rights to the Flemish craftsman John of Utnyam to teach English subjects, only allowing them to practice under his express consent.

39. Scott W. Berg, *Grand Avenues: The Story of the French Visionary Who Designed Washington, D.C.* (New York: Pantheon Books, 2007), 19–29.

40. Gantz, *The Industrialization of Design*, 41.

41. Herbert Hoover, telephone address to the 4th Annual Exposition of Women's Arts and Industries, New York City, September 2, 1925, Hoover Institute Archives, box 7, Stanford University, quoted in Arthur Pulos, *American Design Ethic* (Cambridge, MA: MIT Press, 1983), 304.

42. Charles R. Richards, Henry Creange, and Frank Graham Holmes, *Report of Commission Appointed by the Secretary of Commerce to Visit and Report upon the International Exposition of Modern Decorative and Industrial Art in Paris, 1925* (Washington, DC: Department of Commerce, 1927), 21-23, www.cmog.org/sites/default/files/collections /C2/C287A4A3-05A3-427F-832E-622E96DC189E.pdf. See also Pulos, *American Design Ethic*, 304.

43. Gantz, *The Industrialization of Design*, 122. According to Gantz, the term likely derives from its usage in the influential book by D'Arcy Wentworth Thompson, *On Growth and Form* (Cambridge: Cambridge University Press, 1917). Gantz writes, "Darcy uses the term stream-lining to describe organic structures that offer the least resistance when they are in motion, and how a fluid medium tends to impress its 'stream lines' on a deformable body, like snowdrifts and sand dunes." Making arguments for his parametric architecture, the deconstructivist-era architect Greg Lynn also credits Thompson's early observations. It is worth noting that both Thompson's and Lynn's books fall within the same Strauss-Howe "time locations." See Greg Lynn, *Animate Form* (New York: Princeton Architectural Press, 1999), 26.

44. Gantz, *The Industrialization of Design*, 139–140.

45. Pulos, *American Design Ethic*, 336. AUDAC members took a moral and patriotic

high ground, contending that copying "degrades the producers [and] corrupts the taste of the public," and that without "the placing of American arts and crafts on a basis of honesty, dignity and merit," no truly indigenous style could be expected to mature. See also: Paul Frankl, *Form and Re-Form* (New York: Harper and Brothers, 1930), 187.

46. Jeffrey Meikle, *Twentieth Century Limited: Industrial Design in America, 1925–1939* (Philadelphia: Temple University Press, 1979), 181.

47. This makes Teague, Bel Geddes, and Loewy Lost Generation contemporaries of Le Corbusier, Mies, and Gropius.

48. Meikle, *Twentieth Century Limited*, 39–67.

49. Meikle, 43.

50. Meikle, 60.

51. Gantz, *The Industrialization of Design*, 161.

52. "Both Fish and Fowl," *Fortune*, Feb 1934. Gantz describes the title as alluding to the dual role of industrial designers as artists and businessmen. Written anonymously, the article was by George Nelson, the 1932 winner of the Rome Prize in architecture and at the time an assistant editor of *Architectural Forum*. Nelson would go on to become a formidable industrial design figure after World War II.

53. Norman Bel Geddes, *Horizons* (Boston: Little Brown, 1932), 3.

54. Gantz, *The Industrialization of Design*, 256.

55. This estimate is based on a query to the website Owler (www.owler.com) in 2016. Later that year, IDEO sold a minority stake of its business to Kyu (pronounced "Q"), part of Hakuhodo DY Holdings, one of Japan's largest advertising holding companies. See www.wired.com/2016/02/ideo-sold-part-of-itself-and-joined-a-collective-but-why/. The value as quoted by Owler has since changed.

56. Gantz, *The Industrialization of Design*, 271. Gantz writes, "even at the depth of the recession in November 2009, when national unemployment topped 10 percent, there were over 20 positions advertised on the IDSA Website for industrial designers and thousands more posted on the Internet."

57. IDEO Fact Sheet. Retrieved 1/5/16 from www.ideo.com.

58. Meikle, *Twentieth Century Limited*, 38.

59. Rudolph Rosenthal and Helena L. Ratzka, *The Story of Modern Applied Art* (New York: Harper and Brothers, 1948), 177, quoted in Meikle, *Twentieth Century Limited*, 21.

60. Gantz, *The Industrialization of Design*, 145–148. The 1930 exhibition at the Grand Central Galleries in New York featured modern interiors filled with mass-produced items already on the market rather than the custom-made highly decorative objects favored by museums and driven by taste-making originating in Europe, demonstrating that consumer acceptance, comfort, and practicality were appropriate American design criteria.

61. Robert A. M. Stern, "Relevance of the Decade," *Journal of the Society of Architectural Historians* 24 (March 1965): 7.

62. Meikle, *Twentieth Century Limited*, 180.

63. Catherine Bauer, "Machine Made," *The American Magazine of Art* 27 (May 1934): 270, quoted in Meikle, *Twentieth Century Limited*, 180.

64. Gantz, *The Industrialization of Design*, 172. MOMA's bias at the time against American industrial design by the likes of Teague, Bel Geddes, Dreyfus, and Loewy was categorical. Its director, Alfred H. Barr Jr., writing to Bel Geddes in 1934, referred to streamlining as "an absurdity" (Meikle, *Twentieth Century Limited*, 181). John McAndrew, who later

would inherit Philip Johnson's position, typically resorted to sarcasm when describing streamlining: "Streamlined paper cups, if dropped would fall with less wind resistance," but they were "no better than the old ones for the purposes for which they were actually intended, namely drinking" (Meikle, *Twentieth Century Limited*, 181). In a retrospective exhibit celebrating the tenth anniversary of its founding, MOMA's industrial design section contained none of the commercially successful American work of the decade, only a bathroom by Buckminster Fuller and chairs by Le Corbusier, Mies, Marcel Breur, and Alvar Aalto (Meikle, *Twentieth Century Limited*, 180–181).

65. Meikle, 181.

66. "Industrial Design Comes of Age, Part I," *Business Week* 351 (May 23, 1936): 18; "Industrial Design Comes of Age, Part II," *Business Week* 352 (May 30, 1936): 30.

67. Gantz, *The Industrialization of Design*, 172.

68. The architect Eliot Noyes, who had studied under Gropius at Harvard and later worked for him, was its first director. To underscore its mass market focus, MOMA recruited twelve commercial retail stores to sponsor the competition and offered manufacturing contracts to the winners.

69. Gantz, *The Industrialization of Design*, 222. See also Vance Packard, *The Hidden Persuaders* (New York: D. McKay Co., 1957).

70. Victor Papanek, *Design for the Real World* (New York: Bantam, 1973), quoted in Gantz, *The Industrialization of Design*, 236.

71. Papanek, *Design for the Real World*, 15.

72. Ada Louise Huxtable, "Industrial Design: Invented to Serve and Shape a 20th Century Consumer Economy," Design Notebook, *New York Times*, May 24, 1979, C10.

73. Beginning in 1974, Niels Diffrient (then working at Henry Dreyfuss Associates) and colleagues began publishing a series of ergonomic standards based on extensive human engineering data compiled and organized by the firm. See Niels Diffrient et al., *Humanscale 1/2/3* (Cambridge, MA: MIT Press, 1974). See also Klaus Krippendorff and Reinhardt Butter, "Product Semantics: Exploring the Symbolic Qualities of Form," *Innovation* 3, no. 2 (1984): 4–9, repository.upenn.edu/asc_papers/40.

74. Herbert Simon, *The Sciences of the Artificial* (Cambridge, MA: MIT Press, 1969), 111–138. Simon espouses a theory of design that anticipated the later steps of design thinking: define, research, ideate, prototype, choose, implement, and learn. Simon's work in artificial intelligence is also an important bridge between design and its future computerization in the Internet of Things.

75. Gantz, *The Industrialization of Design*, 240. Patricia Moore went on to teach industrial design at Arizona State University.

76. Frank Gibney Jr. and Belinda Luscombe, "The Redesigning of America," *Time*, March 20, 2000.

77. David Kelley, "Design and Quality: The Designer's View," *Managing Automation*, August 1989, 20.

78. Linda Hales, "Sleek Chic: As the Pendulum Swings," *Washington Post*, June 16, 2001, accessed August 8, 2016, https://www.washingtonpost.com/archive/lifestyle/2001/06/16/sleek-chic-as-the-pendulum-swings/1932cac8-ff44-4e18-b178-c511294f0c60/. Hales is paraphrasing Moggridge.

79. 1997 employment figures are from the Bureau of Labor Statistics as described in "Where The Jobs Are," *Time*, January 20, 1997, as quoted in Gantz, *The Industrialization*

of Design, 259. 2016 figures are from the US Department of Labor, Bureau of Labor Statistics, *Occupational Outlook Handbook*, s.v. "Industrial Designers," accessed August 30, 2018, https://www.bls.gov/ooh/arts-and-design/industrial-designers.htm.

10. Medicine, Law, Architecture

The epigraph is from Andrew Abbott, *The System of Professions: An Essay on the Division of Expert Labor* (Chicago: University of Chicago Press, 1988), 323.

1. Elizabeth Evitts Dickinson, "The Millennials: Children of the Revolution," *Architect*, January 2013, 112.

2. Tomas Rossant, personal interview with author, June 1, 2016. Rossant is a self-avowed member of Generation X, the 2015 AIA-NY past president, and a founding partner at Ennead Architects. See also "Design and Disruption: Millennials in Architecture" (roundtable discussion, Center for Architecture, New York, January 21, 2016). At the roundtable, Rossant spoke with candor about Millennials in his office, noting that their understanding of expertise was often difficult to make use of in a building information modeling environment. Rossant's involvement with leadership succession as Polshek and Partners transitioned into Ennead gives him firsthand insight into the generational transition of a professional organization.

3. Robert Gutman, *Architecture Practice: A Critical View* (New York: Princeton Architectural Press, 1988), 61–69. Dana Cuff focuses more on the ambiguity of authority that causes this; see Dana Cuff, *Architecture: The Story of Practice* (Cambridge, MA: MIT Press, 1991), 85–88.

4. Based on the Bureau of Labor Statistics *Occupational Outlook Handbook*, in 2017 architects earned a median annual income of $78,000, slightly more than registered nurses ($70,000) and less than physical therapists ($86,850). By contrast, physicians and surgeons earned $208,000. US Department of Labor, Bureau of Labor Statistics, *Occupational Outlook Handbook*, accessed August 18, 2018, https://www.bls.gov/ooh/.

5. This passage represents my paraphrasing of Bernstein's arguments in: Phillip Bernstein, "Models for Practice: Past, Present, Future," in *Building (in) the Future: Recasting Labor in Architecture* (New York: Princeton Architectural Press, 2010), 191–198; his presentation entitled "The Evolving Role of the Architect in the Era of Connection," live-streamed at ARCHITECT Live from the American Institute of Architects Convention on May 20, 2016; and a telephone conversation we had on June 14, 2016.

6. Andrew Abbott, *The System of Professions: An Essay on the Division of Expert Labor* (Chicago: University of Chicago Press, 1988), 40-17. For Abbott's specific discussion of diagnosis, inference, and treatment see 40-52, for jurisdictions see 59-85, and for subordination see 69-74.

7. Abbott, *The System of Professions*, 30.

8. Tom Lewis, *Divided Highways: Building the Interstate Highways, Transforming American Life* (Ithaca, NY: Cornell University Press, 2013), 133–136. Lewis describes how, after World War II, jet propulsion and the transistor drew the best students toward programs in electrical, aeronautical, and chemical engineering and away from more traditional and less glamorous careers in civil engineering. And among the remaining civil engineers, the epic scale of the bridges and dams being built based on the standards set by those from the Roosevelt administration diverted the best away from highway departments. A lack of training beyond the technical, including in socioeconomic or environmen-

tal considerations, further hampered the lowest tier of the engineering profession charged with building the interstate system. Lewis argues that these factors contributed to the crude and damaging effects of highway construction.

9. Richard Susskind and Daniel Susskind, *The Future of the Professions* (Oxford: Oxford University Press, 2015), 1-4. Given the subject of this book, the Susskinds are notable for the teaming of a cusping Boomer/Generation X father and a Millennial son to predict the future.

10. Susskind and Susskind, *The Future of the Professions*, 303-308. The Susskinds use Donald Schon's description of the grand bargain: "In return for access to their extraordinary knowledge in matters of great human importance, society has granted [the professions] a mandate for social control in their fields of specialization, a high degree of autonomy in their practice, and a license to determine who shall assume the mantle of professional authority" (p. 21).

11. Stanley Fish, *Doing What Comes Naturally* (Oxford: Oxford University Press, 1989), 200-201, quoted in Susskind and Susskind, *The Future of the Professions*, 28.

12. Harold J. Laski, *The Limitations of the Expert,* Fabian Tract, no. 235 (London: Fabian Society, 1931), 14, https://digital.library.lse.ac.uk/objects/lse:wal303heb, quoted in Susskind and Susskind, *The Future of the Professions*, 141. See also the Susskinds' use of Herbert Hart's even more scathing description of professional mystification (in this case, regarding the profession of law) as practitioners who "are frequently protected from criticism by a veil of mystery thrown over them. This conceals their true nature and effects, perplexes and intimidates the would-be reformer, and so prolongs the life of bad institutions. The forms of mystery . . . include not only glorification by open eulogy and pomp in ceremony; but also, and more importantly, mystification consists in the propagation of a *belief* . . . [that] institutions of society are infinitely complex and difficult to understand, and that this is an invincible fact of nature, so that long-standing institutions cannot be changed without risk of the collapse of society." Herbert L. A. Hart, "Bentham and the Demystification of the Law," *Modern Law Review* 36, no. 1 (1973): 2, quoted in Susskind and Susskind, *The Future of the Professions*, 141.

13. Susskind and Susskind, *The Future of the Professions*, 187.

14. Susskind and Susskind, 281. The Susskinds continue: "in some circumstances, it feels inappropriate, or wrong, to abnegate responsibility and pass it along to a machine, no matter how high-performing."

15. Susskind and Susskind, 42.

16. Carl B. Frey and Michael A. Osborne, "The Future of Employment: How Susceptible are Jobs to Computerisation?" (working paper, Oxford Martin Programme on Technology and Employment, September 17, 2013), www.oxfordmartin.ox.ac.uk/downloads/academic/The_Future_of_Employment.pdf.

17. Frey and Osborne, "The Future of Employment," 44.

18. Frey and Osborne, 57–72. Architectural occupations and drafters rank 305th least computerizable out of 702. Frey and Osborne separate landscape and naval architects from the architectural profession and include civil drafters with architectural occupations.

19. Frey and Osborne, 44–45.

20. James Manyika et al., *A Future That Works: Automation, Employment, and Productivity* (San Francisco: McKinsey Global Institute, 2017).

21. Susskind and Susskind, *The Future of the Professions*, 105. In the Susskinds' notes

they credit "blue oceans" to W. Chan Kim, W. C. and Renee Mauborgne, *Blue Ocean Strategy* (Boston: Harvard Business Review Press, 2005); "disrupting" to Clayton M. Christensen, *The Innovator's Dilemma: When New Technologies Cause Great Firms to Fail* (Boston: Harvard Business School Press, 1997); and "fast second" to Constantinos C. Markides and Paul A. Geroski, *Fast Second: How Smart Companies Bypass Radical Innovation to Enter and Dominate New Markets* (New York: Wiley & Sons, 2005).

22. The first-time enrollment of 8,553 in NAAB-accredited schools in the academic year 2009–2010 fell to 6,597 by the 2013–2014 academic year. See Appendix II on page 263. While the official drop in overall enrollment between 2007 and 2017 was 17.2 percent, the fastest-growing category of ethnicity in architecture schools was nonresident alien. In 2009, this category accounted for 6.4 percent of enrollment overall; by 2015, it had tripled to 18.6 percent. See Appendix II. A 2016 evaluation that includes candidate schools along with NAAB-accredited programs brings the percentage of nonresident alien students to 24 percent. See "Trends in International Student Enrollment in Architectural Education," Association of Collegiate Schools of Architecture, December 2016, www.acsa-arch.org /resources/data-resources/international-students-in-architectural-education/. In effect, American schools are making up for enrollment decline with foreign students who often pay cash and are ineligible for financial aid. If foreign students were not readily available to architecture schools, enrollment declines might exceed 30 percent, putting them in the same range as the law school enrollment declines described later in this chapter.

23. National Architectural Accrediting Board, *2009 Report on Accreditation in Architecture Education*, February 2010, https://ww.naab.org/wp-content/uploads/2009-Report -on-Accreditation-in-Architecture-Education.pdf.

24. National Architectural Accrediting Board, *2015 Annual Report, Part III: 2015 Accreditation Decisions and Other NAAB Activities*, 2015, 8-9, https://www.naab.org /wp-content/uploads/2015-NAAB-Report-on-Accreditation-in-Architecture-part-III.pdf.

25. According to *2016 NCARB by the Numbers*, more than 5,000 architecture students completed internships in 2009, while those passing the licensing exam hovered close to 3,000. Although the number of interns taking the exam has since increased, NCARB writes that the surge is likely due to interns preferring the existing test rather than the new one that will replace it. A similar spike in 2008 for similar reasons returned pass rates to previous levels. See National Council of Architectural Registration Boards, *2016 NCARB by the Numbers* (Washington, DC: NCARB, 2016), https://www.ncarb.org/sites/default/files/2016 -NBTN.pdf.

26. Evelyn Lee, "Casius Pealer: Unlicensed Architect and Real Estate Attorney," Practice of Architecture (website), July 24, 2015, www.practiceofarchitecture.com/2015/07/24 /casius-pealer-unlicensed-architect-and-real-estate-attorney/.

27. Gutman, *Architecture Practice*, 98. Gutman writes: "Principals who run firms find it to their advantage to maintain a substantial flow of architects through the schools. It provides offices of all sizes with an inexpensive supply of young graduates who are well educated but nevertheless are prepared to do low-skilled work. Although architects are embarrassed by their pay levels compared to other old and established professions, without the reserve supply of cheap labor the profitability of firms would be below the current rate."

28. Peter Buchanan, "The Big Rethink Part 1: Towards a Complete Architecture," *Archi-*

tectural Review, December 21, 2011, www.architectural-review.com/rethink/viewpoints
/the-big-rethink-part-1towards-a-complete-architecture/8624049.fullarticle.

29. Thomas Fisher, *In the Scheme of Things: Alternative Thinking on the Practice of Architecture* (Minneapolis, MN: University of Minnesota Press, 2000), 27–37.

30. Gutman, *Architecture Practice,* 110. Gutman refers here not to racial but to programmatic diversity, as in the sentence, "There is no one method that can handle the diverse requirements of an increasingly complex, competitive, and fragmented profession with equal effectiveness."

31. Wendy L. McIntosh et al., "Suicide Rates by Occupational Group—17 States, 2012," *Morbidity and Mortality Weekly Report* 65, no. 25 (July 1, 2016): 641–645, http://dx.doi .org/10.15585/mmwr.mm6525a1. The Centers for Disease Control and Prevention lists architecture with engineering, indicating 32.2 suicides per 100,000 population, as compared to 18.8 for the legal occupation and 17.4 for "healthcare practitioners and technical." If one adds their "construction and extraction" group, the entire architecture, engineering, and construction (AEC) industry would have the highest suicide rate at 85.5 out of 100,000 of any other occupation classification the CDC uses.

32. Cuff, *Architecture,* 26–32.

33. Barbara Barzansky, "Abraham Flexner and the Era of Medical Education Reform," *Academic Medicine* 85, no. 9 (August 2010), S19–S25, https://journals.lww.com/academicmedicine /fulltext/2010/09001/Abraham_Flexner_and_the_Era_of_Medical_Education.3.aspx.

34. Abraham Flexner, "Medical Education in the United States and Canada, Bulletin Number Four," The Carnegie Foundation for the Advancement of Teaching, 1910, 14–16, http://archive.carnegiefoundation.org/pdfs/elibrary/Carnegie_Flexner_Report.pdf.

35. Some universities annexed proprietary schools, although they often did so without supporting or taking responsibility for them.

36. Thomas P. Duffy, "The Flexner Report—100 Years Later," *Yale Journal of Biology and Medicine* 84, no. 3 (Sept. 2011): 269–276, www.ncbi.nlm.nih.gov/pmc/articles /PMC3178858/. Carnegie's Henry Pritchett, believing that those antagonized might be less vengeful if a non-physician were the author, specifically chose Flexner to be "the hatchet man in sweeping clean the medical system of substandard medical schools that were flooding the nation with poorly trained physicians."

37. Abbott, *The System of Professions,* 20. Abbott describes homeopaths as those who "espoused, among other novel ideas, the practice of not killing patients with treatment." See also Paul Starr, *The Social Transformation of American Medicine: The Rise of a Sovereign Profession and the Making of a Vast Industry* (New York: Basic Books, 1982).

38. Duffy, "The Flexner Report—100 Years Later," 269–276. Flexner patterned his pedagogy after one put in place by William Welch at Johns Hopkins. Flexner worked closely with Carnegie director Henry Pritchett, who was passionate about medical reform. Pritchett introduced Flexner to the "Hopkins Circle," a group of medical reformers including Welch, the founding dean at Hopkins, William Osler, its first chief of medicine, and Frederick Gates, a Baptist minister and adviser to John D. Rockefeller. Gates later convinced Rockefeller to provide philanthropic support for medical reform (even though Rockefeller was devoted to homeopathy).

39. "Council on Medical Education of the American Medical Association: First Annual Conference held in Chicago, April 20, 1905. Society Proceedings," *Journal of the American*

Medical Association 44, no. 18 (May 6, 1905): 1470–1475, https://babel.hathitrust.org/cgi
/pt?id=umn.319510027085517;view=1up;seq=68.

40. Mark D. Hiatt and Christopher Stockton, "The Impact of the Flexner Report on the
Fate of Medical Schools in North America after 1909," *Journal of American Physicians and
Surgeons* 8, no. 2 (Summer 2003): 39. Although Flexner sought to ambitiously reduce the
number of schools to thirty-one, the reduction was still dramatic. By 1920, the number of
students decreased from 28,142 to 13,798 while the percentage of schools requiring two
years of college for admission rose to 92 percent.

41. Hiatt and Stockton, "The Impact of the Flexner Report," 39.

42. Abbott, *The System of Professions*, 21.

43. Susan Katcher, "Legal Training in the United States: A Brief History," *Wisconsin
International Law Journal* 24, no. 1 (July 26, 2006): 345–346. The requirement of study in
a lawyer's office for admission to the bar became less strict. "The numbers are revealing:
compared to 1800, when fourteen out of nineteen jurisdictions had required an apprenticeship, by 1860, only nine of thirty-nine jurisdictions required one." See also Robert Stevens, *Law School: Legal Education in America from the 1850's to the 1980's* (Chapel Hill,
NC: The University of North Carolina Press, 1983), 8.

44. Katcher, "Legal Training in the United States," 362–365. Quoting Robert Stevens
and Alfred Reed, Katcher writes, "'The motives behind the urge of the AALS, eventually
joined by the ABA, to reform legal education in the United States are complex' and intrigu-
ing, involving a mixture of market considerations, a desire for exclusivity of the profession,
as well as wanting to raise the standards of legal education itself."

45. Lawrence M. Friedman, *A History of American Law* (New York: Simon & Schuster,
1985), 236–238. In most situations this constituted memorizing laws and transcribing
court proceedings, and if fortunate, an apprentice could actually observe a mentor in
court. Few standards governed this educational system, and becoming a lawyer—passing
the bar—typically involved only oral examination. One could become a lawyer in the US in
the nineteenth century without any exposure to higher education.

46. Stevens, *Law School*, 26. Similar to Flexner's recommendation for medical school
faculty, Langdell also advocated for the professionalization of faculty to be solely devoted
to teaching and not serve as practitioners.

47. Frank L. Ellsworth, *Law on the Midway: The Founding of the University of Chicago
Law School* (Chicago: The Law School of the University of Chicago, 1997), 120, referenced
in David Perry, "How Did Lawyers Become Doctors?" *New York State Bar Journal* 84, no. 5
(June 2012): 20–25.

48. Perry, "How Did Lawyers Become Doctors?" 27–28. Early adopters New York University (1903), Berkeley and Stanford (1905), and Michigan (1909) all discontinued the JD
by the 1930s.

49. Perry, 27–28. The University of Chicago and its neighboring Illinois law schools
were the only holdouts. Other schools treated it as an honor bestowed to the best LLB
graduates, while other postgraduate degrees emerged.

50. Alfred Z. Reed, *Training for the Public Profession of the Law: Historical Development and Principal Contemporary Problems of Legal Education in the United States, with
Some Account of Conditions in England and Canada* (New York: Carnegie Foundation,
1921), 418. Reed wrote that "only in so far as bar examinations are adjusted to the training
that is practicable for the particular type will they be of service in insuring high standards

of proficiency. . . . Only in this way can completely incompetent individuals be prevented from securing the privilege of practicing law."

51. Reed, *Training for the Public Profession of the Law*, 414–415. Reed did recommend eliminating programs of insufficient length and scope. See also Robert Hardaway, who writes that Reed's conclusion that "it was impossible to achieve a 'unitary bar,'" and that "different types of lawyers may be determined by the economic status of the client rather than the nature of the . . . service rendered," was "useless as a basis for reform." Robert M. Hardaway, "Legal and Medical Education Compared: Is It Time for a Flexner Report on Legal Education?" *Washington University Law Review* 59, no. 3 (January 1981): 709.

52. John G. Hervey, "Evaluate J.D. Degree on Merit," *American TRIAL Lawyer*, June/July 1967, 56. See also Joanna Lombard, "LL.B. to J.D. and the Professional Degree in Architecture," in *Architecture: Material and Imagined: Proceedings of the 85th ACSA Annual Meeting and Technology Conference*, ed. Lawrence W. Speck and Dominique Bonnamour-Lloyd (Washington, DC: Association of Collegiate Schools of Architecture, 1997), 586.

53. Section of Legal Education and Admissions to the Bar, *Review of Legal Education* (Chicago: American Bar Association, Fall 1965), 21, www.americanbar.org/content/dam /aba/publications/misc/legal_education/Standards/standardsarchive/1965_review .authcheckdam.pdf. The resolution was considered by the section at its annual meeting on August 11, 1964, and was adopted without a dissenting vote.

54. David Perry, "How Did Lawyers Become 'Doctors'? From the LL.B. to the J.D.," *New York State Bar Association Journal* 84, no. 5 (June 2012): 28.

55. "Comparison of Enrollment and Degrees Awarded with African American J.D. Enrollment 1971–2010," Statistics, Section of Legal Education and Admissions to the Bar, American Bar Association, accessed July 17, 2016, www.americanbar.org/groups/legal _education/resources/statistics.html (report has since been removed); "First Year and Total J.D. Enrollment by Gender 1947–2011," Statistics, Section of Legal Education and Admissions to the Bar, American Bar Association, accessed September 9, 2016, www .americanbar.org/content/dam/aba/administrative/legal_education_and_admissions_to _the_bar/statistics/jd_enrollment_1yr_total_gender.authcheckdam.pdf. The percentage of African Americans in comparison to total enrollment increased from 4 (3,744) to 7 (10,174) percent and women's enrollment increased from 9 (8,567) to 47 (68,502) percent, also in comparison to total enrollment.

56. Tomas Rossant, personal interview with author, June 1, 2016. The degree to which the JD facilitated this latitude has never been proven. Many argue that it was the "realist" critique of Langdell's case law method that led to the expansion of the lawyer's purview.

57. "2015 Law Graduate Employment Data," Section of Legal Education and Admissions to the Bar, American Bar Association, compiled April 26, 2016, www.americanbar.org /content/dam/aba/administrative/legal_education_and_admissions_to_the_bar/reports/2015 _law_graduate_employment_data.authcheckdam.pdf.

58. "LSAC End-Of-Year Summary," Law School Admission Council, accessed July 17, 2016, www.lsac.org/lsacresources/data/lsac-volume-summary.

59. David Barnhizer is a professor emeritus at Cleveland-Marshall College of Law and quoted in Elizabeth Olsen, "Minnesota Law School, Facing Waning Interest, Cuts Admissions," *New York Times*, May 12, 2016.

60. Olsen, "Minnesota Law School."

61. American Bar Association, *Report of the Task Force on the Financing of Legal*

Education, June 2015, https://www.americanbar.org/content/dam/aba/administrative /legal_education_and_admissions_to_the_bar/reports/2015_june_report_of_the_aba_task _force_on_the_financing_of_legal_education.pdf.

62. David Barnhizer, "The Future of Work: Apps, Artificial Intelligence, Automation and Androids" (working paper no. 823, Law Faculty Articles and Essays, Faculty Scholarship, Cleveland State University, January 15, 2016), 3, https://engagedscholarship.csuohio.edu /cgi/viewcontent.cgi?article=1834&context=fac_articles.

63. Turpin C. Bannister, *The Architect at Mid-Century: Evolution and Achievement*, vol.1 (New York: Reinhold, 1954), 151, referenced in Rebecca Williamson, "'Elegant Swords': A Profession in Pursuit of an Academic Identity," in *Architecture School: Three Centuries of Educating Architects in North America*, ed. Joan Ockman (Cambridge, MA: MIT Press, 2012), 270.

64. Association of Collegiate Schools of Architecture, "Minutes of the Second Annual Meeting," New York, December 27, 1913, referenced in Rebecca Williamson, "Collateral Organizations: The Role of Professional and Academic Groups in Architecture Education," in Ockman, *Architecture School*, 248.

65. Williamson, "Collateral Organizations," 249.

66. Francke H. Bosworth Jr. and Roy Childs Jones, *A Study of Architectural Schools*, prepared for the Association of Collegiate Schools of Architecture (New York: Charles Scribner's Sons, 1932), 180, referenced in Joan Ockman, "Introduction: The Turn of Education," *Architecture School*, 19. Releasing their report in the worst year of the Depression, Bosworth and Jones may have found it difficult to criticize schools that were struggling, although they did single out schools for preparing for "an unreal profession of their own imagining, whose vague duties and misty obligations have no possible relation to actuality." See Ockman, "Introduction," 186.

67. Williamson, "Collateral Organizations," 249.

68. Williamson, "'Elegant Swords,'" 272.

69. Bannister, *The Architect at Mid-Century*, 109, 122, referenced in Joan Ockman, "Introduction: The Turn of Education," *Architecture School*, 22.

70. Robert L. Geddes and Bernard P. Spring, *A Study of Education for Environmental Design: Final Report*, sponsored by the American Institute of Architects (Princeton: Princeton University, 1967), 29–35. An undergraduate phase begins the course of study, including general education with some pre-professional training, followed by a graduate phase that contains didactic and clinical experience, and capped by an organized internship and professional concentration. When completed in full, that sequence bears a close resemblance to twentieth-century American medical education as first established by Flexner. To reach the highest level of professional attainment and some form of licensure, a student must complete two modules of postgraduate experience. But given that the sequence may apply to many disciplines with different licensure practices, and because its recommendations are largely educational, the authors make no reference to where along the sequence one becomes licensed. And given that there may be hundreds of design-related careers to consider, licensure may not even be needed.

71. Lombard, "LL.B. to J.D.," 589. See also Rebecca Williamson, "Degree Nomenclature," in Ockman, *Architecture School*, 274. The five collateral organizations include the American Institute of Architects (AIA), American Institute of Architecture Students (AIAS),

Association of Collegiate Schools of Architecture (ACSA), National Architectural Accrediting Board (NAAB), and the National Council of Architectural Registration Boards (NCARB).

72. The AIA also needed to merge three distinct traditions: German (scientific), French (artistic), and English (practical).

73. Magali S. Larson, *The Rise of Professionalism* (Berkeley: University of California Press, 1977), 104–135, quoted in Abbott, *The System of Professions*, 13.

74. Williamson, "Collateral Organizations," 250.

11. What's Next?

1. The epigraph is from Tim Kreider, "Go Ahead, Millennials, Destroy Us," *New York Times*, March 2, 2018, https://www.nytimes.com/2018/03/02/opinion/go-ahead-millennials-destroy-us.html. Kreider's full paragraph, which addresses gun control, is: "As with all historic tipping points, it seems inevitable in retrospect: Of course it was the young people, the actual victims of the slaughter, who have finally begun to turn the tide against guns in this country. Kids don't have money and can't vote, and until now burying a few dozen a year has apparently been a price that lots of Americans were willing to pay to hold onto the props of their pathetic role-playing fantasies. But they forgot what adults always forget: that our children grow up, and remember everything, and forgive nothing."

1. Elizabeth Evitts Dickinson, "The Millennials: Children of the Revolution," *Architect*, January 2013, 110.

2. American Institute of Architects, *The AIA Foresight Report: The Changing Context, Business, and Practice of Architecture 2013* (Washington, DC: AIA, 2013), 11, www.aiacc.org/wp-content/uploads/2013/06/foresight-report.pdf.

3. The AIA's public awareness advertising campaign, developed with The Purpose Institute of Austin, Texas, is a comprehensive three-year plan to emphasize the value that architects bring to shaping the built environment. The I Look Up Film Challenge unites storytellers and the architectural community to describe architects' impact on our built world in YouTube-style videos.

4. Caroline Massie, "13 Architecture Schools to Bring Path to Licensure Into Curricula," *Architect*, August 31, 2015, www.architectmagazine.com/practice/13-architecture-schools-to-bring-path-to-licensure-into-curricula_0/. As of 2015, the National Council of Architectural Registration Boards (NCARB) has begun working with thirteen accredited architectural programs as part of its Integrated Path initiative, which allows students (undergraduate and graduate) to begin the licensure process as a part of an academic curriculum and to take each division of the Architect Registration Examination (ARE) before graduation. NCARB is guiding each school in the process and also coordinating with local state regulators to ensure compliance. Each school will implement the restructured program according to the unique schedule established with its administration and faculty.

5. Edwards & Company, *Final Report + Recommendations for The Association of Collegiate Schools of Architecture*, www.acsa-arch.org/docs/default-source/resources/cccampaignresearchsummary.pdf.

6. Thomas Fisher, *In the Scheme of Things: Alternative Thinking on the Practice of Architecture* (Minneapolis, MN: University of Minnesota Press, 2000), 33.

7. Carl B. Frey and Michael A. Osborne, "The Future of Employment: How Susceptible Are Jobs to Computerisation?" (working paper, Oxford Martin Programme on Technology

and Employment, September 17, 2013), 42, www.oxfordmartin.ox.ac.uk/downloads
/academic/The_Future_of_Employment.pdf.

8. If jurisdictional elasticity is a primary goal, whether a degree be a doctorate or master's seems a matter of semantics; the doctoral designation of the JD and the master's
designation of the MBA have afforded each an equivalent elasticity.

9. See Paul Starr, *The Social Transformation of American Medicine: The Rise of a
Sovereign Profession and the Making of a Vast Industry* (New York: Basic Books, 1982),
24. Starr writes, "Doctors' increasing authority had the twin effects of stimulating and
restricting the market. On the one hand, their growing cultural authority helped draw
the care of the sick out of the family and lay community into the sphere of professional
service. On the other, it also brought political support for the imposition of limits, like
restrictive licensing laws, on the uncontrolled supply of medical services. By augmenting
demand and controlling supply, greater professional authority helped physicians secure
higher returns for their work."

10. Robert Geddes, *Fit: An Architect's Manifesto* (Princeton: Princeton University
Press, 2013), 29.

11. Robert L. Geddes and Bernard P. Spring, *A Study of Education for Environmental
Design; Final Report*, sponsored by the American Institute of Architects (Princeton, NJ:
Princeton University, December 1967), 19–20.

12. Geddes and Spring, *A Study of Education for Environmental Design*, 32. Geddes
and Spring's first postgraduate phase, an organized internship, like a medical residency,
"would be one year long and would involve observation and study of a wide range of professional activity." The following professional internship would be similar to contemporary
medicine's period of specialization, and "would emphasize participation in a specific set
of tasks."

13. Geddes and Spring, 30.

14. For those with the motivation and the academic standards to be admitted, an
honors professional track in architecture can be modeled on those currently offered in
medicine and law and can be of roughly the same duration as the current bachelor of
architecture degree.

15. An undergraduate degree with semesters not dominated by studios may be the
best opportunity for necessary foundation courses, allowing sufficient time to cultivate
the corresponding communication skills and broader sense of cultural knowledge required
for leadership. As rich in experiential learning as studios may be, they tend to monopolize
a student's time, relegating other needs to a lower priority. For the creeping demands of
studios, see Dana Cuff, *Architecture: The Story of Practice* (Cambridge, MA: MIT Press,
1991), 65.

16. Frank H. Wu, "Law Schools Closing," *Huffington Post*, November 7, 2016, www
.huffingtonpost.com/entry/law-schools-closing_us_581fcf1ee4b044f827a78fa2.

17. Robert Gutman, *Architecture Practice: A Critical View* (New York: Princeton Architectural Press, 1988), 110.

18. According to the Susskinds, some professions, notably the law, are currently being
disrupted by dropping demand and are finding clients reluctant to pay for interns, largely
because of the significant multipliers employers apply. Richard Susskind and Daniel Susskind, *The Future of the Professions* (Oxford: Oxford University Press, 2015), 260.

19. The idea of an architectural residency goes back to Bannister and the Princeton

report's postgraduate modules. Turpin C. Bannister, *The Architect at Mid-Century: Evolution and Achievement*, vol.1 (New York: Reinhold, 1954), 447–449. Geddes and Spring, *A Study of Education for Environmental Design*, 35. Recent suggestions include those proposed by Deborah K. Dietsch, "Build a Better Internship," *Architecture*, August 1996, 15; Thomas Fisher, *In the Scheme of Things: Alternative Thinking on the Practice of Architecture* (Minneapolis: University of Minnesota Press, 2000), 116–117; and most recently, in Michael Monti et al., "Infrastructure," in *Goat Rodeo: Practicing Built Environments*, ed. Daniel S. Friedman (San Bernardino, CA: Fried Fish Publishing, 2016), 81.

20. Joanna Lombard, "LL.B. to J.D. and the Professional Degree in Architecture," in *Architecture: Material and Imagined: Proceedings of the 85th ACSA Annual Meeting and Technology Conference*, ed. Lawrence W. Speck and Dominique Bonnamour-Lloyd (Washington, DC: Association of Collegiate Schools of Architecture, 1997), 588–589. In 2015, only 3.8 percent of teaching hospital funding came from tuition. See Association of American Medical Colleges, "Table 1: Revenues Supporting Programs and Activities at Fully-Accredited U.S. Medical Schools FY2015 ($ in Millions)," Tables and Graphs for Fiscal Year 2015, prepared June 2016, from LCME Part I-A Annual Medical School Financial Questionnaire (AFQ), FY2015, www.aamc.org/download/461876/data/fy2015_medical_school _financial_tables.pdf.

21. A two-tiered arrangement was an original component of Flexner's educational model, although what was once a one-year, rotating medical internship has since been absorbed into the larger residency program known as graduate medical education. See "Becoming a Physician," American Medical Association, accessed July 14, 2016, www .ama-assn.org/ama/pub/education-careers/becoming-physician.page.

22. "Becoming a Physician," American Medical Association. As of 2016, medical doctors in the US can optionally pursue board certification in thirty-six general medical specialties and an additional eighty-eight subspecialty fields.

23. Residencies would organize by various foci: building types—schools, hospitals, stadia, etc., components—envelope, structure, interior, etc., scale—domestic, urban, infrastructural, etc., and whether an architect's future practice would engage with the physical, virtual, or organizational.

24. A strict reading of Strauss and Howe suggests that the same time location exists to reprise a Bauhaus Vorkurs in American public schools. See Fern Lerner, "Foundations for Design Education: Continuing the Bauhaus Vorkurs Vision," *Studies in Art Education* 46, no. 3 (Spring 2005): 211–226.

25. Cuff, *Architecture*, 20.

26. The internet computer dictionary Techopedia defines computer architecture as "a specification detailing how a set of software and hardware technology standards interact to form a computer system or platform. [It] refers to how a computer system is designed and what technologies it is compatible with. As with other contexts and meanings of the word architecture, computer architecture is likened to the art of determining the needs of the user/system/technology, and creating a logical design and standards based on those requirements." Techopedia, s.v. "computer architecture," accessed May 6, 2016, www .techopedia.com/definition/26757/computer-architecture.

27. Jon Bentley, "Programming Pearls: Bumper-Sticker Computer Science," *Communications of the ACM* 28, no. 9 (1985): 896–901. The credibility rule, as stated here, combines two aphorisms from Bentley's article. The first is a witticism attributed to Tom

Cargill of Bell Labs which states: "The first 90 percent of the code accounts for the first 90 percent of the development time. The remaining 10 percent of the code accounts for the other 90 percent of the development time." The second clause by May Shaw of Carnegie-Mellon University states: "Less than 10 percent of the code has to do with the ostensible purpose of the system; the rest deals with input-output, data validation, data structure maintenance, and other housekeeping."

28. The manifesto's full title is "The Manifesto for Agile Software Development." See http://agilemanifesto.org.

29. Webopedia, s.v. "aspect-oriented programming," "object-oriented programming," "advice," accessed July 18, 2016, www.webopedia.com/TERM/A/aspect_oriented _programming.html, www.webopedia.com/TERM/O/object_oriented_programming_OOP .htm, www.webopedia.com/TERM/A/advice.html.

30. Andrew Ross Sorkin, "President Obama Weighs His Economic Legacy," *New York Times*, April 28, 2016, http://www.nytimes.com/2016/05/01/magazine/president-obama -weighs-his-economic-legacy.html.

31. Andrew Abbott, *The System of Professions: An Essay on the Division of Expert Labor* (Chicago: University of Chicago Press, 1988), 30.

32. Hudnut's complete motivation for choosing design over architecture remains unclear. Was it anticipation of Bauhaus's multidisciplinary modernism, which would arrive the following year, or a nod to the ascendance of design streamlining? See Anthony Alofsin, *The Struggle for Modernism: Architecture, Landscape Architecture, and City Planning at Harvard* (New York: W. W. Norton, 2002).

33. Geddes, *Fit*, 1.

34. Nomenclature and professional structure for landscape architecture already exists. Others could include urban architecture (physical planning), policy architecture (policy planning), product architecture (product design), preservation architecture (historic preservation), property architecture (real estate), and digital architecture (virtual reality).

35. Earl Pope, telephone conversation with author, September 7, 2018. Pope's explanation for how the firm accomplished this goal is twofold: the partnership never took on debt and they refrained from working with developers, whom Pope felt often reneged on fee obligations as recessions began.

36. Geddes, *Fit*, 1.

Appendix I. Millennials in Architecture Survey

1. NJIT Institutional Review Board: HHS FWA 00003246, Notice of Approval, IRB Protocol Number: F268-16 Principal Investigator: Darius Sollohub, *Millennials in Architecture Survey*, Approval Date: December 8, 2015.

2. Pew Research Center, *Millennials: Confident. Connected. Open to Change*, edited by Paul Taylor and Scott Keeter, February 2010, 18, http://www.pewsocialtrends.org/files /2010/10/millennials-confident-connected-open-to-change.pdf.

3. Pew Research Center, *Millennials in Adulthood: Detached from Institutions, Networked with Friends*, ed. Paul Taylor et al., March 7, 2014, 44-46, http://www .pewsocialtrends.org/2014/03/07/millennials-in-adulthood/.

Index

Note: Page numbers in italics refer to figures.

American Psychological Association, 9, 26, 273n25

American Recovery and Reinvestment Act (ARRA), 131

American Society of Civil Engineers (ASCE), 130–131

American Union of Decorative Arts and Craftsmen (AUDAC), 192, 195

Anastasio, Trey (Phish), 171

Appiah, Kwame Anthony, 116–117

Apple (company), 15, 151; and design, 7, 31, 151–152, 196, 200, 209; Millennials and, 31–33, 151, 186, 188; products, 15, 32–33, *32*, 199

archetypes, generational: 55, 56–58, *57*, *59*, 68, 72, 120; artist (adaptive), 56, 65, 67–68, 119; gray champions, 68, 74, 91–92, 95, 285n44; hero (civic), 13, 56, 57, 64, 68, 90, 91; midgenerational inflections, 58–60, 65, 119, 179; nomad (reactive), 56, 57, 65, 91, 119, 120, 167; prophet (idealist), 56–57, 64, 91, 120; in social moments, 64–65, 70; and turnings, 61, *62*, 64, 66. *See also* generational theory

Archigram (firm), 83, 117

Architect, 19; Millennials in, xii, 6, 23, 71, 93, 205–206

Architect at Mid-Century: Evolution and Achievement (Bannister), 222, 240

Architects Collaborative (firm), 79

Architectural Review, Big Rethink campaign, 117–118

architecture: aestheticism vs. empiricism in, 116, 142, 143, 152, 229–230; awareness of Millennials in, xi–xii, 6–7, 29, 35; design process, 10, 16, 111, 184–185, 186, 187, 208–209; future role of, xii, 4–5, 19, 92–93, 141, 206, 242–243; generational cohorts in, 112–114, 115–119, 120–125, 138–139, 230, 240; generations in, history, 48, 76–78, 78–81, 81–83, 83–87, 87–92, 92–96; haptic practices of, 111, 124, 159, 185, 214; jurisdiction and agency, xiii, 4, 104, 116, 214, 215, 226, 242; mystification of, 118,

122, 211; preseasonality of, 61, 93–94, 104–105, 114, 137, 138, 241; as proto-Millennial, xv, 96, 101, 126; public perception and value of, 194–195, 201, 210, 228, 232, 237, 239; role of architect, 116, 134, 143, 183, 185, 207, 214; sister disciplines of, 205, 215, 221, 223–225, 234–235, 304n4; title and terminology, 236, 237–240, 314n34. *See also* architecture, academy; architecture, practice; *specific architectural styles and subdisciplnes*

architecture, academy: assessments and formalization of, 112–118, 138–141, 183–185, 191, 221–224, 234–235, 240–242; degree reform and diversity in, 206, 213, 221–223, 224, 236, 239, 314n34; fragmentation and diversity in, 114, 116, 214, 224, 232, 307n30; innovations to, 22, 162, 163–164, 166–167, 185–186, 189, 230, 232–234; interdisciplinarity in, 29, 77, 79–80, 140, 185, 222–223; jurisdiction of, 175, 187, 231, 236–237, 239–240; Millennial values and preferences in, 105, 107, 123–124, 127, 166, 184–185; oversupply from, 213–214, 225, 226, 234; the practice of, 113, 209, 222, 223, 230, 306n22; retention in, 101, 105, 202, 209, 225; sister disciplines of, 221–222, 231–232, 234, 235–236, 310n70, 312n12; theory vs. pragmatism, 82, 85, 118, 122, 140, 259, 310n66. *See also* enrollment; learning and pedagogy; studio; *specific architectural styles, reports, and values*

architecture, practice: and the academy, 113, 209, 222, 223, 230, 306n22; compensation in, 107, 181, 210, 229, 234, 304n4, 306n27; innovations to, 228, 229–230, 231, 236, 237–238; interdisciplinarity of, 29, 31, 80, 126, 132, 141, 186; jurisdiction of, 131–132, 158–159, 186, 206–207, 228–230, 238, 239; Millennial Age, values, 33–34, 132–137, 152, 153, 154–159; Millennial characteristics in, 9–10, 19, 24, 29–31, 33–35,